LEADERSHIP EDUCATION 300
LIFE SKILLS & CAREER OPPORTUNITIES

Second Edition

Victor Valley High School
16500 Mojave Drive
Victorville, CA 92395

PEARSON

Pearson Learning Solutions, 501 Boylston Street, Suite 900,
Boston, MA 02116
A Pearson Education Company
www.pearsoned.com

Printed in the United States of America

1 2 3 4 5 6 7 8 9 10 V357 17 16 15 14 13 12

000200010271280643

RG/TB

ISBN 10: 1-256-49296-5
ISBN 13: 978-1-256-49296-2

Contents

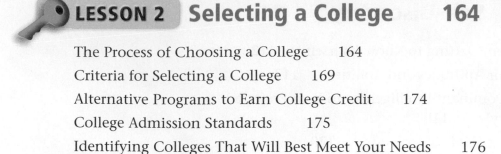

Contents

CHAPTER 7 Working for the Federal Government 305

CHAPTER 8 Developing Your Career Skills   369

LESSON 4 Your Civic Responsibilities   410

Preface

Life Skills and Career Opportunities provides an essential component of leadership education for today's high school students. This book, and the course it is designed for, will prepare you for life after high school in the high-tech, globally oriented, and diverse workplace of the 21st century.

Through reading, discussing, and practical exercises, you will become a more confident financial planner. You will understand how to save, invest, and spend money wisely, as well as how to avoid the credit trap. You will learn about real-life issues such as understanding contracts, leases, warranties, legal notices, and personal bills. For students who may be moving into an apartment of their own, you'll learn practical and money-saving strategies for grocery shopping, apartment selection, and life with roommates.

You will also discover who you can become by investigating who you are. The Holland Interest Inventory and other self-assessments will help you to reveal your attitudes, aptitudes, and personal skills. This self-understanding will allow you to explore career paths and understand requirements that you'll need to be successful at work and in life.

To help you increase your potential for success through education, you will learn how to select a school that is right for you. You'll understand how to apply for admission to a vocational or technical school, community college, or college/university, and how to succeed—and enjoy yourself—in these learning environments.

Information is provided on how to conduct the job search for students who wish to enter the workforce right after high school or after additional education and training. You will learn how to prepare a winning résumé, and how to develop effective interviewing skills. You'll become more skilled at using the Internet for career research and learn how to network safely using social media. For those who are interested in a career in the military, the federal government, or in aerospace, the text provides extensive and current information. Finally, you'll consider the most important elements of life skills for all Americans: civic responsibilities, such as volunteering, registering to vote, jury duty, and draft registration.

All chapters and lessons contain full-color diagrams and pictures, providing visual information to supplement the text. Other features in each lesson include a "Quick Write" exercise for in-class writing activities at the start of each lesson. A "Learn About" box tells students what they should learn and take away from the lesson. A list of vocabulary words ensures that students will understand the terms they encounter throughout the text.

At selected points in each lesson, "Success Tips" highlight specific information that will be useful, including stories from people who have been successful using this information. Each lesson is followed by "Checkpoints" which will allow students to review what they have learned. An "Applying Your Learning" section at the end of each lesson presents one or more discussion questions that give students a chance to use and reinforce what they have learned.

The text has eight chapters, each divided into multiple lessons.

Chapter 1: Charting Your Financial Course explains important concepts in building financial stability and wealth. You will learn how to make a plan for earning money, saving it, and spending it. A personal financial plan can be the difference between the ability to do the things each of us wants and the feeling that you'll never reach your financial goals in life. This chapter will provide you with an overall picture of how to create a budget before the text moves on to examine the specifics of savings, bank accounts, and the real-life issues you will face when buying and selling.

Chapter 2: Managing Your Resources explains the types of credit and discusses positive and negative aspects of using credit, along with monitoring credit to build a positive credit history. By evaluating the types of insurance options available to protect resources, you will learn the importance of insurance and tips for protecting your personal and financial information.

Chapter 3: Career Opportunities examines career opportunities each of you may pursue. It is designed to provide you with an overview of the high-tech, globally oriented, and diverse 21st-century workplace. The chapter discusses the importance of charting a career path, comparing career options, and evaluating key factors when choosing a career path. You will explore who you are by examining your own interests, values, attitudes, and abilities. Your self-discovery will help you choose careers based on you as a unique individual, and help you consider which work environments are best suited for your personal preferences. Finally, you will analyze different career paths available to you immediately after high school graduation or post-secondary vocational training or college education. By linking technical and educational career paths in this chapter, the intent is to communicate that both choices are worthwhile options.

Chapter 4: Aiming Towards a College Degree focuses on selecting and applying for college. You will examine the financial costs of attending college, explore sources of funding, and learn about the criteria, or standards, all students should consider when choosing a college. This chapter also covers college entrance exams and college placement tests; how to write an application essay; how to prepare for an admissions interview; and what to look for during a campus visit.

Chapter 5: Charting Your Course examines aspects of preparing to attend college and charting your course of study. You will explore aspects of campus life, including resources, organizations, and policies. You will also cover ways to ensure success in the college environment, including how to make healthy choices. You will take the information you learned about yourself from Chapter 3 and examine the decision process for choosing a college major. This chapter will also explain the importance of effective time management and how you can avoid procrastination.

Chapter 6: Applying for Jobs evaluates the process of successfully pursuing a desired career. By examining what employers are looking for, you, the career seeker, will be employing the most effective tool needed to sell your skills. You will learn how to organize the job search. You will also consider different résumé types, and be able to prepare a persuasive cover letter and résumé. You will learn about different types of interviews, how an interview is conducted, and effective tips for interview preparation.

Chapter 7: Working for the Federal Government evaluates the benefits of working for the federal government. This chapter provides you with the requirements needed to enlist in the military or to enter as a member of the officer corps. The text also compares educational opportunities for enlisted members from each military service, making military service a career option, and how military training is useful when seeking a civilian career. You will examine educational requirements for careers in aerospace and explore specific career examples in aerospace. Finally, this chapter will provide information for selection and training in careers in criminal justice, fire science, and homeland security.

Chapter 8: Developing Your Career Skills will help you create a plan for successful career development. Students will summarize the process of successfully planning for professional development in the workplace. You will learn to create a professional portfolio, organize personal and organizational values, and maintain effective verbal and nonverbal communication. You will learn how to seek and receive constructive feedback and identify successful tips for earning a promotion. Finally, Chapter 8 will cover civic responsibilities. You will review the Selective Draft system, why it is important to vote, work as a volunteer, and be a productive member in your community.

At the end of the textbook, you will find a glossary defining all the vocabulary words and telling you which page each term appears on. You'll also find an index organized by subject at the end of the text, as well as a list of references.

This textbook has been prepared especially for you, the cadet, the student— to increase your knowledge and appreciation of the skills you'll need to be successful once you have graduated from high school. Students like you are our nation's first responders, teachers, engineers, technicians, corporate leaders: the workforce of the future. The future is in your hands. Are you ready to take up the challenge? Every one of us involved in the production of this book hopes it will prepare you for future challenges.

LEADERSHIP EDUCATION 300

http://www.pearsoncustom.com/us/leadership_education

Login Information to Be Provided by Instructors

Acknowledgments

This new edition of *Life Skills and Career Opportunities* is based in part on suggestions from AFJROTC instructors on meeting the need to update the tools young adults require to succeed in the 21st century. The Jeanne M. Holm Center for Officer Accessions and Citizen Development (Holm Center) Curriculum Directorate team involved in the production effort was under the direction of Dr. Charles Nath III, Ed.D., Director of Curriculum for the Holm Center at Maxwell Air Force Base, Alabama, and Ms. Vickie Helms, M.Ed., Chief, AFJROTC Curriculum. Special thanks and acknowledgment go to Mr. Michael Wetzel, M.Ed., an instructional systems specialist and Academic Credit Liaison for Holm Center Curriculum, who was the primary Air Force editor and reviewer. We commend Michael for his persistent efforts, commitment, and thorough review in producing the best academic materials possible for AFJROTC units worldwide.

We are deeply indebted to those instructors who provided the initial input of suggestions that we used to bring this book and the course up to date. Special thanks go to Chief Master Sergeant Jeffrey Dodson, USAF (Ret) of AFJROTC Unit CA-933, Temecula Valley High School, Temecula, California and Master Sergeant William Poe, USAF (Ret) of AFJROTC Unit WV-20021, Jefferson High School, Shenandoah, West Virginia, for thoroughly reviewing the instructor guide material. We are also indebted to Dr. Kimberly Combs-Hardy, Ph.D., Chief of Educational Technology, Holm Center Curriculum, for her advice and suggestions throughout the project.

We would also like to express our gratitude to the Pearson publishing team, including Dr. Penny Wilkins, DM, and Richard Gomes, for project and production management. As well as Mia Saunders of Gamut & Hue for page layout and design. Thanks also to the Deerpath authoring team, led by Dr. W. Dees Stallings, Ph.D. and principal writer-researcher Bill Noxon, for all their hard work on this textbook revision. Our appreciation also goes to Erin Kelmereit, chief developer of the Instructor Guide, and Heidi Guthrie, who assisted in this aspect of the project.

The AFJROTC mission is to develop citizens of character dedicated to serving their nation and communities. Our goal is to create materials that provide a solid foundation for producing members of society able to productively fulfill their citizenship roles. We believe this course will continue the precedent set forth by previous curriculum materials. All the people identified above came together on this project and combined their efforts to form one great team, providing 21st Century curriculum materials to all our schools.

Checks

Credit Cards

Bank

Loans

Deposits

Accounting

Charting Your Financial Course

"The safest way to double your money
is to fold it over and put it in your pocket."

Kin Hubbard, cartoonist and humorist

Creating a Budget

Quick Write

_____

_____

Why do you think it is important for you to have a financial plan? Do you think a plan is just as important for someone who is wealthy as it is for someone who's just getting by? Why or why not?

"There are plenty of ways to get ahead. The first is so basic I'm almost embarrassed to say it: spend less than you earn."

Paul Clitheroe, financial analyst

The Components of a Personal Financial Plan

Would you put on a big party without planning? Not likely! First, you'd probably decide on the date and time. Then you'd figure out where to have it: at your house? At a restaurant? You would decide on the food, decorations, and music. Of course, you'd have to make a list of guests and send out invitations. Before the plans went too far, you'd have to make sure you could afford everything.

Planning for your financial future is much more important than planning a party. But it, too, involves answering a series of questions. What are your goals? Do you want to go to college? Buy a car? Buy a home? Build up a savings account? Start a family and then help your children become financially secure? Take an early retirement? All these things require money. And if you want to have money, you have to make a plan for how you're going to get it and how you're going to save and spend it.

Learn About

• the components of a personal financial plan
• creating a personal financial plan
• the steps for developing a personal financial plan

Planning for your financial future involves answering a series of questions about your goals.
Courtesy of Lisa F. Young/Shutterstock

This textbook is about life skills and career opportunities. The tools offered in this book and in this chapter provide knowledge about money, how it is used, spent, and invested. They provide a starting point for building an entire set of needed skills in life, as well as finding a good career.

This chapter will provide you with the knowledge and skills to make decisions about how to use money and plan for wise spending and saving throughout your lifetime.

The word finance refers to *management of money*, and personal finance refers to *how you manage your money and other things of financial value*. A personal financial plan can make the difference between being able to do the things you want to do and feeling that you'll never reach your goals in life.

Advantages of Understanding Personal Finance

An understanding of personal finance helps you:

- *Make good financial decisions*—Good financial decisions will increase the wealth you accumulate over time and make it more likely that you'll be able to purchase the products and services you want.

- *Evaluate the opinions of financial advisers*—Financial advisers are experts in financial planning. When you're older, you may want to get advice from such a professional. But it will be up to you to determine whether you're getting good advice. You'll also need to know the right questions to ask to feel more secure. No one can predict the future. The firm you've worked with for years may go out of business. You may become seriously ill and not be able to work. An investment may turn sour. The more you know about financial planning, the better you'll be able to adapt to unexpected circumstances.

And who knows? If you decide, as you study the lessons in this book, that you want to pursue a career path in personal finance, you might want to become a financial adviser yourself.

Vocabulary

- finance
- personal finance
- financial plan
- budget
- income
- expenses
- needs
- wants
- liquidity
- financing
- interest
- compound interest
- asset
- insurance
- investment
- stocks
- shares
- bond
- mutual fund
- retirement
- risk
- spending limits

success TIP ★

Life is a long journey, and financing that journey requires planning. By learning now to make effective decisions about money, you'll be applying a key life skill for a brighter future.

Creating a Personal Financial Plan

The starting point in mastering your personal finance is to create a financial plan, or *a document that outlines your financial goals and how you plan to reach them*. A financial plan sets forth your decisions in six areas:

1. Managing Your Budget

Your budget is *a detailed summary of expected income and expenses during a given period*. Income (money coming in) is *what is earned or made available to you* that you expect to receive on a regular basis. Expenses (money going out) are *amounts of money you spend to pay bills or for other needs and wants*. Needs are *things that you must have to sustain your livelihood*. Basic meals, necessary school expenses, and transportation money to get to school are examples. Wants are *things that you do not have to have, but would like to have, or own*.

Let's take a look at planning a school activity such as an awards banquet. Building a budget will allow you to make an informed decision about how many people to invite, how much food, drink, and decorations you can afford, and what type of entertainment to provide. You'll also want to think about how many tables and chairs you may have to rent. You may have to consider how many tickets to sell. Some additional research will allow you to make better use of available money by checking local stores or catering services for the best deals in food and beverages.

To use a budget as part of a long-term financial plan, rather than for a specific event such as a party, you list your expected expenses and income over a certain period. A financial plan is a long-term document. Creating a plan allows you to set financial goals. The plan can be for next year, the next 10 years, or even a lifetime.

Based on the information in your long-term budget, you can decide if your income will be adequate to enable you to have the standard of living that you want to have. Your goal should be for your income to be greater than, not just equal to, your expenses. If this is the case, you will be able to save, and saving is essential for creating wealth and building a good future.

2. Managing Your Liquidity

A financial plan must take into account your liquidity. Liquidity is *access to funds to cover a short-term cash need*. Even though they've made good plans, people often need money for an unexpected expense. They might own valuable items, such as land, a house, or a car, but those items will be useless if they need cash quickly. In that case, they will need liquidity.

If liquidity is a problem, some people borrow money. Borrowing is usually necessary to finance a major expense, such as a college education, a house, or a new car. But borrowing has risks, as you'll learn later in this lesson.

3. Financing Your Large Purchases

Financing is *obtaining or providing money for a specific purpose*. The person obtaining the money is the borrower, and the provider of the money (usually a bank) is the lender. Financing generally comes in the form of loans.

For example, if you plan to go to college, your parents or guardian may be able to pay part of the cost from their savings. You may be able to contribute something from your earnings. But college can be expensive, and you and your family may not have enough to pay for everything. In this case, you may want to take out a student loan. This loan will cover the difference between what you and your family can give and the total cost of your education.

Most people need to take out loans at one point or another. But you should never get dependent on loans, because you must pay all those loans back. And when you repay them, you'll have to pay interest, which is *a charge on borrowed money*. Interest charges seem small, but they add up.

For example, say you borrowed $10,000 to pay for part of your college tuition. The interest rate on the loan was 5 percent per year. If you didn't make any payments in the year after you got your loan, you would have to add 5 percent, or $500, to the $10,000 that you borrowed. If you made no payments on your loan for 10 years, your interest would total a whopping $6,289. Of that sum, $5,000 would be interest on the $10,000 you had borrowed. The remaining $1,289 would be *interest on accumulated unpaid interest*, which is called compound interest.

Most people pay back their loans gradually. Their interest payments go down, rather than up, over the years. Still, interest payments add up, and you need to be aware of and keep track of them. More importantly, you should not become dependent on loans since interest payments are funds lost to you, and gained by someone else (the lender).

Buying an item like a TV may require you to finance payments over time.
Courtesy of Yuri Arcurs/Shutterstock

4. Protecting Your Assets

An asset is *something of value that you own*. Maybe you own a car. Or you might own stock in a company. Perhaps your collection of baseball cards is valuable. Or you may have inherited a gold ring from your grandmother or a piece of equipment from your grandfather's wood shop. These are tangible assets. *Tangible* means *a physical item that you can touch*.

In making a financial plan, you will want to protect your assets. You can do this by buying insurance. Insurance is *an agreement between two parties under which one party— usually an insurance company—guarantees the other that if an asset is lost or destroyed, the insurance company will pay for it*. To insure an asset of any kind, you must pay a monthly fee, or premium, to the insurance company. We will discuss more about insurance in Chapter 2, Lesson 2.

Insurance also covers *intangible* assets—assets that are not tangible. For example, you can insure your health or your life. Health insurance covers medical benefits. Life insurance pays a certain amount of money, or benefit, should you die.

You will want to insure your most important assets. For example, if you buy a car you will need to buy insurance. Then, if you have an accident and the car is damaged, your insurance policy will pay for the repairs.

5. Investing for the Future

Investments are an important part of a financial plan because they are one of the best ways to help you increase your wealth over a desired period or over your lifetime. An investment is *something you own that you expect to increase in value over time*. At some point, you may buy a house and expect it to increase in value. That's an investment. One type of investment to consider is stocks, which are *funds raised by companies through the sale of shares*. Shares are *equal parts into which company stocks are divided*. Investors may buy shares, thereby giving them part ownership in a company. When you purchase a bond, another kind of investment, you are *investing to help a company or government agency raise funds for a return greater than the money you invested*. A third popular investment is a mutual fund, *an investment that often includes a mix of stocks, bonds, or other securities purchased in shares*.

Some people buy art or jewelry because of its investment value. A car is not an investment because it typically decreases in value over time.

6. Investing in Your Retirement

A financial plan is a long-term document, so retirement should be a part of it. Retirement is *the period (usually later in life) during which you no longer work full time at a job*.

People retire at different ages. In the past, many people retired at age 65, when they qualified for Social Security benefits. However, recent federal law has changed the ages for Social Security eligibility, depending on a person's year of birth. Today, many don't qualify until they are older than 65. In addition, many private retirement plans have changed. In general, retirement ages have gone up because people are living longer and can work longer.

If you entered military service, you could retire after just 20 years of service (although you may need to get another job at that time, possibly allowing you a second retirement income when you reach retirement age).

During retirement, you will not be getting a paycheck as you did when you had a full-time job, but you will still need money to live. So making sure you have enough money for retirement is important. And the better you plan for your future, the more likely you can choose when to retire. If you love your job and want to go on working into your 70s, that's fine. However, if you would rather retire and move on to something else, you will need a steady source of retirement income.

You probably think that retirement seems so far away that it's not worth thinking about. But just ask a grandparent or another older adult. Retirement age comes a lot quicker than most people think it will. If you start planning for retirement now, you'll be glad you did. The longer you save money, the more it will earn for you over the years between the time you save or invest and the time you retire.

The Steps for Developing a Personal Financial Plan

Now that you know the basic ingredients of a financial plan, you should develop your own. Ready to start? Here are the six steps involved in creating a financial plan:

1. Establish Your Financial Goals

Zig Ziglar, the well-known motivational speaker, may have said it well that "money isn't the most important thing in life but it's reasonably close to oxygen on the 'gotta have it' scale."

The first question might sound obvious, but it's important: How important is money to you? Some people get along well with just the basics. Others want a more luxurious lifestyle.

Next, consider what you need money for. Do you want to buy a new car every year? Pay for college, or even graduate school? Help your family? Make a down payment on a home? Contribute to a worthy cause? To make your plan work, you must have goals. After all, as the saying goes, if you do not know where you are headed, any path will take you there.

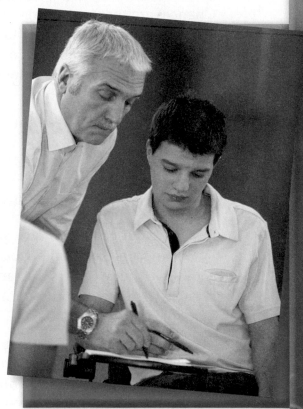

Writing down personal and financial goals is important for planning your future.

Courtesy of auremar/Fotolia LLC

When you set those goals, be realistic. For example, a financial plan that requires you to save more than half your income is probably not realistic, no matter how much you earn. A plan that requires you to accumulate $1 million within one year is certainly not realistic (unless you beat enormous odds and win a state lottery).

Timing is important. A financial plan usually covers three time segments:

- *A short-term plan, usually covering the next year*—the goal of a short-term plan might be to buy a car within six months.

- *An intermediate-term plan, covering one to five years*—for someone your age, the goal of an intermediate-term plan might be to save enough money for college tuition.

- *A long-term plan, which covers more than five years*—a long-term goal might be to save enough to retire by age 55.

2. Consider Your Current Financial Position

Look at your present financial situation. Any future decisions about what you want to buy, how much money to save or borrow, and where to invest your money, depend on it. If you're lucky enough to have plenty of money, your financial decisions will be very different from those of someone who is struggling to make ends meet.

Chances are that your current financial position is limited. But that will change, and you need to know what to do with your finances when it does. The career path you choose and the amount of money you earn will greatly influence your financial position. So if your goals require a lot of money, you will want to choose a well-paying career.

But don't choose a career just for the money. If you don't enjoy your work, you'll be miserable, no matter how much money you've got in the bank. Try to find an equal balance.

3. Identify and Evaluate Alternatives to Achieve Your Goals

If one of your goals is to save $200,000 within 10 years, you could try to do it by putting a big portion of your income each month into a savings account. Or you could put your earnings into an investment. Of these two alternatives, the first choice is safer. The US government insures the money in most bank and credit union savings accounts up to $250,000.

Savings accounts have another advantage. They pay you interest. While you *pay* interest on a loan, you *earn* interest on a savings account. The interest on your savings account will be a small percentage, paid monthly, of the amount that you have saved.

For example, say you deposited $1,000 into a savings account at 3 percent interest. One year later, your balance would be $1,030. Although it's not likely, let's assume that the interest rate stayed the same for the next nine years. Even if you made no additional deposits to your account, you would have a balance of $1,349 by the end of that time—thanks to compound interest.

A second way to reach your goal is to buy stocks or another investment. If you do, you'll face a certain degree of risk, or *uncertainty as to the outcome of an investment.* The government does not insure stocks. You might make a lot of money buying stock from a company—more than you ever could through savings. But if the company has problems, you could lose some, or even all, of the money you invested.

The US government insures deposits in most bank and credit union checking and savings accounts up to $250,000.
Courtesy of Dorling Kindersley

You can also buy bonds. Bonds have much less risk than stocks, but the amount of money you earn from them is usually less. Both bonds and stocks are long-term investments. Many people have both savings accounts and investments in stocks and bonds. The portion of their income that they invest in each depends on how much risk they are willing to accept.

success TIP ★

One lesson that does not require a financial adviser is this: Never invest more money than you can afford to lose.

Financial advisers often advise you to spread your money into different types of investments in order to protect against big losses that may occur in any one type of investment.

4. Select the Best Plan to Achieve Your Goals

Choose the plan you think will best help you reach your goals. It should be a plan you can stick with. It should also have an acceptable level of risk. Set spending limits, or *the amount above which you should not spend if you are to meet your financial goals.*

5. Evaluate Your Plan

Don't put your plan in a drawer and forget about it. Review it regularly to see how you're doing. You may have decided that you want to save $100 a month, but after a year you find that this is impossible. If that's the case, it's time to reevaluate how much you can save.

The Elements of a Budget

Knowing how to draw up budget is a valuable skill. You don't need to be a math wizard. Here are the basics.

Every budget has two main elements: income and expenses. Remember, *income* is money you receive on a regular basis. Income falls into many categories. The main categories for most people are:

- Salary or wages
- Savings
- Investments
- Other (gifts from relatives, income from things you've sold).

An *expense* is money you spend. Major categories of expenses for someone your age include:

- Clothing
- Entertainment
- Travel
- Books and CDs
- Food
- Car (payments, insurance, fuel, repair).

success TIP ★

Follow the 70–20–10 rule to improve your budget planning. Spend 70 percent of your income on living expenses, save or invest 20 percent, and spend the final 10 percent on paying off debt. With what's left over, you can buy something you want.

success TIP ★

The most important expense is— SAVINGS. Pay Yourself First!

6. Revise Your Plan

Look over each item on your plan. Note where it's worked and where it hasn't. Then think about how your financial situation and goals have changed since you drew up your plan. Perhaps you've gotten a new job, with a 15 percent increase in pay. Or maybe you've just gotten married or had a baby. Major life changes will require changes in your financial plan.

No one can predict the future. You can only make an educated guess. When reality says you need to change, don't be afraid to do so. Flexibility is a sign of strength, not of weakness. You'll get better at planning with each plan you make. Financial planning should become a part of your life.

Conclusion

The point of having a budget is to compare your income versus your expenses. It helps you see what you are spending money on, and where you need to lower your spending—so you will have enough for expenses and still have money left over for savings.

Remember to set spending limits; you do not want your expenses to exceed your income.

Figure 1.1 shows a sample monthly budget for Steve Johnston. Steve is 20 years old. He's an electrician apprentice. He's living on his own for the first time, and finances are tight. Steve earns $24,000 a year after taxes and withholding, and wants to save at least $200 per month. His budget is in balance. In other words, the total income and total expenses are the same. That doesn't mean that Steve is spending all the money he gets. Look closely and you'll see that Steve has set a spending limit of $200 less than his income. In keeping with his financial plan, he's putting $200 a month into a savings account. The next lessons will discuss how to save and invest your money, and how to make good buying decisions.

INCOME	
Salary	$2,000
Savings interest	10
Investment income	50
Total Income	**$2,060**

EXPENSES	
Rent	$ 500
Electricity and water	50
Telephone (home and cell)	80
Cable TV	60
Food	250
Entertainment and recreation	150
Health care insurance and expenses	300
Clothing	170
Car expenses	300
Savings	200
Total Expenses	**$2,060**

FIGURE 1.1

Sample Monthly Budget for Steve Johnston

✔ CHECKPOINTS

Lesson 1 Review

Using complete sentences, answer the following questions on a sheet of paper.

1. Why is a personal financial plan important?

2. What are the six areas for decision making when creating a personal financial plan?

3. What are the six steps for developing a personal financial plan?

4. What is a budget, and why is it important?

APPLYING BUDGET SKILLS

5. List your three financial goals for the next year, and for the next five years.

Savings and Bank Accounts

Quick Write

_____

_____

Your summer part-time job has allowed you to save $300, and your grandparents sent $300 for your birthday. You have soccer gear you want to purchase for $90. The rest, $510, you have in your bedroom. Should you feel comfortable with this? Explain why you would consider a bank account at this time. What type of account would you open, savings or checking, and why?

Learn About

- the advantages of bank services
- types of bank services
- how to choose a bank
- how to conduct banking transactions
- electronic banking

> "I saw a bank that said '24 Hour Banking,' but I don't have that much time."
>
> Stephen Wright, famous writer

The Advantages of Bank Services

After you graduate from high school, you might get a job and move into your own apartment. Or, if you go to college, you'll probably live in a dormitory or an off-campus apartment.

Most high school graduates are excited about setting out on their own. However, they sometimes don't take time to think enough about the responsibilities that go along with independence. Knowing how to manage your money is one of these responsibilities.

You may already have some savings. You may have a part-time job and receive a regular paycheck. Or perhaps you've saved some of the money that your parents, a guardian, or a relative may have given you on birthdays or other occasions.

To keep your money safe and to conduct financial transactions such as check writing, you'll need to open a bank account.

Courtesy of Konstantin Chagin/Shutterstock

No matter where your money comes from, you'll need a safe place to keep your extra cash. That's where banks come in. Banks help keep the flow of money safe and orderly in society. Without banks, our economy couldn't function.

To keep your money safe and to conduct financial transactions such as check writing, you will need to open a bank account. A bank account is *a formal relationship between you and a bank, where the bank keeps your money for you until you need it.*

Owning a bank account has several advantages:

- You know your money is safe—if someone breaks into your home, or if you lose your wallet, you won't lose all your money.
- The US government protects the customers of licensed banks—if something happens to the bank, the government will pay you the amount you had deposited in the bank, up to $250,000.
- You can get your money if you need it.
- You can keep track of how much money you've used and how much you still have.
- You can cash checks, get loans, and perform many other financial transactions more easily than people without bank accounts can.
- You will receive *interest* on the money you have in certain accounts. As you remember from Chapter 1, Lesson 1, interest is money that the bank pays you each month—the interest is a small percentage of the amount you have in your account.
- You will be able to show that you are responsible with your money. This is important, for example, if you want to get a credit card or take out a loan.

Types of Bank Services

Banks offer two main types of accounts: *savings* accounts and *checking* accounts. Banks also offer a number of other financial services, as described below.

Vocabulary

- bank account
- savings account
- checking account
- check
- debit card
- checkbook register
- balance
- account statement
- automated teller machine (ATM)
- personal identification number (PIN)
- certificate of deposit (CD)
- direct deposit
- loans
- credit cards
- credit
- credit union
- balancing
- reconcile
- electronic banking
- online banking
- electronic funds transfer (EFT)
- pay-by-phone
- electronic check conversion
- prepaid debit card

Savings Accounts

Even before they reach adulthood and financial independence, many people establish savings accounts. A savings account is *an account for depositing money that you want to keep*. Perhaps your parent or guardian has already created a savings account for you. If you received cash as a gift, someone probably encouraged you to put some of that money into your savings. Or you may have established a savings account so that you could deposit part of your earnings from a part-time job. A big advantage of a savings account is that your bank will pay you interest on the money you deposit. It will even pay interest on the interest, which is called *compound* interest. The money grows by itself if left alone!

Many banks enable you to access your account information online.

Courtesy of Supri Suharjoto/Shutterstock

Checking Accounts

A checking account is *a bank account into which you deposit money, and from which you can withdraw money by writing checks or using a debit card*. A check is *a written order that directs a bank to pay money*. A debit card is *a card that allows the automatic withdrawal of money you request from your checking account*. We will discuss more about debit cards later in this lesson.

A checking account provides a means of storing your money safely and using it to pay bills or buy things.

To open a checking account, bring to the bank some cash or a check that is made out to you. The bank representative who opens your account will explain the requirements and benefits of the account. Some checking accounts pay interest; others don't. If the checking account offers interest, you may have to keep a minimum amount in your account. Find out what this minimum is from your bank representative. The bank may also charge a monthly fee, which it will deduct from the amount in your account. This may also depend on how much money you keep in the account. The bank representative will ask you to sign a signature card or an electronic pad so that the bank knows what your signature looks like.

When you open your account, the bank will give you some temporary checks. You can use these checks as soon as you've established your account. Within a week or so, you'll receive your own checks. These checks will have your name and address on them. They will also be numbered in sequence.

Included with the checks will be a checkbook register, which is *a form on which you keep track of the money you deposit or withdraw*. You will write the amount of your first deposit in your checkbook register so that you know how much money you are starting with.

That amount will be your beginning balance, which is *the amount of money after expenses that is left in your checking account.* From that point on, you'll either add to or subtract from that number to get a new balance. If you make a deposit, you'll add to the balance. If you write a check or take out money, you will subtract from it.

As you make each additional deposit or withdrawal, you will make an entry in the checkbook register. You will include the date of the transaction, the person or company to which the payment was made, the check number (if applicable), and the amount involved. Using the current balance as the basis, you'll add or subtract to get your new balance.

success TIP ⭐

Make your entry to your checkbook register immediately after a transaction—or you may forget to do it later!

A checkbook register is useful only if you enter information that's up to date and accurate. A checkbook register is useful only if you make accurate entries. If you keep it up to date, it can help prevent you from writing checks when you do not have enough money in your account to cover them. You do not want a check to be returned for insufficient funds. The bank will charge you a fee for these checks, and the store or payee may refuse to accept any more checks from you.

Once a month, your bank will send you an account statement or *a list of transactions in your checking account over the month.* Through your checkbook register and your statement, you can keep track of how much you deposit in your account and how much you spend. The checkbook register and statement should agree. You'll find more information on how to balance your account later in this lesson.

If you need to know your balance and your statement isn't due to arrive for a while, you may be able to check your balance online. Most banks offer this service. It lets you know instantly how much money the bank says you have in your account. However, if you have written checks that haven't been cashed, you have less money in your account than the bank's record shows. Be careful! The only way to know for sure how much money you have in your account is to keep an accurate, up-to-date record in your checkbook register.

Many banks offer debit cards to their checking account customers. Debit cards are a convenient way to get cash or to pay for things from your checking account. Think of a debit card as a plastic check that you don't have to write.

Debit cards are a convenient way to get cash or pay for things from your checking account.
Courtesy of Jutta Klee/ableimages/Corbis Images

If your checking account doesn't have enough to cover the transaction, the debit card will not work. This is another reason you must keep an accurate record in your checkbook register of how much money you have in your account.

If you need cash when your bank isn't open, or you just want to save time, you can use your debit card to withdraw cash from your account at an automated teller machine (ATM), *a 24-hour electronic terminal that lets you bank almost any time to withdraw cash, make deposits, or transfer funds between accounts.* You will need your debit card and a personal identification number (PIN), *a code you enter to use credit or debit cards to make banking transactions like withdrawing cash, making deposits, or transferring funds between accounts from an ATM.* You can access your account from nearly anywhere in the world through ATMs. They are very convenient. However, if you use a card at a bank where you do not have an account, you may be charged a fee of up to several dollars to use their banking services.

Other Bank Services

Most banks offer other services besides checking and savings accounts. For example, you can rent a safe deposit box, where you can store valuable documents or other items. You can purchase certificates of deposit, which are like savings accounts. A bank certificate of deposit (CD) is *a type of bank deposit that typically pays higher rates of interest than a savings account, on the condition that you agree not to withdraw your money for a certain amount of time.*

Banks offer many additional services, including certificates of deposit, safe deposit boxes, and credit cards.

Courtesy of Christopher Oates/Shutterstock

Banks also offer a direct deposit service, *a payment that is electronically deposited into an individual's account.* Using this service, your employer can deposit your paycheck directly into your account. That way, you don't have to worry about making a special trip to the bank—or spending your check before you get home! We will discuss more about direct deposits later in the lesson.

Loans, *sums of money borrowed with interest,* are one of the most important services that banks offer. Banks lend people money to buy cars, homes, and other things. To get a loan, you have to prove that you can handle your money responsibly. You must have a good credit history, which means that you repay on time the money you owe.

Minimum Payments

Credit cards often allow you to make a minimum monthly payment. Many people wrongly believe that if they make this minimum payment they are paying down their loan. However, this is not always so—often the minimum payment is less than the interest on the loan for that month. This means that if you pay only the minimum payment, the amount you owe the bank actually goes up! The best way to use a credit card is to pay off the full amount you owe at the end of every billing period, usually each month.

Banks also offer credit cards, *cards that represent a promise that the bank will give you credit to buy things*. A bank that gives you credit is *offering to lend you money*. Banks limit the amount of credit they will offer their customers—you can't continue to borrow more and more money. However, if you pay your bills on time, the bank may raise your credit limit.

Because they make money on interest from credit cards, banks advertise them heavily. After you turn 18, you may receive offers for credit cards in the mail. Be careful about applying for and using these cards. When you use a debit card, you're using money you already have. The bank deducts the amount of your purchase from your checking account. However, using a credit card is like taking out a loan. You are borrowing money from the bank that issued the card. If you don't pay what you owe right away, you'll be charged interest. Credit card interest rates can be quite high. If you let your debt grow and cannot repay the loan, you can run into financial trouble quickly.

> **success TIP** ★
>
> Credit cards can give you a false sense of financial security. Get a credit card only if you are sure you can handle the responsibility.

How to Choose a Bank

When you choose a bank, you should consider several things:

- You may need to go to your bank a lot, so it should be conveniently located.

- How friendly is the staff? The staff should be willing to explain anything that you don't understand.

- What are the hours? Banks are famous for having short hours (Monday through Friday, 9 a.m. until 3 p.m. used to be common). However, today banks are extending their hours. They are often open in the evenings and on weekends. Make sure the bank is open at times when you'll be able to visit.

- What are the fees? If the bank wants to charge you a monthly fee for maintaining your account, make sure you understand why and how much. Are you comfortable with the reason? If not, shop around for another bank. You may end up back at this bank, but at least you'll know your options.

- What kinds of accounts does the bank offer? Some banks pay interest on checking accounts as well as on savings accounts. This is a good option for some people. However, if you have such an account, the bank may charge a fee if you do not keep a minimum amount of money in it at all times. If you don't have a lot of money to spare, an interest-bearing checking account may not be a good option.

- Does the bank offer online services? If you want to access your account information from your home computer, make sure the bank has such a service. Some banking services, especially savings services, are available only online.

- What is the interest rate? Banks pay different rates of interest on savings and other accounts. Shop around to make sure that your money is earning as much as it can. For example, if a bank pays 3 percent interest and you deposit $1,000, you will have $1,030 in the account at the end of the year. If a bank pays 4 percent, you will have 10 dollars more, or $1,040.

- Finally, make sure the bank has a good reputation. This is especially important for newer banks, such as those that offer only online banking services. Make sure the bank you choose is insured by the US government's Federal Deposit Insurance Corporation (FDIC).

How to Conduct Banking Transactions

Writing a Check

Although electronic banking has become the preferred way and even a convenient method of purchasing items or accessing your money, there are still occasions where you will find it necessary to write a check. In this next section, we will discussion the actual process of how to properly write a check. This important task must be completed properly; you do not want more money taken out of your bank account than what you have signed for. We will discuss more about electronic banking later in the lesson.

Here's how you write a check:

- Check your balance in your checkbook register. Make sure you have enough in your account to cover the check you're about to write.

- On the line in the upper-right corner, fill in the date.

- On the line stating "Pay to the order of," fill in the name of the person or company (called the "payee") who will receive your money.

- To the right of the payee line, write the amount of the check in numbers; include both dollars and cents, such as $12.92. Make sure the dot between the dollars and cents is clear, so someone doesn't think it says $1,292!

Always write your checks in ink. If you make a mistake, tear up the check and start over.
Courtesy of Anna/Fotolia LLC

- On the line under the payee, write the amount of the check in words. Write the cents as a fraction. You would write $12.92 as "Twelve and 92/100." Then draw a line all the way to the right, where "dollars" is printed on the check. The bank will compare the number you've written on the previous line and the words you write on this line to make sure it pays the amount that you request.

- On the "For" line at the bottom left, write the reason for the check (for your own information) or the account number that the company to which you're making the payment has assigned you (this is optional).

- At the bottom right, sign the check in the same way you did when you signed the signature card at the bank.

Figure 1.2 is an example of a written check.

FIGURE 1.2

Example of a Written Check

Adapted from Mitchell, N.L. (1999). *Leadership Education III: Life Skills*. Maxwell Airforce Base, AL: Air Force Reserve Officer Training Corps

Other Information on Your Check

If you've never looked at a check closely, you may be surprised to see that it has other information printed on it. The bank uses this information to process your check. Look again at Figure 1.2. Your check number appears at the top right of the check. The bank's name will appear somewhere on the check. At the bottom of the check are a bank-identifying routing number and your account number. The number on the check that appears to the right of your account number is the check number. The strange-looking numbers at the bottom of the check are designed so a scanner can read them.

Filling Out a Deposit Slip

You'll have to fill out a deposit slip each time you add money to your checking or savings account (except for direct deposits). The bank usually includes a supply of deposit slips in the back of your checkbook. If you do not have your own deposit slips, you can use the bank's, which are available for checking and savings accounts on a counter in the bank. Fill in the form with your account number, and hand it and the money you are depositing to the teller. The teller may ask for identification when you make a deposit. Figure 1.3 is an example of a deposit slip.

The bank does not immediately credit money that you deposit to your account. It usually takes one working day for the bank to process your transaction. So if you plan to write a big check right after you've made a deposit, make sure the deposit has been credited to your account.

DEPOSIT TICKET

	Dollars	Cents	
CURRENCY			07-123 / 456
COIN			
Checks			
Total from other side			
SUBTOTAL			
Less Cash			
TOTAL			
Total number items			

NAME _____
123 Anywhere Street
Somewhere US 30244

DATE _____ 20 __

_____
(Signature)

ADVENTURE BANK
ANYWHERE, USA

⑈262262955⑈ 712399328222

FIGURE 1.3

Sample Deposit Slip

Adapted from Mitchell, N.L. (1999). *Leadership Education III: Life Skills.* Maxwell Airforce Base, AL: Air Force Reserve Officer Training Corps

CHAPTER 1 Charting Your Financial Course

Balancing a Checkbook

Each month, the bank will send you a statement. The statement will show your deposits, withdrawals, bank charges, debit transactions, and canceled checks (or pictures of them). Check right away to see if the bank's records and your records agree.

Comparing the bank statement to your checkbook register is called balancing your checkbook. The purpose of balancing is to make sure the deposits and withdrawals, the checks you wrote and payees cashed, and the debit transactions you made are the same on the statement and on the register. In short, it's the best way to ensure that you and the bank agree on how much money is in your account.

You may find an error as you reconcile the account (reconcile means to *verify that your checkbook register balances*). Common problems are:

- Addition or subtraction errors
- Failing to record a deposit or withdrawal
- Failing to record the amount of a check or debit transaction

When you review your monthly statement:

- Some banks may still send you a paper copy of your monthly statement or you may review your monthly statement online.
- Sort the canceled checks (checks that have been cashed) by number. (You will not be able to do this if your bank sends photocopies or just lists the checks.) Match the checks against your checkbook register and against your bank's list of checks cashed.
- Match the deposits you have recorded in your register with the deposits the bank says you made. Do you and your bank agree? If not, figure out why. Did you forget to record a deposit? Did the bank make a mistake? (Not likely, but it can happen.)
- Go through the same matching process for any withdrawals and debit card transactions you made during the month.
- Make sure the bank has charged you the appropriate fees, if any, and that you have recorded them in your register. If your checking account pays you interest, add it to your checkbook register.

Once you have confirmed that all transactions on the statement and all transactions in your register match, you can balance your checkbook.

- Start with the "New Balance" shown on your statement—this is the amount that the bank says you had on the date it prepared your statement.
- Subtract any checks that you've written but that have not been cashed or recorded by the bank as of the date of the statement.
- Subtract any withdrawals or debit card transactions that the bank had not recorded as of the date of your statement.
- Add any deposits you made after the statement was prepared.

The resulting number should be the same as the current balance that appears in your checkbook register. If it does not match, you need to find the source of the mistake.

Try again. If you still can't find the mistake, visit your bank and see if a representative there can help you. Keep your statements and canceled checks in a safe place. They are a financial record—your receipts for purchases made. You may also need them for tax purposes.

Electronic Banking

Electronic banking is now widely and easily used by almost everyone with Internet access in their homes. Electronic banking is *a group of services that allows you to obtain account information and manage certain banking transactions.*

Online Banking

Online banking is one of two major categories of services offered as part of electronic banking. Online banking is *a way to manage many banking transactions on your personal computer or other electronic device by signing on to your bank's website through the Internet.* You can log on to your Internet account with a user name and a password. Once there, you can view your checking and savings account activity. You can also set up ways to pay bills and transfer money between accounts.

Some people depend solely on online banking without referring to any other written record of their account balance. To them, it's a matter of trust that the bank will always be right, and there's some peace of mind in that. However, if there is a bank error, a lot of confusion can arise. Why do you think this practice may not be a good idea?

The better practice is to combine online banking with maintaining an accurate checkbook register manually. Here's why. Online banking allows you to verify everything the bank has done with your account daily. This practice allows better management of your account within the checkbook register itself. You can record things like interest and fees daily online, rather than wait for a monthly statement from the bank. You also get to exercise your math skills by checking your record against that of the bank. This skill is a valuable tool as you learn to manage your budget.

All electronic banking services offer these advantages:

- The convenience of keeping track of, or getting to, your money almost anytime, anywhere

- The personal safety of not having to carry a lot of cash

- The time saved by not having to visit a bank, leaving you more time for other things you want to do

Online banking has made keeping records easier because you can log into your account and compare your daily transactions and account balances with those on your bank's website. Most banks are making account statements available this way instead of mailing monthly statements. An online system helps you better understand how to easily fix mistakes and re-balance your checking account on a daily basis. However, if the bank does make an error, an accurate manual checkbook register will help you resolve the issue by contacting the bank and verifying the error with a bank representative.

There are two reasons why online banking and bank statements aren't as accurate as your checkbook register.

First, the checks you write on any given day will take some time to "clear" the bank—in other words, to show up on your daily balance. Therefore, you really may have less money in your account than you believe. If you rely only on your online banking source you may accidently overdraw your account. Your checkbook register, if you maintain it daily, will help you avoid possible complicated problems in balancing your account.

Second, monthly bank statements do not account for your banking activity for the past several days because of printing and mailing delays for the printed statements.

Electronic Funds Transfer

Another major category of electronic banking is electronic funds transfer (EFT). This is *a way to manage many banking transactions on your personal computer or other electronic device by accessing your bank account through the Internet.*

Your bank may offer ATM machines that require personal identification numbers (PINs). Some banks use a form of debit card that may require, at the most, your signature or a scan. However, you should be comfortable about the security of such a system before using it.

Let's look at some of the more popular EFT services.

Direct Deposit

Many people use *direct deposit* to have their paychecks and other recurring income payments recorded into their bank accounts automatically. There's no card to touch. There's no need to carry money to a bank or an ATM and no need to fill out a deposit slip.

You can get direct deposit forms from your employer or at a bank if you want to set up electronic deposit. In either case, there should be some form of brochure or instructional guide for how to fill out the forms correctly.

For direct deposit, you need your checking or savings account number and the bank's routing or routing transit number, which is the code for your employer or income provider to set up the direct payments.

If you're asked for the bank's address to which you are making a deposit, do not be surprised. In a situation where someone needs to contact you, knowing from which branch you service your account is helpful.

In some cases, you will have to submit a voided check or other relevant document in order to set up your direct deposit or withdrawal. This allows for security and verification that all information is entered correctly. The goal is to make sure that money only goes into the correct account.

Once you have decided to set up a direct deposit or automatic withdrawal, you should record in your checkbook register a deposit or withdrawal on the day you know it is being added to or subtracted from your bank account.

<table>
<tr><td>

success **TIP** ★

Do not get so wrapped up in the receipt or taking money from the machine that you walk or drive off without taking your ATM card back. Most machines will *swallow or capture* your ATM card if you do not pull it out within a few minutes. *This means the ATM will ingest and hold the card until you retrieve it from the bank.* However, if the ATM has not captured your card yet, someone can take your card and use it at your expense.

</td></tr>
</table>

Automated Teller Machines (ATMs)

Automated teller machines (ATMs) are very convenient. They are used most often with debit cards to conduct deposits and withdrawals from your bank account(s). Withdrawals usually are limited to a daily maximum. You can also use the ATM for transferring funds from one account to another or to pay certain monthly bills.

You must use your PIN number at an ATM to initiate your transaction. When your transaction is complete, you can ask for a summarized detailed receipt.

Identity theft can also result from someone getting your ATM card. If your ATM/debit card is stolen and you report it within two days, the Electronic Funds Protection Act protects your losses. Within that time period, you will only be responsible for losses up to $50. If you wait from two to 60 days to report the loss, you can be responsible for up to $500. After 60 days, you could be responsible for everything lost on a stolen card.

Automated teller machines (ATMs) are very convenient, but require caution.

Courtesy of Tony Souter/DK Images

One other caution: If you use an ATM facility not affiliated with your bank, you can incur a fee. Some banks charge several dollars for transactions made at an ATM by those who are not account holders with that bank or credit union.

Debit Card

A debit card, described earlier in the lesson, is an electronic transfer function that can be very handy for use at ATMs or making purchases at most stores, on the Internet, or by phone.

A debit card directly deducts money immediately from your bank account. So make sure that you have funds in your account to cover your purchase. The debit card won't work if you fail to have enough money in your account to cover your purchase or cash request. It's like overdrawing your account except you're told before you spend money that your account is too low to cover your request.

There are some other EFT services that you may choose to use at some point.

Pay-by-Phone

You may initiate a pay-by-phone *system that lets you call your bank with instructions to pay certain bills or to transfer funds between accounts.* You must have an agreement with the institution to make such transfers.

Electronic Check Conversion

You may also do an electronic check conversion that *converts a paper check into an electronic payment in a store.* In the store, when you give your check to a cashier, the check is scanned through an electronic system that transfers funds into the merchant's account, like a debit. You get back a voided check. You should keep the voided check for when you balance your checkbook because the number of your voided check will not likely appear on your monthly banking statement. Instead, the merchant name will appear for an amount of an electronic transfer.

Prepaid Debit Card

A prepaid debit card, *a debit card for use at retail stores or cash withdrawals,* is growing in popularity for those whose jobs move them around, or for students living away from home who sometimes do not have checking or savings accounts. This kind of card allows for a strict limit on spending, and can be *preloaded,* or increased in amount by, say, a parent, who can better control a child's spending. Like any such card, the prepaid debit card should be kept safe to prevent someone from using part, or the entire amount on the card if it is lost or stolen.

Conclusion

However you conduct your banking and other financial transactions, always be conscious of security and privacy.

For online banking, be sure to keep secure your user identification (ID) and password. Keep them secret and stored in a safe place.

If your credit card is lost or stolen, and if you report the loss promptly, your maximum liability is $50, according to the Fair Credit Billing Act. If someone uses your ATM or debit card without your permission, you are also protected against loss under the Electronic Funds Transfer Act. However, the rules are a little stricter. You must report your loss within two business days in order to keep your losses to no more than $50. If you don't report the loss until more than two business days have passed, you could lose up to $500 for an unauthorized ATM use.

Every privilege carries with it a responsibility, and banking services, especially electronic ones, should be considered a privilege, not a necessity, and be used cautiously and responsibly.

✔ CHECKPOINTS

Lesson 2 Review

Using complete sentences, answer the following questions on a sheet of paper.

1. What are the two major types of banking institutions? Explain the differences between them.

2. Why would you choose to have a savings account?

3. Why would you choose to have a checking account?

4. How do you set up a checking account? Be specific.

5. Why is it important to keep a checkbook register accurate and up-to-date?

6. What are the main entries you make on a deposit slip, and why is math important in filling one out?

7. What are the main advantages and disadvantages you can think of for using electronic banking?

8. What are three types of electronic banking systems you might choose to use, and why?

APPLYING BANKING SKILLS

9. Fill out a sample deposit slip with the following: three checks totaling $45.00 (from a parent), $34.40 from selling a card collection to a friend, $58.00 from a part-time job, and currency amounting to $34.00. This is only a deposit. You are not withdrawing anything. Check your figures and fill in the TOTAL.

10. Suppose you deposit $275.00 in your savings account on December 31. Your bank pays 3 percent annual interest on savings accounts. If you do not deposit any more money into the account, what would be the balance on December 31 of the following year?

Real-Life Issues in Buying and Selling

Quick Write

_____

_____

You have finally earned enough money to purchase your first car. List four things on a separate sheet of paper that you would consider prior to purchasing a car, and be prepared to share your list with the rest of the class.

Learn About

- shopping issues in daily life
- renting or leasing an apartment
- buying or leasing a car

success TIP

Separate your *wants* from your *needs*.

"The amount of money you have has got nothing to do with what you earn. People earning a million dollars a year can have no money and people earning $35,000 a year can be quite well off. It's not what you earn, it's what you spend."

Paul Clitheroe, financial analyst

Shopping Issues in Daily Life

In Chapter 1, Lesson 2, you learned about bank accounts. You've also learned how to create a budget. This lesson focuses on the decisions you'll have to make about buying everyday items such as groceries and clothing. You'll also learn about making big decisions that don't come up every day—decisions about such things as renting an apartment or buying or leasing a car. This lesson, in short, is about learning how to be a smart consumer. The smarter you are, the more money you'll save.

Four Steps to Smart Shopping in the 21st Century

Just as you work hard to earn money, you should also work hard when deciding where to spend it. Apply these steps to any purchasing decision—especially major items—and you'll be more likely to get products that meet your needs for the best price.

A big benefit of this approach: It helps eliminate impulse buying, which is the quickest route to an empty bank account.

Step 1: Separate your *wants* from your *needs*. You may want a new cell phone to keep in touch with your friends. However, will it interfere with your ability to pay for the things that you need, such as gas to get to school or work?

Step 2: Do your research. Purchase wisely. Let's say you're in the market for a flat screen TV. First, you need to find out how much your budget will allow. Then, do some *comparison-shopping*. The Internet is a convenient way to compare brands and models, and to access useful resources such as the *Consumer Action Handbook*, downloadable at www.consumeraction.gov. Also online, in bookstores, and most libraries, is *Consumer Reports*, a publication that provides unbiased ratings and recommendations for a wide range of products and services.

Step 3: Make your purchase. Once you've decided on the item, decide where to buy it. In today's high-tech, global economy, you have the opportunity to search online for the best bargains. When shopping in stores, and occasionally online, you may be able to negotiate a better price than the one listed. The key to good negotiation is research. If you know the markup, *the price added on above what the dealer paid for the product*, you can sometimes convince the seller to reduce the price. If you are paying for your purchase over time, carefully evaluate the financing alternatives. Some stores offer layaway or "90 days same as cash" options, helping you to spread out your payments without incurring interest or finance charges.

Step 4: Maintain your purchase. Smart buying also means maintaining your purchase, which includes physically maintaining what you've bought, as well as resolving any complaints or issues about the purchase or product. If you have a problem, the first thing to do is to contact the seller. If that doesn't resolve the issue, contact the headquarters of the company that made the product. Most large companies have a toll-free 800 number, and almost all companies have a website.

Vocabulary

- markup
- comparison shopping
- unit price
- product expiration date
- brand
- produce
- prime
- choice and select
- tenant
- landlord
- gross income
- real estate agent
- lease
- security deposit
- utilities
- net income
- interest rate
- down payment
- equity

Shopping online can be convenient and fun, but requires careful purchasing decisions.
Courtesy of Elena Elisseeva/Shutterstock

Shopping Online

Internet shopping has become available to almost everyone with a computer. Internet retail sales reached almost $200 billion dollars in 2011. In the same year, growth in Internet sales almost doubled that of other retail sales trends. Since online shopping is so common now, you should understand that retail-shopping convenience on the Internet is sometimes not a good thing. Some bad purchasing decisions have been made because online shoppers have failed to heed certain cautions about untrustworthy business ventures and practices. To ensure you're shopping safely, you should pay attention to these shopping tips offered by the American Bar Association:

1. *Trust your instincts when you shop online*—Don't feel pressured to make an order quickly.

2. *Be knowledgeable about web-based auction activities such as eBay®*—Understand rules of the site and legal terms about warranties and refunds, for example.

3. *Be suspicious of prices that are too good to be true, or overpricing*—Compare products online, as you would in normal retail stores.

4. *Find and read the privacy policy of any potential seller*—If the seller is going to use your information, find out how it will be used, as well as how you can stop the process.

5. *Understand fully the return, refund, and shipping policies*—Somewhere there should be a link to "legal terms."

6. *Make sure the Internet connection is secure*—There should be an indicator that security software is in place on the site.

7. *Use the safest way to pay on the Internet*—Use a credit card rather than a debit card, when possible.

8. *Print or save the terms, conditions, warranties, and all other records of your contact with the online seller*—and save them with a record of your purchase.

If you have an item delivered, you should find out if a signature is required so that the package can be delivered to you and not left at the door while you're away. You should also carefully inspect your purchase immediately, and if there's a problem, contact the seller as soon as possible. Put the complaint in writing, if necessary, to ask for a repair or refund, and keep the correspondence until the issue is resolved.

Shopping for Groceries

Studies show that the average person uses at least 15 products every morning before he or she even leaves home. These products include toothpaste, soap, shampoo, and other bathroom products. They also include food—cereal, bread, eggs, juice, and milk, for example. All these products are available on the shelves of your favorite grocery store. Although none of them is expensive by itself, their combined costs quickly add up, especially for a shopper without a list. Therefore, it's important to shop intelligently. Being a smart shopper takes a lot of thinking, as you'll find out below.

Starting Off Right: Some Basic Tips

You'll be a smarter shopper if you follow these basic rules:

- *Plan your meals, and make a shopping list*—Write down items when you think of them. Don't wait until you're ready to head out for the store.

- *Watch for sales*—Check the current ads in your newspaper or the flyers at the store for special deals. Compare weekly ads of stores in your community to find the best bargains.

- *Buy store brands rather than nationally known manufacturers' brands whenever you can*—There's often little or no difference in quality, but a big difference in price.

- *Have a grocery budget and stick to it.*

- *Don't go to the store hungry*—If you do, you may buy too much.

- *Don't buy on impulse*—The spur-of-the moment items you throw into the cart can be budget breakers.

- *Minimize purchases of processed foods, such as instant potatoes*—Instead, buy raw foods, such as real potatoes. Raw foods often cost less than processed foods. They also tend to be more nutritious.

- *If you have a freezer and the prices are right, buy more than you need*—Store the extra items in your freezer. For example, if the store is offering a "buy one, get one free" sale on bread, buy two loaves and stick one in the freezer.

- *Clip coupons from newspapers and magazines*—They are great money savers. Sort the coupons by type (for example, cleaning supplies, canned foods, or pet food). Then place a "C" beside each item on your list for which you have a coupon. This will help you remember the coupon at the checkout counter. Finally, make sure to look at the expiration dates on the coupons. If you have two coupons for the same item, use the coupon with the shortest expiration date first.

> **success TIP** ★
>
> Place a "C" beside each item on your list for which you have a coupon. This will help you remember the coupon at the checkout counter.

Comparison Shopping

Smart shoppers don't buy the first thing they see. Instead, they make it a habit to do comparison shopping, which means *comparing the prices and quality of different items to see which one is a better deal.*

Consider how Sara handles her grocery shopping. With her shopping list in hand, Sara heads to the frozen-food section to find the first item on the list: corn. She sees that a 16-ounce bag of Brand A corn costs $1.36. A 24-ounce bag of Brand B corn sells for $2.20. Which brand is the better buy?

If you answered Brand A, you are right. How did you know? The bags are different sizes, so you can't tell which one is cheaper by comparing the prices. To know which brand is the better buy, you must know the cost of one ounce of each brand of corn.

To calculate the cost per ounce, you divide the cost of the item by the total number of ounces.

For Brand A, divide $1.36 by 16 ounces, and you get $0.85 per ounce. For Brand B, divide $2.20 by 24 ounces, and you get $0.91 per ounce. Since Brand A costs less per ounce than Brand B, Brand A is the better buy, at least in terms of price.

You don't necessarily need to bring a calculator to the store to determine the cost of an ounce of most foods today. Beneath each stack of items on many supermarket shelves is a label that provides the unit price, or *cost per serving*. The grocer has divided the price of each item by the number of servings, or units, in each package. (Unit pricing also works for nonfood items. The unit price for facial tissues, for example, is the cost of a single tissue.)

Unit pricing is very helpful when you're comparing two sizes of a product. You'd expect that the larger size would be a better deal, and it often is. This may not always be true; the only way to be sure is to look at the unit price.

Even if you've decided that the larger size is a better deal, don't drop it into your cart too fast. Look at the product expiration date. The product expiration date is *the date after which the item will be stale or no longer be at its finest quality*. You'll usually see it stamped on the bottom or side of the package. If you think you won't use the product by the expiration date, it's probably better to buy the smaller quantity. Otherwise, you may have to throw away the remaining food and you will not have saved any money.

Price is not the only thing to consider when comparison shopping. Quality is important. You may trust one brand, or *distinctive name identifying a product or manufacturer*, more than you trust another. Therefore, if you knew, based on experience, that the more expensive brand tasted a lot better, or that it was more nutritious, you might buy it despite the higher cost.

Tips for Buying Particular Food Items

Fruits and Vegetables

Produce, or *fresh fruits and vegetables*, is an excellent source of vitamins. The rule of thumb is, "The darker the green or brighter the orange, the more the vitamins." In other words, vegetables such as broccoli and carrots have many times more vitamins than pale vegetables such as celery.

Eating a variety of fresh fruits and vegetables may be expensive, however, unless you are careful to purchase produce when it's in season in your area. In other words, buying a watermelon in July is cheaper than buying it in December. It's usually less expensive to buy canned or frozen fruits and vegetables in the winter months, when prices of fresh produce increase. Frozen fruits and vegetables have the benefit of consistent quality, and they will keep longer than fresh fruits and vegetables. Dried fruits are also an option.

Other ideas for saving money on produce include:

- Buy certain items in bulk. For example, buy potatoes in five- or 10-pound bags, not by the piece or by the pound. However, when you buy in bulk, don't overdo it. Potatoes, for example, may spoil if you keep them more than two weeks.

- If you buy produce in bulk, keep it refrigerated. Store produce in plastic bags so they will not dry out.

Fresh produce costs less when it's in season.
Courtesy of lightpoet/Shutterstock

- Don't be put off by appearance. For example, did you ever notice the dark-brown bananas that the grocer puts in bags and sells half-price? They may not look great, but they taste fine. Buy them and store the extras in the refrigerator. Although the cold will darken the skin, the fruit is not affected.

- Test green beans for freshness by snapping one in half. It should break easily.

- Buy oranges not by their color (most oranges are dyed) but by their firm skin.

- Lemons are best when they're slightly green on the ends and with a smooth skin. Store lemons in a sealed container of water to keep them moist. If you need just a few drops of juice, puncture the lemon and squeeze them out; don't slice the whole lemon.

- Wash and drain salad greens, then refrigerate them in a plastic container or bag. Tear the greens; don't cut them. They'll stay fresh longer. A bag of salad greens will remain fresh in the refrigerator for several days. However, don't try to save time by making a whole salad in advance. If you add tomatoes or cucumbers to the bag, the salad will become soggy. Add these extras just before serving.

- Store strawberries in the refrigerator in the plastic basket the grocer provided. This allows air to circulate around them and keep them firm. To make sure that strawberries keep their sweetness, don't wash them until just before serving.

Meat Products

As a US Department of Agriculture (USDA) bulletin states, "Consumers buy meat because they like its taste and flexibility for being prepared in a variety of ways for just about any occasion." The USDA oversees the safety of America's meat through regular inspection of facilities where meat is prepared.

Fresh and frozen meats require cooking before you can eat them. It is important to cook meats to the appropriate temperature. You can find information on these temperatures on the package or in a good cookbook.

Processed meats, such as cold cuts, do not require cooking. They contain several added ingredients, such as salt and preservatives. They also have a high fat content. If you're watching your salt or fat intake, you might want to avoid them. You can store processed meats in the refrigerator up to a week or in the freezer for up to a month. Always check the product expiration date and read the label when you buy processed meats.

The most popular types of meat sold in the United States are beef, pork, and lamb. Here are some details on each of these types of meat.

Beef

Beef is a popular red meat for grilling and broiling. Whether you are shopping for hamburger, steak, roast, or other cuts of beef, you do not have to be an expert to choose the right grade of beef, since many cuts of meat, from hamburger to steaks to roasts, are labeled with a USDA grade.

The best grade is prime, *a cut of beef that has the greatest degree of marbling, or flecks of fat, that help make meat tender, juicy, and flavorful*. It is the most expensive cut of beef. You can find prime beef in restaurants and better grocery stores. Choice and select grades are *less expensive grades with less marbling in select than in choice grade*. The protein, vitamin, and mineral content of beef are similar regardless of the grade.

Pork

The most popular cuts of pork are *ribs*, *roasts*, and *chops*. All these cuts come from the *loin*, the meat that runs along either size of the backbone. The *tenderloin* is a strip of choice meat that is cut from the center of the loin. Pork chops come from the rib. The *shoulder* is cut from the front leg. The lower section of a shoulder cut is often labeled a *picnic cut*. The upper section of the shoulder is *pork butt* or *Boston butt*. The *ham* is cut from the back leg. Shoulder cuts and hams are sold both fresh and smoked. *Bacon* and *spare ribs* come from the underside of the animal.

Lamb

The most popular cuts of lamb are *leg*, *chops*, *rack*, and *loin*. *Leg of lamb*, a choice cut, comes from the hind leg of the animal. Lamb *chops* come from the rib. The *rack* is the rib section of the lamb. Lamb *loins* run along either side of the backbone.

Poultry

The word *poultry* refers to a farm-raised bird, as opposed to one that a hunter shoots in the wild. The main types of poultry are chicken and turkey. Most chicken is sold fresh; turkeys are sold both fresh and frozen. The USDA oversees the safety of poultry. Poultry is a nutritious, economical food. It is generally less expensive than meat.

You can buy a chicken whole and roast it in the oven or cook it on the grill. You can also buy chicken parts, such as *breast, legs (drumsticks), thighs,* and *wings.* Breast meat is white and is the most expensive cut. Chicken wings, which have little meat, have become a popular snack item. Turkeys are usually sold by the whole bird, although you can buy turkey breast, legs, and frozen ground turkey.

Fish

The National Oceanic and Atmospheric Administration (NOAA) oversees the management of fisheries in the United States. It also maintains a voluntary seafood-inspection program. Fish that has passed NOAA inspection bears a special mark that may read "US Grade A," "processed under federal inspection (PUFI)," or "lot inspection." Nevertheless, the sale of seafood, unlike that of poultry and meat, is not regulated by the US government.

The two main types of fish are *fin fish* and *shellfish.* Fin fish include salmon, cod, halibut, flounder, tuna, trout, catfish, and many others. The two main cuts of fish are steaks and fillets. A steak is cut crosswise across the fish's body. A fillet is cut down the length of the body of the fish. Popular shellfish include shrimp, lobster, crabs, clams, scallops, and oysters.

Most fish is sold fresh or frozen. Both are equally nutritious and tasty, provided they have been properly stored and handled. Beware of fish that smells "fishy." Fish should have a fresh, natural aroma. Some fish, such as salmon and tuna, may also be sold canned.

Canned and Packaged Goods

Canned goods have a long shelf life. The product expiration dates may be one year or more from the date of purchase. This means that you can stock up when these items are on sale. Again, buying food in quantity will not save you money if you never eat it.

When buying canned or packaged goods take the time to read the labels. Federal law requires that every package of food display the name of the product, the name and address of the manufacturer, net amount of contents by weight (or by weight and volume if it's a liquid), a Nutrition Facts label, and a list of ingredients.

Labels on canned and prepackaged goods contain useful information.
Courtesy of Lucian Coman/Shutterstock

The *Nutrition Facts label* is full of valuable information. If you check out this label before you make a purchase, you can make better decisions about healthy eating. At the top, the label shows serving size (for example, one cup for dry cereal) and the amount of servings per container (a 15-ounce box of dry cereal has around 14 servings). The label then lists the calories, as well as total amount of fat, carbohydrates, and protein, in a serving. Finally, the label has information on the product's vitamin and mineral content. It tells you what percentages of your daily requirements of these nutrients are in one serving. For example, a cup of oat cereal provides 3 percent of your daily recommended fat content, 7 percent of your daily recommended carbohydrate intake, and no protein. It contains 45 percent of your daily requirement of iron and 10 percent of your daily requirement for vitamin C, as well as other vitamins and minerals. Add milk to the cereal, and those percentages go up considerably, as the label for cereal also shows.

The ingredients list may be quite informative for both your physical health and the health of your budget. By law, it must begin with the main ingredient and then move on, item by item, to the ingredient used least. For example, suppose you're comparing two bottles of pasta sauce. Both contain 28 ounces of sauce, and both cost $2.99. The first ingredient on one label is water. The first ingredient on the label of the other bottle is tomato puree. Which do you think is the better deal? The ingredients list also tells you what chemical additives and dyes are in the food.

Dairy Products

Milk is a low-cost source of calcium, important for healthy bones. However, some types of milk have more fat than others. If you're concerned about consuming too much fat, check out the fat content. Milk with the highest fat content is labeled "4 percent butterfat." Skim milk, at the other extreme, has no fat.

You can also find eggs, cheese, butter, sour cream, and other products in the dairy section. Eggs come in several sizes. Check the price of each size. If the price difference between two sizes of eggs, say medium and large, is less than five cents per dozen, buy the larger size. Always check the expiration date before buying eggs.

You can buy cheese in several forms; for example, in blocks, sliced, and grated. Sliced or grated cheese may have a higher unit price than block cheese does. Save money by buying cheese in blocks and slicing or grating it yourself. Hard cheeses may turn green as they age. This is a natural process. Just cut off the mold before eating. Store extra cheese, butter, or margarine in the freezer to reduce spoilage.

Frozen Foods

Americans today have less time to cook than ever before, and sales of frozen foods have increased dramatically. The frozen-foods section in the grocery store has fruits, vegetables, breads, and desserts, as well as main dishes and low-calorie meals. Although frozen meals are usually more expensive than home-prepared meals, people depend on them because they are so convenient—particularly when you have a microwave oven.

You can save money buying these foods by comparing ads from various stores. Since frozen foods are so popular, many grocers regularly put them on sale to increase business. You can also use manufacturers' coupons to reduce the cost of these items.

Other Foods

You can buy breads fresh off the shelf, frozen, or partially baked. Many supermarkets have in-store bakeries. These bakery products vary in cost, depending on their quality and other factors. Compare costs by reading labels and determining the cost per serving.

Cereals appeal to kids, and they're heavily advertised. You can save money by clipping coupons. You can also buy store brands rather than name brands. The packaging of the store brand may not be as glitzy, but the product is often just as good as the name brand.

Baking needs such as flour, sugar, spices, and oils usually are in the same aisle of the grocery store. Again, look for store brands, which vary little from national brands in quality. When selecting flour, consider the unbleached variety, even though it costs a bit more. The nutritional content is higher.

Rice and pasta are good sources of carbohydrates. They supply quick energy. Some people call them "meat extenders" because they satisfy hunger but cost less than meat. Pasta comes in various forms, both fresh and dried. The labels provide excellent cooking ideas. Rice and pasta store well. Buying them in large quantities can save money.

Condiments include pickles, sauces, and spreads. These items add zest to meals, but they are usually expensive. Again, compare the national and the store brands for quality and price. Consider mixing your own salad dressings. It doesn't take long, and the result is often more flavorful and less expensive per serving.

Many shoppers spend a large percentage of their grocery budget on snack foods and soft drinks. These items provide little or no nutritional value, but they may have lots of calories. If you include these on your grocery list, look for specials and volume discounts. Since they are popular items, grocers tend to offer competitive prices.

Eating on a Budget—The US Department of Agriculture's 3 Ps

PLAN

- Plan meals and snacks for the week according to an established budget.
- Find quick and easy recipes online.
- Include meals that will "stretch" expensive food items (stews, casseroles, stir-fried dishes).
- Make a grocery list.
- Check for sales and coupons in the local paper or online and consider discount stores.
- Ask about a loyalty card at your grocery store.

PURCHASE

- Buy groceries when you are not hungry and when you are not too rushed.
- Stick to the grocery list and stay out of the aisles that don't contain items on your list.
- Buy store brands if cheaper.
- Find and compare unit prices listed on shelves to get the best price.
- Purchase some items in bulk or as family packs, which usually cost less.
- Choose fresh fruits and vegetables in season; buy canned vegetables with less salt.
- Pre-cut fruits and vegetables, individual cups of yogurt, and instant rice and hot cereals are convenient, but usually cost more than those that require a bit more prep time.
- Good low-cost items available all year include:
  Protein—beans (garbanzo, black, cannellini)
  Vegetables—carrots, greens, potatoes
  Fruit—apples, bananas

PREPARE

- Some meal items can be prepared in advance; pre-cook on days when you have time.
- Double or triple up on recipes and freeze meal-sized containers of soups and casseroles or divide into individual portions.
- Try a few meatless meals by substituting with beans and peas or try "no-cook" meals like salads.
- Incorporate leftovers into a subsequent meal.
- Be creative with a fruit or vegetable and use it in different ways during the week.

---

success TIP ★

Over a lifetime, most people will make thousands of trips to the supermarket. Try to avoid unnecessary trips, and always use a list. It will pay off over time to learn to shop efficiently.

Nonfood Items

Supermarkets are "super" because they offer more than just food. You can rent movies, buy flowers, medicines, and cosmetics, or even buy furniture, tires, and appliances in some supermarkets. Buying nonfood items while grocery shopping may save you a trip to another store. Remember, impulse purchases are tough on the budget. Avoid browsing and stick to your list.

Shopping for Clothing

When you have your own money, you may be tempted to spend a lot on clothing. Dressing well is important: It makes a big difference in how you feel. You also need to dress well to get a good job. However, clothing can be expensive. When shopping for clothing, keep these tips in mind:

You shop more efficiently when you plan your purchases rather than buying on impulse.

Courtesy of Andresr/Shutterstock

- *Don't overspend*—Think about the gaps in your wardrobe and buy only what you need.

- *Buy pieces you can mix and match*— A shirt or blouse that you can wear with several outfits is more economical than one you can wear only with a certain skirt or pair of pants.

- *Shop at discount stores rather than at malls whenever possible*—They often have good clothes at bargain prices.

- *Shop online to save time and money*—But be careful to shop at secure sites. The American Bar Association's informational site at *http://www.safeshopping.org/* will help you order safely when shopping.

- *Don't buy something just because it's the latest fashion*—The best bargain is what looks good on you, not what's trendy.

- *Even if you find a good sale, be careful*—You don't want to fill your closet with things you can't use. Sale items also may be of lower quality than items not on sale.

- *Don't shop just for shopping's sake*—Some people shop just to feel good—that's an expensive way to calm your nerves.

- *Try to buy clothing at the end of a season*—For example, the best time to find a winter coat at a bargain price is in February, not November.

Spending on Entertainment

Many teenagers spend a good deal of their money on entertainment, such as movies, CDs, downloading music, and video games. The key issue here is budget: Decide how much you can afford to spend each month on entertainment, and then stick to it. Do not get distracted by what's new or in the mall, what your friends have, or what you see on TV or the Internet.

Renting or Leasing an Apartment

While you are in high school, you probably live at home with your parents or guardian and don't pay any rent. However, even if you still are one or two years from graduation, it is important for you to learn the ropes of finding a place of your own - one of life's most important personal and financial decisions.

Renting or leasing an apartment is often less expensive, at least over the short term, than buying a house. Renting is often necessary for young people who are just starting out and don't have enough money for a down payment on a house. Renting is also a good idea if you're not sure whether you'll be staying in an area for more than a year or two.

Apartments are often clustered in complexes on a large piece of property. Apartments offer amenities such as tennis courts, pools, clubhouses, and laundry facilities for their tenants. A tenant is *a person who rents an apartment*. Tenants pay a monthly fee to the landlord, or *apartment owner*. Tenants are responsible for keeping their units safe and clean, but they are not responsible for the maintenance of the apartment. If something goes wrong, they call the landlord, who arranges for the repair.

If you've decided to rent an apartment, the next thing to do is to choose where you want to live. Explore various neighborhoods. Think about such factors as neighborhood safety, as well as access to public transportation, shopping, libraries, and other community services.

Some apartment complexes have professionals on the property who can show and rent apartments.

Courtesy of Corbis Images

Determine what size apartment you want. The smallest apartment is called a studio or efficiency. It has one large room, a bathroom, and a kitchen. Landlords typically refer to apartments based on how many bedrooms, and in some cases bathrooms, they have.

Rental fees of apartments vary widely. They can range from a few hundred dollars a month to thousands, depending on where you live and how upscale the building is. One important thing to think about before you even start looking is how much you can afford to spend on rent. Experts recommend that you pay no more than 30 percent of your gross income, or *income before taxes and other deductions*, on rent, gas, heat, and electricity. This will allow you to have enough extra money for other living needs.

To find an apartment, look at newspaper and online advertisements. These are usually the best sources of information on apartments currently available. Some apartment complexes have professionals on the property who can show and rent apartments. Another option is to call a real estate agent. A real estate agent is *a professional who helps people buy, sell, or rent homes and apartments*. Many real estate agents prefer to deal with people who are buying rather than renting. If you are interested in using a real estate agent, ask which type is his or her primary focus. If the agent doesn't usually help renters, you may want to find another agent who does. If you use a real estate agent, he or she may charge a fee. Be sure to inquire what the fee is before you use the agent.

If you are interested in a particular apartment building, try to find out information about the landlord from the previous tenant or other people in the building. For example, does the landlord fix things promptly? Does the landlord have a habit of showing up unannounced to inspect the apartment? If so, living there could be difficult.

When you agree to rent an apartment, you will sign a lease, or *an agreement to pay rent and fulfill other obligations for a certain length of time*. A lease is usually for one year, but it can be longer. Some apartments have monthly leases, but this is relatively rare.

A lease is a legal document. When you sign it, you are legally bound to its terms. Read it carefully, and ask about any terms that you do not understand. The lease will spell out your responsibilities and those of your landlord. If you break the lease and move out early, do not pay your rent, or don't follow the terms of the lease in any other way, the landlord has grounds for taking legal action against you. Items covered in a lease may include the amount of the rent, the security deposit and utilities (see below), the number of people who may live in the unit, where you can park your car, responsibilities for maintenance of the apartment, a policy on pets, and similar items.

One of the terms of the lease may be that you leave the apartment in good shape when you move out. If you have not kept the apartment in good shape (for example, if there are spills on the carpet, holes in the walls, or structural damage), the landlord may withhold some or all of your security deposit A security deposit is *a payment to make sure you meet your obligations as a tenant*. Deposits vary widely. Some landlords require a first and last month's rent; some require only one month's rent. The landlord will refund your security deposit at the end of the lease if you have met the terms of the lease.

Young people often share an apartment with one or more roommates. This helps cut the cost of living. If you and a friend want to rent an apartment together, ask yourself, and each other, two big questions:

1. Who will sign the lease? If you both sign, you are *both* legally responsible for fulfilling *all* its terms. If everything goes as planned, you'll both save money. However, if your roommate decides to move out early or breaks one of the requirements of the lease, you will be responsible for the rent and other obligations. If one of you expects to leave earlier, it might be best for the one who intends to stay longer to sign the lease alone. The bottom line is to have a roommate you can trust.

2. Do you have similar living habits? For example, if you like to have loud parties on weekends and your roommate values privacy, you may have problems. If dirty dishes in the sink, a messy bedroom, and dust and grime don't bother your roommate but you're a very organized person, watch out.

Discuss both questions in advance. If you can't agree, you'd better decide to live alone or find another roommate. Saving money is important, but it's not your only consideration. You don't want to risk losing a friend or getting into the legal problems that a broken lease might create.

Tips for Apartment Hunting

Shopping for an apartment is a big deal. Here are some tips to help you succeed.

- Don't rush into anything. Spend enough time searching for an apartment to be sure you will be happy.

- Know whether utilities are included in your rental rate. Utilities are *electricity, heat, gas, and water*. They can be expensive. If they are not included in your rent, you will need to pay for them separately (Try to find out from the landlord or the previous tenant how much utilities will cost.) You will always have to pay separately for things such as your telephone and cable TV. You may also have to pay a deposit to the telephone company or another utility company. You'll get your deposit back when you move out, as long as you have paid your bills, but you need to count it in when you are planning your budget.

- Before you sign the lease, figure out your monthly rent and utilities expenses. Make sure they total no more than 30 percent of your gross income. For example, if you're earning $24,000 a year, your rent and utilities should total no more than $8,000. A rent of $650 a month ($7,800 per year) is too high.

- Apartments usually have basic kitchen appliances, such as a refrigerator and oven. Many, however, do not include a microwave or laundry facilities.

- Most apartments are unfurnished. If you need to buy your own furniture, figure that into your budget. Rental fees for furnished apartments are usually higher than fees for unfurnished apartments.

- Calculate the costs associated with moving. If you have some furniture, you will probably want to rent a truck, get some friends, and move it yourself. Moving companies can be expensive. Check their rates, and do comparison shopping. Also, be sure to see if the building has specified move-in times.

- Bring someone with you to look at apartments you are thinking of renting. Sometimes a second party can point out things you may not have noticed.

- If you are concerned about safety, you might want to rent an apartment on the second floor or above. Make sure the locks are strong and that they work well. Better yet, install a new lock. This is because the previous tenant might have given out keys to other people. If being in the neighborhood makes you nervous, no matter how good a deal the apartment is, you should probably rent somewhere else. You want to be able to walk around outside without fear and sleep peacefully.

When renting an apartment, select a location that is both convenient and safe.
Courtesy of AISPIX by Image Source/Shutterstock

Pets

Many apartment buildings don't allow their tenants to have pets. Ask about this when you visit the apartment. If you have a pet, don't lie about it. Instead, find an apartment with a "pet-friendly" policy. Some landlords require a pet deposit or an extra security deposit to cover damage that your pet could cause.

Buying or Leasing a Car

Getting a car is a major goal for many young people. When you're ready to take this step, you'll need to decide what kind of car to get, how much you can afford to pay, and whether to buy or lease.

Selecting a Car

When you're ready to choose a car, think about the following questions:

- What kind do you *need*? The car you need may be different from the car you *want*. Be realistic. Do you need a small car that is easy to park and gets good gas mileage? Do you need an SUV that holds lots of people and equipment? The SUV will use much more gas, but if you really need a big car, then you'll have to be willing to pay for fuel. As gas prices climb, that becomes an even more serious consideration.

- How much can you afford? Stay within your budget. Don't buy or lease a car that will require you to get a second job or borrow more money than you can afford. Remember, if you borrow money to buy the car, you will probably be making monthly payments for the next several years. A good rule of thumb is to spend no more than 20 percent of your net income, or *income after taxes and other deductions*, on monthly car payments.

- Should you get a new car or a used one? New cars require less maintenance, but they're much more expensive than used ones. A compromise may be a well-maintained car that is a few years old.

When you're hunting for a car, think about what kind of car you need, how much you can afford to pay, and whether you should get a new car or a used one.

Courtesy of Lee White/Corbis Images

- If you've decided on a used car, what kind of condition is it in? Check the outside: Is the paint worn or chipped? Is it rusty? Is there body damage? Are the tires in good shape? Then check the inside: Is the upholstery worn? Do the electronic devices work? Finally, look under the hood: Does everything work, particularly the engine? If you don't have the knowledge to inspect the engine, hire a mechanic to do it for you. This will cost you some money, but if it prevents you from buying a car that needs lots of repair, it will be worth it.

- What kind of insurance will you need? Insurance rates for some cars, usually more-expensive ones, sports cars, or models that are popular targets of car thieves are higher than rates for other cars. Get an insurance estimate before buying a car.

- What kind of resale value will the car have? You cannot perfectly predict the resale value of a car, but you can get a rough idea from various websites, such as the Kelly Blue Book site at www.kbb.com. Compare cars and choose the one that has a good resale value.

- How much will repairs cost? Some cars cost more to maintain than others do. Generally, the more expensive the car when it is new, the more expensive it is to repair. It usually costs more to fix a Mercedes, for example, than a Chevy.

- What is the financing rate? If you'll need a loan to pay for your car, visit several dealers and banks and see which one will give you the best interest rate, *the seller's or lending institution's charge on borrowed money.* You may have to make trade-offs: For example, one dealer may charge a lower price for the car but charge a higher interest rate.

Should You Lease or Buy?

For some drivers, leasing is an attractive option. An advantage of leasing is that you may not need a down payment, or *partial payment that you make when purchasing something.* Your monthly payment may be less than a loan payment would be. Another advantage is that you return the car to the dealer at the end of the lease period, so you don't need to worry about finding a buyer.

However, leasing a car also has serious disadvantages. Since you do not own the car, you do not have equity in it, or *the difference between the market value and the unpaid balance,* though you are still responsible for maintenance costs. You will have to pay for repairing any damage to the car over the lease period. You will have to pay an extra fee if you drive more than the maximum number of miles specified in the lease. You may have to pay a fee if you return the car before the end of the lease. In addition, you may be charged "lease acquisition fees" or "lease disposal fees" of several hundred dollars to cover costs of obtaining a credit report, verifying insurance coverage, and other administrative costs to process your lease. One authoritative source, the nonprofit magazine *Consumer Reports,*® says that for many reasons it usually costs more to lease than to buy a car.

Let's say Stephanie is considering whether to buy or lease a car. The model she wants costs $18,000. As you see in Figure 1.4, if she purchased the car, she would make a down payment of $1,000. If she had no other money to put down on the car at that time, she'd need to take out a $17,000 loan. To pay off that loan, she would make payments of $412 per month for 48 months. Considering these expenses, and the fact that she would not be able to collect the $160 in interest that she would earn if that $1,000 remained in her savings account, the car would cost her $20,936.

In this example, if she leased the car, Stephanie would not have to make a down payment. She would give the dealer a security deposit of $800, which she would receive back at the end of the lease period. She would not collect $128 in interest on that $800. She would make monthly payments of $300 for the 48 months. Her cost would be $14,528.

However, the story isn't complete. At the end of the lease period, Stephanie would have to return the car to the dealer. She would not be able to sell it. If Stephanie had bought the car and could sell it for $10,000, her total cost for purchasing would be $10,936.

In this case, buying would be a better deal. It would save Stephanie more than $3,500.

COST OF PURCHASING THE CAR

	COST
1. Down payment	$1,000
2. Down payment of $1,000 results in foregone interst income:	
Forgone Interest:	
Income per Year = Down Payment × Annual Interest Rate	
= $1,000 × 0.04	
= $40	
Forgone Interest over Four Years = $40 × 4	
= $160	$160
3. Total monthly payments are:	
Total Monthly Payments = Monthly Payment × Number of Months	
= $412 × 48	
= $19,776	$19,776
Total	$20,936
Minus: Expected amount to be received when car is sold in four years	−$10,000
Total Cost	**$10,936**

COST OF LEASING THE CAR FOR FOUR YEARS

	COST
1. Security deposit of $800 results in forgone interest income (although she will receive her deposit back in four years):	
Forgone Interest:	
Income per Year = Down Payment × Annual Interest Rate	
= $800 × 0.04	
= $32	
Forgone Interest over Four Years = $32 × 4	
= 128	$128
2. Total monthly payments are:	
Total Monthly Payments = Monthly Payment × Number of Months	
= $300 × 48	
= $14,400	$14,400
Total Cost	**$14,528**

FIGURE 1.4

Comparison of the Cost of Purchasing Versus Leasing a Car

Reprinted from *Personal Finance*, edited by Jeff Madura (2011), by permission of Pearson Education

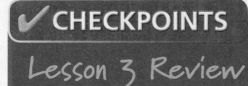

✔ CHECKPOINTS

Lesson 3 Review

Using complete sentences, answer the following questions on a sheet of paper.

1. What are the four steps to smart buying?

2. What is comparison shopping?

3. What are the three Ps for eating on a budget?

4. What are three ways you can make sure you are spending wisely on clothing?

5. What are three of the most important things to consider when renting an apartment?

6. What are the advantages of buying a car? What are the advantages of leasing a car?

APPLYING BUYING AND SELLING SKILLS

7. Look online or in the classified section of your newspaper and find two apartments that sound like great places to live. On the basis of the ads, compare the apartments. Consider their prices and features (such as air conditioning, size, parking), plus what you know about their location. Which one sounds better to you?

CHAPTER 2

Courtesy of Monkey Business Images/Shutterstock

Managing Your Resources

"There is no dignity quite so impressive,
and no independence quite so important,
as living within your means."

Calvin Coolidge, 30th President of the United States

Avoiding the Credit Trap

Quick Write

_____

_____

Terry is interested in buying a new cell phone, costing $200. However, he has only $50 in his checking account and $40 in savings. He is considering how to borrow the rest he needs to cover the cost. In a short paragraph, explain which of these three kinds of credit would work best for Terry: a retail card, an installment loan, or a layaway plan. From what you know already, how would you purchase this new cell phone?

"If you would like to know the value of money, go and try to borrow some."

Benjamin Franklin, scientist, author, politician, musician, postmaster, inventor, Founding Father of the US

What Is Credit?

The American economy is built on credit. Americans have $2.68 trillion in consumer credit, according to the US Department of the Treasury. If people didn't use credit, they'd have to give up many of the things they now take for granted—a car, a home, a college education, a great vacation. Few people have $20,000 or so on hand to buy a new car. But they can't get along without one. So they have to use credit to get the money.

Here's a good math problem. What is 2.68 trillion divided by 300 million? That's how much consumer credit each American has amassed on average. The answer will come later in the lesson.

Credit, or *providing or lending money with the expectation of future repayment*, enables you to postpone payment for something you buy. The creditor, usually *a bank, credit union, or financing company that loans money*, makes the purchase for you. You promise to pay the creditor back what you've borrowed within a certain time period, with interest.

How Credit Works

Once you're 18, you may qualify to apply for a credit card and many other kinds of loans. This lesson is to help you prepare for that day. The more knowledge and information you have about credit, the better you'll be prepared for the time when you have to manage money on a larger scale.

Learn About

- what is credit?
- important credit terms
- positive and negative aspects of using credit
- sources of credit
- how credit works
- using credit responsibly
- credit and credit card options
- building your credit history
- avoiding credit card fraud
- the consequences of deficit spending

(As you may remember from Chapter 1, Lesson 1, *interest* is a charge on borrowed money.) An annual percentage rate (APR), is *the yearly interest rate.* Finance charge is *another term for interest and APR.* Credit may come through a direct loan; for example, the bank may loan you money to buy a car. Credit may also come through a credit card that you use to purchase goods and services. Suppose you need a loan of $15,000 to buy a new car. *The money you borrow* is called the principal. A direct loan will have a maturity date, which is *the date by which you must repay the money you borrowed.* You cannot wait until the maturity date to make payments on your loan. You must make monthly payments, which include both the principal and interest. Credit card loans have no maturity date. You simply pay a minimum amount each month on your credit card bill. If you don't pay the remaining balance of your bill each month, you'll also pay interest.

Some people think that it's never a good idea to buy things on credit. They don't like the idea of being in debt. However, virtually no one today can get along without borrowing money at some point. Furthermore, if you never borrow, you won't establish a credit rating, or *an assessment of how trustworthy you are in paying your bills.*

It's actually a good idea to get one or two credit cards— as long as you have an income from steady employment. However, do not overspend, and do make your payments on time. That way, you will establish a good credit rating. Then creditors will be more likely to give you a loan when you need one for a big purchase, such as a car or a house.

Good credit can help you reach your goals. In this lesson, you'll learn how using credit wisely can be an important part of managing your finances.

Vocabulary

- credit
- creditor
- annual percentage rate (APR)
- finance charge
- principal
- maturity date
- credit rating
- minimum payment
- bankruptcy
- installments
- cash advance
- annual fee
- collateral
- credit history
- periodic rate
- variable rate
- grace period
- default
- unsecured loan
- cosigner
- credit bureau
- credit score
- deficit spending

A Credit Dictionary

Account statement—a summary of the activity in your credit card or other account. It includes how much you charged, borrowed, and paid during the past month, as well as updated information on the overall status of your account.

Annual percentage rate (APR)—the yearly interest rate you must pay for the use of the money loaned to you. If you have a $10,000 loan and the APR is 5 percent, you'll pay $500 a year in interest.

Annual fee—a yearly fee that some credit card companies charge in addition to the interest charge

Bankruptcy—a situation in which a court rules that a person is not able to pay his or her bills

Collateral—possessions such as a home or car that a borrower pledges in return for a loan. If a borrower does not repay a loan, the lender has the right to take possession of an item used for collateral. You can also use the money in a savings account as collateral.

Cosigner—a person with a good credit rating who signs a loan note along with a borrower— the cosigner agrees to be responsible for repaying the loan if the borrower defaults

Credit bureau—a public or private agency that gathers credit information on people— the information includes where, when, and how much you have borrowed and whether you made your payments on time

Credit history—the record of a person's use of credit, often compiled by a credit bureau

Credit rating—a rating that a credit bureau gives you based on your history of borrowing and repaying money, your character, and your assets

Default—failure to make a loan payment as scheduled

Important Credit Terms

Credit is a complex subject. If you know the meanings of some basic terms, you will find it easier to understand. The "Credit Dictionary" in this lesson defines some of the words that come up most in discussions of credit. Perhaps you've heard some of them before. Others will probably be new. Most of the words on this list appear in bold text in this lesson. Check back to this list if necessary as you go through the lesson. Then keep the list handy and refer to it when you need it.

Positive and Negative Aspects of Using Credit

Credit has one big advantage: You can buy something you need, even if you don't have the money right now. There are also other advantages to using credit. For example, using a credit card makes day-to-day purchases more convenient. You don't have to carry a lot of cash with you. Credit can be useful in emergencies, also. Using credit has many disadvantages, however. If you borrow too much money, you may have difficulty making your payments. Having credit can tempt you to make impulse purchases that you cannot afford.

Delinquent—an account for which payment is overdue

Down payment—an initial cash sum that a buyer must pay in order to make a credit purchase or get a loan, usually a small percentage of the total amount of the purchase

Finance charge—a charge for using credit—another term for APR or interest

Grace period—the time during which you can pay a credit card bill on new purchases without being charged interest

Installment—a partial payment of a loan, usually paid monthly

Interest—the cost of borrowing money, expressed as a percentage—you *earn* interest when you invest your money in a savings account; you *pay* interest when you borrow money

Maturity date—the date by which you must repay your loan

Minimum payment—the smallest amount you must pay in any given month in order to keep your credit account in good standing—usually a great deal less than the total amount you have charged on your account

Periodic rate—the monthly interest rate on a credit card—for example, the periodic rate on a credit card with an 18 percent APR is 18 divided by 12, for a periodic rate of 1.5 percent

Principal—the amount of the money borrowed—payment of the principal is usually spread out over the term of the loan

Variable rate—an interest rate that changes over time

Here is the answer to the earlier math problem on how much consumer credit debt Americans have acquired. By using 300 million as the base population estimate, and $2.68 trillion as the total amount of consumer credit spread among the population, every American has about $8,933 in acquired credit debt, on average.

Young adults, especially those who have borrowed to finance a college education, may be in worse shape. Many young people accumulate considerable debt by the time they graduate from college. The average new college graduate today has more than $25,000 in debts, including credit cards, student loans, and other debts, such as car loans.

Because they have big debts and are always struggling to get by financially, many people make only the minimum payment—*the smallest amount due to the lender to keep your credit in good standing*—on their credit cards each month. They're always hoping that they'll be able to pay off their balance when they get more money. This frequently does not work—the accumulating interest fees catch many people by surprise. Their debt grows each month instead of decreasing and can quickly become difficult to manage. Almost 1.5 million people in the United States file for bankruptcy each year. Bankruptcy is *a situation in which a court rules that a person is not able to pay his or her bills*. A primary reason for these bankruptcies is that the individuals obtain more credit than they can repay.

Sources of Credit

Credit is available from a variety of sources. Some of the most common sources are store charge accounts, credit cards, charge cards, installment loans, and layaway plans.

Charge Account or Retail Account

These accounts let you buy goods or services at a specific store on credit. For example, a charge account from Sears allows you to charge purchases, but nowhere else. In return for your promise to pay in full by a later date, the store lets you pay in *monthly payments*, or installments. The store will charge interest on the amount that you have not yet paid. If you fail to pay on time, the store may charge you a late fee.

Credit Card

You can use a credit card to pay for goods or services at any business establishment that accepts the card. The credit card has a code number that tells the issuing company who you are and where to send your bill. If you pay your entire bill at the end of the month, you may not have to pay interest. If you pay your bill in monthly installments, you will be charged interest.

A credit card gives a consumer more flexibility on purchases, but should be used in a responsible manner.
Courtesy of Media Bakery13/Shutterstock

With credit cards, you may be able to get a cash advance, or *borrowed cash*, through the card. If you get a cash advance, you will usually have to pay a higher interest rate than if you bought something with your credit card. Thus, it's a good idea to avoid taking cash advances. In addition to interest, the credit card company may charge you an annual fee, *a yearly fee that some companies charge in addition to the interest charge.*

Charge Card

A charge card looks like a credit card, but it is quite different. If you buy something with a charge card, you must pay the entire balance very quickly, usually within 30 days or less.

Installment Loan

People usually use installment loans when they need to make a single expensive purchase, such as a car or a home. You may use the item, but the lender holds ownership until you repay the loan. Installment loans may require you to make a down payment or pledge collateral, *possessions* (such as a home, car, or savings) *that a borrower pledges in return for a loan*. (Often the collateral will be the item you are taking out the loan to buy.) You will make fixed payments over a set period. The interest rate may be lower than that of other kinds of credit.

Layaway Plan

When you buy something on layaway, the store holds it until you have paid for it in full. You must usually make a down payment and then make regular payments according to a contract. The store may add a service charge. If you fail to pay on time, the store may no longer hold the item for you.

How Credit Works

How does all this work? Say you have a credit card with an APR of 18 percent. You want to buy a $650 iPad.® When you make the purchase, you hand your credit card to the store clerk. The clerk contacts the credit card company (usually by swiping your card into a computer reader) to make sure you have sufficient credit to cover the purchase. He or she then checks your signature and the card expiration date, and sells you the item. The store charges $650, plus any sales tax, to your account.

When you receive your credit card account statement the following month, you make the minimum monthly payment. Suppose that minimum is 10 percent of the balance. In that case, you'd pay $65 within the specified time. This would leave you with a balance of $585.

So far, so good. However, it's at this point that many people get into trouble. That's because for each month that you do not pay your entire balance, the company adds interest to the remaining balance. Thus, once you make your initial $65 minimum monthly payment, you will be charged an APR of 18 percent on your remaining balance. As long as you didn't pay off your total debt, your interest would continue to accumulate. If you continued to charge additional items on your card and pay only the minimum amount required, your interest and principal would continue to grow each month. If you have several credit cards and pay only the minimum monthly balance on each, your interest will really add up, overwhelming your ability to pay.

SIMPLE INTEREST RATE	SIMPLE INTEREST PAYMENT PER YEAR	TOTAL SIMPLE INTEREST PAYMENTS OVER 4 YEARS
6%	$600	$2,400
8%	$800	$3,200
10%	$1,000	$4,000
12%	$1,200	$4,800
14%	$1,400	$5,600
16%	$1,600	$6,400
18%	$1,800	$7,200
20%	$2,000	$8,000

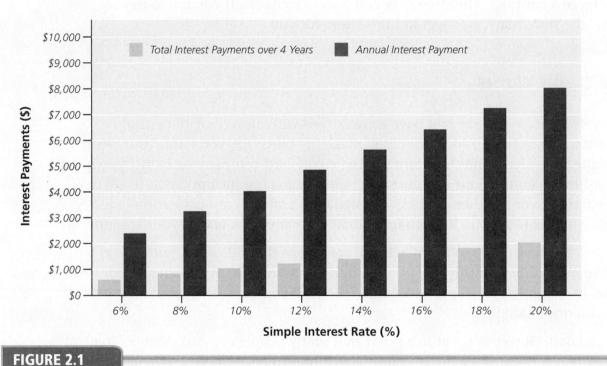

FIGURE 2.1

How Interest Payments Are Influenced by Interest Rates

Reprinted from *Personal Finance*, edited by Jeff Madura (2011), by permission of Pearson Education

To see what effect interest can have on your financial situation and what difference the interest rate can make, look at Figure 2.1. It shows what happens with a $10,000 loan at various interest rates. If you borrow money at an 8 percent rate, your interest, or finance charge, will be $800 during a year. However, if you borrow at an 18 percent APR—the standard interest rate for credit cards today—the charge will be $1,800. If you don't make any payments for four years, you will owe $7,200 just in interest. Most people are responsible, and they make monthly payments. But again, they often make only the minimum monthly payments. That means that their debt will quickly grow.

CHAPTER 2 Managing Your Resources

Using Credit Responsibly

Using credit wisely is an essential part of managing your finances. You should use it within the limits of your resources and your overall financial plan. Here are some tips for managing your credit:

- *Pay all your bills on time*—Remember that you will be able to get credit only as long as your credit history, or *record of paying your bills*, is good.

- *Don't think of a credit card as extra cash*—When you use your card, think of it as borrowing money. Before charging a purchase, ask yourself, "If I had to pay cash, would I still buy it?"

- *Never borrow more than your budget shows you can pay back*—Never get into the position of having to borrow money to pay credit debts.

- *Always pay your other regular monthly bills, such as rent, utility, and telephone on time*—Try to pay more than your monthly minimum on your credit card bills. Whenever possible, avoid paying high finance charges by paying off your balance each month.

- *Limit yourself to no more than two credit cards*—Make sure that one card has the lowest interest rate available. Use this card for purchases or services that you plan to pay for over a period of time, if that's really necessary. If the other card has a higher interest rate, pay the full balance on it each month.

Paying off your credit card in full is the best way to avoid falling into a credit trap.
Courtesy of Blend Images/Shutterstock

success TIP ★

A good rule of thumb is never to borrow more than 20 percent of your net income.

Remember, pay yourself first. Get into a savings habit so that you rarely need the support of credit.

Credit and Credit Card Options

When you're looking for credit, you need to be a smart shopper, just as when you buy groceries, clothing, or anything else. You need to comparison shop.

Say you're like most people and don't pay the balance of your credit card bill each month. If so, you should look at either the annual interest rate or the periodic rate, or *monthly rate*, the card issuer uses to calculate your finance charge (Figure 2.2).

INTEREST RATES AND INTEREST CHARGES

Annual Percentage Rate (APR) for Purchases	**8.99%**, **10.99%**, or **12.99%** introductory APR for one year, based on your creditworthiness. After that, your APR will be **14.99%**. This APR will vary with the market based on the Prime Rate.
APR for Balance Transfers	**15.99%** This APR will vary with the market based on the Prime Rate.
APR for Cash Advances	**21.99%** This APR will vary with the market based on the Prime Rate.
Penalty APR and When It Applies	**28.99%** This APR may be applied to your account if you: 1) Make a late payment; 2) Go over your credit limit; 3) Make a payment that is returned; or 4) Do any of the above on another account that you have with us. **How Long Will the Penalty APR Apply?**: If your APRs are increased for any of these reasons, the Penalty APR will apply until you make six consecutive minimum payments when due.
How to Avoid Paying Interest on Purchases	Your due date is at least 25 days after the close of each billing cycle. We will not charge you any interest on purchases if you pay your entire balance by the due date each month.
Minimum Interest Charge	If you are charged interest, the charge will be no less than $1.50.
For Credit Card Tips from the Federal Reserve Board	To learn more about factors to consider when applying for or using a credit card, visit the website of the Federal Reserve Board at *http://www.federalreserve.gov/creditcard*.

FEES

Set-up and Maintenance Fees	NOTICE: Some of these set-up and maintenance feels will be assessed before you begin using your card and will reduce the amount of credit you initially have available. For example, if you are assigned the minimum credit limit of $250, your initial available credit will be only about $209 (or about $204 if you choose to have an additional card).
• Annual Fee	**$20**
• Account Set-up Fee	**$20** (one-time fee)
• Participation Fee	**$12** annually ($1 per month)
• Additional Card Fee	**$5** annually (if applicable)
Transaction Fees • Balance Transfer	Either **5%** or **3%** of the amount of each transfer, whichever is greater (maximum fee: $100).
• Cash Advance	Either **5%** or **3%** of the amount of each transfer, whichever is greater.
• Foreign Transaction	**2%** of each transaction in U.S. dollars.
Penalty Fees • Late Payment	**$29** if balance is less than or equal to $1,000; **$35** if balance is more than $1,000
• Over-the-Credit Limit	**$29**
• Returned Payment	**$35**

How We Will Calculate Your Balance: We use a method called "average daily balance (including new purchases)."

Loss of Introductory APR: We may end your introductory APR and apply the Penalty APR if you become more than 60 days late in paying your bill.

FIGURE 2.2

Sample Credit Card Disclosure Box

Source: *www.federalreserve.gov*

That rate is fixed. Some credit card companies offer a variable rate, *an interest rate that changes over time*. It starts low, but the company can then raise it after you've had the card for a while. Variable rates can also go down, although this does not happen often with credit cards.

Are you a person who pays off your bills each month? Then the credit card that has no annual fee and offers a grace period, *the time during which you can pay a credit card bill on new purchases without being charged interest*, is good for you. Other questions to ask when shopping for credit include the following:

- Which kind of credit is appropriate for your purchase? Should you put the item on a credit card or take out a loan, which would usually have a lower interest rate?

- What kind of maturity period do you want? A longer maturity means smaller monthly bills. A shorter period costs less interest. Which plan best fits your budget? Is there a penalty if you pay off the loan before the maturity date?

- Do you have to pledge collateral? What collateral do you have?

- Does one credit card have a higher annual fee than another?

Applying for a Credit Card

You must be 18 years old to get a credit card. In most cases, in order to get credit, you must show that you have steady employment; a checking or savings account; a history of paying your bills on time; an income that exceeds your budgeted expenses; and a permanent residence.

You must fill out an application from the store or bank offering the card. Be honest on the application. The company has its requirements for a reason. If you are tempted not to be fully honest about your income or expenses, you probably cannot afford credit at this time.

Once you've applied, the company has 30 days to respond to your application. If the company does not approve your application, it must tell you why.

Visit with a bank official or store manager when you apply for a credit card to ensure you fully understand the card's benefits and potential costs.
Courtesy of auremar/Shutterstock

LESSON 1 Avoiding the Credit Trap

If your application is accepted, the company will ask you to sign a credit agreement. Read this very carefully. The Truth in Lending Act, a federal law, requires that any company issuing the credit card disclose the following information to you:

- Annual fee if applicable
- Annual percentage rate (APR) for purchases
- Other APRs (balance transfer, cash advances, default APRs)
- Grace period
- Finance calculation method
- Other transaction fees (balance transfers, late payments, exceeding credit limit fee, cash advances)

All credit card companies use the same format, making comparison shopping for credit cards easy. Although the disclosure box contains the basic terms of the credit card, there are other terms that you should look for in the fine print. For example,

- *Universal default clause*—If you are reported late by another creditor, your APR can be increased even if you are paying your bills on time with that creditor.
- *Dispute resolutions, binding arbitrations*—Disputes are settled by an independent third party body instead of a judge or court. The arbitrator's decision is final and cannot be disputed or appealed. There are two types of arbitrations—voluntary and mandatory. In mandatory arbitration, a consumer waives the right to sue and must use an arbitrator instead to resolve disputes. In voluntary arbitration, the consumer and company may mutually agree to allow a third party to intervene.

Questions to Ask Yourself When Applying for a Credit Card

When it comes time to apply for a credit card for the first time, ask yourself these 10 questions:

1. Do I really need to establish this account? What will I use it for?
2. Can I qualify for credit?
3. What is the interest rate?
4. Are there additional fees?
5. What percentage is the monthly minimum payment, and when is it due?
6. Can I afford to make the monthly payments?
7. What will happen if I don't make the payments on time?
8. Are there any nontangible costs if I use credit? That is, can I sleep at night, or will I worry about my debts?
9. Given my current earnings and other regular expenses, what is the maximum credit card debt that I can handle?
10. All things considered, is using a credit card worth it?

- *Double Billing Cycles*—You are charged interest on your current billing cycle and the previous one. As such, even though you may have paid your previous balance in full, you are still charged interest on it.

- *Fees*—Read your contract for other fees you may incur. For example, some credit card companies charge a fee for not updating your account every year

Do not sign the agreement until you fully understand it. If you need help, ask the lending officer to explain what you want to know. Ask that person to confirm how much is due each payment, how long the grace period is, and what happens if you default, or *fail to pay your bill on time*. In short, know what you are getting into. If the creditor has not filled out all the blanks on the form, do not sign until the company has filled out all the information.

How the Creditor Evaluates Your Application

Credit institutions use various guidelines to determine who qualifies for credit. Most lenders look at three things. These are sometimes referred to as the *"three Cs of credit."*

- *Character*—Are you reliable? Do you pay your bills on time? The application form may ask you for references or the names of other creditors.

- *Capacity*—Is your income enough to pay the debt? Do you have a job? Do you have other debts? Is it likely you can continue to earn your present salary, or even more, in the future? If you don't hold a job and have no regular income, you'll probably have a hard time obtaining credit.

- *Collateral*—Do you have enough assets? What do you own that has value and that you could use to repay the debt? A car? A savings account? Another word for collateral is *security*. *A loan that does not require collateral* is called an unsecured loan.

Building Your Credit History

The *"three Cs"* sound good, but what if you're just starting out? What if you don't have collateral or sufficient capacity? There are many ways to start building good credit. Most banks are willing to work with small loans. A good practice is to borrow a small amount of money from a bank and pay it back quickly.

The best collateral you could probably use for your first loan is your savings account. For example, if you had $750 saved, you could borrow $675 for a sofa and pledge your $750 savings against the loan as collateral. Be sure to make regular payments on your loan and be on time. When you pay off the loan, you have started a good credit history.

Another way to establish credit is to apply for a credit card or charge account at a local business or bank. Charge a few items that you would normally buy with cash, and pay the bill in full when it is due.

A third alternative is to have someone cosign your loan. The cosigner, *a person with a good credit rating who signs a loan note along with a borrower*, should be a relative or other responsible adult who has a good credit history and the ability to pay. If you are unable to make payments on the loan, the person who cosigned is responsible for paying the debt.

Still another way to start credit would be to purchase something on the installment plan. Many stores, such as furniture stores, encourage first-time credit for such purchases.

How Credit Bureaus Function

Once you borrow money and pay it back on time, the credit bureau, *a public or private agency that gathers credit information on people*, will have a record of your credit history. That's a good beginning, because other companies will then be more likely to give you credit.

Your credit report shows every time you apply for credit, your payment history, late fees that are assessed if you miss a payment, and other notations about your accounts. Out of this comes a credit score, *a rating that helps lenders decide whether and/or how much credit to approve to a borrower*. Your credit score gives a lender an idea of how creditworthy you may be.

Using a Credit Bureau

If a company turns you down for a loan or a credit card, you will want to find out why. Under federal law, you are entitled to a free report if a company takes adverse action against you, such as denying your application for credit, insurance, or employment, and you ask for your report within 60 days of receiving notice of the action. The notice will give you the name, address, and phone number of the consumer reporting company.

If you find errors on your credit report, write the credit bureau giving proof of the error. The credit bureau will then correct your report. It will send the corrected information to any company that requested your credit report in the previous six months.

Credit Bureaus

TransUnion: *www.tuc.com*

Experian: *www.experian.com*

Equifax: *www.equifax.com*

There are three main credit bureaus in the United States: TransUnion, Experian, and Equifax. Each bureau covers a different region of the country, but since credit card and other companies have offices nationwide, you will likely deal with all three at some point in your life. You can find out more at the companies' websites. It's good practice to check your credit rating every year or so, even if you don't have any problems.

Avoiding Credit Card Fraud

Credit card fraud is a growing problem. It's all too easy for dishonest people to find ways to use your credit for their own purchases. They can do this by stealing your card, of course. But people who engage in fraud have more tricks up their sleeves.

Preventing Misuse of Your Credit Card

Follow these steps to reduce your risk of credit card fraud:

- *Always sign a new credit card as soon as you receive it*— When you buy something, the salesperson will compare the signature on the back of the card with your signature at the bottom of the receipt for your purchase.

- *Save your receipts from credit card purchases*— Compare them with the charge amounts on each month's account statement.

- *Never give out a credit card number to someone who has called you on the phone*— Give out your number only if you have made the call and you're sure you're dealing with a reputable company.

Saving your purchase receipts and adding up your credit card purchases will help you manage your spending.
Courtesy of Andrey Popov/Shutterstock

- *If you're purchasing on the Internet make sure you're using a secure site*—Look for the little lock on your browser's status bar.

- *Destroy any preapproved credit offers you receive in the mail*—A dishonest person might pull the blank application from your trash and apply for the card in your name.

- *Destroy any old or canceled credit cards*—Dishonest practices have made even canceled credit cards susceptible to misuse.

If Your Credit Card is Stolen

What if your card or card number is stolen and a thief runs up charges? Federal law protects you. It states that credit card holders who are victims of theft or fraud are not responsible for more than $50 *if* they report the theft promptly.

Keep a record of all your account numbers and the phone numbers for any credit card or charge card companies you deal with. If you lose your card, if someone steals it, or if someone uses your credit card number fraudulently, contact the company immediately.

You have the option to buy credit card insurance protection, but it's expensive for a young person. Often, credit card companies offer it by making exaggerated claims about the protections that are offered. The Federal Trade Commission says that if you follow your credit card company's procedures for disputing charges you haven't authorized, or lose a credit card and report it promptly, your liability for unauthorized charges is limited to $50. We will cover how to protect your personal and financial information in more detail in Chapter 2, Lesson 2, "Insurance for Protecting Your Resources."

The Consequences of Deficit Spending

Cutting your spending and borrowing can help you work your way out of a credit crunch..

Courtesy of Orange Line Media/Shutterstock

If you make a habit of deficit spending, or *spending more than you earn*, sooner or later you'll wind up in a credit crunch. This inability to make all your payments can strain more than your wallet. Money worries can bring stress and low morale, hurt family and social life, and cause poor performance at your job or in school. The minute you think you're getting into trouble, take the following steps:

- *Stop borrowing*—Leave your credit cards at home. Carry only enough money to get through the day.

- *Cut expenses both big and small*—Limit trips to snack machines. Clip coupons for shopping, but only for items you really need. Borrow CDs or books at the library instead of buying them. Make do with what you have instead of buying something new.

- *Talk to creditors*—Explain your problem. They may be willing to work out an easier payment schedule for you.

Bankruptcy

This is the last resort when you get too deeply in debt. The reason it is a last resort is that it stays on your credit record for up to 10 years and affects your ability to seek credit for any reason. Here are the types of bankruptcy actions:

Chapter 7 allows you to erase most of your debt, but to qualify, you must be unemployed or on a very low income, and you must go to financial counseling.

Chapter 13 allows you to set a plan to repay debts over five years or less, but a court will oversee the process.

A few important notes:

- Congress changed the bankruptcy law in 2005 to make Chapter 7 bankruptcy more difficult to declare.
- Bankruptcy does not erase certain kinds of debt, such as school loans or penalties and fines because of a crime you may have committed.
- The "clean slate" is given only to people who have serious unforeseen and unavoidable misfortune that bankruptcy helps in rebuilding their lives.

Source: NEFE High School Financial Planning Program Student Guide, *p.55*

- *Learn from your mistakes*—Did an emergency throw you off course? Was your budget unrealistic? In both cases, you probably need to revise your budget, as discussed in the previous lesson. But if your problems result from spending money irresponsibly, you need to get serious about your financial future.

The Importance of a Financial Plan

It's up to you to make sure your credit decisions fit your financial plan. The key question to ask yourself is: How will buying something through credit affect my future? By making proper decisions, you can keep a lid on your credit. This will increase the amount of money you have available now and enable you to buy the things you need.

Figure 2.3 shows a good example of how to manage credit. Stephanie Spratt has had to make the same decisions regarding credit that you will have to make soon. Note how she first set out in words her goals for managing credit. Then she figured out how much money ($1,100) she had left each month after paying basic bills. She explained to herself why this $1,100 could be used for credit card purchases, if necessary. Finally, she decided to make a real effort to reduce her debt. She decided that any extra money she gets will go first to paying back credit card bills. She wants to reduce her debt. This is because credit cards charge a higher rate of interest than she would earn by putting that money into savings account.

1. Spend on my credit card only what I can pay back in the same month.
2. Avoid large expenses on my credit card.

ANALYSIS

Monthly income	$2,500	
Monthly expenses (paid by check)	−$1,400	
Total Money Available	=$1,100	

Sources of Assets	**Balance**	**Interest Rate**
Cash	$100	0.0%
Checking Account Balance	$800	0.0%
Money Market Fund	$400	3.0%
30-day CD	$1,200	4.3%
Sources of Debt		
Credit Card Balance	$600	20.0%

DECISIONS

Credit limit: With $1,100 available after taxes on my income and regular monthly expenses, I can spend up to $1,000 and no more on my credit card to be able to pay it off the following month. If my income goes up, I can continue to spend up to $100 below my total money available each month after expenses, as long as I continue to pay off the credit card fully.

Credit balances: My interest rates on savings accounts are much lower than my interest payments on my credit card, so I will always pay off my credit card, even if I have to withdraw money from my savings to do so. But if that happens, I'll reconsider my highest spending limit on my credit card each month to avoid dipping into savings.

FIGURE 2.3

How Credit Management Fits with Stephanie Spratt's Financial Plan

Reprinted from *Personal Finance*, edited by Jeff Madura (2011), by permission of Pearson Education

✔ CHECKPOINTS

Lesson 1 Review

Using complete sentences, answer the following questions on a sheet of paper.

1. List three positive benefits and three possible negative results of using credit.

2. Name three sources of credit and describe the differences between each.

3. Explain why a credit card is different from a direct loan in terms of interest rates and in how they are "paid off."

4. What are three ways you can start to build a credit history?

5. What are three ways that your identity could be stolen? Give an explanation of how you can prevent it from happening.

6. What are the main consequences of deficit spending?

7. Develop and explain a three-point method you might employ to reduce deficit spending.

APPLYING CREDIT SKILLS

8. Study the sample credit card disclosure box in Figure 2.2. Read it and analyze its terms. What is the interest rate? Are there other fees? Is there a grace period? What is the penalty rate? Get used to reading and understanding such information in credit card agreements. You will read many over your lifetime.

Insurance for Protecting Your Resources

Quick Write

_____

_____

What do you think is the purpose of having insurance? How many types of insurance can you name? Discuss this with another student in the class and be prepared to share your answers with the rest of the class.

Learn About

- what insurance is and why it is necessary
- major types of insurance
- how to protect your personal and financial information

"Property is the fruit of labor; property is desirable; it is a positive good in the world."

Abraham Lincoln, 16th President of the United States

What Insurance Is and Why It Is Necessary

As you grow older, you'll take on more responsibilities. These responsibilities will probably include having a full-time job and owning a car, a home, and other valuable property. But what would happen if you were injured and couldn't work? Who would pay your medical bills? What would you live on? What if your house and its contents were damaged by a fire or a flood? How would you repair or replace your car if it were damaged or stolen?

Bad as these situations are, you might find yourself in even bigger problems. What if you accidentally injured someone and a court determined that you had liability, or *legal responsibility*, for causing the injury? The injured person could sue you, and you could lose a lot of money.

Accidents happen. You have to expect the unexpected. This is where insurance comes in. Insurance is *the means by which people protect themselves financially against losses or liability incurred as a result of unexpected events*.

Insurance works on the principle of shared risk. For example, suppose that 100 people buy auto insurance. Each person pays a premium, or *fee for being protected by the insurance*, of $50 per month. In exchange for these monthly premiums, the insurance company provides each person with a policy, or *contract that promises to pay for any losses*.

Along with those other 99 policyholders, you share the risk of damaging your car. Some of those car owners probably will have accidents, but the insurance company doesn't know which ones will be the unlucky few. Therefore, the company collects premiums from everyone.

If all 100 people are paying the same premiums, in just one month, the company will create a reserve of $5,000 (100 × $50). It will then draw on that reserve to cover car repairs that policy holders might need if their vehicles are damaged. When a policy owner has an accident that is covered by insurance, he or she will make a claim, or *demand for payment in accordance with the policy.* The insurance company will then pay for the repairs.

You may never damage your car and may never have to file a claim. And you certainly hope that you won't. No one wants to be in an accident. But an investment in insurance is still a good one. It's not money wasted. This is because insurance gives you financial security and peace of mind. You can drive (or live in your home, go to work, or do just about anything else in life) without worrying about the financial loss that may result from an unexpected event.

One more thing: Although the insurance company will reimburse you for a major part of your claim, an insurance policy doesn't usually cover the entire loss. Most policies have a deductible, or *amount that you must pay before the insurance company pays anything.*

Deductibles vary. If you choose a low deductible, you'll probably have higher premiums. If your deductible is higher, your premiums will be lower. This is the company's way of rewarding you for accepting a greater share of the up-front financial responsibility for loss. It makes sense to choose a deductible that is large enough to reduce premiums. But the deductible needs to be small enough to prevent financial hardship if you suffer a loss.

Major Types of Insurance

People face many kinds of risks that they can share through insurance. As Table 2.1 shows, the major types of insurance are: automobile; property (for homeowners and renters); liability; health; disability; and life.

Vocabulary

- liability
- insurance
- premium
- policy
- claim
- deductible
- no-fault
- insurance agent
- inventory
- copayments
- indemnity plan
- managed care plan
- workers' compensation
- life insurance
- beneficiary
- term life insurance
- whole life insurance
- universal life insurance
- identity theft
- phishing

"The joke is on us. We thought we had you covered for every kind of accident."

Courtesy of John Morris/CartoonStock

Table 2.1 Common Events That Could Cause a Financial Loss

Event that could cause a financial loss:	Your financial loss is due to:	You can protect against this financial loss by having:
You have a car accident and damage your car	Car repairs	Auto insurance
You have a car accident in which another person in your car is injured	Medical bills and liability	Auto insurance
You have a car accident in which another person in the other driver's car is injured	Medical bills and liability	Auto insurance
Your home or condo is damaged by a fire	Home or condo repairs	Homeowners' insurance
Your neighbor is injured while in your home or condo	Medical bills and liability	Homeowners' insurance
You become ill and need medical attention	Medical bills	Health insurance
You develop an illness that requires long-term care	Medical bills	Long-term care insurance
You become disabled	Loss of income	Disability insurance
You die while family members rely on your income	Loss of income	Life insurance

Reprinted from *Personal Finance*, edited by Jeff Madura (2011), by permission of Pearson Education

Earlier in life, you'll probably need auto, health and property (renters) insurance. A little later on, as you establish your independent life as an adult, you'll probably consider other kinds of insurance, such as life, homeowners, and liability. While it's hard to think about it now, you may have to consider disability insurance or workman's compensation.

Automobile Insurance

Automobile insurance protects car owners from financial loss. This loss may be caused by damage to their cars or the cars of other drivers. The loss may also result from medical expenses related to an accident.

For example, suppose you are in a two-car accident. If a court decides that you are liable, you will have to pay for any damages to the other car. If people in the other car are injured, the court may also require you to pay for their medical bills, lost income, and any related pain and suffering. These damages could amount to millions of dollars. The right type of auto insurance will protect you from most of those expenses.

To protect its residents from heavy losses, almost every state requires that car owners have some type of auto insurance before they can register a car.

Types of Automobile Insurance

The major types of auto insurance are:

1. *Collision*—this pays for repair costs for your car if it rolls over or collides with something.

2. *Comprehensive*—pays for repairing damage to your car that is caused by something other than collision or rolling over—these damages might be caused by a fire, a falling object, or vandalism, for example.

A Lesson Learned

Rebecca was leaving her apartment for community college classes when she discovered her car had been vandalized. The driver's window had been broken and her entire CD collection was taken, along with the CD player, which had been stripped from the dashboard of the car. She also lost a gym bag with an expensive pair of running shoes inside.

She reported the incident to police, who came out to file a report. Then she called her insurance agent. The agent, trying to be helpful, asked Rebecca what damage was done to the car. After she explained, she asked the agent, "What about all of the stuff stolen from inside?"

"Well, we can cover the CD player," said the agent. "But did you ever come in to get your renters' insurance policy?"

While comprehensive auto insurance covers vandalism, it may not cover belongings that are considered your personal property..
Courtesy of Dariush M./Shutterstock

"No," Rebecca replied. "I didn't do that yet."

The insurance agent then explained, "The reason I wanted you to come in for renters' insurance was that your CD collection, your gym bag and shoes can't be covered on your auto policy because they aren't part of the vehicle, and would normally be located in your apartment as your personal possessions."

He went on to explain that having the renters' policy would have qualified her for reimbursement under her renters' policy.

The lesson learned from this story is that for any belongings in your car that are considered your personal property—not part of the vehicle's options or equipment—you need to have a separate homeowners' or renters' insurance policy to cover their loss.

3. *Liability*—helps pay the expenses of other people involved in an accident. It also protects you from lawsuits resulting from an accident. The two major types of liability coverage are:

   a. *Property damage* insurance, which helps pay the cost of repairing damage to other people's property.

   b. *Bodily injury* insurance, which helps cover medical expenses for injuries to other people.

4. *Uninsured motorist protection*—protects you if your car is damaged by a driver who has no auto insurance.

5. *Emergency road service*—covers the cost of towing your car to a repair shop in an emergency.

Of those five major areas of insurance coverage, the first four are almost universally taken by people to keep themselves protected from incidents on the road. Some states have no-fault automobile insurance, *laws that make each person responsible for his or her own damages and injuries*, so liability coverage isn't required. Most states, however, still use the courts to determine liability. Once fault is determined, the one who is liable must pay the costs for the accident through his or her insurance company.

Automobile Insurance Rates

The cost of insurance premiums varies. Each insurance company sets its own rates based on a number of factors. One of the most important factors is your driving record and the driving record of people with characteristics similar to yours. You can help keep your premiums low by driving carefully and not getting traffic tickets. Teenagers as a group, however, are poorer drivers because they're inexperienced and take more risks than people who've been driving for a while. In fact, statistics show that 16-year-olds have 10 times as many accidents as people between the ages of 30 and 59 have. So younger drivers usually have to pay higher premiums than other drivers do, no matter how good their individual driving records.

In setting your premium, the insurance company also looks at where you live. Accident rates are higher in cities than in rural areas, so people who live in the country often have lower premiums than people who live in urban areas.

In addition, the company takes into account what type of car you drive. One reason is that some cars cost more to repair than others do. Another reason is that some car models are the specific targets of thieves.

The company will want to know if you are a good student, because records show that good students are more careful drivers. They will even consider your gender, because girls between 16 and 25 tend to be better drivers than boys of the same age are. (Sorry, guys!)

Distracted Driving

In 2009, nearly 5,500 people were killed and 450,000 more were injured in distracted driving incidents involving activities such as texting; using a phone; eating and drinking; talking to passengers; grooming; reading maps or newspapers; using a navigation system; watching a video; or adjusting a radio, CD player, or MP3 player. In 2009, the latest year for which data is available, texting alone made it 23 times more likely for a driver to have an accident.

The use of cell phones and other handheld devices in moving vehicles is a major cause of distractions leading to injuries and deaths on the nation's roadways.

Courtesy of Poulsons Photography/Shutterstock

Once you have insurance, the company will keep a record of your driving habits and any claims you file. If the insurance company sees that you drive recklessly, and they will know when they run your driving record before selling you insurance and at renewal time. If they choose to sell or renew your policy, it may certainly increase your premium. If you have too many accidents, it might refuse to renew your policy.

Buying Auto Insurance

When you're ready to buy insurance, you should choose a reputable company. Ask friends or relatives if they can recommend one. You want to be sure the company will stand behind you if you have an accident.

The next step is to find out what type of coverage your state requires. In many states, collision and liability insurance are mandatory. Then decide which additional insurance, if any, you want to purchase. Keep in mind that car repairs are expensive. Although the cost of the premiums might seem high, it will be much less expensive than repair costs if you do have a serious accident. For this reason, comprehensive insurance is usually a good idea, especially if you have a fairly new car. Also think about deductibles. If you want to keep your premiums low, get a high deductible. However, do not forget that this means you will have to pay more if you do have an accident.

Narrow your search as much as you can and compare rates. Ask whether lower rates are offered to good students and people with safe driving records. You might get a lower rate if you've taken a driver's training course. Companies also offer discounts for people who insure more than one car.

At some point you may want to find an insurance agent, or *a person who sells insurance*. You will need an agent if you don't buy insurance directly from an insurance company. Many agents sell policies for several companies. Ask friends or relatives if they can recommend an agent. A good agent may know about the benefits offered by several companies. Remember, however, that the agent makes some money from selling you a policy. Don't let the agent sell you more than your budget will allow.

Property Insurance

Property insurance covers valuable items you own, such as clothing and furniture. It also covers real estate, such as a house or condominium. Your first experience with this kind of insurance may be as a renter. Having an apartment is one of the first steps you take in life to live independently away from your family home. Even if you have lived all your life in an apartment, having your own apartment brings with it some new responsibilities.

Losing personal property may be expensive to replace without property insurance.
Courtesy of Elliott Kaufman/Beateworks/Corbis Images

How do you decide how much property insurance to purchase? The basic rule of thumb is simple: Have enough insurance to cover the replacement value of your goods. You might think that your property doesn't have much value, but things add up. In addition, it may cost you more to replace something than it did when you originally bought it. That's why it's a good idea to keep an inventory, or *list of your property and its value*, and update it yearly.

If you have an apartment, you do not have to worry about insurance on the apartment building in which you live. However, the contents you bring with you, or buy, are your responsibility. If a fire breaks out, you will need a way to protect your belongings because the apartment owner does not cover personal property of renters.

The good news is that renters' insurance is among the cheapest to buy, and if you have a policy that covers the full amount of the worth of your apartment contents, you can be reimbursed for your possessions in case of fire or other events causing the loss of your property.

Liability Insurance

Liability insurance is a good idea for homeowners and renters, as well as auto owners. It covers the costs associated with injuries resulting from slips, falls, or other accidents that might happen when someone is on your property.

Liability insurance premiums are based on the company's assessment of the degree to which your home poses a risk to others. For example, if your home has a swimming pool, your rates will be higher than they would be otherwise. Even having a pet can increase your liability premiums.

> **success TIP** ⭐
>
> Your best insurance policy is a healthy lifestyle. Physical fitness and careful driving will pay off in lower insurance premiums.

Health Insurance

In recent years, the trend in the United States toward obesity and weight-related diseases means that it's no longer true that younger people don't have to worry much about medical bills.

In 2007 researchers reported that in just over one generation, the number of overweight American children tripled among preschoolers and quadrupled among 6- to 11-year-olds. This group has a higher risk of weight-related disease. Not only is this becoming a burden on the health care system, this *epidemic* has long-term medical, psychological, social, and financial consequences. Controlling the epidemic, the scientists said, is going to have to be done through many social and behavioral changes, as well as in medical practices.

> **are you AWARE?**
>
> Over the past 30 years, while adult rates of obesity have doubled, childhood obesity rates have tripled.

Having a health insurance policy is important for the unexpected, but maintaining a healthy lifestyle is even more important.

Courtesy of .shock/Shutterstock

In 2010 a group of high-ranking retired US military officers filed a report saying that at least nine million 17- to 24-year-olds in the United States are too overweight to serve in the military. That's 27 percent of all young adults. The report also quoted a survey from the Center for Disease Control (CDC) that 42 percent of young adults aged 18 to 24 were either overweight or obese, 11 million in all. Even more dramatic was that within a decade, most of the period coming after 2000, the number of states with 40 percent of young adults considered by the CDC to be overweight or obesity rose from just one state to 39 states, an alarming rate of increase.

The impact of weight-related health issues is no longer limited to adults and older people. It means that health insurance has, for some, become much more expensive. For others, it's not available at all. Many companies have been dropping health care insurance plans to stay in business. Others have had to drastically limit their health care coverage for employees. The more forward-thinking companies have created wellness programs to help people reduce their intake of foods that lack proper nutrition. Some school systems have moved toward much healthier dining selections for students.

Once you're on your own, you will need your own health insurance. The alternative is to go without, which can be risky. You can buy health insurance yourself, but since it's so expensive, it's better if you can get it through your employer. Always inquire about health insurance when interviewing for a job—it's an important benefit. Some companies pay the entire cost of their employees' health insurance, while others pay part of the premium and deduct the rest from the employee's wages.

If your employer provides your health insurance, you may or may not have a choice of plans. If you pay for your own health insurance, you'll have more choices, but your premiums will cost more than they would if you got your insurance through your employer. If you have any choices about your health insurance, you will need to do some comparison shopping.

Some plans have limited optical or dental care options, and most offer reduced prices on prescription medicines. Many plans also have deductibles, like car insurance. As an individual or for a family, you would have to pay a certain amount before your health

Government Health Care Plans

Medicare, a federal government program, provides health insurance to people who are aged 65 and older and qualify for Social Security benefits, or who are disabled. There is no fee for Part A coverage (hospitalization insurance) because that's paid for by the Medicare tax deducted from everybody's paycheck. Part B is optional medical insurance for which participants pay a monthly premium.

Medicaid provides health insurance for people with low incomes and those in need of public assistance. It is administered on a state-by-state basis under federal guidelines. People who receive Medicare may also receive Medicaid if they need public assistance.

plan picks up the rest. There are also copayments, *money paid for each doctor visit or other health service* that is usually a small percentage of the actual cost of a visit. Your health insurance pays the rest of the cost.

There are two basic types of health insurance plans. One is an indemnity plan, which is *a plan that provides payment to the insured for the cost of medical care but makes no arrangement for providing care itself.* An indemnity plan allows you to go to any health care provider to receive care. You can visit a general practitioner who handles basic medical needs, or go directly to a specialist. The second is a managed care plan, which *requires you to consult a primary care physician when you need medical care.* One of his or her roles is to reduce the number of unnecessary visits to specialists. That saves money and makes better use of resources. Under a managed care plan, the doctor bills the insurance company directly.

Some managed care plans pay only for visits to certain doctors or medical facilities. These plans are called *health maintenance organizations*, or HMOs. Other plans, called *preferred provider organizations*, or PPOs, offer you greater flexibility in choosing a doctor. Both HMOs and PPOs publish the lists of their providers. You choose your doctor from this list. The cost of health insurance varies. Indemnity plans are generally more expensive than managed care plans, and HMOs are less expensive than PPOs (Table 2.2).

Table 2.2 Comparison of Private Health Insurance Plans

Type of Private Health Plan	Premium	Selection of Physician
Indemnity Plan	High	Flexibility to select physician or specialist
Managed Care: HMOs	Relatively low	Primary care physician refers patients to specialist
Managed Care: PPOs	Low, but usually higher than HMOs	There is a greater number of physicians to choose from in PPOs than HMOs.

Reprinted from *Personal Finance*, edited by Jeff Madura (2011), by permission of Pearson Education

Disability Insurance

When you're young, one of the last things on your mind is the possibility of becoming disabled.

More than even your car or home, your ability to earn a living is your most critical asset. If you're injured on the job or become extremely ill, either one causing you to lose a lot of work time, that's a lot of lost income.

The purpose of disability insurance is to replace part of your income if you cannot work because of injury or illness. The amount of coverage is usually limited to one half to two-thirds of your earnings at the time of the disability. Coverage is limited in order to encourage you to return to work as soon as you are able. Some employers offer this insurance to their workers. You can also purchase it on your own. *Short-term* disability insurance usually covers illness or injuries that last up to one year. Long-term disability insurance covers from one year to retirement, which is usually age 65.

Most states require that companies provide workers' compensation, *a type of disability insurance that covers medical expenses and part, or most, of income lost due to injury in the workplace.* Most workers nationwide are covered by this plan, but the payments made under this disability plan vary widely state-to-state.

The US government is another source of disability coverage. If you have contributed to Social Security and you have an injury that lasts for more than a year, you may be eligible for payments through the Federal Insurance Contributions Act (FICA) program. However, these payments are not likely to be enough income for you to maintain your standard of living. *Long-term care insurance* protects you from financial loss in the case of a disabling long-term illness. You may get this insurance from your employer or buy it from an agent.

Sometimes people are not sure about the difference between long-term care insurance and long-term disability insurance. Long-term care insurance covers the costs of health care services in your home, a nursing home, or some other facility. Long-term disability insurance replaces lost wages.

Both disability insurance and long-term care insurance protect you from major expenses when you are disabled by saving you from having to pay large sums of money from your savings and other financial assets to pay for expensive care.

Life Insurance

Life insurance provides *a way to protect your family and loved ones from financial losses if you should die.* No one wants to think about dying, but having the right type and amount of life insurance is an important part of your financial plan.

You may have heard this old saying, "There's nothing sure in life except death and taxes." Truthfully, it should say, "taxes and death." That's because you have already paid tax somewhere, even as a child on a 50-cent package of gum or candy.

Like taxes, death is inevitable, and for many young people, death often comes suddenly and too early in life: a car accident, falling from a high place, a severe sports injury, maybe a heroic action to save someone else, or a terminal illness.

Young persons are not immune from the possibility of life being taken away. It may be the hardest subject to speak about, but it's one that is better to deal with early.

Life insurance transfers to your insurer the risk associated with your loss. When you purchase a life insurance policy, you transfer to your insurance company the risk that you may die at a younger age than most people do, causing your family to lose your income. Your family can use the proceeds from your life insurance policy to pay bills such as home mortgages and taxes, as well as to meet day-to-day living expenses.

When you purchase a life insurance policy, you will need to specify your beneficiaries. A beneficiary is *a person who will receive insurance benefits*. If you name more than one beneficiary, you will also need to decide what percentage of the money each person will receive.

If you have a full-time job, your employer may offer life insurance as a benefit. If you decide to buy a policy on your own, find a good agent who can discuss all types of life insurance and help you choose the best.

Many young people wait until they're married and have children to select a life insurance plan. Your long-term financial plan should include a well-constructed grouping of insurance needs, including life insurance, and how you intend to select and pay for them.

Types of Life Insurance

There are three main types of life insurance: *term*, *whole life*, and *universal life*.

- Term life insurance is *a policy that you buy to cover a certain period of time*. Term insurance is the least expensive kind of life insurance. If you buy a term insurance policy for $100,000 for 20 years and you die within that time, your beneficiaries will receive $100,000. If you do not die in that time, you won't receive anything. Term insurance premiums are low for people under 40, since most people do not die before that age. Premiums get higher as you get older. If you get a term life insurance policy on your own you will probably have to undergo a physical examination to make sure you are healthy. If you get such a policy through your employer, you probably will not have an exam, since the employer buys insurance for all its employees at once.

- Whole life insurance *provides coverage for your entire lifetime*. A whole life insurance policy is more valuable than a term policy because it does not expire, as long as you keep paying the premiums on time. A whole life insurance policy accumulates a cash value as it gets older; a term policy does not. Whole life insurance, however, has much higher premiums than term insurance does. The premium and the value of the policy remain the same, unless you use the cash value to buy more insurance. You can cash in your policy and collect the money it has accumulated or borrow against its value.

- Universal life insurance is *insurance for a specific period that accumulates savings for policyholders during this period*. It's a combination of term insurance and a savings plan. Because it allows the policyholder to accumulate savings, it's considered a cash-value life insurance policy. Universal life insurance allows you to alter your payments over time. You have a choice of investments that the company administers, and you can decide how to invest the savings plan funds. If you skip premium payments, the company will withdraw the amount needed to cover the term insurance portions from the savings plan.

So how much life insurance do you really need? If you are single and have no dependents, you might be able to do without it. When you have financial obligations and a family, you'll want to make sure you have enough insurance to provide your family a few years' income if you die unexpectedly.

How to Protect Your Personal and Financial Information

In Chapter 2, Lesson 1, "Avoiding the Credit Trap," you learned about how to protect yourself if your credit card is lost or stolen. However, there's also a real possibility that if you don't protect your bank cards, you could be victimized by identity theft. Protecting your identity from being stolen is a major concern for millions of people and it should be for you also. In this section, we will examine *identity theft*, what you can do to prevent it, and if it happens, the steps you will need to take to correct the problem.

Identity Theft

Identity theft is *when someone uses your personal information without your permission to commit fraud or other crimes*. Identity thieves are on the lookout for information such as your name, credit card number, Social Security number, and driver's license number. You may have given this information on a job application, a credit card application, or an online transaction. The thief steals this information, then can use your name to: apply for telephone service; apply for a credit card or loan; buy merchandise; lease a car or apartment; and even obtain medical care.

A crafty identity thief can even live under your name!

In the year 2010, more than eight million people were victims of identity theft. That's 3.5 percent of the U.S. population. Their total loss was $37 billion, and in an annual survey of consumer fraud from Javelin Strategy & Research, the average out-of-pocket loss to victims soared to $631 from $387—an increase of more than 60 percent over the previous year.

Preventing Identity Theft

You can do several things to protect yourself against identity theft:

- Keep track of your financial statements—when you get your monthly bank or credit card statement, check it immediately to make sure it matches your receipts.

- Check your credit report at least once a year and make sure it is accurate.

- Never give account numbers or personal information to someone you don't know—if someone telephones you and asks for such information, hang up.

Using credit cards on unsecure websites may expose you to identity theft.
Courtesy of Odua Images/Shutterstock

- Destroy all financial documents with personal information on them, including credit card offers you receive in the mail—don't just throw them in the trash, where identity thieves can find and steal them.

- Do not give out your Social Security number or other sensitive information over a cordless or a cell phone.

- Get a locking mailbox so people cannot steal your mail and get access to your financial information.

Many states use your Social Security number as your driver's license number. However, they are supposed to provide you the option to use a different number.

People often demand to see your driver's license as proof of your identity. By using a different number on your driver's license, you protect your Social Security number from people who have no business seeing it. So when you apply for a driver's license, ask if the state can issue you a different number instead of using your Social Security number.

With online accounts, it's especially important to create a password that you'll surely remember, but won't be easy for someone else to guess. However, if you forget a password, remember to keep a record of it in a safe place, as you would for bank account information and other documents that are important to keep secure.

are you AWARE ?

For more information on how to protect yourself from identity theft, visit the government website: *www.consumer.gov/idtheft*.

Reporting Identify Theft

If you think you are a victim of identity theft, take the following steps immediately:

- Report the identity theft to your bank.

- Report the identity theft to each of your credit card companies—cancel all your credit cards and ask for new ones with new numbers.

- File a report with the local police.

- Contact the Federal Trade Commission at *https://www.ftccomplaintassistant.gov/* to report a complaint.

- Contact one of the major credit bureaus (Equifax, Experian, or TransUnion) and ask them to place a fraud alert on all your accounts—you only need to contact one bureau, because each company is required to share its information with the other two.

- Visit the Identity Theft Resource Center website at *www.idtheftcenter.org* for assistance in how to clear your name if you become a victim of identity theft.

- There are companies that will provide credit monitoring and assistance in case your credit card or identity is stolen. These companies will also provide financial insurance for a fee that will help protect your financial assets in the event that your identity is stolen.

A Word About Phishing

Identity theft is not a new phenomenon anymore in our electronic communications. Criminals trying to steal your identity come up with creative ways to target your personal information. One of them is phishing, *the creating of a website replica in order to trick users into submitting personal, financial, or password data online.*

A phishing expedition is a two-pronged attack. First, the phisher creates and sends a fake e-mail message. Posing as a legitimate source, such as a bank, the phisher tries to lure you into clicking on a hyperlink that will take you to a bogus website. This website will appear legitimate; for example, it may have the same logo and other information that an authentic site would have.

When you log on to the website, the phisher will try to get you to enter your Social Security number, credit card information, passwords, or other personal data. It may do this, for example, by telling you that you need to update your information for the company's files in order to maintain an open account. The reasoning can sound very persuasive.

As with fake websites, the phisher may call your cell or home phone falsely representing your bank, credit card company, or some other financial institution. The phisher may tell you that they suspect your account has been compromised and ask you to verify your account number, pin number, address, and even your social security number.

How can you know if you are dealing with a phisher? Keep these points in mind:

- *Look for clues that the message is fake*—if the message has no phone number or return e-mail address, be suspicious. Grammar, spelling, or punctuation mistakes are another good clue that it's not legitimate.

- *Do not be hasty*—even if the e-mail appears to come from a source you trust, think before you click on a hyperlink.

- *Use common sense and trust your instincts*—if you suspect something's amiss, chances are you are right.

- *Never give your personal information over the phone*—unless you are absolutely sure the person you are talking to is who they say they are.

Conclusion

By now you should understand the importance of having insurance for yourself and your family, as well as some ideas of what to look for in an insurance policy, and how to make it affordable and effective in your life's planning.

As your life changes, so will your needs. So as you look to find a career, try to look beyond the hourly wage or yearly salary. Focus on how employer benefits fit into the life you want, then, stick with that goal as you move forward.

In this lesson, *identity theft* was also covered; safeguarding your identity protects your financial assets. The importance of taking necessary precautions to prevent identity theft cannot be stressed enough here; millions of Americans suffer from this crime yearly. You do not want to become a victim.

Lesson 2 Review

Using complete sentences, answer the following questions on a sheet of paper.

1. Why is insurance different from other investments like savings accounts or stocks?

2. Explain how insurance works, describing the key elements of premiums, deductibles, and how you obtain benefits.

3. Why is liability an especially important type of car insurance?

4. What are three ways to reduce your car insurance premiums?

5. What are the differences between the two major types of health insurance plans in terms of costs and how you get care when you need it?

6. What are the differences between term and whole life insurance plans?

7. As a young person just starting out on your own, what factors would you consider in deciding whether to buy life insurance right away?

8. What is phishing? What are two things you can do to avoid becoming a victim of phishing?

APPLYING INSURANCE SKILLS

9. Assume you have been on your own for a year. In your apartment, you have a computer, a CD player, a high-definition TV, your bedroom and living room furniture, and some kitchenware. Evaluate how much money these things are worth and discuss why it would be important to have renters' insurance. For how much would you insure your personal items?

CHAPTER 3

Courtesy of: (left) *wavebreakmedia/Shutterstock;* (top) *Yuri Arcurs/Alamy;* (right) *Hemis/Alamy*

Career Opportunities

Chapter Outline

"The main thing I tell the kids is to study hard, do their best, and stay in school. I also tell them not to ever give up on their dream if it is something that they really want to do in life. Rejection and failure [are] likely, but persistence can pay off in the end."

Astronaut Don Thomas

Researching Careers

Learn About

- selecting and charting a career path
- careers versus jobs
- career options
- career factors
- career planning and information sources

> "If you wish to achieve worthwhile things in your personal and career life, you must become a worthwhile person in your own self-development."
>
> Brian Tracy, self-help author and motivational speaker

Selecting and Charting a Career Path

You want a good career—one that's fulfilling, rewarding, and enjoyable—almost everyone does. After all, you'll probably spend 8 to 10 hours a day or more on the job. That's two-thirds of your waking hours!

Finding the right career isn't easy. If you want to have a career that will carry you through life, finding your passion will be crucial. Remember what the first lesson in financial planning told you. The concepts of success and fulfillment aren't satisfied necessarily by just making a lot of money.

Finding your passion for life's work is a combination of research, self-discovery, and creating a career path, which is _a sequence of rigorous academic and career or technical courses leading to an associate's degree, baccalaureate degree and beyond, or an industry-recognized certificate and/or license._

This lesson will cover some aspects of how to research careers. The next lesson will explain more about self-discovery. The final lesson of the chapter will look into pathways toward your career goals.

As a young person, you would be making a wise move to start now in doing some early research to seek your own needs and wants in a career. The results may give you a great source of satisfaction and contentment later in life. Your research should take into account some self-discovery about what makes you tick. It's not so much a question of analyzing strengths and weaknesses as it is about developing those strengths you do have to be successful at what you love to do. Finally, as you chart your path forward, remember that there will always be someone willing to tell you how to work within your limitations, emphasizing your weaknesses. However, instead of thinking about limitations that have you looking downward, why not think about possibilities? Possibilities are what will push you upward.

Limitations are a way out. Possibilities are a way in. That's how to think about a good path to a rewarding career. You can always do a job eight hours a day that gets you a paycheck. Alternatively, you can work many more hours on a career you love, and find many rewards in doing so!

The way to a good career starts with knowledge. Good grades are an important first step. The world is now more competitive and more technical than it has ever been. Most highly skilled occupations now require a greater understanding of science and math. The Bureau of Labor Statistics reported that the growth of high-paying jobs between now and 2020 will favor those in technical and medical fields, almost all of which require a substantial level of science and math education. Even those jobs requiring only a high school diploma are becoming more technical and require some knowledge in these subjects.

College graduation and a job probably seem a long way off right now. However, this is the time to figure out the direction you want to take and how to get there. This doesn't mean that you'll be stuck forever with the decision you make now. Most people change their life goals several times as they get older. The average person undergoes several career changes in a lifetime.

Decisions you make now are still very important. If you can develop an idea of the direction you want your life to take, it will help you focus. This will improve your ability to succeed in school and in life.

Vocabulary

- career path
- job
- career
- education
- training
- vacancy announcement
- closing date
- networking
- lead
- social network

Though often used interchangeably, the words *career* and *job* have different meanings. The difference is one of attitude and lifestyle. A job is *work you do to make a living*. A career is much more. A career is *a chosen field of work that has the potential for continuous growth and advancement by incorporating your interests, values, skills, and strengths to provide long-term fulfillment.*

If you have a career, you are willing to put in some extra effort to get ahead—go back to school, take training programs offered by your employer, or work extra hours so you can do your job better. Having a career means having a plan to get more skilled at your job as time goes on. Careers offer opportunities for advancement.

A career often involves five or six positions, perhaps in several industries. Each position has a different level of responsibility and difficulty, as well as salary. In each step, you'll have an opportunity to apply your increased experience.

Studs Terkel's book, *Working*, written decades ago, has held true right on through to the most recent annual surveys by *US News and World Report* and Gallup, which show that more than half of all American workers are dissatisfied with their jobs. Maybe it's because that's all they are—jobs.

"To love what you do and feel that it matters— how could anything be more fun?"

Katherine Graham,
publisher, *Washington Post*
Courtesy of Jurgen Frank/Corbis Images

Jobs are positions in which employees perform specific duties within designated hours for specific pay. Generally, these duties are similar from one day to the next. A job generally provides a basic living. It pays for food and shelter. It may not give you a chance to improve your lifestyle or afford many luxuries.

With respect to jobs and careers, what counts is not where you start but what you do once you've started. As an example, at age 16 you might get a job bussing tables at a local restaurant. If you like it, you may decide to make your career in the food industry. Over your working life, you could move on to a succession of positions as a short-order cook, assistant chef, head chef, and manager. You might one day own your own restaurant. These positions all fit the definition of a career. They do not have to be within the same company. They do not always require a college degree. Each does, however, require more training and a higher level of performance. The experience gained in one job helps prepare you for the succeeding position. At some point, you can say that you have a career.

You may also enter the job market bussing tables and not turn that job into a career step. You may move on to be a gas station attendant, then a cashier, then something else. Over 40 years of working life, you may hold many jobs but none of these jobs would prepare you directly for your next job. Each position is unrelated to the next. At the end of 40 years, you would have held a series of jobs, but you would not have had a career.

Most careers offer better salaries over time as you gain more experience. However, while money is an important factor in selecting a job or career, it is not the only consideration.

Career or job: The choice is up to you. If you choose a career, your only limits will be how much you are willing and able to learn, how much authority and responsibility you want, and what lifestyle changes you wish to strive for. If you choose to have a series of jobs, you will provide for your daily needs, but your ability to advance will be more limited.

Find something that you enjoy. Work doesn't have to be boring! And if you find something you like to do, you'll probably do it well. That's a good recipe for success in the workplace.

So who knows what you'll do? Whatever it is, try to think about possibilities, not limits. That's how a career is built. When you think in terms of limitations over 40 years of a working life, there is a point at which finding your passion and a good career can be lost. For many, it means a 40-year working life of no more than only a series of jobs held, and not much fulfillment.

Tim McGraw's Success Story

Tim McGraw, popular country music recording star, has sold 40 million CDs and won three Grammy Awards. He failed so badly in his first few attempts at selling his singles that he was told to give up his dream of becoming a country singer. A well-known producer told him, "You'll never make it, son. Go home and find yourself a job." McGraw didn't take the advice.

Courtesy of Michael Hurcomb/Corbis Images

In Chapter 1, you were asked to create a financial plan. You should now extend that plan. As you read this lesson, try to develop a clear statement in your plan about how you intend to spend your working life to build financial and personal security.

Listing a series of jobs will do very little to provide for your long-term financial security. But a career goal will allow you to build a level of satisfaction you achieve from that career. It will also provide for how to achieve increased responsibility and monetary rewards. Just remember that money isn't the only thing to consider in choosing a career. You are limited only by how much you are willing and able to learn, how much authority and responsibility you want, and what lifestyle you wish for yourself and your family.

Doing work you like is important not only because it releases you from possible boredom but it allows you to do a job well. When you do a job well, you can see the difference. If you do a job well often enough, you will you build a career. Better still, you will build a reputation. A solid reputation allows you satisfaction and peace of mind.

Training Versus Education

As you prepare for any career, you'll need both education and training. Although people sometimes use these two words interchangeably, they have different meanings.

Education involves *broad-based learning*. When you earn a college degree, you sample many fields of knowledge, and then concentrate on one specific field. Because of its broad basis, education prepares you for a variety of career possibilities.

Training has a narrower focus. It *prepares you to perform a function that requires a specific set of skills*. Training can prepare you, for example, to work on jet engines or (computer repair—to replace aircraft radios).

Different careers need people with different mixes of education and training. But it's not an "either/or" situation. Even the most highly educated people need training, and even entry-level trainees need some education.

Career Options

Many possible career options lie ahead of you. The path you take will influence the amount of education you will need and the experience you must gain to prepare for your chosen career. Among your options are working in the private sector; working for the federal, state, or local government (including as a teacher); or serving in the military.

Each option provides employment in a fascinating variety of fields. Some will require a high school diploma; others might demand years of postgraduate university study.

Currently a large number of Americans are aging. The retirement of many millions of baby-boomers has opened up many opportunities in the next decade. At about the time you graduate from high school you may find many new career options available to you. Check the latest trends from the US Department of Labor's Bureau of Labor Statistics. In Tables 3.1 and 3.2, you'll see that between now and 2020, there will be a huge growth in available jobs and careers, especially in medical technologies and health sciences.

Table 3.1 The 20 Fastest Growing Occupations in the United States Requiring at Least a High School Diploma, Through 2020

Occupation	Percentage Growth
Biomedical engineers	+61.7%
Veterinary technicians/technologists	+52 .0%
Reinforcing iron and rebar workers	+48.6%
Physical therapist assistants	+45.7%
Helpers—pipe layers, plumbers, pipefitters and steamfitters	+45.4%
Meeting, convention, event planners	+43.7%
Diagnostic medical sonographers	+43.5%
Occupational therapist assistants	+43.3%
Physical therapist aides	+43.1%
Glaziers	+42.4%
Interpreters and translators	+42.2%
Medical secretaries	+41.3%
Marketing research specialists and analysts	+41.2%
Marriage and family therapists	+41.2%
Brick and block masons	+40.5%
Physical therapists	+39.0%
Dental hygienists	+37.7%
Audiologists	+36.8%
Health educators	+36.5%
Stonemasons	+36.5%

Source: http://www.bls.gov/news.release/ecopro.t07.htm

Table 3.2 The 20 Occupations with the Largest Numerical Increases in Employment Requiring at Least a High School Diploma, Through 2020

Occupation	Growth (rounded to nearest 1000)
Registered nurses	+712,000
General office clerks	+490,000
Customer service representatives	+338,000
Heavy tractor-trailer and truck drivers	+330,000
Postsecondary teachers	+306,000
Nursing aides, orderlies and attendants	+302,000
Child care workers	+262,000
Bookkeeping, auditing and accounting clerks	+259,000
Elementary school teachers (except special education)	+249,000
Receptionists/information clerks	+249,000
Sales reps, wholesale and manufacturing	+223,000
Medical secretaries	+210,000
First-line supervisors of office and administrative support workers	+203,000
Carpenters	+196,000
Security guards	+195,000
Teacher assistants	+191,000
Accountants and auditors	+191,000
Licensed practical nurse and licensed vocational nurse	+169,000
Physicians and surgeons	+169,000
Medical assistants	+163,000

Source: *http://www.bls.gov/news.release/ecopro.t06.htm*

Some fields are expected to lose jobs, and you'll want to know which ones they are. Table 3.3 shows some of these. Economic sectors lose jobs because of technological advances or changes in business practices, among other factors. For example, machines now enable farmers to produce more food with fewer people. At the same time, larger farms are constantly absorbing smaller ones. As a result, there are fewer and fewer jobs for farmers and ranchers.

Table 3.3 The 20 Occupations with the Largest Numerical Declines, Through 2020 (all education levels)

Occupation	Decline
Farmers, ranchers, and other agricultural managers	−96,100
US Postal Service mail sorters, processors and processing machine operators	−68,900
Sewing machine operators	−42,100
US Postal Service mail carriers	−38,100
Switchboard operators, including answering service	−33,200
Postal Service clerks	−31,600
Cooks, fast food	−19,100
Miscellaneous agricultural workers	−19,100
Data entry keyers	−15,900
Word processors and typists	−13,200
Door-to-door sales, news and street vendors and related workers	−11,500
Food service managers	−10,600
Electrical and electronic equipment assemblers	−10,400
File clerks	−8,800
Prepress technicians and workers	−8,100
Computer operators	−7,400
Postmasters and mail superintendents	−6,800
Office machine operators, except computer	−6,800
Pressers, textile, garment, and related materials	−6,800
Floral designers and petroleum pump system and refinery operators and gaugers (tie)	−6,200

Source: *http://www.bls.gov/news.release/ecopro.t08.htm*

Farming, by the numbers, may not look attractive. But as population growth continues, food producing will still be very important. Thus, if you have the desire to be a farmer, there will always be a need. Not only that, but by increasing your knowledge of farming, you may find yourself creating a path toward working in agribusiness. Or, by going back to school you may decide to learn about the science of agriculture as another pathway to advance in your working career.

In the end, however, statistics are just statistics. Be aware of them, but don't give them too much weight. Consider all the types of positions that interest you, regardless of overall employment prospects in that field. Try to understand what draws you to these particular jobs. If you are drawn to a career that seems to have a bleak future, maybe you'll be the one who changes that future for the better!

In any event, achieving a high school diploma should be your first priority. A diploma will get you the biggest percentage jump in your potential earnings—82 percent more than if you drop out. According to a recent study by Georgetown University's Center on Education and the Workforce, earnings become even greater for those who have a bachelor's degree or higher.

The growing technical job market makes it necessary for most Americans to have at least some collegiate experience. A postsecondary certificate or an associate's degree will help you earn above the median income for the nation as a whole. Postsecondary education, according to the researchers, "is no longer the preferred pathway to middle-class jobs—it is...the only pathway." So think of your future this way. Creating a fulfilling career will require continued study—finding postsecondary education and training opportunities wherever and whenever possible.

By 2018, almost 47 million job openings will be created. Almost 14 million will be new jobs. Thirty-three million more jobs will be established to replace workers who are retiring. About 63 percent of these jobs will require people who have at least some college education. The other third will require workers with a high school diploma or less. Those jobs will be most certainly on the low end of the wage scale.

Computer animation, requiring a combination of creativity and technical skills, is a growth area for jobs today and careers into the future.

Courtesy of Ton Koene/Alamy

Career Examples

Computer Animation

Computer animation has been a growing field because of advances in computer technologies that have eliminated most mechanical functions. Sketches and illustrations are now enhanced by computers, which have made it easier to produce animated characters and scenes.

The Payoff: Movie and television studios, advertising, Internet, and multimedia firms now pay top dollar for technology-savvy animators. There is work in both two-dimensional (cartoons, for example) and three-dimensional animation.

How You Prepare for a Career: Your talents should be in the arts, with a background in painting and drawing, enhanced by a creative mind.

What You Need: A bachelor's degree in art, computer animation, or graphics is ideal for this kind of work.

Customer Service Representatives

Customer service representatives have become extremely important in recent years. Retail consumers became increasingly unhappy with customer call centers being run from other countries. So many companies are bringing more of these jobs back to the states.

Customer service representatives answer questions about products or services and handle or resolve complaints. They communicate with customers by telephone; by e-mail, fax, US mail, or in person. Some customer service representatives handle general questions and complaints. Others specialize in a particular area. Some customer service professionals have important titles, like account manager. These professionals are often found at advertising agencies. They often handle accounts worth millions of dollars.

Computer animators draw sketches by hand, transfer the images to a computer, and add movement.
Courtesy of Kim Kulish/Corbis Images

The Payoff: This field will grow much faster than the average. More than 2.25 million people work in customer service. The number will be more than 3.25 million by 2020. These jobs will cover the entire range from the lowest to highest levels in responsibilities and pay.

How You Prepare for a Career: High school courses in computers, English, or business can help you prepare for a career in customer service. Good communications skills with people are important at all levels in customer relations. Your state employment service offices can provide information about job opportunities for customer service representatives.

What You Need: Most customer service representative jobs until recently required only a high school diploma. But employers are now demanding more skills. So many jobs are requiring at least an associate's degree. You need basic-to-intermediate computer knowledge and have good interpersonal skills. Some positions require as high as a master's degree in marketing or business, like account representatives who handle big clients or a large volume of customers.

Veterinary Technicians and Technologists

Veterinary technicians and technologists are expected to grow rapidly in number through 2020. These assistants to veterinarians do very important tasks. They do lab tests to help treat and diagnose disease in animals. They prepare vaccines and serums to prevent disease. They take tissue and blood samples and they do urinalysis and blood counts. They assist a veterinarian during surgical and dental procedures. They also clean and sterilize instruments, and maintain equipment and machines.

The Payoff: While not particularly high-paying, these jobs often offer a lot of personal satisfaction. If you love animals and enjoy taking care of them you will do well in these jobs. The ability to understand problems, communicate with customers and be sensitive to their needs is very important. These professionals make around $30,000 per year on average. There are 80,000 people working in these positions within the United States. That number will grow by more than 20 percent from 2010–2020.

How You Prepare for a Career: You need some knowledge of plants and animals. If you are good in chemistry and can handle administrative details, those are important. Being able to use word processing to manage files, records, and forms is very helpful, too.

What You Need: You will likely need at least some college, such as an associate's degree. This is a field where the love of animals often overshadows issues of how much money can be made.

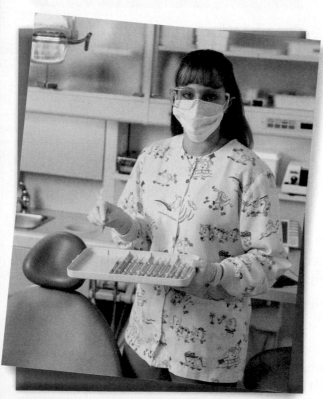

Dental assistants sterilize and disinfect instruments and equipment. They also prepare trays of instruments for dental procedures.

Courtesy of Guy Cali/Corbis Images

Dental Assistants

Dental assistants, like many other professionals in the health care industry, will be in great demand over the coming decade. There are about 300,000 dental assistants currently, and by 2020, the need will be for 400,000. Dental assistants are important to a dentist's work. Assistants examine and treat patients, mostly doing cleanings and scaling. But they also make patients more comfortable before dental procedures and treatments. They also do X-rays, interpreting them for the dentist when needed. They update patients' dental records. Assistants also prepare the trays of instruments and instruct patients on postoperative and general oral health.

The Payoff: Dental assistants make, on average, about $33,500 per year, and the work is usually stable.

How You Prepare for a Career: High school students interested in a career as a dental assistant need courses in biology, chemistry, health, and office practices. The American Dental Association offers information on dental assistant careers at *http://www.ada.org/public/education/careers/assistant_bro.asp.*

What You Need: As a dental assistant, you may learn skills on the job. Nevertheless, you may be required to enroll in a dental-assisting program at a community college, trade school, technical institute. Some are trained through the armed forces. Some college is usually a prerequisite for these positions, but more important are: skills in communicating effectively with patients and with dentists; listening attentively—hearing what people are saying about their conditions; being service oriented—finding ways to help people; and perceptiveness—being aware of others' reactions, and being understanding.

Meeting, Convention, and Event Planners

Meeting, convention, and event planners will be among the most-in-demand professions over the next decade. You need to be highly organized to succeed as a planner. You must coordinate the activities of a staff, convention personnel, caterers, and clients to prepare for group meetings, events, or conventions. Your major skills should include communicating, problem-solving, good judgment, and time management. You will juggle many details as a planner to assure a smooth-running event.

The Payoff: An experienced event planner can easily earn $50,000 per year. The field will grow by almost 44 percent through 2020.

How You Prepare for a Career: Some know-how in sales and marketing is helpful. If you are good at presenting, promoting, and selling services, you are headed for success. Skill in managing money, an ability to work with consumers, and understanding how to provide quality service is also important to be a successful meeting planner.

What You Need: Courses in high school English and communications should be followed by postsecondary courses in marketing, public relations, or business. A bachelor's degree is the primary path to a career in these fields.

Cybersecurity

Cybersecurity is growing faster than most careers. Protecting the public, and in some cases the nation, from computer-related threats requires special skills. If you choose this field, you would protect the data and systems connected to the Internet. There are some in the field who work to secure large networks. Others develop software security programs.

The Payoff: You can make a career in information security without a college degree. But the higher paying jobs go to those who have more advanced education. Annual salaries can range from $70,000 to more than $100,000, depending on your skills, where you want to work, and the kind of industry you choose.

Victor Valley H.S. Textbook

How You Prepare for a Career: Understanding computers is important. You can pick up enough knowledge to do computer jobs that pay very well without a degree. Some have earned an unrelated academic degree to one in computers. However, they found that their knowledge of computers allowed them to switch careers altogether into cybersecurity. Many switch to careers in information security because they are patriotic. They feel they are contributing to the safety of our nation.

Independent computer schools no longer dominate the training of computer and network security people. Many traditional colleges and universities are reacting to the post–9/11 era by using government grants to create advanced education programs.

What You Need: This is a field that can be very sophisticated. Often, a bachelor's or advanced degree is required. Many workers still learn their skills on the job or in classes offered by schools that offer certificates. Be careful of on-line sources that make promises that can't be kept. Before you enroll and pay any fees, check out any organization's accreditation status.

Interpreters and Translators

Interpreters and translators are another group of professionals needed in the coming decade. As an interpreter, you can work with oral or sign language. As a translator, you can take something written in one language and translate it into another. You could edit and revise translated materials. You might also rewrite material into different languages. You might be required to listen to a speaker's statement and then prepare a translation using electronic listening systems. If you become a tour guide, you may have to be multi-lingual.

The Payoff: You can earn over $43,000 per year as a professional, and there is opportunity for advancement. The 51,000 now employed in these positions is expected to grow to almost 75,000 by 2020.

Interpreters and translators are in demand in today's globally-oriented economy.

Courtesy of Steve Skjold/Alamy

How You Prepare for a Career: Good grades in English and in one or more foreign languages will help prepare you for these opportunities. Strong reading, oral and writing skills are important for a career.

What You Need: Education requirements differ quite a bit. About one-fourth of the jobs require associate's degrees, another fourth require advanced or professional degrees. Another 16 percent require bachelor's degrees. There is a wide variety of organizations and geographic locations in which you can work. You can work with tour companies and educational organizations. You might work at the US State Department, National Security Agency, or in an international association.

Brick or Block Masons

If you like the construction industry, one of the better paying, more specialized jobs is a brick or block mason. This is a field expecting to grow by more than 40 percent over the next several years. Masons lay and bind building materials, such as brick, structural tile, concrete block, cinder block, and other materials to construct or repair walls, partitions, arches, sewers, and other kinds of structures.

The Payoff: The average income for brick and block masons is about $47,000 per year. A good masonry worker can command a pretty good income and have work stability as the demand continues to grow in this field.

How to Prepare for a Career: Having skill with tools is very helpful, as well as the ability to work quickly. Being precise and neat with use of materials is important. A year or two working as a helper is beneficial, as is the completion of a recognized apprenticeship program.

What You Need: More than half the jobs do not normally require a high school diploma. However, if you want to get into better-paying and supervisory positions, the education and training requirements go up. A recognized apprenticeship program is important for career preparation. You'll find apprenticeships in bricklaying for masonry, construction, firebrick and refractory tile, and other related areas.

Teachers

Teachers will be needed at almost every level from preschool through college. High school teachers, especially, will be needed between now and 2020. The number of positions, according to estimates, will grow by more than 410,000 in that time. Elementary school teacher positions will grow by almost 250,000. The same demand is expected for middle school teachers. Postsecondary-level teaching positions will jump by 300,000.

The Payoff: At the postsecondary level, you can easily earn $60,000. Because there's such a big need, a career will be not only rewarding but can contribute to a very critical national need. Middle school and elementary school teachers now make close to $52,000 a year, on average, and high school teachers, slightly more.

How to Prepare for a Career: Mastering core subjects in high school will prepare you well for teaching. College courses in understanding and handling the group dynamics of a classroom are part of the preparation. You will need to learn how to work with individual personalities and problems of students. Being a good observer of your own teachers will help you understand how classes are organized. You'll learn how to be creative in passing on knowledge. You will also see that safety and security issues are part of the teaching experience.

What You Need: For postsecondary teachers, most need a PhD. Fewer than 25 percent of the positions require a master's instead of a doctorate. At the high school level and below, the majority of teachers have master's degrees and some have bachelor's degrees with significant other professional training.

Physical Therapists

Physical therapy is growing because there are many older baby boomers needing help with injuries, muscular ailments, and flexibility. The profession is also growing because of returning military service members from the wars in Iraq and Afghanistan. Many service members lost limbs or had other serious injuries requiring therapy to help them improve their quality of life. Much of this therapy will require a long-term commitment to these veterans.

The Payoff: Therapists are highly trained and paid. About half have master's degrees, and the rest are split pretty evenly between doctorates and bachelor's degrees. A $70,000 income is average for a therapist. Physical therapy assistants can be paid well, too, into the upper 40-thousands. Physical therapy aides, while the demand for them is high also, are not formally trained, and make about half as much money as an assistant.

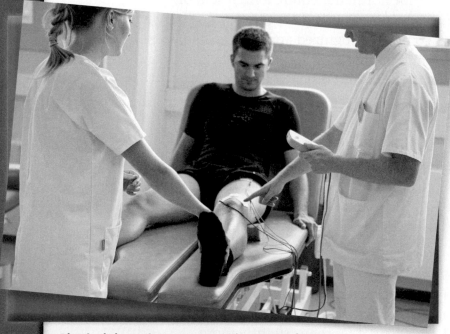

Physical therapists serve a wide range of patients.

Courtesy of Chassenet/BSIP/Corbis Images

How to Prepare for a Career: A hospital is the best place to volunteer some time to learn some basics. However, opportunities are everywhere, including health centers, sports facilities, and nursing homes. Therapists work with a variety of assistants and aides because the patient load can become very heavy. Physical therapy assistants are important to the therapist because they are trained to assist in the development of treatment plans, to carry out routine functions, document the progress of treatment, and modify specific treatments within the scope of treatment plans established by a physical therapist. Generally, this requires formal education, at least an associate's degree. Aides, meanwhile, do not have as much responsibility, working under the close supervision of a physical therapist or physical therapy assistant. Aides perform only delegated or routine tasks in specific situations. Usually, these include preparing the patient and the treatment area.

What You Need: Almost 150 colleges offer a four-year degree in physical therapy. Many offer advanced degrees. To practice, you have to pass a state examination. As a physical therapy assistant, a bachelor's degree is better to have in terms of responsibility and pay. But it can be a rewarding experience to be able to work with patients and see them make progress to a better quality of life.

Telecommunications Engineering Specialists

Telecommunications engineering specialists is another big growth area. Within these positions, you might design or configure voice, video, and data communications systems, and possibly supervise installation and post-installation service and maintenance. Also, you may be installing software, configuring modems, and setting up cables and networks.

The Payoff: Salaries are very good for skilled specialists in telecommunications. Not quite 300,000 people work in these fields now, but by 2020, there will be a need for almost 500,000. Currently, salaries are about $75,000 per year.

How to Prepare for a Career: An ability in electronics and computers, the ability to use tools, and a good understanding of science and math are good starting points.

What You Need: No degree or license is needed to become a technician. But some significant study of computer systems networking and telecommunications is important.

Some Other Noteworthy Careers on the Rise

Registered nurses (RNs) are already in short supply. The need for them will be even greater over the next decade. As many as 700,000 new RNs will be needed to provide medical care. RNs are the closest link between patient and doctor. They carry a lot of responsibility. They care for ill, injured, convalescent, or disabled patients. They provide advice to patients on maintaining health and preventing disease.

Women have traditionally filled most of these skilled positions, but more men are entering the profession, and many have proven to be very effective. RNs need a genuine sensitivity to patients' medical problems and must communicate effectively with patients to provide them aid and comfort.

As the critical link between doctors and patients, registered nurses are highly valued in the health services field.
Courtesy of Yuri Arcurs/Shutterstock

Usually an associate's degree is required for nursing. Some skills require a bachelor's degree. The hours and shifts can be long, but RNs make on the average about $65,000 a year.

Other health-related jobs in the high-growth category are dental hygienists, medical secretaries, biomedical engineers, and health educators.

Working for the Federal Government

The federal government is still the largest employer in the United States, some 2,630,000 people—military and civilian. It hires hundreds of thousands of people each year.

Federal jobs are found in every state and every large city, as well as in 200 countries around the world. Working for the federal government can be very fulfilling. The Office of Personnel Management (OPM) is the employment agency for the US Government. It is headquartered in Washington, DC.

OPM maintains a website (*www.usajobs.opm.gov*) that lists all federal jobs. When a federal department or agency has a position available, it issues a vacancy announcement. OPM posts it to the USAJobs website. The vacancy announcement *describes the skills and experience required to perform in a position.* It is usually posted with information about the job title, salary, duties, and application procedures. It also says where and when to apply. It will also list a closing date. This is *the cutoff point for an application,* or the date it must either reach or be mailed to the agency hiring for the position.

You can also visit this site: *www.federaljobs.net/employme.htm* for a listing of federal jobs and other helpful information on how to apply for federal employment.

Two workers with the US Department of Agriculture inspect a row of plants at a government research facility.
Courtesy of Winkler/Corbis Images

Student Educational Employment Program

The Student Educational Employment Program is a way for you to get into government work. The program offers students who finish their education on-the-job experience leading to possible full-time careers. You can be hired under this program if you are working at least half-time toward a diploma, academic or vocational certificate, or a degree.

The Student Temporary Employment Program introduces students to the work environment and teaches basic workplace skills.

The Student Career Experience Program provides experience related to your academic and career goals. Complete information on federal student employment opportunities is at: *www.opm.gov/employ/students/intro.asp*.

Career Factors

You'll need to consider many factors as you decide on a career path or specific job. Table 3.4 lists some of the primary career factors that will influence your choice.

Table 3.4 Primary Career Factors

Factor	Description
EDUCATION	Your level of formal knowledge and training. Education greatly increases your career potential.
EXPERIENCE	Your combined knowledge, skills, and self-confidence gained through events and activities. Experience adds to your earning potential and can come from jobs, internships, and volunteer work.
SKILLS AND TALENTS	Abilities you possess. Education and training enhance your abilities.
INTERESTS AND TEMPERAMENT	Aspects of your personality that affect the kinds of work you prefer and the settings in which you can work effectively.
JOB AVAILABILITY	Positions available at a given time and place that match your skills, experience, and education. Some jobs are available only in specific locations, such as large cities or company headquarters.
EARNING POTENTIAL	Certain professions or careers have higher earning potential than others.
PERSONAL NEEDS	Fringe benefits and other factors that influence job satisfaction, such as insurance, vacation, on-site child care, and sick leave.

Career Planning and Information Sources

What is right for you? A job or a career? Will you enter the work force right out of high school, or pursue higher education? Will you join the military?

You should be constantly weighing those options, but also be willing to change if a particular direction doesn't seem right. When you find a path that's good for you, go for it!

Good career planning includes four tasks:

1. Evaluating your attitudes, interests, abilities, and preferences
2. Gathering information on different career options
3. Matching your interests with possible occupations
4. Taking the steps necessary to reach your career and life goals.

Later lessons in class and in this book will discuss the job-search process in detail, including writing a résumé, applying for a job, what employers are looking for, and job interviewing.

The remainder of this lesson will help you as you gather the information you'll need for good decision-making.

Online Job Information Sources

In the Internet age, you have more information available to you than most high school students have ever had.

- *The Occupational Outlook Handbook*, the career-information resource guide cited above for the 20 fastest-growing and fastest declining occupations is produced by the US Department of Labor, and you can find it at *www.bls.gov/oco/*.

- *The Dictionary of Occupational Titles* gives titles for thousands of jobs. It may be a good source of ideas if you are having a hard time imagining what you might do for a career. You can find it at *www.wave.net/upg/immigration/dot_index.html*.

Other Sources of Information

Dozens of books give career and job-seeking advice. Check out a couple of them from the library or buy a couple that look interesting and read them to compare the differences.

You also have easy access to a state or local job services office. They have updated information on jobs that are available.

Newspapers are a good source of job availabilities. The business section of your local newspaper may give you an idea of what kinds of new businesses may be opening in or moving to your area. Larger national newspapers have significant job sections, or if you subscribe online, you can get access to these job openings on your home computer.

Visit the local chamber of commerce. Attend trade shows if there are any in your area. Visit the local branch of a union if the members work in an area that interests you.

You will also hear the word "networking" a lot during your working life. Networking is *the process of making contacts and building relationships that can help you obtain leads, referrals, advice, information, and support.* But even in high school, this could be one of the best ways you can learn about job or career openings. Relatives or neighbors may know about potential careers. People who are working often hear about job openings before their businesses make them public. Those are people who may be able to give you a good lead to a job, that is, *an inroad or route to information before it is otherwise widely known.*

Networking is important to success in your job search and career plan.
Courtesy of Warren Jennings/Shutterstock

The most widely used form of networking now is on the Internet. Social networks such as LinkedIn and Facebook are the most popular. Generally, a social network is *a website that provides a virtual community for people to share their daily activities or interests, or to widen their circle of professional acquaintances.* To become a member of a social network, you go to the network web page and create an online "profile" with your personal or biographical information, pictures, and other information you choose to "post." You can communicate with others in your network in many ways. You can offer comments in a blog, or by e-mail, instant messaging, even by audio or video.

As a career tool, you can join a professional-oriented network like LinkedIn and obtain many free services that are not available on other such sites. You can post your own resume, or profile, and connect to others who are in your area of career interest. You do this by looking for people you already know, or by reviewing company profiles that can tell you a lot about what the company or organization does, who works there, and how the organization is doing, from its career offerings to its financial status.

As with other forms of electronic communication, you should follow some guidelines about social networking. Do not allow just anyone to join your network. Know the individual or group to whom or which you decide to connect. Be careful about career or business social networks that do not offer a variety of services but charge you for your participation. Some of these "connections" could also be someone *phishing*, looking to steal personal information to compromise it in some way. So, always be wary of unfamiliar sources of friends and business connections.

Consumer Reports magazine has listed several cautions about social networking, things that should be avoided:

- *Using a weak password*

- *Leaving your full birth date in your profile*—This is an ideal target for identity thieves. You should change that by choosing an option to show only the month and day, or no birthday at all.

- *Failing to use privacy controls*— Almost 13 million Facebook users in 2012 said they had never set, or did not know about the site's privacy tools. Twenty-eight percent shared all or almost all of their wall posts with an audience wider than just their friends.

- *Mentioning that you'll be away from home*—That's like putting a "no one's home" sign on your door.

- *Letting search engines find you*—This can help unwanted strangers to access your page.

Finally, as you look to start your career or job search, talk with professionals and the people who visit your school during career days. If possible, attend the career days at other schools, including those at colleges and universities in your areas. Use these events to learn about the requirements for entering various occupations or professions.

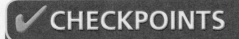

✔ CHECKPOINTS

Lesson 1 Review

Using complete sentences, answer the following questions on a sheet of paper.

1. What are some of the considerations in selecting the right career?

2. What is the difference between a job and a career? Why is a career better?

3. What is a career path? When you set a career path, does it mean you have to stick with one kind of job? Explain your answer.

4. What careers sound most appealing to you? Look to see if the career is in a fast-growth or slow-growth area. What would your strategy be to become better prepared to succeed in that career choice?

5. What qualities do you have that employers will appreciate?

6. What qualities do you think you need to develop to become more valuable to employers?

APPLYING CAREER-CHOOSING SKILLS

7. Take the list of three types of jobs you wrote for the Quick Write. Look up each job in *The Occupational Outlook Handbook*. If one or more aren't listed there, look on O*Net, the Department of Labor site, and write down the educational qualifications and salary information. Then write a list of the advantages and disadvantages of each position and rank them in your order of preference. Which factors helped you decide the rankings?

Self-Discovery

> "Ninety percent of the world's misery comes from people not knowing themselves, their abilities, their frailties, and even their real virtues. Most of us go almost all the way through life complete strangers to ourselves."
>
> Sydney J. Harris, journalist

Learn About

- career direction: getting to know yourself
- identifying your aptitudes and abilities
- linking your dominant intelligences to your preferred learning style
- identifying your fields of interests
- linking your aptitudes and interests to career paths

Career Direction: Getting to Know Yourself

In the previous lesson, you considered some aspects of how to research careers. You now know about some of the most potentially rewarding career paths for the 21st century. In this lesson, you will learn techniques of self-discovery that can reveal pathways to success for your education and your career.

During this lesson, you will learn about three personal inventories. The first allows you to identify the relative strengths of your multiple intelligences (MI), *the eight distinct areas of intelligence that everyone possesses.* The second will help you identify your preferred learning style—*the way an individual learns best.* These two inventories will help you develop study and career exploration strategies. They will also allow you to effectively apply a third tool for self-discovery, the Holland Interest Environments, *a technique for exploring the ways that your interests can be grouped into job categories so you can begin to select specific career paths to investigate.* Once you have taken these inventories, you'll learn about career clusters, *an organized way to get information about a variety of different careers.*

These inventories are not intended to label you, nor are they a measure of how smart you are. They do not measure your worth or your capabilities as a student or citizen. They are offered so that you might gain a better understanding of your multiple intelligences, your preferred style for learning and working, and your fields of interest. Using these tools for self-discovery, you can start today to improve how you learn. You'll also be more equipped to make career path choices for tomorrow.

Identifying Your Aptitudes and Abilities

You Have More Than One Type of Intelligence

Scientists and educators used to believe that intelligence, *the ability to acquire, understand, and use knowledge*, consisted of only two basic areas: verbal or mathematical. More recently, the research of Dr. Howard Gardner (1999) has shown that there are at least eight distinct areas of intelligence. Gardner proposes that each person possesses all eight intelligences to a greater or lesser degree, and can more fully develop each of the eight. As you read the descriptions below, ask yourself which ones you think are already well developed and which you would like to develop further:

- Visual/spatial intelligence (Picture Smart) *includes the ability to create mental images and transform them into an art form or useful product.* People with this intelligence enjoy art, shop, drafting, and photography. They enjoy projects such as designing brochures, ceramics, costumes, structures, and websites.

- Verbal/linguistic intelligence (Word Smart) *focuses on the use of language and words.* Individuals with this type of intelligence tend to enjoy school subjects such as English, foreign languages, history, and social sciences. They enjoy debate, drama, TV, and radio work, newspaper and yearbook editing, writing blogs, newsletters, and magazine articles.

- Musical/rhythmic intelligence (Music Smart) *focuses on the ability to be aware of patterns in pitch, sound, rhythm, and timbre.* These individuals enjoy such school subjects as music and dance. They are involved in band, orchestra, choir, and dance productions.

Vocabulary

- multiple intelligences (MI)
- learning style
- Holland Interest Environments
- career clusters
- intelligence
- visual/spatial intelligence
- verbal/linguistic intelligence
- musical/rhythmic intelligence
- logical/mathematical intelligence
- bodily/kinesthetic intelligence
- intrapersonal intelligence
- interpersonal intelligence
- naturalistic intelligence

A good chef might combine "picture smart" with "body smart" by being able to visualize an appealing dish and then prepare it.

Courtesy of Jon Feingersh/Corbis Images

- Logical/mathematical intelligence (Number Smart) *includes the ability to think abstractly, to problem-solve, and to think critically.* Favorite school subjects for these individuals include math, science, economics, and computer programming. They tend to be involved in science projects and enjoy reading maps, spreadsheets, budgets, and blueprints.

- Bodily/kinesthetic intelligence (Body Smart) *relates to the ability to connect mind and body, and often relates to excelling at sports.* Popular subjects include dance, drama, sports, and culinary arts.

- Intrapersonal intelligence (Self-Smart) *involves the ability to comprehend your own feelings.* Popular school subjects related to this intelligence include psychology and creative writing. These individuals enjoy reading and journal writing.

- Interpersonal intelligence (People Smart) *involves the ability to comprehend others' feelings.* Individuals who possess this intelligence enjoy such school subjects as literature, psychology, and sociology.

- Naturalistic intelligence (Environment Smart) *involves the ability to understand and work effectively in the natural world of plants and animals.* Popular school subjects related to this intelligence include science and agriculture.

Self-Discovery Through the Multiple Intelligences Survey (MIS)

Each person possesses all of these eight intelligences. When you can recognize which of your eight intelligences are most highly developed, and which come naturally, you can apply this knowledge to many activities, including your studies and career planning.

Research on career satisfaction suggests that to be satisfied with your career, you need to identify and capitalize on areas that seem to come naturally and take advantage of your multiple intelligence preferences.

If you had to make a career choice right now, just considering this information on multiple intelligences and the various careers listed under each, which of the eight areas would be in your top three? Which careers might fit you best? How you respond to these questions will indicate how these various intelligences might affect your future career. You are likely to be more satisfied and less stressed in a career that uses your natural preferences.

The Multiple Intelligences Survey (MIS) allows you to begin to answer these questions. You'll be able to complete the MIS either in class or online at the LE-300 companion website. There is also a version of the MIS at the Literacyworks site (*http://www. literacyworks.org/mi/assessment/findyourstrengths.html*) that will identify your top three intelligences based on your responses, and make recommendations for further building your strengths. Once you have taken the survey, you'll learn how it can improve your studies and career decisions. You'll also be more prepared to relate your intelligences to your preferred learning styles and fields of interest.

Using Your Knowledge of Multiple Intelligences in Your Studies and Career Planning

Study Habits

Once you know your scores in the MIS, you can put this knowledge into practice. Use the list below to help create a study environment and habits that will be more comfortable and more efficient for you. Read each category, because you may need to use your less dominant intelligences in some of the classes you take.

VISUAL/SPATIAL

- Use visuals in your notes such as timelines, charts, graphs, and geometric shapes.
- Work to create a mental or visual picture of the information at hand.
- Use colored markers to make associations or to group items together.
- Use mapping or webbing so that your main points are easily recognized.
- When taking notes, draw pictures in the margins to illustrate the main points.
- Visualize the information in your mind.

VERBAL/LINGUISTIC

- Establish study groups so that you can talk about the information.
- Use the information you studied to create a story or a skit.
- Read as much information about related areas as possible.
- As you read chapters, outline them in your own words.
- Summarize and recite your notes aloud.

MUSICAL/RHYTHMIC

- Listen to music while studying (if it does not distract you).
- Write a song or rap about the chapter or information.
- Take short breaks from studying to listen to music.
- Commit the information being studied to the music from your favorite song.

LOGICAL/MATHEMATICAL

- Strive to make connections between subjects.
- Don't just memorize the facts; apply them to real-life situations.
- As you study the information, think of problems in society and how this information could solve those problems.
- Create analyzing charts. Draw a line down the center of the page, put the information at hand in the left column and analyze, discuss, relate, and synthesize it in the right column.
- Allow yourself some time to reflect after studying.

BODILY/KINESTHETIC

- Don't confine your study area to a desk or chair; move around, explore, go outside.
- Act out the information.
- Study in a group of people and change groups often.
- Use charts, posters, flash cards, and chalkboards to study.
- When appropriate or possible, build models using the information studied.
- Verbalize the information to others.
- Use games such as chess, Monopoly, Twister, or Clue when studying.
- Trace words as you study them.
- Use repetition to learn facts; write them many times.
- Make study sheets.

INTRAPERSONAL

- Study in a quiet area.
- Study by yourself.
- Allow time for reflection and meditation about the subject matter.
- Study in short time blocks and then spend some time absorbing the information.
- Work at your own pace.

INTERPERSONAL

- Study in groups.
- Share the information with other people.
- Teach the information to others.
- Interview outside sources to learn more about the material at hand.
- Have a debate with others about the information.

NATURALISTIC

- Study outside whenever possible.
- Relate the information to the effect on the environment whenever possible.
- When given the opportunity to choose your own topics or research projects, choose something related to nature.
- Collect your own study data and resources.
- Organize and label your information.
- Keep separate notebooks on individual topics so that you can add new information

Knowing your dominant intelligences can help you understand how you learn best and the kinds of careers you would prefer.
Courtesy of mangostock/Shutterstock

Career Planning

There are at least four benefits in applying your knowledge of MI to career planning:

1. You increase the chances for maximum career development when job tasks closely match your MI strengths.

2. The strength and development of intrapersonal intelligence is a key factor in positive career selection and advancement.

3. Career development will be enhanced when your parents, teachers, counselors, and friends are aware and supportive of the growth of your particular strengths.

4. The negative impact of weaknesses on career success will be lessened when your knowledge of MI allows you to emphasize your strengths while understanding areas for improvement.

Consider this short list of occupations categorized by primary intelligence. Which seem most suitable for you?

- *Visual/spatial intelligence*—engineer, surveyor, architect, urban planner, graphic artist, interior decorator, photographer, pilot.

- *Verbal/linguistic intelligence*—librarian, curator, speech pathologist, writer, radio or TV announcer, journalist, lawyer.

- *Musical/rhythmic intelligence*—musician, piano tuner, music therapist, choral director, conductor.

- *Logical/mathematical intelligence*—auditor, accountant, mathematician, scientist, statistician, computer analyst, technician.

- *Bodily/kinesthetic intelligence*—physical therapist, dancer, actor, mechanic, carpenter, forest ranger, jeweler.

- *Intrapersonal intelligence*—psychologist, therapist, counselor, theologian, program planner, entrepreneur.

- *Interpersonal intelligence*—administrator, manager, personnel worker, psychologist, nurse, public relations person, social director, teacher.

- *Naturalist intelligence*—botanist, astronomer, wildlife illustrator, meteorologist, chef, geologist, landscape architect.

Linking Your Dominant Intelligences to Your Preferred Learning Style

Learning Styles

Have you ever been in a class where you felt inadequate or out of place? Where it seems that others are understanding what's being taught but you are lost? It may be that your instructor and the materials were not compatible with your learning style. (*Learning styles* are the way an individual learns best.) On the other hand, if you are doing very well in a class, it may be because the instructor, the materials, or the class environment matches the way you process information best.

How do you learn best? Do you prefer lectures or group discussions? Role playing or case studies? Guided field trips or hands-on exercises? Some students learn best by touching and doing, while others learn best by listening and reflecting. Some students prefer working with a group of people sitting outside under the trees, while others would rather be alone in the library.

You may be asking yourself, "Is there one 'best' way of learning?" The answer is no. The way you learn new information depends on many variables. Your learning style, intelligences, personality, experiences, and attitude all play a part in the way you process new information. However, understanding these variables will help you learn more efficiently, and discover which career path is best for you.

There are three learning styles: visual, auditory, and tactile. The Learning Evaluation and Assessment Directory (LEAD) will help you determine your dominant learning style. As with the MIS, you can take the LEAD survey either in class or online at the LE-300 companion website.

Analyzing Your Learning Styles

When analyzing your scores on the LEAD, first look at your top score. If you learn best by *seeing information*, you have a more dominant *visual* learning style. If you learn best by *hearing information*, you have a more dominant *auditory* learning style. If you learn best by *touching or doing*, you have a more dominant *tactile* learning style. You may also hear the tactile learning style referred to as kinesthetic or hands-on.

Here are brief descriptions of how the three styles relate to a person's approach to learning:

- *Visual (Eye Dominant)*—Thinks in pictures; enjoys visual instructions, demonstrations, and descriptions; would rather read a text than listen to a lecture; avid note taker; needs visual references; enjoys using charts, graphs, and pictures.

- *Auditory (Ear Dominant)*—Prefers oral instructions; would rather listen than read; often tapes lectures and listens to them in the car or at home; recites information out loud; enjoys talking, discussing issues, and verbal stimuli; talks out problems.

- *Tactile (Action Dominant)*—Prefers hands-on approaches to learning; likes to take notes and uses a great deal of scratch paper; learns best by doing something, by touching it, or manipulating it; learns best while moving or while in action; often does not concentrate well when sitting and reading.

A Successful Decision

Brandon knew that he has always learned best when he could see the information in pictures, charts, graphs, PowerPoints, videos, or other visuals. He did not know what this was called. However, he also knew that he was a good "hands-on" learner.

When he discovered that different people have different ways of learning and instructors have different ways of teaching, things began to make more sense. He wondered why he had also done poorly in classes that were all lecture—like his history class.

This semester, he was becoming increasingly worried about his Medical Terminology class. It too, was all lecture—term after term after term. He decided to go to the Tutoring Center to find out what he could do to retain the information more effectively.

The tutor told Brandon about learning styles. He also showed Brandon how to make the terms more "visual" by drawing pictures beside each term, using colors, and creating storyboards with visual images of the definitions.

This strategy worked. Brandon's retention became easier because he learned to convert a "lecture" class into "visual" study time.

Brandon had made a successful decision.

Some of the most successful students have learned to use all three styles. If you are learning how to skateboard, you might learn best by hearing someone talk about the different styles or techniques. Others might learn best by watching a video where someone demonstrates the techniques. Still others would learn best by actually getting on theboard and trying it.

However, the student who involves all of his or her senses might gain the most. They might listen to the instructor tell about skateboarding, watch the video, and then go do it. Therefore, they would have involved all of their learning styles: visual, auditory, and tactile.

Identifying Your Fields of Interests

The rest of this lesson explores the ways that interests can be grouped into career categories or clusters so you can begin to select specific fields of interest to investigate. In this lesson, we highlight two different, widely-used approaches to identify interests.

The first is the Holland Interest Environments (or categories), which are Realistic, Investigative, Artistic, Social, Enterprising, and Conventional (Table 3.5). The second system, career clusters, is provided by the American College Testing (ACT) Program. The ACT clusters, as well as the tech-prep and school-to-career clusters listed later in this chapter, are used in secondary-school career centers.

Although you may have access to career inventories, remember that the information gathered by printed or online assessments is not magic. Assessments simply provide a quick, efficient way of gathering and organizing the information that you know about yourself—the answers come from you, that's why it's important to be honest when answering these questions. In the absence of an inventory, you are still able to collect the same information by completing the exercises, activities, and links to available inventories online provided throughout this book.

Linking Your Aptitudes and Interests to Career Paths

As you have seen in this lesson, understanding your interests can be very useful to you in making satisfying educational and career choices. The more you are able to incorporate your interests into your schoolwork and career planning, the more you will enjoy your life's work. Once you have completed the Holland Interest Inventory, you should use the framework of *career clusters* to explore those occupations associated with your interests. Find out what people actually do, and compare these jobs to your interests.

Table 3.5 Holland Interest Environments: Realistic, Investigative, Artistic, Social, Enterprising, and Conventional (RIASEC)

Instructions: Using the descriptions in each section, select which of the six Holland categories best describes you.

DOERS

(Realistic—R)	Doers like jobs such as automobile mechanic, air traffic controller, surveyor, farmer, and electrician. They like to work outdoors and to work with tools. They prefer to deal with things rather than with people. They are described as:			
	conforming frank honest	humble materialistic modest	natural persistent practical	shy stable thrifty
Hobbies	Building things	Growing	Repairing	Using hands
Abilities/ Interests	Operating tools	Planting	Playing sports	Repairing
Sample Careers	Air conditioning mechanic (RIE) Anthropologist (IRE) Archaeologist (IRE) Architectural drafter (RCI) Athletic Trainer (SRE) Automotive engineer (RIE) Automotive mechanic (RIE)	Baker/chef (RSE) Biochemist (IRS) Carpenter (RCI) Commercial airline pilot (RIE) Construction worker (REC) Dental assistant (RES) Electrical engineer (RIE) Fiber-optics technician (RSE)	Floral designer (RAE) Forester (RIS) Industrial arts teacher (IER) Optician (REI) Petroleum engineer (RIE) Police officer (SER) Radio/TV repairer (REI) Software technician (RCI)	Truck driver (RSE) Ultrasound technologist (RSI) Veterinarian (IRS)

THINKERS

(Investigative—I)	Thinkers like jobs such as biologist, chemist, physicist, anthropologist, geologist, and medical technologist. They are task oriented and prefer to work alone. They enjoy solving abstract problems and understanding the physical world. They are described as:			
	analytical cautious critical	curious independent intellectual	introverted methodical modest	precise rational reserved
Hobbies	Collecting rocks Collecting stamps	Doing puzzles	Participating in book clubs	Visiting museums

Source: *The Career Fitness Program: Exercising Your Options*, 7th edition, by Diane J. Sukiennik, William Bendat, and Lisa Raufman. Copyright 2004 Pearson Prentice-Hall.

Table 3.5 Holland Interest Environments, continued

Abilities/ Interests	Doing complex calculations	Interpreting formulas	Solving math problems	Using a microscope or scientific instrument
Sample Careers	Actuary (ISE) Anesthesiologist (IRS) Anthropologist (IRE) Archeologist (IRE) Automotive engineer (RIE) Baker/chef (RSE) Biochemist (IRS) Biologist (ISR) Chemical engineer (IRE)	Chemical technician (IRE) Commercial airline pilot (RIE) Computer analyst (IER) Dentist (ISR) Ecologist (IRE) Electrical engineer (RIE) Industrial arts teacher (IER)	Geologist (IRE) Landscape architect (AIR) Librarian (SAI) Medical technologist (ISA) Nurse practitioner (ISA) Petroleum engineer (RIE) Physician (ISE)	Psychologist (IES) Statistician (IRE) Technical writer (IRS) Ultrasound technologist (RSI) Veterinarian (IRS) Writer (ASI)

CREATORS

(Artistic—A)	Creators like jobs such as composer, musician, stage director, writer, interior designer, and actor/actress. They like to work in artistic settings that offer opportunities for self-expression. They are described as:

	complicated emotional expressive	idealistic imaginative impractical	impulsive independent intuitive	
Hobbies	Drawing/ photography	Performing Playing music	Sewing/designing Visiting museums	Writing stories, poems
Abilities/ Interests	Designing fashions or interiors	Playing a musical instrument	Singing, dancing, acting	Writing stories, poems, music; being creative, unique
Sample Careers	Actor (AES) Advertising (AES) Artist (AES) Broadcasting executive (EAS) Clothing designer (ASR) Copy writer (ASI) Dancer (AES)	Drama/music/art teacher (ASE) Economist (IAS) English teacher Fashion designer (ASR) Fashion illustrator (ASR) Floral Designer (RAE)	Furniture Designer (AES) Graphic Designer (AES) Interior designer (AES) Journalist (ASE) Landscape architect (ASR)	Librarian (SAI) Medical illustrator (AIE) Museum curator (AES) Nurse practitioner (ISA) Writer (ASI)

Table 3.5 Holland Interest Environments, *continued*

HELPERS

(Social—S)	Helpers like jobs such as teacher, clergy, counselor, nurse, personnel director, and speech therapist. They are sociable, responsible, and concerned with the welfare of others. They have little interest in machinery or physical skills. They are described as:			
	convincing cooperative friendly	generous helpful idealistic	insightful kind responsible	sociable tactful understanding
Hobbies	Caring for children	Participating in religious activities	Playing team sports	Volunteering
Abilities/ Interests	Expressing oneself	Leading a group discussion	Mediating disputes	Teaching/ training others
Sample Careers	Air traffic controller (SER) Athletic coach (SRE) Chaplain (SAI) College faculty (SEI) Consumer affairs director (SER) Cosmetologist (SAE) Counselor (SAE)	Dental hygienist (SAI) Historian (SEI) Homemaker (S) Hospital administrator (SER) Mail carrier (SRC) Medical records administrator (SIE) Nurse (SIR)	Occupational therapist (SRE) Paralegal (SCE) Police Officer (SER) Radiological technologist (SRI) Real estate appraiser (SCE) Schoolteacher (SEC)	Social worker (SEA) Speech pathologist (SAI) Youth services worker (SEC)

PERSUADERS

(Enterprising—E)	Persuaders like jobs such as salesperson, manager, business executive, television producer, sports promoter, and buyer. They enjoy leading, speaking, and selling. They are impatient with precise work. They are described as:			
	adventurous ambitious attention-getting	domineering energetic impulsive	optimistic pleasure-seeking popular	risk-taking self-confident sociable
Hobbies	Campaigning	Leading organizations	Promoting ideas	Starting own service or business
Abilities/ Interests	Initiating projects	Organizing activities	Persuading people	Selling things or promoting ideas

Table 3.5 Holland Interest Environments, continued

Sample Careers	Advertising executive (ESA)	Financial planner (ESR)	Insurance agent (ECS)	Stockbroker (ESI)
	Automobile sales worker (ESR)	Flight attendant (ESA)	Journalist (EAS)	Urban planner (ESI)
	Banker/financial planner (ESR)	Food service manager (ESI)	Lawyer (ESA)	
	Buyer (ESA)	Funeral director (ESR)	Office manager (ESR)	
	Claims adjuster (ESR)	Hotel manager (ESR)	Politician (ESA)	
	Credit manager (ERS)	Industrial engineer (EIR)	Public relations representative (EAS)	
			Real estate agent (ESR)	

ORGANIZERS

(Conventional—C)	Organizers like jobs such as bookkeeper, computer technician, banker, cost estimator, and tax expert. They prefer highly ordered activities, both verbal and numerical, that characterize office work. They have little interest in artistic or physical skills. They are described as:			
	careful	conservative	orderly	reserved
	conforming	efficient	persistent	self-controlled
	conscientious	obedient	practical	structured
Hobbies	Arranging and organizing household	Collecting memorabilia	Playing computer or card games	Studying tax laws
				Writing family history
Abilities/ Interests	Keeping accurate records	Organizing	Using a computer	Working within a system
				Writing
Sample Careers	Accountant (CSE)	Clerk (CSE)	Financial analyst (CSI)	Paralegal (SCE)
	Administrative assistant (ESC)	Computer operator (CSR)	Insurance underwriter (CSE)	Tax consultant (CSE)
	Bank teller (CSE)	Congressional-district aide (CES)	Internal auditor (ICR)	Travel agent (ECS)
	Budget analyst (CER)	Court reporter (CSE)	Legal secretary (???)	
	Building inspector (CSE)	Customer inspector (CEI)	Librarian (CSE)	
	Business teacher (CSE)	Elementary school teacher (SEC)	Medical records technician (CSE)	
	Claims adjuster (SEC)			

State and local career centers across the country often base their pathways on 16 career clusters developed by the US Department of Education (DOE). For example, the state of Georgia currently recognizes the following 11 career pathways related to these clusters.

- *Agriculture Pathway*—includes Agribusiness Management, Agriscience, Agricultural Mechanics, Animal Science, Forestry/Natural Resources, Plant Science/Horticulture, and Veterinary Science.

- *Architecture, Construction, Communications and Transportation Pathway*—includes Aircraft Support, Broadcasting/Video Production, Construction, Engineering Drawing and Design, Flight Operations, Graphic Communications, Metals, Transportation Logistical Operations, Transportation Logistical Support, and Graphic Design.

- *Arts & Humanities Pathway*—includes Foreign Languages, Journalism, Performing Arts, and Visual Arts.

- *Business and Computer Science Pathway*—includes Administrative/Information Support, Computer Networking, Computing, Computing Systems and Support, Financial Management-Accounting, Financial Management-Services, Interactive Media, and Small Business Development.

- *Culinary Arts Pathway*—includes Culinary Arts.

- *Education Pathway*—includes Early Childhood Education and Teaching as a Profession.

- *Engineering and Technology Pathway*—includes Electronics, Energy Systems, Engineering, and Manufacturing.

- *Family and Consumer Sciences Pathway*—includes Consumer Science; Family, Community and Global Leadership; Interior Design; and Nutrition and Food Science.

- *Government and Public Safety Pathway*—includes Homeland Security and Emergency Services, JROTC—Air Force, JROTC—Army, JROTC—Marines, JROTC—Navy, and Law and Justice.

- *Healthcare Science Pathway*—includes Biotechnology Research and Development, Diagnostic Services, Health Informatics, Therapeutic Services—Emergency Services, Therapeutic Services—Medical Services, and Therapeutic Services—Nursing.

- *Marketing, Sales and Service Pathway*—includes Fashion Marketing, Marketing Communications and Promotion, Marketing and Management, Sports and Event Marketing, and Travel Marketing and Lodging Management.

Each state has created their own career pathway model based on the 16 career clusters provided by the US DOE.

Career clusters and pathways are tools for investigation and self-discovery, and not intended to force you into a final career path decision. As the Georgia Career Resource Network site states, "When a student selects a career cluster, they are simply choosing a direction upon which to build a plan....Assessment and exploration will provide the knowledge to decide if that occupation 'fits' the individual."

Career Paths Based on Your Aptitudes and Interests

Many states have provided websites that allow students to explore their own career interest, values, and skills through online assessments. One such website used by the state of New York Department of Labor is CareerZone, which can be found at *careerzone.ny.gov*. Another website provided by The American College Testing Program (ACT) has also devised a useful system of organizing jobs into career clusters. If you are trying to choose a major field of study, you might research the cluster in which your major falls or your interests are located. You should also explore the area that seems to relate to your interests, values, and skills. The definitions of each cluster found at the ACT website *http://www.act.org/wwm/overview.html* will help you identify career interest areas.

If you've taken the time to use the tools for self-discovery in this lesson, you're on the road to a lifelong pattern of rewarding learning and working. The career lists on CareerZone and the ACT site are a good starting point for further investigation. They are far from complete. Use them to help you begin to think about career choices. Many people have found such lists helpful. You can take the information and working environments found in Table 3.5 and combine it with the careers listed on CareerZone and the ACT site to create a more complete picture of the career paths and work environments you are most likely to prefer.

Remember: There's no guarantee that any of these careers will be appropriate for you or that your best career match is among those listed in the MIS or the Holland Interest Environments. That's because, more than anything else, you need to understand yourself and the aptitudes and interests that will have an impact on your career. You need to know what is really important to you. This lesson has provided you with some powerful tools that can help you do that. Once you understand your strengths and weaknesses and are aware of what you truly value, you'll be in an excellent position to pick a rewarding career.

Another thing to keep in mind: Once you choose a career, you may face lots of pressure from family, friends, and others to go in a different direction. For example, on the basis of your aptitudes, personality preferences and interests, you may decide on a career as an actor, but your family may want you to be a doctor. Or you may want to be a military officer, and your friends think you should stay in the private sector and become a business executive.

success TIP ★

Once you have identified your interests, you should notice how enthusiastic and alive you feel when you are involved in activities involving your interests. Ideally, your work and studies will relate to your interests. To help you set a lifelong pattern, get involved in something that interests you for at least four hours per week—for example, if you enjoy helping kids, tutor a child or volunteer at a childcare center.

It's not always easy to resolve conflicts such as these. It might help to realize that most people pursue several careers over their lifetimes, and there may be a way to do both. For example, a doctor may be able to act in plays in his or her spare time, and then pursue acting as a full-time career later in life. A military member may retire in 20 years and become an executive for an airplane manufacturer.

The lessons that follow will help you further explore your options in career and educational paths. Later you'll learn about how to apply for college, how to find and apply for a job, and how to develop your career skills.

✔ CHECKPOINTS

Lesson 2 Review

Using complete sentences, answer the following questions on a sheet of paper.

1. Based on your responses to the MIS and LEAD surveys, describe three new strategies you can use to improve your grades and work performance.

2. Review the Holland Interest Environment category that seems to best fit you and describe some specific examples from your studies and work that support your choice.

3. On the basis of what you've learned about your aptitudes and interests, describe the work environment in which you might do best.

4. Name three career clusters that fit your aptitudes and interests, and explain why each might be a good option for you.

5. In today's workplace, lifelong learning is a key to success. How will your self-discovery activities help you succeed over the long term?

APPLYING SELF-DISCOVERY SKILLS

6. Based on your findings in the Multiple Intelligences Survey (MIS) and the LEAD survey on learning styles, talk with a friend about your abilities and interests. Does your friend agree with your findings?

Career Paths

Quick Write

_____

_____

Based on what you've read in previous lessons, which factors do you think are important when deciding whether to choose a technically oriented career or one that requires a college degree? As you write, think about the issues of earning money versus other factors. In your answer, also take into account your personal strengths and preferences.

Learn About

- advantages of a technically oriented career path
- types of job classifications for technically oriented career paths
- earnings potential for technically oriented career paths
- ways to pursue a technical career
- advantages of pursuing post-secondary degrees
- careers associated with educational tracks
- earnings potential of college-educated professionals
- how to pursue an education-oriented career

"The information age is going to produce millions of new jobs for the so-called 'middle-skill' occupations. These jobs require employees to have more than a high school diploma but less than a bachelor's degree."

Arne Duncan, US Secretary of Education, 2011

The Advantages of a Technically Oriented Career Path

Some people follow career paths that require a college or university education. What if you think that college is not right for you, at least at this point in your life?

You have many other options, as you're about to learn. You can choose a technically oriented career path, *a career path focused on mastering technical skills that do not require a college or university education.*

Many good careers, including those in construction, can be found through technical education and training.

Courtesy of Ariel Skelley/Corbis Images

A technically oriented career path has at least three important advantages:

- You can achieve a good standard of living without pursuing a college education.

- You have an opportunity to learn a trade that's fulfilling to you and is a benefit to society.

- You can develop your knowledge of science and technology, which is important in today's interconnected world.

Individuals who follow a technically oriented career path will achieve better success when they think about their choice, define their goals, and then work hard to achieve them. Follow your heart, but then follow a logical plan for your career goals.

Sources of Information on Technically Oriented Career Paths

Several sources are available online to help you learn details about jobs and career paths within technical fields.

One of the best overall sources is the US Department of Labor's *Occupational Outlook Handbook* from the Bureau of Labor Statistics.

The *Occupational Outlook Handbook*

The US Department of Labor's Bureau of Labor Statistics *Occupational Outlook Handbook* is a great resource on jobs. You can find it online at *http://www.bls.gov/oco/*. The government updates it every two years. In the *Handbook*, you can learn about careers in such areas as information technology; management; sales; administration; agriculture; construction; and transportation. The *Handbook* also provides information about careers in the armed forces. It covers training and education you need for a specific job, earning potential, employment prospects, as well as typical job activities, responsibilities, and working conditions. The *Handbook* also contains job-search tips, links to information about the job market in each state, and more.

Vocabulary

- technically oriented career path
- median
- technical training program
- cooperative education (co-op) programs
- junior and community colleges
- vocational school
- apprenticeship
- internship
- volunteer
- reference
- mentor
- higher education
- white-collar job
- blue-collar job
- open-admissions policy
- continuing and adult education
- graduate school
- major

Additional Resources

A second helpful Department of Labor website is the Employment and Training Administration's O*Net at *http://www.onetonline.org/*.

Another valuable, nongovernment resource is the Vocational Information Center at *www.khake.com*.

Types of Job Classifications for Technically Oriented Career Paths

If you decide to pursue a technically oriented career, you have many choices. Table 3.6 lists some technically oriented career paths, or career fields, and it's just the beginning. That's because each of the fields in Table 3.6 has dozens of possible careers within it. As an example, Table 3.7 shows a few of the types of jobs you can pursue in just six of the career paths listed in Table 3.6.

Table 3.6 Examples of Technically Oriented Job Classifications

- Agricultural/Food Science and Inspections
- Architectural Design/Drafting/Planning
- Automotive Service Technology
- Aviation and Aerospace
- Broadcast Media/Engineering
- Business Analysts
- Construction Trades
- Computer Systems/Programmers/Analysts
- Dieticians/Nutritionists
- Electrical/Electronics
- Energy/Power/Utilities
- Engine Technology
- Engineering
- Environment/Green Jobs
- Forensics
- Foresters
- Graphic Arts
- Health Information/Safety Technicians

- Horticulture and Landscape Design
- Heating, Ventilation, and Air Conditioner Repair
- Industrial Production Managers
- Journalism
- Machining
- Manufacturing
- Masonry
- Military Service
- Painting and Repair
- Paralegal/Legal Assistants
- Photography/Film Production/Editing
- Plumbing
- Printing
- Protection and Investigation
- Security and Risk Management
- Telecommunications
- Transportation/Logistics
- Visual Arts Crafts and Design
- Welding and Metal Arts

Source: *http://www.bls.gov/oes/current/oes_stru.htm#29-0000*

Table 3.7 Examples of Jobs Within Six Different Technically Oriented Career Paths

Arts, Design, Media
- Animators, Illustrators, Graphic/Scenic Designers
- Communications Equipment Workers
- Broadcast Technicians/Engineers
- Convention/Event/Exhibit Planning

Health
- Optometrists/Opticians
- Physical Therapists/Therapy Assistants
- Paramedics
- Pharmacy Technicians

Legal
- Court Reporters
- Paralegals and Assistants
- Title Examiners
- Arbiters/Mediators

Community and Social Services
- Health Educators
- Behavioral Counselors
- Marriage/Family Therapists
- Healthcare Social Workers

Production
- Aircraft Assemblers
- Fiberglass Fabricators/Laminators
- Electromagnetic Equipment Operators
- Machinists

Computers
- Systems Analysts
- Database Administrators
- Software Developers
- Statisticians

Source: *http://www.bls.gov/oes/current/oes_stru.htm#15-0000*

Earnings Potential for Technically Oriented Career Paths

If you decide on a technical career, there's a good living and a satisfying work life ahead if you continue to gain new skills and advance. Table 3.8 shows the earning potential for six such careers.

These salaries may not be current by the time you enter the job market. They do provide estimates of what you might expect in relative earnings for these six areas. Some salaries will be higher or lower based on where the job is, how much experience you have, and how hard you're willing to work to move into the higher salary ranges.

You can employ your math skills to compare the hourly wages of jobs within Table 3.8. For example, a typical workweek is 40 hours, and a year has 52 weeks. If you multiply those two numbers, you get 2,080 hours, the standard work year used by the government and many industries. Try dividing any of the salaries in the top half of Table 3.8 by 2,080. That will tell you how much you'll make by the hour. (Median means that *half the salaries are above the amount stated, while half are below.*)

Table 3.8 Earnings Potential for Technically Oriented Career Paths

Position	Median Earnings (2008)
Computer Support Specialist	$46,400
Veterinary Technician	$31,000
Structural Metal Fabricators	$35,900
Sound Engineering Technicians	$54,000
Brick and Block Masons	$51,100
Physical Therapy Assistants	$49,800

Other Salary Ranges for Graduates with Associates' Degrees (rounded to the nearest $100)

Position	Median Earnings (2008)
Maintenance Technician PC	$23,100–49,800
Registered nurse	$40,000–52,000
Radiology Technician	$35,000–56,800
Respiratory Technician	$27,700–55,300
Engineering Technology	$28,700–55,400

Sources: *http://www.bls.gov/oes/current/oes_stru.htm*; *The Career Fitness Program*, Pearson

Ways to Pursue a Technical Career

Several types of training programs are available for these careers. You can take advantage of some while you're still in high school. Below, we discuss technical training, apprenticeships, pre-apprenticeships, job shadowing, and internships.

Technical Training Programs

A technical training program is *a learning experience that will give you the knowledge and skills you need to start a technically oriented career.* Technical training programs cover a wide variety of career fields, such as:

- Agriculture (careers related to food and fiber production, food inspections, and agricultural business specialties)

- Health occupations (nurses, dental assistants, medical technicians, physical therapy assistants)

- Trade and industrial skills (such as automotive technicians, carpenters, construction specialties, electricians, plumbers, and computer technicians)

- Specialized fields within transportation, manufacturing, electronics, communications, aviation, computer graphics, and graphic or engineering design

Of course, many more career fields offer technical training. The Association for Career and Technical Education estimates that there are about 16 million students enrolled in technical education in the United States.

Here are some of the ways to obtain technical training.

Many high schools have technical education programs. They are usually designed for high school juniors and seniors; some programs accept high school sophomores. A few other programs begin in the ninth grade. When high school technical courses are linked to community college programs, students can earn college credit while they're still in high school. Some high schools offer technical education and cooperative education (co-op) programs, *programs in which you can work part-time in a career field in which you are interested while taking job-related courses at school.* You receive school credit for both your work-related classes and your real-world work experience.

Technical training programs will give you the knowledge and skills required for a technically oriented career.
Courtesy of Peter Muller/Corbis Images

Two-year junior and community colleges, *institutions that offer courses and programs leading to associate's degrees and training certificates,* provide a wealth of options. Many of these programs are offered in conjunction with high schools and four-year colleges. Such programs generally last two years, but can be shorter if students earn college credits while still in high school.

Another way to use a community college's course offerings to your advantage is to take a course or two after being hired for a full-time job. Increasing your skills during your off time will be helpful later when you seek higher-paying jobs within your company or industry.

success TIP ★

A person with an associate's degree or two-year credential will earn, on average, over $5,000 a year more than a person with just a high school diploma. A person with a Career Technical Education (CTE)-related associate's degree or credential may earn between $5,000 and $15,000 more a year than a person with a humanities or social sciences associate's degree will earn.

Since the Recession of 2009, more temporary workers will be hired than ever before. The challenge when looking for a good career is to know how to enter the job market, and stay there. Temporary workers usually have few benefits. But by gaining skills that your company or industry needs, you can move forward toward beyond temporary work into a successful career.

Another option is a vocational school, *a school that offers courses to prepare students in specific skills to enter a technical career field*. Most of these schools combine coursework with work-based experiences such as internships, apprenticeships, pre-apprenticeships, and job shadowing.

Many private companies offer technical training. Courses can last from two weeks to several years. For example, a California company trains workers for the construction industry at locations around the state in skills such as carpentry; painting; plumbing; and electrical contracting. These courses teach job skills and safety rules. A training company in Arizona, Texas, California, and Illinois provides courses to young people aiming for careers in the automotive industry. Courses cover such topics as automotive and diesel technology.

Before you enroll in a privately operated school, check the school's references with your state board of education. Also be aware that private organizations usually charge fees for trainees. To find out more about technical training programs, see your high school guidance counselor, or go to the website of the Association for Career and Technical Education at *www.acteonline.org*.

If you have a specific career path in mind, you can also contact a company or an industry association in your area to ask about where to attend a training program.

Apprenticeship Programs

An apprenticeship is *an opportunity to learn a trade on the job while also learning in class*. Apprenticeship programs are available in the United States for more than 1,000 occupations and vary in length from one to six years. Almost a half million people are enrolled each year in some kind of apprenticeship program.

Apprentices work and learn as employees. Construction and manufacturing apprenticeships are among the most common, but apprenticeships are available in many other fields including most of those mentioned above in the section on technical training programs.

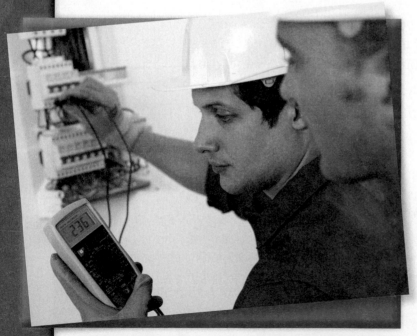

Electrical workers often go through apprenticeships, both formal and on-the-job, to acquire needed skills.

Courtesy of auremar/Shutterstock

While most apprenticeships are in the civilian sector, the military also offers them. Some career fields, such as firefighter or engine mechanic, feature apprenticeships during military training. Many fields in the military have a civilian equivalent. This means that you can carry the skills you've gained in the military into a career elsewhere.

What Apprentices Do

Apprentices start by learning simple, repetitive tasks, and then gradually progress to duties that are more complex. Electrician apprentices, for example, might begin by learning to cut and install wire. Eventually, they learn to plan projects; set up, wire, and test entire construction sites; and diagnose and fix electrical problems.

In addition to learning by doing, apprentices take classes to learn the basics in their field. The first class might teach the names and uses of the equipment a student will see on a job site. Later, students learn skills such as drafting, estimating costs, or reading blueprints.

A beginning apprentice earns one-third to one-half of what an experienced, fully trained worker in that field earns. For example, a trained electrician currently earns about $23.71 per hour while apprentices earn about $13.83 per hour.

Finding an Apprenticeship Program

Finding apprenticeship programs that have openings can be a challenge, especially in occupations that don't employ large numbers of workers. To locate a program, check several sources, including career-counseling offices. Many apprenticeship sponsors publicize openings at career centers and local high schools. Career counselors usually know about the programs in their community. You can also find information on apprenticeships in newspapers and on job boards.

For lists of current programs, contact your state's Bureau of Apprenticeship. You can also go online to the Office of Apprenticeship Services at the US Department of Labor (DOL) website at *http://www.doleta.gov/oa*. The DOL updates its list periodically to reflect the changing workforce; for example, wind turbine technician was added recently as the first apprentice-able "green" occupation.

Trade unions and industry associations have information on apprenticeships, too. These organizations often recruit apprentices once or twice a year. Union training programs cover many areas. They include building trades; communications; electricians; roofers; painters; air traffic controllers; steel workers; chemical workers; and transit workers, among others. You can get information about applying for such an apprenticeship from a local union office, the national union headquarters, or the national industry association headquarters.

Apprenticeship programs give you an opportunity to learn a trade on the job and in the classroom.

Courtesy of Exotica.im 13/Alamy

If you are interested in an apprenticeship in the armed forces, contact your local recruitment office or check out the military branch's website. Each branch of the military has its own rules about apprenticeships.

For general information on apprenticeships, check the *Encyclopedia of Associations* or the DOL's *Occupational Outlook Handbook*. Both are available at libraries and career centers. If you can't find an apprenticeship program that fits you, consider studying at a community college or vocational school. Later, you might be able to transfer credits you've earned in one of these schools to an apprenticeship program.

Applying for an Apprenticeship Program

Once you find a good apprentice program, you have to apply for entrance. Request an application from the organization conducting the apprenticeship and follow the instructions.

Qualifications

Most apprenticeship programs require that applicants be at least 18 years old, and have a high school diploma or a passing score on the high school equivalency exam. Some programs require applicants to complete specific classes related to the occupation.

Interview

If you meet the basic qualifications, you may be invited for an interview. At that time, you will probably meet with the head of the organization sponsoring the apprenticeship as well as a few other people. During the interview, they will ask you about your work and school experience. They may ask why you want to be an apprentice. The interviewers will also probably ask questions that will reveal your personality traits. Interviewers want to hire people who have determination and commitment to the occupation. Curiosity is also important. Interviewers might ask questions such as:

- Why do you think you would be good at this job?
- Have you ever worked as part of a team?
- Do you know what the work is like?
- What do you think you'll be doing in 5 or 10 years?
- How dependable and resourceful are you? For example, how would you get to work if your car broke down?

Work-Experience Options

The following organizations can provide more information on work-experience options for high school students. Some of them have local high school chapters you can join.

- National Mentoring Center at: *www.nwrel.org/mentoring*
- National Service-Learning Clearinghouse at: *www.servicelcarning.org*
- Junior Achievement at: *www.ja.org*
- Future Business Leaders of America (FBLA) at: *www.fbla-pbl.org*
- Future Farmers of America (FFA) at: *www.ffa.org*
- Distributive Education Clubs of America (DECA) at: *www.deca.org*

Tour of the Work Site

Before deciding to join a program, you'll want to see what life will be like on the job. Tour the worksite for clues about the quality of training and the work environment. Is the equipment modern? Is the work site comfortable and safe? Do workers seem willing to demonstrate and teach skills? What would the work schedule be like? How would you get to the work site? If you don't have a car, is public transportation available? A tour is an excellent opportunity to ask employees about their jobs. By asking questions, you can learn a lot about the occupation and the program sponsor. Dress neatly and behave professionally when visiting potential employers. Each conversation you have during a tour of the work site is like an interview.

Pre-Apprenticeship Programs

Many nonprofits, schools, and government agencies help people qualify for apprenticeships. They do this by offering pre-apprenticeship programs. The goal of these programs is to help young people get jobs and stay employed. The programs focus on specific groups, including high school students, disadvantaged youth, veterans, and women.

School-to-apprenticeships allow high school students to begin their apprenticeships as juniors and seniors. These programs allow students to take occupational classes in addition to their regular high school courses. These classes cover math, science, and other topics important for specific careers. Students in school-to-apprenticeship programs work part-time,

In a pre-apprenticeship program, students take occupational classes in addition to their regular high school courses.

Courtesy of Spencer Grant/PhotoEdit

often earning school credit for on-the-job training. After graduation, they become full-time apprentices, with the advantage of having already completed many of the requirements.

A few states have a large number of pre-apprenticeship programs. Washington, California, Oregon, and Ohio had the largest number of programs prior to 2010. Ask your high school guidance counselor or call your school district office to find out about the school-to-apprenticeship programs in your local area.

Job Shadowing

Job shadowing can lead to a good job if you're interested in a field and know someone you respect in that field. This person may allow you to follow him or her around during the workday. Most often, a parent or friend is the first source to make a contact to get such a job shadowing opportunity.

Many job shadowing programs, however, are a little more formal. They also may be connected to technical coursework. These programs make it possible for students to earn tuition-free college credits and industry certifications in many fields while still in high school.

Some job shadowing programs are now connected with online technical skills courses. In these programs, virtual job shadowing is offered to enrich the course's basic curriculum. See *http://www.virtualjobshadow.com*.

Technical and College Internship Programs

Once you've narrowed your decision about the career you want to pursue after high school, think about an internship. An internship is *a low-paying or volunteer job that provides supervised practical training in a field or skill*. For example, if you think you might want to be a plumber, contact a local plumbing company to see if you can be a part-time intern with the company while you're still in school. The company may pay you a small wage. If the company does not offer a paid internship, you may still want to offer to be a volunteer, or *unpaid worker*. A company manager may interpret your offer as a volunteer in a positive light, and may hire you later for a skilled position, if you learn quickly.

A summer internship is a good way to get work experience while attending college. In these internships, students learn details about a job and get practice doing it. They also make valuable contacts that can lead to a permanent position. Many internships offer college credit. Just as with technically oriented internships, these positions may be low paying or a volunteer job that provides supervised practical training in a field or skill. During an internship, you may do work that is useful to the organization such as research. The person who oversees your internship may give you assignments relevant to your college studies. When your internship ends, the organization usually submits a brief report about your experience to your college.

Whether you're a paid worker or volunteer, an internship gives you real-life experience that can help you decide whether a particular career path is right for you.

In addition, an internship can:

- Boost your self-esteem

- Give you references—a reference is *a person future employers can contact to ask about what kind of worker you are*

- Give you the chance to meet a mentor, *a life coach who guides, advises, and advocates for you in your individual life path*

- Help you grow and learn your true interests and talents

Summer internships allow college students to learn the details about a job and get practice doing it.
Courtesy of Keith Morris/Alamy

To see if you qualify for an internship, contact a company, organization, or government agency that you're interested in. Many of these maintain websites where you can learn how to apply for an internship.

Advantages of Pursuing Post-Secondary Degrees

Should you continue your education after high school? If your goal is to become a more informed citizen, to be well-rounded, or to earn a better living, a college education can help you achieve that goal. Maybe you've dreamed of going into a particular career such as teaching or the entertainment industry. You may also be interested in law, marketing, medicine, or being a military officer. Whatever your dream job, a higher education, or *study at a college or university—perhaps starting at a community or junior college*—can open doors to more possibilities and choices than you ever imagined. If that's not enough, you will also have a chance to make friends for a lifetime, and have a great time doing so.

Colleges and universities are exciting places to be. They have social and cultural centers with much to offer students of any age, nationality, or social background.

You'll see that in this lesson the words *college*, *university*, and *higher education* are used interchangeably. Although universities are generally larger than colleges, they both offer higher education courses and cover roughly the same subjects. A degree from a four-year college is the same as a university degree. A degree from a two-year community or junior college, however, is not the same as a four-year college or university degree.

Here are some good reasons for beginning and completing a course of study in higher education:

- The difference between what you can earn with a college degree and what you can earn with just a high school diploma is substantial. If you don't complete high school, your earning potential is even less.

- Whatever you do in life, your career opportunities will be greater if you get a college degree.

A person who has attended college usually works in a white-collar job, or *a job that does not involve manual labor and for which people generally do not have to wear uniforms or protective clothing.* This differs from a blue-collar job, or *a job that often involves manual labor and for which people may need to wear a uniform or protective clothing.*

The term *white collar* originally referred to a person wearing a suit, shirt, and tie, but dress is often less formal today. The term *blue collar* originally referred to a blue work shirt or worker's coverall. Today the term *blue collar* might be used more accurately to describe those whose jobs are done primarily in clothing like jeans and work boots.

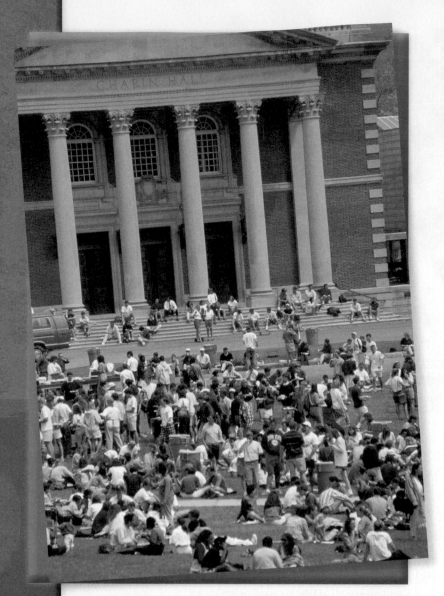

Attending a four-year college can be a life-changing experience where higher levels of learning, teamwork and social skills, and career goals all come together.

Courtesy of Bob Krist/Corbis Images

White-collar workers tend to work in air-conditioned settings. They have conveniences ranging from computers to on-site childcare. They often have consistent work hours. This makes their work environment more appealing and productive. White-collar jobs also tend to offer more benefits, such as pension plans and paid vacations.

Blue-collar jobs are more likely to be outdoors, as with construction jobs. They may be in dangerous locations (for example, in mining). Blue-collar workers are also often in factories, warehouses, or driving vehicles.

Junior and Community Colleges

As stated earlier, junior and community colleges offer courses and programs that lead to associate's degrees and training certificates. Community colleges may fit your needs because:

- They are often less expensive than four-year colleges.

- Their entrance requirements aren't as difficult as many state and private four-year colleges, which have become more selective in recent years. Many have an open-admissions policy, or *a policy that permits enrollment of a student who has a high school diploma or equivalent, or in some cases, regardless of academic qualifications.*

- They are often more willing to accommodate part-time students.

- They often tailor their programs to the needs of local employers.

- They arrange their schedules to fit those of working adults.

Students who aren't able to enroll in a college or university because of their academic record, limited finances, or distance from such an institution, can enroll at a junior or community college and earn credits that they can apply toward a degree at a four-year college.

Junior and community colleges also have important roles in continuing and adult education, that is, *evening or weekend courses for working adults who are not able to enroll in college full-time.* (Many four-year schools also offer weekend, evening, and online classes—sometimes off-campus—for working adults. Some four-year schools cater specifically to people who are working.)

If you earn a certificate or two-year degree, careers such as the following will probably be open to you:

- Auto mechanic
- Hair stylist or barber
- Broadcast technician
- Computer support specialist
- Cosmetologist
- Dental hygienist
- Electrician
- Medical records and health information technician
- Registered nurse
- Physical therapist assistant
- Plumber
- Veterinary technologist or technician
- Welder

Four-Year Colleges and Universities

The degree that will enable you to call yourself a college graduate comes from a four-year college or university. These institutions provide courses in a wide variety of subjects, both theoretical and practical. Colleges and universities offer their students the knowledge to succeed in many fields. They also can help place you in internships, where you will gain work-related experience that will help you get a better job after graduation. A wealth of information on colleges and universities is available at your local library and online. Be sure to talk with your high school guidance counselor, and contact individual colleges. A good place to start is by visiting college websites. To make your search a little easier, get some tips on how to find a college that's right for you from the US Department of Education at *http://nces.ed.gov/collegenavigator* and from the College Board (which administers the SAT exam) at *apps.collegeboard.com/ search/index.jsp*.

Careers Associated with Educational Tracks

A degree from a four-year college or university opens many more career paths than does a high school education.

You will need a degree from a four-year college or university to enter careers such as those listed below. In some cases, you'll need education beyond a four-year college degree to progress to higher levels in a career. This education will come from graduate school, or *formal education after you graduate from college, which will give you in-depth knowledge about your specific career area*. Here are some of the fields in which a bachelor's degree or higher is required:

A scientist usually needs an advanced degree, and even many technicians who assist in a scientific lab need at least a bachelor's degree.

Courtesy of Alexander Raths/Shutterstock

- Accountant
- Business executive
- Doctor or dentist
- Computer systems analyst
- Engineer
- Environmental or natural sciences manager
- Financial manager
- Lawyer
- Military officer
- Rehabilitation counselor
- Scientist
- Social worker
- Teacher

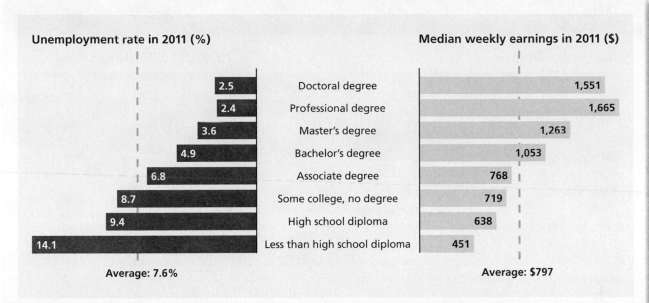

Unemployment rate in 2011 (%)   Median weekly earnings in 2011 ($)

Degree	Unemployment rate	Median weekly earnings
Doctoral degree	2.5	1,551
Professional degree	2.4	1,665
Master's degree	3.6	1,263
Bachelor's degree	4.9	1,053
Associate degree	6.8	768
Some college, no degree	8.7	719
High school diploma	9.4	638
Less than high school diploma	14.1	451

Average: 7.6%   Average: $797

Note: Data are for persons age 25 and over. Earnings are for full-time wage and salary workers.

FIGURE 3.1

Median Income and Unemployment Rates, by Education Level

Source: *Bureau of Labor Statistics, Current Population Survey*

Earnings Potential of College-Educated Professionals

A hundred years ago, a college education was not necessary, even for high-level jobs. Most people could find good, well-paying jobs, regardless of their education, and training. In those days, many people saw a college education as a luxury. Today, however, higher education is often necessary to achieve a better living.

By the year 2020, experts say, there will be 15 million new jobs requiring college preparation. As the skill requirements of jobs continue to rise, more and more young people will need to go to college.

Figure 3.1 shows how the *median* income and unemployment rates differ by the level of education. In 2011, the *median* salary for a worker with a high school diploma was $638 per week. The *median* salary for a person with a bachelor's degree was $1,053 per week, almost twice that of a high school graduate. The *median* unemployment rate for high school graduates in 2011 (9.4 percent) was also nearly double that of a person with a bachelor's degree (4.9 percent).

success TIP

What can you expect to earn when you start out as a college graduate?

According to recent surveys, people in their first year of full-time work after receiving a bachelor's degree average earnings between $32,000–$51,000 a year.

Table 3.9 Representative Starting Salaries for College Graduates

Bachelor's Degree		2007–2010 Starting Salary
ENGINEERING	Electrical	$55,000–$65,000
	Mechanical	$54,000–$62,000
	Civil	$45,170–$55,120
	Chemical	$60,000–$70,000
	Computer Science	$55,000–$65,000
BUSINESS	Business Administration	$33,280–$52,000
	Accounting	$45,000–$53,000
OTHER	History	$28,000–$42,000
	Economics	$44,000–$55,698

Source: Bureau of Labor Statistics

Table 3.10 Fastest-Growing Careers Through 2020

Job	Growth	New Jobs	Salary	Training Needed
Biomedical Engineers	+ 72	11,600	$51,540	Bachelor's Degree
Network Systems and Data Communications Analysts	+ 53	155,800	$51,540	Bachelor's Degree
Financial Examiners	+ 41.2	11,100	$51,530	Bachelor's Degree
Athletic Trainers	+ 37	6,000	$32,390–$51,530	Bachelor's Degree
Computer Software Engineers, Applications	+ 34	175,100	$51,540 and higher	Bachelor's Degree
Environmental Engineers	+ 30.6	16,600	$51,540 and higher	Bachelor's Degree
Computer Software Engineers, System Software	+ 30.4	120,200	$51,540 and higher	Bachelor's Degree
Survey Researchers	+ 30.3	7,100	$32,390–$51,530	Bachelor's Degree
Personal Financial Advisors	+ 30.13	62,800	$51,540 and higher	Bachelor's Degree

Source: Bureau of Labor Statistics

Salaries vary depending on many things, such as location. Salaries tend to be higher near big cities and in many areas along the coasts. The cost of living, however, also tends to be higher there.

Table 3.9 shows some other representative starting salaries for individual career fields.

Table 3.10 shows which careers will be the fastest growing requiring a bachelor's degree through 2020.

Finally, although it may seem a long way off, it's important to think of salary in terms of your lifetime earning potential. A recent study by Georgetown University's Center on Education and the Workforce reveals that over their working lives, high school graduates earn an average of $1.3 million; associate's degree holders earn about $1.73 million; and bachelor's degree holders earn about $2.27 million.

How to Pursue an Education-Oriented Career

If you've already settled on two or three possible career choices, you should also explore whether the colleges that you are considering have strong programs in those areas. That's because when you enroll in college, you will need to select a major, or *subject area on which you want to focus*. The courses you complete in your major will give you the knowledge you need to start your career in your chosen field.

Table 3.11 shows all the majors (more than 170!) at The Ohio State University, one of the largest state universities in the country. The college or university you eventually choose may have many of these majors, or it may specialize in different areas. Georgia Tech, Purdue University, and Virginia Tech are known for engineering programs, for example. However, these schools also offer many other kinds of general degrees in various fields, much like Ohio State.

Table 3.11 Undergraduate Majors at The Ohio State University*

A

- Accounting
- Actuarial Science
- Aeronautical and Astronautical Engineering
- African-American and African Studies
- Agribusiness and Applied Economics
- Agricultural Business
- Agricultural Commerce
- Agricultural Communication
- Agricultural Systems Management
- Agriscience Education
- Agronomy
- Allied Medical Professions
- Ancient History and Classics
- Animal Sciences
- Anthropological Sciences
- Anthropology
- Arabic
- Architecture
- Art
- Art Education
- Arts Management
- Astronomy and Astrophysics
- Athletic Training
- Atmospheric Sciences
- Aviation

B

- Biochemical Sciences
- Biochemistry
- Biology
- Biomedical Engineering
- Biomedical Science
- Biotechnology
- Business Administration General Information
- Business Management
- Business Pathways Brochure

C

- Chemical Engineering
- Chemistry
- Chinese
- City and Regional Planning

- Civil Engineering
- Classics
- Communication
- Community Leadership
- Comparative Studies
- Computer and Information Science
- Computer Science and Engineering
- Construction Management
- Construction Systems Management
- Consumer and Family Financial Services
- Criminology and Criminal Justice Studies
- Crop Management and Soil Conservation
- Culinary Science

D

- Dairy Cattle Production and Management
- Dairy Science
- Dance
- Dental Hygiene

E

- Early and Middle Childhood Studies
- Earth Sciences
- Economics
- Education—Early Childhood Education
- Education—Foreign Language Education
- Education—Integrated Language Arts/English Education
- Education—Middle Childhood Education
- Education—Science and Mathematics Education
- Education—Special Education
- Education—Teaching English to Speakers of Other Languages
- Education—Teaching English to Speakers of Other Languages
- Electrical and Computer Engineering
- Engineering, General Information
- Engineering Physics
- English
- Entomology
- Environment and Natural Resources
- Environment Resources Management
- Environment, Economy, Development, and Sustainability

*As of fall 2012. Taken from *http://majors.osu.edu/*

Table 3.11 Undergraduate Majors at The Ohio State University, *continued*

- Environmental Engineering
- Environmental Policy and Decision Making
- Environmental Science
- Evolution and Ecology
- Exercise Science Education
- Exploration

F

- Family and Consumer Sciences Education
- Family Financial Services
- Fashion and Retail Studies
- Film Studies
- Finance
- Floral Design and Marketing
- Food, Agricultural, and Biological Engineering
- Food Business Management
- Food Science and Technology
- Forestry, Fisheries, and Wildlife
- French

G

- Geographic Information Science
- Geography
- German
- Globalization Studies
- Greenhouse and Nursery Management

H

- Health and Rehabilitation Sciences General Information
- Health Information Management and Systems
- Health Professions Exploration
- Health Promotion, Nutrition, and Exercise Science
- Health Sciences Management
- Health Sciences Program
- Health-Care Professions Pathways Brochure
- Hebrew
- History
- History of Art
- Horse Production and Management

- Horse Science
- Horticultural Science
- Hospitality Management
- Human Development and Family Science
- Human Nutrition
- Human Resources
- Hydraulic Power and Motion Control
- Hydraulic Service and Repair

I

- Industrial and Systems Engineering
- Industrial Design
- Information Systems
- Insurance
- Interior Design
- International Business Administration
- International Studies
- Introduction to Pre-Professional Programs
- Islamic Studies
- Italian

J

- Japanese
- Jewish Studies
- Journalism

K

- Korean

L

- Landscape Architecture
- Landscape Horticulture
- Linguistics
- Livestock Production and Management
- Livestock Science
- Logistics Management

M

- Management and Industry Exploration
- Marketing
- Materials Science and Engineering
- Mathematics
- Meat Science
- Mechanical Engineering
- Medical Dietetics

continued on next page

Table 3.11 Undergraduate Majors at The Ohio State University, continued

- Medical Laboratory Science
- Medieval and Renaissance Studies
- Microbiology
- Middle Childhood Education (pre-licensure)
- Modern Greek
- Molecular Genetics
- Music—Composition
- Music—Education
- Music—Jazz Studies
- Music—Musicology
- Music Performance—Orchestral Instruments
- Music Performance—Piano
- Music—Theory
- Music—Voice

N

- Natural Resource Management
- Neuroscience
- Nursing
- Nursing (RN to BSN)

O

- Operations Management

P

- Pharmaceutical Sciences
- Philosophy
- Physical Education, Sport, and Physical Activity
- Physics
- Plant Health Management
- Plant Pathology
- Political Science
- Portuguese
- Power Equipment
- Pre-Dentistry
- Pre-Law
- Pre-Medicine
- Pre-Occupational Therapy
- Pre-Optometry
- Pre-Pharmacy
- Pre-Physical Therapy
- Pre-Veterinary Medicine
- Professional Golf Management

- Psychology
- Public Affairs
- Public Health

R

- Radiologic Sciences and Therapy
- Real Estate and Urban Analysis
- Religious Studies
- Renewable Energy
- Respiratory Therapy
- Romance Studies
- Russian

S

- Science and Technology Exploration
- Sexuality Studies
- Social Science Air Transportation
- Social Work
- Sociology
- Spanish
- Speech and Hearing Science
- Sport Industry
- Sports/Commercial Turf Equipment
- STEM Pathways Brochure
- Sustainable Agriculture
- Sustainable Plant Systems
- Swine Production and Management

T

- Theatre
- Turfgrass Management

U

- University Exploration General Information

V

- Visual Communication Design

W

- Welding Engineering
- Women's, Gender, and Sexuality Studies
- World Literatures

Z

- Zoology

✔ CHECKPOINTS

Lesson 3 Review

Using complete sentences, answer the following questions on a sheet of paper.

1. What are three main advantages of a technically oriented career path?

2. What are three fields in which you can have a technically oriented career?

3. What are the three types of programs that can prepare you for a technically oriented career?

4. Pick a technically oriented career path that you are interested in. Then find out what you could earn at the beginning of your career and what you might earn when you reach the top of your profession. You may need to do some research on the Internet to find the answers.

5. Why does it make sense to pursue a higher education if you want a satisfying career?

6. What is the difference between a college and a university? Between a university and a community college?

7. What are five types of jobs that will be open to you with the proper certificate from a junior or community college?

8. What are five types of jobs that typically require a four-year degree?

APPLYING CAREER SKILLS

9. Contact a four-year college or university by mail or through its website. Find out what undergraduate majors it offers. Pick three majors that you can see yourself studying. Then make a list of careers you could enter with that educational background.

CHAPTER 4

Courtesy of Peter Dazeley/Getty Images

Aiming Towards a College Degree

Chapter Outline

"Education is the best provision for old age."

Aristotle, ancient Greek philosopher, whose writings covered many
subjects, including physics, poetry, theater, music, and logic

Financing for College

Quick Write

How much do you think it costs to go to a college or university? Make a short list of ways you can get the money you need to attend a school of your choice. Try to cover all possible expenses, and reflecting on what you've learned about financial planning, separate your *needs* from your *wants*.

Learn About

- costs of college
- sources of college funds
- planning to finance a college education

"Next in importance to freedom and justice is popular education, without which neither freedom nor justice can be permanently maintained."

James A. Garfield, 20th President of the United States

Costs of College

A college degree can lead to a great future. As you know, it can open the door to hundreds of careers—as a doctor, a lawyer, an engineer, or a military officer, for example. But you've probably heard that college can cost a lot. In some cases, that's true. At some colleges, tuition, or *the fee for instruction*, can cost over $50,000 a year. Most colleges, however, cost far less. In fact, only a small fraction of US students attend colleges where the annual tuition is $33,000 or higher. According to the College Board, a nonprofit organization, 50 percent of full-time students pay less than $10,000 for tuition per year.

Tuition is not the only cost of college. If you're no longer living at home, you will also have to pay room, *the cost of a place to live*, and board, *the cost of food*. You'll have other expenses as well. In college, unlike high school, you'll have to pay for books. You will pay laboratory, library, and medical fees. And then there's the cost of transportation. Some students have cars on campus. That means fuel, repair, parking fees, and insurance costs. If you don't have a car and your college is a good distance from your home, you'll have long-distance travel expenses whenever you go home for vacation.

But if you want to go to college, don't be discouraged by all those costs. In 2011–2012, $178 billion in financial aid was awarded to help students pay for college. This financial aid is available from a variety of sources. In this lesson, you'll learn about the costs of college and how to get financial aid to cover those costs.

Two-Year Colleges

The least expensive option for higher education is usually a two-year college. This can be a community, junior, or technical college. Technical colleges are often more expensive than community colleges. If you attend a two-year college, you can earn an associate's degree after two years of study. A two-year degree does not prepare you for as many careers as a four-year degree does. However, if you are not sure whether a four-year college is right for you, this option is worth considering.

Attending a two-year college, then transferring to a four-year school can help keep your costs down. In addition, attending a two-year college to take general education requirements such as math and science can give you some additional time to decide on a major prior to transferring to a four-year college. It can also provide additional sources to help you decide on a direction for a career path, and a four-year college you would like to attend to help meet your career path goals.

Attending a two-year college, then transferring to a four-year school, can help you keep your costs down.

Courtesy of David Butow/Corbis Images

Additionally, two-year colleges often have convenient options for students with jobs and other obligations, including online degree programs. According to The American Association of Community Colleges, forty-four percent of all college students attend two-year colleges.

A year of tuition at a public community college in the United States in 2011–2012 cost an average of $2,963. This was the average fee for an in-state resident, or *a legal resident of the state in which the college is located*. Out-of-state students, or *students who are not legal residents of the state in which the college is located*, paid on average an additional $5,175 for tuition at community colleges. For example, if you live in Illinois and go to a community college in Illinois, you will pay the in-state rate. But if you live in Indiana and go to a school in Illinois, you will pay a much higher out-of-state rate, unless the states have special agreements. Since most students at community colleges live at home, they save a lot on room and board as well as tuition (see the tuition averages for four-year schools below). If you make that choice, you may be able to use the money you save to complete the last two years of your education at a four-year college.

Four-Year Colleges and Universities

Four-year colleges and universities are more expensive than two-year schools. For the 2011–2012 school year, average tuition at a public university, or *an institution of higher learning that is operated and funded by the state in which it is located*, was $8,244 for in-state residents. Out-of-state residents paid an average of $20,770—that's $12,526 more. Average annual tuition at a private university, or *an institution of higher learning that is operated by a private organization*, was $21,235.

Private universities have to charge higher tuition costs than public schools because they receive no money from the state. Because these schools do not receive state funds, they charge all students the same rate, regardless of where they are from. Therefore, the amount you'll have to pay depends on which college you attend.

It's a good idea to start thinking about your preferences now. Will it be a two-year or a four-year school? Public or private? In-state or out-of-state? Start to put together a list of possibilities, and then get cost information from the website of each college you're thinking about. And don't forget that while tuition is usually the biggest cost, it's not the only one.

Sources of College Funds

You or your family may already have saved enough money to pay for your college. If so, you have a lot for which to be grateful. Most young people, however, have to find the money to finance their college educations. Fortunately, once they start looking, they find many sources of financial aid—so many, in fact, that it takes time and patience to sort through them. According to the College Board, the average undergraduate received $12,000 in financial aid in 2011. There is plenty of financial assistance available out there! However, finding and applying for the right form of the help will take a lot of work on your part. If you are planning to go to college, start your financial preparation early—at least by the spring of your junior year. This section describes the major sources of financial assistance for college students. They include scholarships, grants, and loans.

Scholarships and Grants

Scholarships and grants are *types of student financial aid that you do not have to repay. Scholarship* recipients are usually selected based on academic, athletic, or artistic merit. *Grant* recipients are usually selected based on their financial need. College students receive millions of dollars in scholarships and grants each year.

Most scholarships go to students with special qualifications, such as academic, athletic, or artistic talent. Scholarships are also available for students who want to pursue a particular field of study, such as architecture, chemistry, or literature. Members of particular groups, such as religious, ethnic, military, or community groups, may also be eligible for certain scholarships. For example, your church denomination may offer a scholarship to a private college affiliated with your denomination. Or the local Elks Lodge or Rotary Club very likely offers scholarships for students from the local community. Scholarships are available for students who live in certain areas of the country or who demonstrate financial need. Good grades are important, but you don't have to have a 4.0 grade point average (GPA) to get a scholarship. Scholarships are out there, but finding the one that is right for you will take some work.

Good grades are important, but you don't need a 4.0 grade point average to get a college scholarship.
Courtesy of: (left) Jannis Werner/Alamy; (right) Andresr/Shutterstock

Scholarship Information Resources

Scholarship information is free, and there's lots of it out there on the Web. Two good places to start are:

- *www.deca.collegeoptionsfoundation.net/*—This website, provided by the College Options Foundation, allows parents and students to order DVD packages that assist in the search for college financing. (These materials are presently available for JROTC programs through WINGS.)

- *http://hsfpp.nefe.org*—The National Endowment for Financial Education (NEFE) provides free materials to assist with career preparation. This foundation supports JROTC programs with educational materials.

- *www.fastweb.com*—This website, affiliated with Monster.com, matches students to scholarships at no charge

- *https://bigfuture.collegeboard.org/scholarship-search* —This College Board website also helps you search for financial aid

To find more sources of scholarship information online, just type "scholarships" into your favorite search engine and go from there.

Finding Information on Scholarships

To find out which scholarships you might qualify for, talk to your high school guidance counselor, campus career center, or go to your school library or a public library. You can also search the Internet for scholarships. In doing your own search, however, beware of information overload. Ask someone with a little experience (a parent, librarian, teacher, or even a friend who has applied for scholarships before) to help you get started on your search. Even though the Internet puts a tremendous amount of information at your fingertips, you still have to sort through it to determine which information applies to you.

If you have already decided which colleges you will apply to, contact each school's financial aid office for lists of their scholarship programs. Many schools also have their own financial aid programs.

Many small local scholarships sometimes aren't listed in books or databases. To learn about these opportunities, look for notices on bulletin boards at your school's guidance office, in a public library, or outside the financial aid office at nearby colleges and universities.

Applying for a Scholarship

Once you've identified scholarships for which you think you are eligible, request the application forms. Look carefully at the application requirements. Do you meet all of them? If not, is there a way you can? For example, if an application calls for a 3.7 GPA and you have a 3.6, can you raise your GPA before the deadline? Many scholarships are very competitive—with one award for every 500 applicants.

On the other hand, your chances of getting some kind of scholarship as a full-time undergraduate are about 1 in 8, according to FinAid, a free financial aid planning resource. Whatever kind of scholarship you might pursue, you should do everything you can throughout high school to make your academic record look good to the people who will evaluate your application. Answer all the questions completely. Don't give up if you are rejected. Apply for multiple scholarships. One thing is for sure: If you never apply for a scholarship, you'll never get one.

In your quest for a scholarship, **be careful**! Every year, scholarship scams defraud several hundred thousand students and parents. The victims of these scams lose more than $100 million annually. Scam operations often imitate legitimate government agencies, grant-giving foundations, education lenders, and scholarship matching services. They use official-sounding names containing words such as National, Federal, Foundation, or Administration. In general, be wary of scholarships with an application fee, scholarship services that guarantee success, scholarship-search services that charge a fee, advance-fee loan offers, and sales pitches disguised as "financial aid seminars."

To apply for a Pell grant or any other federal government student loan, you must complete the Free Application for Federal Student Aid (FAFSA).

Courtesy of Bob Daemmrich/PhotoEdit

US Government Grants

Pell Grants

If you need money to finance your education, a federal *Pell grant* might be one of your best options. Pell grants are need based, which means *funds are given to students who have a documented need*. To apply for a Pell grant, you must complete the **Free Application for Federal Student Aid (FAFSA)** form. It is available online at *www.fafsa .ed.gov*. Fill out the FAFSA form as soon as you can after January 1 of the year you will start college. To complete the form, you'll need your most recent tax forms along with those of your parents or guardian, as well as your Social Security number. Once you submit your application, the US Department of Education will determine whether you are eligible. In reviewing your application, it will look at the amount that your family can afford to contribute to your education. It will take into account your family's income during the past year, current assets, and expenses. The maximum Pell grant for the 2012 school year was $5,700. This maximum can change from year to year.

Federal Supplemental Educational Opportunity Grants

Another US government grant is the Federal Supplemental Educational Opportunity Grant (FSEOG). The FSEOG is for students with exceptional financial need. It gives priority to students who receive Pell grants. You can receive between $100 and $4,000 a year for a FSEOG, depending on when you apply, your need, and the policies of your school's financial aid office. But you have no guarantee of a FSEOG, even if you qualify. Each school receives enough money from the government to pay for all its Pell grantees, but the government does not guarantee money for every FSEOG applicant.

US Government Loans

Scholarships and grants often don't cover all college expenses, and many students do not receive them at all. Federal government loans offer another means of financing your education. These loans have low interest rates and do not require credit checks or collateral. They have a variety of repayment terms. Such loans are very popular—in fact, two-thirds of undergraduate students graduate with some debt. The average federal student loan debt among those who graduated in a recent year was $20,500, according to the 2007–2008 National Postsecondary Student Aid Study. Keep in mind that these loans are only for tuition and other education-related expenses, and you cannot borrow any more than you need to cover those expenses. That means, for example, that even if you qualify for $10,000 more than your tuition and fees, you cannot borrow an extra $10,000 in order to buy a car.

To learn more details about the following guidelines and the most current limits and rates, visit the Department of Education's Student Aid website (*studentaid.ed.gov*). The following describes federal loans available for students and students' families.

Stafford Loans

The most common federal loan for students is the Stafford loan. A Stafford loan may either be subsidized, meaning *the government pays the interest while you're in school*, or unsubsidized, meaning *you pay all the interest*. Unsubsidized Stafford loans are available to all students. To receive a subsidized Stafford loan, you must demonstrate financial need.

Many students combine subsidized loans with unsubsidized loans to borrow the maximum amount permitted each year. These limits vary based on whether or not you are financially and legally a dependent of your parents (or someone else). Through a Stafford loan, you can borrow up to $5,500 your first year and a little more each year after that, up to a maximum *subsidized* loan of $23,000 for four years, with an interest rate (before July 1, 2012) of 3.4 percent. The maximum *unsubsidized* (or combined) loan amount is $31,000 for those students receiving financial support from another person such as a family member, or $57,000 with a current interest rate of 6.8 percent for independent students who receive no financial support. Many of these limits and rates change from year to year.

You can defer payments on an unsubsidized Stafford loan until after graduation by capitalizing the interest. Capitalizing means *adding the interest payments to the loan balance*. Capitalizing will relieve you from repaying your debt while you are still in college, but it will increase the overall amount of your debt. Keep in mind as well that although you can receive a much higher loan if it is unsubsidized, the interest rate is double that of the subsidized loans.

Perkins Loans

Perkins loans are awarded to students with exceptional financial need. Although funded through the federal government, they are offered through a college or university's financial aid office. Perkins loans are subsidized—the federal government pays the interest while you are in school. In 2012, the interest rate was 5 percent. The student financial aid office at your college or university will determine the amount of a Perkins loan you receive. The maximum is $5,500 per year for undergraduate students, for a maximum total loan of $27,500.

Parent Loans for Undergraduate Students (PLUS)

Your parents or a stepparent can also take out loans to help with your education. They can do this through the Parent Loan for Undergraduate Students (PLUS) program. Like Stafford loans, PLUS loans come from the Department of Education. PLUS loans have variable interest rates, with a current maximum of 7.9 percent. Repaying them is the parent's financial responsibility, not the student's.

Applying for US Government Loans

To apply for a Stafford, Perkins, PLUS, or any other federal government loan, you must submit the FAFSA, the same form that you fill out for the Pell grant. The form is online at *www.fafsa.ed.gov*. You only have to fill out the FAFSA once, even if you are applying for several loans and grants.

Private Loans

Government loans are the best deal for students because of their lower interest rates and because of the opportunity to have all or a portion of the loan subsidized. If you've taken maximum advantage of these loans and still need money, however, you may consider a private lender such as a bank, credit union, or other private company.

Private lenders sometimes charge fees (in addition to interest) when they make loans. These fees can substantially increase the cost of the loan. If you can get a loan with a low interest rate but high fees, you might end up paying more for the loan than if you had a higher interest rate with no fees. A good rule of thumb is that fees equal to 3 percent of the total you are borrowing will cost you about the same as a loan with a 1 percent higher interest rate.

success TIP ⭐

For more information about student loans, contact:

- Sallie Mae, the nation's No. 1 paying-for-college company, at *www.salliemae.com*
- The US Department of Education at *http://.studentaid.ed.gov*

You can learn about the military's loan-repayment benefits at

- *www.todaysmilitary.com/military -benefits/education-support*

Just how much are those lending fees? To illustrate, if a student wants to borrow $9,000 with a fee of 1 percent, he or she will pay a fee of $90; if the fee is 8 percent, the fee will be...got your math gears turning?...$720. Remember, these add to your loan repayment amount *in addition to the interest*, so think carefully through the pros and cons of each loan you are considering. The difference in fees depends on the student's credit rating or that of his or her parents, guardian, or cosigner. In an effort to do business with students, lenders sometimes advertise a low interest rate during the in-school and grace period. After you graduate, however, they raise the rate. Be sure to read the loan agreement very carefully.

Other Sources of Financial Aid

In addition to the scholarships, grants, and loans described above, there are several other sources of financial aid:

- *Federal aid*—The US government offers a number of student aid programs in addition to those described above. To find out about any federally supported student grant or loan program, contact the Federal Student Aid Information Center. The center's phone number is 1-800-4-FED-AID (1-800-433-3243). Its website is *www.studentaid.ed.gov*.

- *State aid*—Your state may offer scholarship or grant money for education. When you complete the FAFSA, the federal government will automatically forward your information to the appropriate agency in your state.

- *Federal Work-Study Program*—This program provides part-time jobs for college students with financial need, which allows them to earn money to help pay their education expenses. You'll earn at least the current federal minimum wage or more, depending on the type of work you do and the skills required. You can apply for a work-study program through the FAFSA.

Many colleges offer their own scholarships, tuition-payment plans, and other forms of aid.
Courtesy of Blake Little/Getty Images

- *Military programs*—Military service members are also eligible for several tuition-support programs. ROTC scholarships can be a great advantage for someone who wants to enter the armed forces after college, offering full or partial tuition and a commission as a United States military officer. In addition, service academies such as the US Naval Academy, US Military Academy (West Point), US Coast Guard Academy, and US Air Force Academy offer a high quality, fully funded education and a commission as an officer. Military members, both current and veterans, can also receive tuition support in exchange for a term of service. For further information on veterans' education benefits, visit *http://www.gibill.va.gov/resources/student_handouts/*.

- *College-controlled aid*—Many colleges offer their own scholarships, tuition-payment plans, and other forms of aid. Contact the financial aid office of the colleges you intend to apply to for information.

- *Scholarship lotteries*—A number of websites give money away to students for their college education. Your chances of winning are small, however, because so many people participate. You can access these sites free of charge, but if you do, they will probably sell your e-mail address, and you may receive unsolicited messages.

Planning to Finance a College Education

Now that you have the basic information on college costs and sources of funds, how should you start planning? As mentioned above, the best place to start out is your high school guidance counselor or career center. Your public library will also have information. Surfing the Web will yield lots of good information as well.

Once you've completed this background research, decide what kind of college you want to attend. If it's a community college and you intend to live at home, your costs will be relatively low. If it's a public college in another state or a private college, your costs will be much higher. If you're not sure which college is best for you, choose your highest-cost option, and start planning for that. Then if it turns out you need less money than you thought, you'll be in great shape.

Next, talk to people in the financial aid offices of the schools you intend to apply to. Ask them what kinds of aid they offer. Once you are accepted at a college, they should work closely with you to make sure you have the funds you need. In most cases, the college wouldn't accept you for admission if it weren't willing to help you find the money to pay for your education. At the same time, start collecting information on specific scholarships, grants, loans, and other sources of money. Note the requirements and application dates of each source. Talk to your high school counselor or career center about aid sources available in your community.

Then start applying. Complete the FAFSA shortly after January 1 of your senior year. This form opens the door to many sources of financial aid. The government will forward your information to the schools you are applying to as well as to several sources of funding. When completing the form, be honest. You may use student loans for educational purposes only. Giving false information is a criminal offense. Be sure to keep copies of all the application forms that you submit.

Finally, borrow only what you need. Remember, you or your family must repay any loans you take out. And when you begin repaying, keep your payments up to date—failing to do so will affect your credit rating.

As part of your planning, you should talk to people in the financial aid offices of the schools you intend to apply to.

Courtesy of Davis Barber/PhotoEdit

CHECKPOINTS

Lesson 1 Review

Using complete sentences, answer the following questions on a sheet of paper.

1. What do the basic costs of college include?

2. What is the difference between a public university and a private university?

3. What is the main advantage of a scholarship over a loan?

4. What is the difference between a subsidized and an unsubsidized loan?

5. What are three financial aid programs you can apply for through the FAFSA?

6. What are three sources of aid other than scholarships, grants, and loans?

APPLYING FINANCIAL-AID SKILLS

7. Say you need a $10,000-a-year loan to cover costs at the college you've decided to attend. Do research to identify scholarships that you might qualify for that would enable you to obtain the funds you need.

LESSON 2

Selecting a College

Quick Write

_____

_____

Write down the names of five colleges or universities you think you would like to attend. Why do you think these schools would be good choices for you? What factors influenced your choices?

Learn About

- the process of choosing a college
- criteria for selecting a college
- alternative programs to earn college credit
- college admission standards
- identifying colleges that will best meet your needs

"The whole purpose of education is to turn mirrors into windows."

Sydney J. Harris, journalist/author

The Process of Choosing a College

Selecting a college takes a lot of thought and hard work. You may think you already know where you would like to go to school. If so, you may want to stop and reconsider. Don't make the decision too quickly. Students often look for a single, perfect school, when, in fact, they could get a great education at any of a number of schools. Just because your dad, an older friend, or a famous athlete went to a certain school doesn't necessarily mean that it's the best place for you. And even if the local community college sounds appealing because it's close to home, you should think about more than convenience. Your goal should be to find the kind of institution where you will get the best education possible.

Your choices are many: In 2012, there were almost 7,000 colleges and universities in the United States. It's likely that more than a few of these schools will meet your educational needs and help complete your career path. So begin the search for a college by casting a wide net. You might end up deciding that your friend's school—or the school in your community—is your best choice. You should be confident that you made your decision the right way.

This is the second of four lessons about planning and applying for college. In this lesson, you'll learn about the *criteria*, or standards, you should think about when choosing a college. You'll learn how to apply these criteria to come up with a list of a half-dozen or so colleges that will best meet your needs. You'll learn a strategy for applying to the colleges you've selected. Lesson 3 will cover college entrance exams and college placement tests. In Lesson 4, you'll learn how to write your application essay, which is often an important entrance requirement. You will also learn how to prepare for an admissions interview and what to look for during a campus visit. It is important to get started right away on the college admissions process. As early as September of your junior year you should be taking the first steps.

Vocabulary

- accredited
- faculty
- curriculum
- alumni
- dual enrollment/ concurrent enrollment
- asynchronous-mode course
- early-admissions policy
- rolling-admissions policy
- waiting list

Regardless of where other people went to college, you must find the place that is best for you.

Courtesy of Ocean/Corbis Images

College Preparation Calendar for High School Students

Here is a simple checklist, season by season, of things you can do in your junior and senior years to prepare for college. For a more detailed list, visit the National Association for College Admission Counseling website at *http://www.nacacnet.org/studentinfo/Pages/Default.aspx.*

Junior Year

FALL

- Register for and take the October Preliminary Scholastic Aptitude Test (PSAT). Junior-year PSAT scores may qualify you for the National Merit Scholarship competition and the National Achievement and the National Hispanic Scholars programs. Many students also consider the PSAT a good practice run. The more times you take standardized tests, the more familiar you will become with the format and the types of questions asked, and the better you'll probably do.

- If you will require financial aid, start looking into options for grants, scholarships, and work-study programs.

WINTER

- Begin to make a list of colleges you would like to investigate. Surf the Internet and use the resources in your school guidance office or public library. The Department of Education's College Navigator offers a great starting point to have a direct link to all colleges and universities in the United States. If you are thinking about a large university, a small liberal arts college, a specialized college, a community college, a technical, or a trade school, you can find information on all of them. Visit the College Navigator at: *http://nces.ed.gov/ collegenavigator/.*

- Meet with your guidance counselor to discuss your preliminary list of colleges.

- Register for and take the SAT, the ACT, or any other tests required by the schools you're thinking of applying to.

SPRNG

- Write, telephone, email, or use the Internet to request admission and financial aid information from the colleges on your list.

- Continue to refine your list. Eliminate schools that no longer interest you and add others as appropriate.

- Look into summer jobs or apply for summer academic or enrichment programs. Students who participate in such activities impress colleges.

- By the end of your junior year, you should have taken any required tests, probably including the SAT or the ACT. If you haven't already looked into these, ask your guidance counselor right away about application deadlines, procedures, and dates of administration.

- Your test scores are an important part of your application at most schools, and you will want to make sure they arrive in the college admissions offices on time.

SUMMER

- Visit college campuses, take tours, have interviews, and ask questions. Make visiting colleges a family event.

- Begin preparing for the application process. Draft essays, collect writing samples, and assemble portfolios or audition tapes if appropriate. If you are an athlete and plan to play in college, contact the coaches at the schools you are applying to. Ask them about sports programs and athletic scholarships.

success TIP ★

The summer between your junior and senior years—

Practice writing online applications, filling out rough drafts of each application, without submitting them. Write some essay drafts, and then review your applications, especially the essay components. Get help from teachers to review your essays for grammar, punctuation, readability, and content.

For schools with early admission policies, submit your applications early, between October and December of your senior year. The college's decision may come early, too, possibly before January 1. If you aren't accepted, you have had the experience of much practice and you will be ready for the next round of applications you submit.

Senior Year

FALL

- Beginning in the fall and throughout most of your senior year, make sure that you get all the application forms required for admission and financial aid for the schools to which you will apply. Mark all deadlines in your calendar. Register for and take the SAT, the ACT, and any other required tests if you have not done so already. Have the testing agency send the scores to the colleges you apply to.

- Ask people to write your recommendations. Give them at least three weeks' notice to do this, and provide them copies of all the necessary guidelines and forms. Include a stamped envelope addressed to the college admissions office you are applying to. Make sure to write a thank-you note to these people afterward.

- Visit any colleges that you did not see over the summer. Schedule interviews with admissions staff.

- Make sure that your guidance counselor has forwarded your transcripts to the schools to which you'll apply.

- If you plan to apply for early admissions, send in your application now.

WINTER

- File any remaining applications. Make sure these applications, as well as any you have filed earlier, are updated to include your first-semester grades.

- If you will need financial aid, complete the Free Application for Federal Student Aid (FAFSA) form early in the year (see Chapter 4, Lesson 1, "Financing for College"). Have your parents or guardian complete their income tax forms as soon as possible; you will need this information for the FAFSA.

- Check over your Student Aid Report, which you should receive from FAFSA within four weeks of applying. Make sure the report is correct. If you don't get your report, call the Federal Student Aid Information Center toll free (800- 433-3243). For the hearing-impaired (TTY users), call (800-730-8913). The alternate toll number is (319-337-5665). (Review companion website for current contact information)

- Complete scholarship applications.

- If you have applied for early admission, you should receive the results by early winter.If you are accepted and you want to enroll in that college, your search is over! Contact the school and move forward with final plans for enrollment. If you are not accepted, continue to pursue other choices.

SPRNG

- As you hear from the colleges to which you have applied, begin to rank them. Compare the financial aid packages they offer. If you're sure that you do not want to go to one or more of the colleges that have accepted you, write to tell them this. This will let them know to give your spot to someone else.

- By 1 May, decide on the college you will attend. Send in your tuition deposit. Notify the other colleges that you are enrolling elsewhere.

- If a college puts you on a waiting list, write to the admissions office and emphasize your continued interest.

- Take advanced placement (AP) exams if relevant, and have the results forwarded to your college.

- Notify the college of any scholarships that you have received.

- Find out when final payments for tuition, room, and board are due. If necessary, talk to the financial aid office to see if you can make installment payments.

success TIP ★

The summer after your senior year—

Participate in summer orientation programs for incoming freshmen. These are critical to a successful first year, and will give you an opportunity to meet future classmates and professors in a relaxed environment.

Respond promptly to any correspondence you get from the college. These letters will ask you, for example, about course selection, housing preferences, and roommates. Prepare for a big change in your life. Set out for campus with confidence and a determination to succeed academically and personally.

Criteria for Selecting a College

The first step in choosing a college is to decide on your selection criteria. Here are some criteria that every prospective college student should consider.

1. Accreditation

According to the Education Writers' Association, there are three basic kinds of accredited colleges and universities:

- Public colleges and universities, both four-year and two-year

- Private, non-profit four-year and two-year institutions

- Proprietary, for-profit schools, including on-line institutions, which have grown sharply in number during the last decade.

A college that is accredited is *a college that is approved as meeting certain standards.* These standards cover such matters as the qualifications of the faculty, *the teachers or professors*; the content and range of the courses; grading; and the adequacy of a school's libraries and laboratories. An accredited college also has sufficient funds to meet its needs. The US Department of Education oversees the accreditation of colleges by delegating accrediting authority to national or regional organizations.

A degree from a non-accredited college is much less valuable than a degree from an accredited school. Many employers will not hire graduates of non-accredited schools because they believe that such students do not have a valid education. Moreover, if you transfer from a non-accredited school to an accredited one, you will have to start over. An accredited college will not accept the credits you have earned from courses taken in a non-accredited school, even if you have earned good grades.

2. Length of Degree Program

If your goal is a bachelor's degree from a four-year institution, it's usually best to enroll in a four-year college right from the start. You could, of course, earn a two-year associate's degree from a community college and then transfer to a four-year institution. In some cases, this approach makes sense. For example, if you are not sure that you can handle college or being on your own, attending a local community college might be a good first step. But if possible, you should enroll directly in the school from which you plan to get your four-year degree.

The size of a campus often determines such things as the size of the library collection.
Courtesy of Andresr/Shutterstock

3. Reputation

Ask your parents or guardian, a school guidance counselor, and other adults about schools that interest you. Although reputation doesn't always equal excellence, you will probably want to consider it. Attending a prestigious institution does not guarantee success, but it will likely make it easier to get a job interview after college.

4. Breadth and Depth of the Curriculum

The main purpose of going to college is to learn. You want to attend a school that has a curriculum, or *course of study*, that is broad enough to challenge you and to make you feel sure you have received a solid education, whatever your area of study. Of course, you can't study everything. At some point, you will have to decide on a major, or area of academic focus. If you want to concentrate on history, for example, you should attend a school that has a respected program in historical studies. That means it has a variety of general courses in the history of the United States, Europe, Africa, Asia, and other areas of the world. It also has courses covering certain eras, such as the Renaissance, or on certain topics, such as women's history. A college with a rich curriculum in your field of interest will give you a variety of courses to choose from. It will have faculty who are experienced and knowledgeable in their areas of specialty. It should also have many graduates who have gone on to good jobs or graduate school to earn a Master's degree in your field of interest. Employers and graduate school faculty will probably know some of these students. If these students have done well, you may find it easier to get a good job or gain acceptance into a top graduate school.

If you know what you want to study, talk to people in the field that interests you and ask them which schools they would recommend. If you are undecided about your major at this point, don't worry. Pick a school that offers a range of majors and programs. Most colleges offer admissions counseling to help you pick a major. If you enter college without a major, by the time you have completed a year or so of general study, you may feel better prepared to select one. Remember, most colleges will require you to decide on a major by the time you enter your junior year of college.

5. Size

The size of colleges and universities varies widely. Some private liberal arts colleges have only a few hundred students and a few dozen faculty members. State-supported schools may have tens of thousands of students and hundreds of faculty members. In addition to the number of faculty and students, the size of the college will determine such things as:

- The number of majors offered
- The range of extracurricular activities
- The amount of personal attention students receive from faculty and advisers
- The size of the library collection
- The availability of computer and science labs
- The diversity and backgrounds of the student body.

6. Academic Admission Standards

Some colleges have strict admission criteria. They accept less than 10 percent of the students who apply. Other schools accept a greater percentage of applicants. Schools consider many things in evaluating students for admission, including the essays written for their applications, references, and interviews. Nevertheless, academic qualifications are probably the first thing colleges explore. They will look at your grade point average (GPA) in your core classes and, in most cases, your scores on standardized college entrance tests.

It is never too early to start working to make sure your GPA is as high as possible. Your GPA is important because it represents your cumulative effort in high school. It is also considered a fair estimate of your future performance.

Your scores on standardized tests are important because they let a school see how you rank with all other students who take the tests. Most schools require applicants to take either the SAT or the ACT. You will learn more details about standardized tests and how to prepare for them in Lesson 3, "Navigating the Testing Maze."

Criteria for Selecting a College

1. Accreditation
2. Length of degree program
3. Reputation
4. Breadth and depth of the curriculum
5. Size
6. Academic admission standards
7. Cost
8. Location
9. Special programs and employment opportunities
10. Student body
11. Role of alumni
12. Employment services

If parts of your academic record are weak, you may still have a chance for admission. Colleges want students with good well-rounded records, not just top grades and test scores. The best thing to do is to aim high but also to be realistic. Applying to college takes time and money. Don't apply to a college unless you are reasonably sure that you meet its academic admission requirements. Typically, there are application fees each time you apply to a college.

7. Cost

College costs, as you learned in an earlier lesson, include much more than tuition. You need to think about costs of room and board, and these vary from school to school. As higher education expenses continue to be on an upward spiral everywhere, this will make your decision making much more critically focused on what you can or cannot afford. For example, the Department of Education reported for the 2009–2010 academic year, prices for undergraduate tuition, room, and board were estimated to be over $12,800 at public institutions and over $32,100 at private institutions. In the ten-year-period between the 2000 and 2010, prices for undergraduate tuition, room, and board at public institutions rose 37 percent. At private institutions, the costs rose 25 percent.

Don't forget daily living expenses. Include the costs of entertainment, such as tickets for movies and athletic events. Also remember that city living is more expensive than country living. A college in an urban area offers many attractions, but the cost of living will be higher, especially if you live in off-campus housing. Travel expenses also must also be considered between campus and your home; it could be as cheap as a half-tank of gas or as expensive as a cross-country plane ticket.

As you learned in Lesson 1, there are many ways to finance an education. Schools want to attract different types of students, and they offer a number of options for financial aid. If a school seems perfect, but the cost is on the high side, don't give up. Talk things over with your parents or guardian and your guidance counselor, as well as people in the college's financial aid office.

When it is time for the final decision, however, make sure that you think seriously about cost. If you've narrowed your decision to two schools and one is much less expensive than the other, it's probably better to choose the cheaper school. You want as little debt as possible when you graduate.

8. Location

Do you want to come home frequently while you're a student, or do you see college as a time to experience a new part of the country? Perhaps you like an urban environment with access to museums, ethnic foods, diverse people, or major league ball games. On the other hand, maybe you value access to the outdoors or the serenity of a small town. You will probably want to find an area where you will feel comfortable but that is also stimulating. That's because part of a quality college experience is meeting a wide variety of people and enjoying new experiences. College is a place for social and emotional growth as well as intellectual growth.

9. Special Programs and Employment Opportunities

Some colleges offer students from diverse ethnic or cultural backgrounds an opportunity to take advantage of programs designed to meet their unique needs. These include everything from campus social organizations to entire schools geared to a specific ethnic group, such as historically black colleges and universities. If you want to work part-time while you're a student, you'll need to look into job opportunities on campus and in the community. You may also want to explore the possibility of internships and work-study programs.

10. Student Body

While you're a student, you will spend a lot of time in classrooms and labs. The drive for academic excellence will be powerful. The atmosphere will be competitive. For this reason, you probably won't want to attend a school where your academic ability is too far above or too far below that of the average student. But you need to think about social relationships, too. Would you be comfortable in an atmosphere where everyone had a lot more money than you do? Or a place where you were surrounded by people of different ethnic, religious, or racial backgrounds? How important are political issues to you? If you choose a school where everyone thinks exactly the same way as you, then you may be missing an important part of what the college experience provides—expanding your knowledge about how others think and why they think that way.

Think about social relationships also when choosing a college— you need to feel comfortable in the campus atmosphere.

Courtesy of Matt Bird/Corbis Images

11. Role of Alumni

How loyal are the alumni, or *people who have graduated from a certain school*? This is important for a variety of reasons. First, alumni support often translates into money for laboratory equipment, computers, athletic facilities, library materials, and other necessities. Loyal alumni can also help a school's new graduates find job and career opportunities.

Once you've identified a few colleges that interest you, talk to some of their alumni. Ask them tough questions about academic rigor or prospects for employment after you graduate. Such conversations can give you a good indication of whether the school is right for you.

12. Employment Services

Many schools take active roles in helping their graduates find jobs. They have student employment offices. Many companies will send recruiters to a campus to interview candidates who are about to graduate. Some schools have internship or cooperative (co-op) programs that allow students to gain practical work experience for class credit. Depending on your expectations and needs, these may be important selection criteria for you.

Alternative Programs to Earn College Credit

1. Earning College Credit While Still in High School

One way to earn college credit while you are still in high school is through dual enrollment. Dual enrollment or concurrent enrollment is beneficial to students seeking to get a head start on their college education. *Students enroll in college classes and if they earn a passing grade, they receive credit that may be applied toward their high school diploma, a college degree, or a certificate.* In some cases, the student may even be able to attain an Associates or equivalent degree shortly before or after their high school graduation. Furthermore, participation in dual enrollment may help with the transition from high school to college by giving students a sense of what college academics are like. In addition, dual enrollment may be a cost-efficient way for students to accumulate college credits because courses are often paid for through an agreement between the local high school and college. However, students who are dual enrolled will typically have to cover the cost of course materials such as textbooks and in some cases will have to pay an enrollment fee for classes taken through a local college.

Another way to earn college credit while you are still in high school is a program offered by educational services that partner with accredited universities and colleges. This may allow you to earn continuing education credits and degrees by taking high school courses that transfer to college credits through completion of additional college level requirements from collaborating postsecondary schools. The awarding of college credit may require additional course readings or written papers. These courses are often completed on-line once the student has enrolled with a collaborating college or university. One such educational service, RTG and Associates.org, can be contacted at *www.leadershipcredit.net*, where you will also find other courses offering honors credit.

2. Online Colleges and Distance Learning

As you consider which college you would like to attend, you may also want to think about online college degree programs. With new technologies, you can get (or complete) your degree via the Internet, usually going to an asynchronous-mode course, in which students "go to class" at a distance, *participating in the course activities and assignments whenever and from wherever it is convenient during the school week*. This fast-growing "alone but together" form of college education is especially popular with busy working students, including those in the military.

Many students are turning to online schools because the cost of tuition and fees has more than tripled at live-in public colleges during the past three decades. Community colleges, too, are so crowded that some hold classes almost around the clock. Though the tuition cost may be about the same as attending classes on a college campus, students will save money by not having to pay daily living expenses such as meals, room, or parking fees. So online learning is becoming not just convenient, but often necessary.

You can find help in your search for accredited online schools at *www.schools.com*; you will find plenty of information for school options and how to be a smart consumer about your education. Another good website for distance learning is located at *www.distancelearning.com/about*; this website will give you advice and information for online colleges.

If you want to go to an online school or attend a for-profit educational institution, use the same guidelines mentioned from the previous section to assist your decision-making.

College Admission Standards

All colleges and universities evaluate applications for admission using several key factors. Although we have touched on some of this material, because of its importance, let's review the following information again:

- *Scores on standardized entrance examinations*—How well did you do on the SAT or ACT? Some schools seek students with outstanding test scores, while others are open to students with more-modest scores.

- *Grades*—What's your GPA? Many schools believe that a student's grades are more important than scores on standardized tests. This is because the GPA indicates a student's academic abilities over four years.

- *Extracurricular activities*—Which clubs, sports, and volunteer activities have you participated in during high school? Are you active in community groups? A college will be more likely to accept a student who has a 3.8 GPA and who was an athlete, participated in plays, and worked in the community than a student with a 4.0 GPA who did nothing but hit the books. Colleges want well-rounded students.

- *Interview*—An interview is a key part of the admissions process at most schools. If possible, you should schedule an interview with every school you apply to. In some communities, college alumni conduct these interviews. If that's the case for a school that you're interested in, you won't need to travel to the campus.

- *Admission essay*—The essay is a critical part of the written application for almost every college. An essay helps college admissions staff see how you write, but it also gives them insight into your character. You'll learn about how to write a good essay in Lesson 4, "Essays, Interviews, and Campus Visits."

- *Recommendations*—Every college will ask you for letters of recommendations from teachers, counselors, or other adults. Pick people who know you well. The longer they have known you, the better. Resist the temptation to ask someone who is famous but does not know you well. The school won't find such a letter nearly as impressive as one from a person who has known you for a long time and can provide an honest picture of your character, abilities, and interests.

Identifying Colleges That Will Best Meet Your Needs

Once you have defined your selection criteria, you will have a good idea of the type of school you would like to attend. The next step is to make a list with which you can identify the schools that best meet your criteria.

Making a List

Make an appointment with your guidance counselor. Do this early, because you want to make your decision based on current and reliable information; this may require some time-consuming research on the part of you and your counselor. Bring a list of those things that are important to you based on what you have read in this section. Keep the list reasonably short, and ask the counselor to help you find colleges that meet your criteria.

You should also go to an online database and create a list of possibilities. In addition to the Department of Education's College Navigator mentioned previously in the lesson, you can find another good college-matching database at *www.collegeboard.com*. Check out others, too, by typing phrases such as "college matching" or "college choices" into a search engine.

College admissions officers sometimes visit high schools to tell students about their institutions. Take advantage of as many of these visits as you can. Be prepared with a list of questions. The answers can help you decide where to apply. Begin by creating a fairly long list. Then narrow your list to five to ten schools. Request information, catalogs, applications, and other necessary forms from these schools. You can do this by US mail or online.

Making the Decision: A Strategic Plan

By now, you have a stack of application forms on your desk. The big moment has arrived. It's time to decide where you'll apply and to start filling out your applications. Your goal should be to apply to enough schools so that you will have a choice— but not to overdo it. You don't want to spend time applying for schools that really don't interest you or where your chances of being accepted are too low.

It's also a matter of money, too, although given the importance of this decision, the application fees are not too high by themselves. The average application fee is under $50. For some, paying this fee may present a hardship for the family, especially if applying to a half dozen schools. This could cost your parents as much as $250–$300 just to turn in applications. You may be able to request a fee waiver. You can usually find information on fee waivers in a school's application packet. If you can't find information there, check with the admissions office. Think strategically at this point. Try to apply for admission to at least three types of schools:

1. *A "safe" school*—This is a school whose qualifications you probably exceed. It's one you have a strong chance of being admitted to. It's a school that you like, although it may not be your first choice. Nevertheless, you'll feel comfortable having it as a fallback if your top choices don't work out.

2. *Two or more "match" schools*—These are schools with standards and requirements that are pretty much in line with your grades, qualifications, and career goals. You think you have a reasonable chance of being admitted to these schools and you're confident that they will meet your educational needs and other criteria.

3. *Two or more "reach" schools*—Your acceptance at these schools is a long shot. Perhaps your GPA and test scores are below the school's average, or these schools are very expensive. But stretching your limits, financially and academically, gives you an opportunity to be accepted by a more select program. Many students are surprised to learn about scholarships or other opportunities that help them gain admission to schools they thought were beyond their reach. You never know until you try.

Filing Your Application

Colleges set their own application dates, and it's up to you to learn the deadlines of the colleges to which you will apply. Colleges' customary deadline for informing applicants of their decision is May 1 of the student's senior year.

Some schools, however, have an early-admissions policy, *whereby you are informed by December whether or not you are accepted.* The application deadline for early admission is usually in the fall of your senior year. Many students like this approach because they want to know where they will be going to college as soon as possible. But if you choose this route, one disadvantage is that you'll have to make your decision whether or not to accept the school's offer promptly.

If you are sure this is the school for you, you're set. But if you are undecided, you may want to wait until May 1st, by which time you may have more than one college to choose from. If you have applied for early admission and the school doesn't accept you in December, you may still have a chance to be admitted. This is because the school will put your application with those of students who have applied under its normal schedule. Schools usually make early-admission offers only to their highest-ranking applicants. In addition, some schools have a rolling-admissions policy, *under which they make acceptance decisions as students apply.* If the school you're interested in has a rolling admissions policy, you should apply as early as you can; otherwise, the school may fill all the positions in its freshman class before it even receives your application.

The Application Process

Photocopy or print additional application forms before filling them out, so you can practice perfecting the information before you write on the original you plan to submit. Never mail the completed application without making a photocopy of it. If the application gets lost in the mail or the college misplaces it, you will have to start over. Mark all application deadlines, test dates, and interview times on your calendar. Keep track of which colleges will be sending representatives to your high school, and arrange to meet with people from the schools you are applying to.

It's up to you to learn the application deadlines for applying to the colleges on your list.
Courtesy of Kate Deioma/PhotoEdit

Playing the Waiting Game

Throughout the last few months of your senior year, trips to the mailbox will probably be both uplifting and disappointing. If you get a few rejections, don't be discouraged. You will eventually find the school that's right for you. If a school doesn't accept you right away, it might place your name on a waiting list, or *list of students who will be admitted if others choose not to come*. Take this as a good sign: The school would not put your name on the list if it didn't think you were qualified. Write to the admissions officer to let them know how much you would like to attend the school, and emphasize why you are qualified to do so.

As you hear back from schools to which you have applied, inform your guidance counselor. What if you aren't accepted into any of the schools to which you applied? Don't panic—there are still plenty of other colleges that are looking for someone with your qualifications. Reexamine your list of potential colleges and call the admissions offices of some you did not apply to. They might accept late applications. Even if they do not, they might be able to provide helpful advice.

"The aim of all education is, or should be, to teach people to educate themselves".

Arnold Toynbee,
Surviving the Future, 1971

✔ CHECKPOINTS

Lesson 2 Review

Using complete sentences, answer the following questions on a sheet of paper.

1. List at least five college selection criteria and describe how each one applies to your potential choice of a college.

2. What are the basic factors that colleges use to judge an applicant's suitability for admission?

3. What can you do to improve your chances that the colleges that interest you most will accept you?

APPLYING COLLEGE-SELECTION SKILLS

4. Using the 12 criteria described in this lesson, write a paragraph describing your ideal college. Then go to the Internet and find five colleges that match your profile. (You've just started your college list!)

Navigating the Testing Maze

Quick Write

_____

_____

Are you a good test taker? If not, why? What difficulties do you usually face? How could you solve them?

Learn About

- college entrance examinations
- college placement examinations
- conquering test anxiety
- test-taking strategies
- procedures for taking standardized tests

"Neither you nor the world knows what you can do until you have tried."

Ralph Waldo Emerson, essayist, lecturer, and poet

College Entrance Examinations

As you learned in the last lesson, one of the important parts of applying to college is taking an entrance examination, _a standardized test that helps admissions officers determine who is qualified to attend their schools._ A standardized test is _one that is given and scored under the same conditions for all students._ A standardized test is carefully constructed by a testing agency. The College Board, for example, creates, scores, and oversees the administration of the Scholastic Aptitude Test (SAT).

Most colleges in the United States require applicants to take at least one entrance examination.

Courtesy of Jack Hollingsworth/Getty Images

As many as 2 million students take the SAT each year. A college to which you've applied can compare your score on such a test with the scores of all its other applicants.

Most schools look both at a student's grade point average (GPA) and at scores on standardized tests when evaluating candidates for admissions. A GPA is a good indication of how well you do in your own school, while standardized test scores show how well you stack up against students your age across the country who are applying for college. Colleges need both types of information to make fair decisions.

For this reason, most colleges in the United States require applicants to take at least one college entrance exam. You can find information on a school's test requirements in its catalog or on its website. Your guidance counselor will have information about test dates, locations, and registration procedures.

Scholastic Aptitude Test (SAT)

The Scholastic Aptitude Test (SAT) is *a widely used entrance exam that measures the academic skills and knowledge students most need for success in college.* In previous lessons, you learned that an aptitude is a talent or skill. An aptitude test is *designed to assess a student's talent, skill, or potential for learning, rather than his or her accumulated knowledge.* Both private and public colleges use SAT scores in evaluating students for admission. They also use SAT results as a basis for granting scholarships. Many educators believe that SAT scores are the best predictors of how well a student will perform in college. According to the College Board, "The SAT and SAT Subject Tests keep pace with what colleges are looking for today, measuring the skills required for success in the 21st century."

Vocabulary

- entrance examination
- standardized test
- Scholastic Aptitude Test (SAT)
- aptitude test
- American College Testing (ACT)
- achievement test
- College Placement Test (CPT)
- Preliminary SAT (PSAT)

The SAT is offered several times a year at locations across the country. It takes 3 hours and 45 minutes to administer. Students can start taking this test in their junior year. If their scores are not as high as they would like, they can repeat it again and again until they are satisfied with the scores. Students should have the SAT completed by the fall of their senior year, so that interested colleges will have time to receive latest scores. The College Board submits all scores to the colleges a student has applied to; the college will then generally use the higher score in its evaluation of the student's qualifications.

The SAT gives students three scores—one for critical reading, one for writing, and one for mathematics. The highest-possible score on each part is 800, meaning that the entire test has a maximum of 2,400 points. The cumulative average SAT score is around 1,500.

In addition to a numerical score, students receive percentile rankings on the SAT. Your percentile ranking tells you what percentage of students scored below you. For instance, if you score in the 80th percentile, then you have scored better than 80 out of every 100 students who took the SAT.

SAT subject tests are one-hour tests in specific areas such as science, English, math, history, or foreign languages. Schools with strict admission standards may require that applicants take two or three subject tests as well as the overall SAT. They use the scores to place students in the most appropriate classes. For example, if you do well on the English SAT, you may be able to take an advanced English course during your freshman year of college. You'll be able to skip the entry-level course required for freshmen.

To take the SAT, you must register and pay a fee each time you take the SAT. You can apply for a waiver of the registration fee if you can't afford it. To find out more information, you can visit the SAT website at *http://sat.collegeboard.org*.

Sample SAT Questions*

As you have read, questions on the most common entrance exam, the SAT, cover three areas: writing, critical reading, and math. This section describes the types of questions you'll find in each area. It also gives examples from previous tests.

WRITING

The questions in the writing section test your skills in the following areas:

Improving sentences. These sentences test correctness and effectiveness of expression. Part of each sentence or the entire sentence is underlined; beneath each sentence are five ways of phrasing the underlined material. Choice A repeats the original phrasing; the other four choices are different. If you think the original phrasing produces a better sentence than any of the alternatives, select choice A; if not, select one of the other choices.

In making your selection, follow the requirements of standard written English; that is, pay attention to grammar, choice of words, sentence construction, and punctuation. Your selection should result in the most effective sentence— clear and precise, without awkwardness or ambiguity.

Example: According to the study, as the body ages, the chance that medications will cause harmful side effects <u>are on the increase</u>.

(A) are on the increase
(B) are increasing
(C) has increased
(D) increase
(E) increases

(*Correct answer: E, increases*)

Identifying sentence errors. This section tests your ability to recognize grammar and usage errors. Each sentence contains either a single error or no error at all. No sentence contains more than one error. The error, if there is one, is underlined and lettered. If the sentence contains an error, select the one underlined part that must be changed to make the sentence correct. If the sentence is correct, select choice E. In choosing answers, follow the requirements of standard written English.

Example: In 1772, <u>four years before</u> the Declaration of Independence,
                  A
Mercy Otis Warren <u>published</u> *The Adulateur*, a satiric play that cast
            B
the colonial governor <u>to be</u> a villain intent <u>on robbing</u> the colony.
           C   D
<u>No error</u>
 E

(*Correct answer: C, to be*)

*SAT test material selected from the SAT Reasoning Test, the College Board. Reprinted by permission of the College Board, the copyright owner.

Improving paragraphs. This section tests your ability to revise sentences in the context of a paragraph or an entire essay, organize and develop paragraphs in a coherent and logical manner, and apply the conventions of Standard Written English.

Essay writing. The SAT® begins with an essay. You'll be asked to present and support a point of view on a specific issue. Because you have only 25 minutes, your essay is not expected to be polished—it is meant to be a first draft.

CRITICAL READING

Critical-reading questions test your skills in the following areas:

Sentence completion. For each question in this section, select the best answer from among the choices given and fill in the corresponding circle on the answer sheet.

Example: Having inherited a staff known for _____ resources, the new chairman had no choice but to introduce a number of more efficient practices.

(A) defining
(B) harboring
(C) neglecting
(D) bolstering
(E) squandering

(*Correct answer: E, squandering*)

Passage-based reading. Some of the reading passages in the SAT are as short as a paragraph or two, about 100 words in length. You will also find one or more pairs of related short passages in each edition of the test. Such material can be followed by two to five questions that measure the same kinds of reading skills as are measured by the questions following longer passages. The questions are based on the content of the passages; questions following a pair of related passages may also be based on the relationship between the paired passages. Answer the questions based on what is stated or implied in the passages and in any introductory material that may be provided.

Sample SAT Questions, continued

MATHEMATICS

Items in the math test are of two types: multiple-choice questions and student produced responses.

Multiple-choice questions

Example: Emily's school offers 3 English classes and 4 History classes for her to choose from. She must choose 3 of these classes to complete her schedule. If exactly one of these must be an English class, how many different combinations of classes are possible for Emily?

(A) 7
(B) 12
(C) 18
(D) 21
(E) 35

(Correct answer: C, 18)

Student-produced responses.

In this section you compute your own answers to math questions. These are not multiple-choice questions.

Example: Of the 6 courses offered by the biology department at his college, Shawn must choose exactly 2 of them. How many different combinations of 2 courses are possible for Shawn if there are no restrictions on which 2 courses he can choose?

(Correct answer: 15)

Below are three possible methods of finding the solution (there are more):

1. There are 6 courses offered; let us refer to them as 1, 2, 3, 4, 5, and 6. One way to find the number of combinations is to list all possible pairings. They are 1-2, 1-3, 1-4, 1-5, 1-6, 2-3, 2-4, 2-5, 2-6, 3-4, 3-5, 3-6, 4-5, 4-6, and 5-6. There are therefore 15 combinations. Note that 1-2 and 2-1 represent the same combination.

2. You could also notice that there are 5 pairings that start with course 1, and 4 additional pairings that start with course 2, and so forth. The total number of combinations using this method is 5 + 4 + 3 + 2 + 1 = 15.

3. You could also solve the problem by noting that the total number of permutations (that is, the number of different ways 2 of 6 courses could be selected) is 6 for the first course selected times 5 for the second course selected, or 6 × 5 = 30. To find the number of combinations, you must divide the number of permutations by the number of arrangements. For each pair of courses A-B selected, the arrangement B-A is also possible. Therefore, there are 2 arrangements. Therefore, the number of combinations is 30 ÷ 2 = 15.

American College Testing (ACT)

The American College Testing (ACT) exam is *a college entrance examination that is an alternative to the SAT*. Whereas the SAT primarily measures a student's aptitude, or learning potential, the ACT is an achievement test that *tests what a student has actually learned*. Most schools require either the SAT or ACT.

The ACT has four sections: English, mathematics, reading, and science reasoning. It is two hours and 55 minutes long and is composed entirely of multiple-choice questions. There is an optional 30-minute writing test. (The writing test on the SAT is mandatory.) Scores on each of the four sections range from 1 to 36. These scores are averaged to produce a composite score.

Colleges use ACT scores, just as they use SAT scores, in making decisions regarding admissions and scholarships as well as in placing students in special programs and honors or remedial courses. Like the SAT, the ACT has a waiver of registration fees for students who can demonstrate financial hardship.

Most students take the ACT during the winter or spring of their junior year. If they think they can improve their scores, they should take the test again in the fall of their senior year. If a college gives you the option of taking either the SAT or the ACT, you may want to take both. Then you can decide which score you want to have submitted to the college. You can learn more about the ACT at *www.actstudent.org*.

Sample ACT Questions

MATHEMATICS

A car averages 27 miles per gallon. If gas costs $4.04 per gallon, which of the following is closest to how much the gas would cost for this car to travel 2,727 typical miles?

(A) $44.44
(B) $109.08
(C) $118.80
(D) $408.04
(E) $444.40

The correct answer is D: If you divide 2,727 miles by 27 miles per gallon, you will get the number of gallons: $2{,}727 \div 27 = 101$. Then, multiply the number of gallons by the cost per gallon: $101(4.04) = 408.04$. This gives the cost of gas for this car to travel 2,727 typical miles.

ENGLISH, READING, SCIENCE, OR WRITING

These sections of the ACT require the test taker to read passages on the subject matter and answer questions from information contained in these passages. You can learn more about the ACT test prep at *www.actstudent.org*.

College Placement Examinations

As you've learned, colleges often use the results of students' performance on college entrance exams such as the SAT or ACT to place them in particular classes. But there are other types of exams. One of the most common is the College Placement Test (CPT), which is *designed to help schools place, or assign, students in classes where they'll learn most.*

Advanced Placement Examinations

Colleges give advanced placement (AP) exams to students who have taken AP courses in high school. Doing well on these exams gives students the opportunity to earn credit or advanced standing at most colleges and universities. AP exams cover 34 courses across 22 subject areas, including history, government, English, music, art, some sciences, and foreign languages.

College-Level Examination Program

The College-Level Examination Program (CLEP) enables new college students to receive college credit without taking a basic or introductory course if they can show they already know the information covered in that course. Around 2,900 colleges grant credit or advanced standing for CLEP exams. Receiving such credit enables a student to move on more quickly to studying advanced topics. Business, industry, government, and professional groups use the CLEP to decide whom to admit to training programs.

ACT ASSET

ACT ASSET is a series of short placement tests designed to measure a student's strengths and needs in language, reading comprehension, mathematics (numerical skills, elementary algebra, and geometry), and study skills. ACT ASSET takes two to three hours to complete. It is used primarily by community and technical colleges. For more information on ACT ASSET, visit *www.act.org/asset*.

ACT COMPASS

The ACT Computerized Adaptive Placement Assessment and Support System (COMPASS) is a series of tests in mathematics, reading, and writing. It also has a component that determines placement levels for students who want to take classes in English as a Second Language. Like ASSET, COMPASS is used primarily by community colleges. You can find out more about COMPASS at *www.act.org/compass*.

Institutional Challenge Examinations

Some colleges allow students to take an institutional challenge exam to qualify for course credits. If a student demonstrates proficiency on this exam, he or she receives college credit for the course without having to enroll. For more information on institutional challenge examinations, consult individual colleges and universities.

Conquering Test Anxiety

The thought of taking any test fills some students with dread. A major test such as the SAT or ACT—one that has major consequences for a student's future—can produce even greater anxiety. Many students are sure they will not do well. They may fear the test so much that they question their decision to go to college in the first place.

Do these thoughts occur to you? Don't despair. You can't study for entrance exams the way you study for a math quiz, but you can do several things to overcome your fears and make sure you get the highest-possible score.

Helpful Reminders for Reducing Test Anxiety

- Approach the test with an "I can" attitude
- Prepare yourself emotionally for the test; control what you say to yourself, and be positive
- Remind yourself that you studied and that you know the material
- "Overlearn" the material—you can't study too much
- Chew gum or eat hard candy during the test if allowed; it may help you relax
- Go to bed early. Do not pull an all-nighter before the test
- Eat a healthy meal before the test
- Arrive early for the test (at least 15 minutes early)
- Sit back, relax, breathe, and clear your mind if you become nervous
- Come to the test with everything you need: pencils, calculator, and other supplies
- Read over the entire test first; read all the directions; highlight the directions
- Listen to the teacher/proctor before the test begins.
- Keep an eye on the clock
- Answer what you know first, the questions that are easiest for you
- Check your answers, but remember, your first response is usually correct
- Find out about the test before it is given; ask the teacher/proctor what types of questions will be on the test
- Find out exactly what the test will cover ahead of time
- Ask the teacher/proctor for a study sheet—you may not get one, but it doesn't hurt to ask
- Know the test's rules and the teacher's/proctor's rules
- Attend the review session if the instructor/teacher offers one
- Know what grade value the test holds
- Ask about extra credit or bonus questions on the test
- When you get the test, jot down any mnemonic (memory device) you might have developed on the back or at the top of a page
- Never look at another student's test or let anyone see your test.

1. Take the Preliminary SAT (PSAT), *a standardized test that covers the same areas the SAT does*. The PSAT measures reading skills, math problem-solving skills, and writing skills. It will help you prepare for the SAT by showing you the kinds of questions you will see on the SAT. Taking the PSAT also gives you a chance to compete in the National Merit Scholarship Program. Students should take the PSAT in their junior year.

2. Take a test-preparation course to get ready for specific college entrance exams such as the SAT and ACT. Your school may offer such courses. Commercial courses are also available. To take commercial courses, however, you must pay a tuition fee. Just type a phrase such as "SAT prep" into an Internet search engine to find out some of the possibilities, or talk to your guidance counselor.

3. In 2011 The College Foundation released The Total College Solutions (DVD) containing SAT and ACT E-Book Study Guide with Peer to Peer Coaching and Zero Hour Threat SAT and ACT prep games.

You can't be sure that test-prep courses will make a major difference in your test performance. They can, however, ease your anxiety. They will introduce you to the test format. They'll give you a chance to apply basic strategies involved in analyzing and answering different types of questions. They'll provide opportunities to practice and increase your speed. And they'll give you a chance to analyze your test-taking strengths and weaknesses.

> **success TIP** ★
>
> **Reduce Stress, Improve your Scores by Taking the Full SAT Practice Test**
> The College Board website has free complete SAT Practice Tests at *http://sat.collegeboard.org/practice/*. This is a convenient way to get comfortable with the testing process and improve your scores on the SAT and PSAT. You can test online, or you can print it out.

If nothing else, taking the PSAT or a test-prep course will give you a psychological boost and the assurance that you've done all the preparation you can. You'll feel more in control of the situation.

Test-Taking Strategies

Here are some test-taking tips that other students and the experts have found helpful. You may find them useful for an upcoming quiz or final exam, as well as for a standardized test.

- *Don't jump the gun*—When you first read a question, you may think you know the answer immediately. This is called a *quick-time response*. But take your time. Read the whole question, and then read it again. You may find that the wording is a little tricky, and that the answer is not what you thought.

- *Keep moving*—Suppose you read a question and have no idea what the answer is. You reread it: Nothing comes to mind. When that happens, move to the next question. You don't have to answer the questions in order. An idea may occur to you later—perhaps while you are reading another question. This is called a *lag-time response*.

- *Guess smart*—Sometimes neither quick-time nor lag-time responses work for a question. What if you have no idea what the answer is? Should you guess or leave the item blank? Don't guess unless you know you won't be penalized for wrong answers. For example, the SAT penalizes you for wrong answers, but the ACT does not.

  So if you are taking the ACT or any other test that does not penalize you for wrong answers, go ahead and do some intelligent guessing. For example, if it's a multiple-choice question, do you know that some of the answers are obviously wrong? Then narrow the choices, and make your best guess. You can also try this strategy for multiple-choice questions on the SAT, although you'll be doing it at a greater risk.

- *Relax*—Don't cram the night before the exam. If you're not ready by that time, you never will be. Get a good night's sleep. Take time for breakfast. Get to the exam site a bit early. Do the best you can. If you don't do as well as you think you should, don't be too hard on yourself. Learn from the experience, and you'll do better next time around.

Tips for Answering Multiple-Choice and Essay Questions

Multiple-Choice Questions

- Try to answer the question before you read the options provided; that will get your mind set in the right direction.
- Be aware that answers containing extreme modifiers, such as *always*, *every*, and *never*, are usually wrong.
- Read all the options before selecting your answer.
- Cross off answers that you know are incorrect.

Essay Questions

- Realize that bigger is not always better—be as concise and informative as possible (the person who grades your essay would rather see one or two pages of substance than five pages of fluff).
- Outline your thoughts before you begin writing.
- Be careful about spelling, grammar, and punctuation.
- Use details, such as times, dates, places, and proper names, where appropriate.
- Write neatly.
- Proofread your answer.

Procedures for Taking Standardized Tests

Consult the colleges you are applying to and ask which tests they require. Then talk to your guidance counselor about when and where the test will be given in your area.

If you decide to take a test-prep course, schedule it well before the test date. This will give the studying and test-taking tips you learn time to sink in. You'll be able to apply at least some of them to taking quizzes and class tests in the meantime.

Even if you don't take a course, reading books a half-hour or so per day will help you develop a good sense of English usage. Also, practice working a variety of math problems every day.

As the test day draws near, relax. Remember that the test is only one of the factors that the school will look at in evaluating you. They'll look at your GPA. Your references, essay, and interview are also important, as you'll learn in Lesson 4, "Essays, Interviews, and Campus Visits."

✔ CHECKPOINTS

Lesson 3 Review

Using complete sentences, answer the following questions on a sheet of paper.

1. What is the main purpose of college entrance exams?

2. What are the two basic entrance exams used by colleges in the United States?

3. Why do you think some students have trouble taking tests?

4. What are two tips for reducing test-taking anxiety?

5. Give three strategies named in this lesson for improving your test-taking ability. Add any other strategies that may have helped you.

APPLYING TEST-TAKING SKILLS

6. Ask your guidance counselor for a sample of SAT questions, or go to *www.collegeboard.com*. The College Board administers the SAT and has sample questions on its website. See how well you can answer them.

Essays, Interviews, and Campus Visits

Quick Write

_____

_____

Write a paragraph about yourself that would be suitable to submit to a college admissions officer. What are your strong points? What are your ambitions? Why do you want to go to college?

Learn About

- the personal side of the college application process
- writing a college application essay
- how to have a successful interview
- campus visits

"College [application] essays are essentially columns, little bits of persuasive prose designed to be both personal and instructive, without too much wear-and-tear on the reader."

Jay Mathews, education columnist, _Washington Post_

The Personal Side of the College Application Process

As you are finding out, applying to college is a multistep process. You must decide which criteria are most important to you and make a list of schools that meet those criteria.

Then you must prepare for and take college entrance exams and other tests. Finally, you must deal with the personal side of college applications. That's what this lesson is about.

The personal side of the application process is important because most colleges want to know more about you than just your test results and high school records. They want to get to know you as a person. To do this, they rely on two main things: 1) an essay that you include with your written application; and 2) what they learn about you during an interview. The interview, along with a third element, the campus visit, also provides you an opportunity to learn more about the college.

Writing a College Application Essay

Most colleges require that prospective students submit an essay with their applications. By reading your essay, an admissions officer, or _a person who helps decide whom to admit to a college_, can discover how you think and what is important to you. Reading the essay also enables the admissions officer to determine how you organize and express your thoughts.

This information helps the admissions officer decide why the college should, or should not, admit you.

If you are not a good writer, get guidance in advance from your English teacher, your parents, guardian, or a tutor as you write your essay. If your English teacher has read and graded several papers you've written, ask for specific tips on how to improve your style.

Write a draft, edit it, put it aside a day or two, and then look at it again. You may have to write several drafts before you become satisfied. Remember, this is an important piece of work. It is not a routine homework assignment. One or more of the college admissions staff will examine it carefully for spelling and grammar, as well as for content and style.

If the college specifies a length, stick to it. Even if the college places no limits on length, you should keep the essay as short as possible, while still covering the topic completely. If the reader sees you can make a point clearly and succinctly, it's a definite plus.

Essay Questions

Many colleges have their own application forms, while others use a common form. You can download an example of the common form from *https://www.commonapp.org/CommonApp/DownloadForms.aspx*.

The essay topics on this form are good examples of the types of questions colleges ask applicants to write about. Some examples include:

- "Evaluate a significant experience, achievement or risk that you have taken and its impact on you."

- "Discuss some issue of personal, local, or national concern and its importance to you."

- "Indicate a person who has had a significant influence on you, and describe that influence."

Vocabulary

- admissions officer
- transcript
- itinerary
- teaching assistant

Sometimes a college application essay will ask you to choose your own topic to discuss. Choose it with care. If you think of a topic too quickly, like "The Big Game," chances are many of your peers will have the same idea. Select a topic that distinguishes you from other students, maybe a personally moving experience, or an issue that you had to solve within your class, peer group or among those close to you.

- "Describe a character in fiction, a historical figure, or a creative work (as in art, music, science, etc.) that has had an influence on you."

- "Describe an experience that illustrates what you would bring to the diversity in a college community or an encounter that demonstrated the importance of diversity to you."

"Notice that the common theme in all these questions is you," writes Madeleine R. Eagon, Vice President, Strategic Communications and Financial Aid at DePauw University in Indiana. "Regardless of your choice of topic, your essay should provide the reader insight into who you are, how you think and what matters in your life."

Tips on Writing a Great Essay

The Cambridge Essay Service gives the following general tips for writing any type of essay:

1. Don't Strive for Perfection

Writing a college application essay is not like competing in an Olympic diving match. You don't start with a perfect score and then lose points for every error. The admissions officers who read these essays are not tyrants with red pencils. They are smart, busy people who know their colleges well and who want to learn whether you'd be a good fit. They are looking for an impression. That impression is mostly emotional. Their goal is to reach a conclusion about you, not about the intellectual content of your essay. The best conclusion that a reader can reach is, "I really like this kid."

2. Focus on One Great Idea

The person who reads your essay will want to get the gist of what you have to say quickly. Focus your essay on one point and express your ideas clearly. If you have more than one point, or if you try to be too complex, the reader might get confused.

3. Keep It Personal

Avoid big topics. This is not the place to set forth your ideas on global warming or peace in the Middle East. Don't introduce heavy-duty moral principles. If you must have a moral, make it fresh and right for you.

4. Be Yourself

On hearing that you have to write an essay, someone may say, "Don't worry—just be yourself." That may sound like good advice, but it's not realistic. Just who is "yourself"? You have several selves—one for your family, one for friends, one for formal occasions, one for when you're alone. Should you tell the admissions officer about yourself alone or as part of a group? Think about this carefully. Then pick the "self" that is honest and that presents you in the best possible light—the self that can present you as unique and passionate about something important.

Your essay should provide insight into who you are and what matters in your life.

Courtesy of Supri Suharjoto/Shutterstock

5. Be Upbeat

If you have a choice of topics, select something upbeat. Write about a passion, not a doubt. Teen anxiety and cynicism are tiresome to admissions officers. If you love something or someone and can convey that love with detail and conviction, do it.

6. Use Dialogue

If it's appropriate for your topic, use dialogue instead of a third-person narrative. Dialogue is livelier and more direct, and will demonstrate a higher level of writing skill. Suppose, for example, that you were writing about Ms. Von Crabbe, your beloved childhood piano teacher. Which of the following passages is more effective?

- Ms. Von Crabbe, my piano teacher, taught me more than just how to play the piano. Her lessons were filled with advice that one could use in life. Even though her English was often just a little off, and her manner seemed odd, she will always be memorable to me.

- "Alex," Ms. Von Crabbe would say, "the concert is starting even before you sit down on the bench." She had warned us the first day, "Never call me 'Ms. Von Crabapple,' even if my back is turned to you." At first, we were too afraid to try to call her that. Then, we came to love her teaching too much to do so.

The second essay is rich in quotation and detail. It helps the reader identify with Alex, the writer, and like him. Making the reader like you is an important goal of a college essay. The second essay also demonstrates an important principle of good writing: "Show, don't tell." While the first essay *tells* the reader that Ms. Von Crabbe's English was a little off and her manner odd, the second essay *shows* both mannerisms by quoting Ms. Von Crabbe in her own words.

7. Use Details

Journalists and other good writers know the importance of detail. Details create sharp, memorable images. Which of these sentences is more memorable?

- I live in a suburb outside a big city where half the property is conservation land, and the other half is large plot houses.

- I live in Lincoln, Massachusetts, a small town 15 miles west of Boston, where half the property is conservation evergreen forests and the other is large houses on small lots.

The second sentence is better than the first because it has more detail. It also helps the reader see you in a real place. In the process, you become a real person. Notice that these details don't make the sentence significantly longer, even though they do make it much more interesting. Choose each word with care, especially if the number of words you can write is limited.

There are several online sources that will help you in writing your application essay:

- At *http://www.college-admission-essay.com/* you will find information about writing a good essay, application assistance, school reviews, and other information.

- Peterson's College Search site at *http://www.petersons.com/college-search/writing-college-application-essay.aspx* also provides some good guidance.

- The College Board has tips at *http://collegeboard.com/student/apply/essay-skills/109.html* with video segments about the application process and what admissions officers say they are looking for at *http://www.collegeboard.com/student/apply/essay-skills9406.html*.

Use Social Media to Show Your Best Side to Colleges

Social media help colleges get to know prospective students.

Courtesy of moodboard/Corbis Images

Social media tools and networking systems are making it more possible than ever for anyone who wants to find out about you to do so with a basic Internet search. According to a 2011 survey of admissions officers at 359 colleges and universities, the use of social media as part of the admissions process is on the rise. This annual report found that "nearly a quarter (24 percent) of respondents from the schools surveyed have gone to an applicant's Facebook® or other social networking page to learn more about them, while 20 percent have Googled® them."

Tips for Prospective Students

- **Do a little housekeeping**—Google your name and see what comes up on the results page. Are there pictures or posts you need to delete?

- **Check your settings**—What you thought was private may now be public, as platforms continue to update their terms of service and setting options. To protect your privacy, periodically go into each of your accounts to review these terms and confirm your settings.

- **Consider your audience**—It may be larger than you think. What things do you want your audience, particularly college recruiters and admissions counselors, to know about you?

- **Participate in conversations with your favorite schools!**—Once you find these schools online and active in social media, don't stop there. Engage in ongoing conversations taking place in discussion forums and live chat sessions.

These numbers show an increase from the 10 percent of schools reviewing applicants' online profiles in 2008. It is extremely important for you to be careful how you come across on the Web! While your first thought is often about how social media profiles can be full of negative information, keep in mind that these searches can be a positive thing, bringing an applicant's qualifications and potential to the attention of college recruiters and application reviewers.

It's a Two-way Street

You can find out more about the schools you are considering via social media as they become more active with their own social media accounts. Colleges today are increasingly active in promoting their school programs and reaching out to prospective, current, and former students. According to the Kaplan Test Prep Report, Facebook® (85 percent) and YouTube (66 percent) are two of the most popular tools schools are using to build virtual communities and make these connections. For you, the applicant, reviewing the social media profiles of colleges and universities can be a time saver, providing answers to frequently asked questions about the school and the admission process. According to a 2010 survey of 1,000 college-bound high school students conducted by the higher education consulting firm Noel-Levitz, online access to information is very important to prospective students. This study found that 76 percent of students used Facebook® and the same percentage "supported schools creating their own private social networks for prospective students." There is a growing expectation that schools will have a presence online, not only with websites and videos, but also in social networking systems.

How to Have a Successful Interview

Your essay shows how you think and how well you express yourself in writing. But it is one-way communication. An essay is not interactive. An interview is your chance to interact with a representative of a college. It's an exchange of information: You learn about the college, and the college learns about you. Many colleges require interviews. But even if a college doesn't require one, it should be willing to set one up at your request.

A face-to-face meeting with an admissions officer benefits both you and the college. The interview will give you a chance to broach issues regarding your application and background more effectively than you could in writing or on the phone. Some of these may involve your transcript, or *official record of your grades*. The interview will also give the college admissions officer a chance to ask an in-depth question on something that you've said in your essay or your application.

Here are some things the College Board suggests you do before the interview:

- Make an interview appointment with one of the colleges you want to attend
- Mark the date and time on my calendar (this is not something you want to forget)
- Research the college by checking out its website, brochures, and catalog
- Make notes about why you want to attend this college
- Make notes about your life outside the classroom, including activities, community service, and hobbies
- Get familiar with common interview questions and do some practice interviews with a friend of family member
- Prepare questions about the school to ask the interviewer
- Get directions to the interview.

Gather documents you may need, such as test scores and a high school transcript. Practicing with a friend who is also applying to college can be especially helpful. Ask each other questions, taking turns playing the roles of student and interviewer. It might even help to have someone sit in on these sessions and then offer feedback.

are you AWARE ?

Alumnus is the singular of the Latin word, *alumni*, which you learned in a previous lesson means graduates of a school (or college).

Most interviews don't last more than an hour. The interviewer will most likely be an admissions officer but could also be a faculty member, a college *alumnus*, or a student.

The interview might even be a group session with admissions staff and current students. If your college requires an interview, and you can't afford a trip to campus, the college may arrange for one of its representatives or alumni to interview you in your home town.

CHAPTER 4 Aiming Towards a College Degree

Also, think back about other interviews you may have had—perhaps for a summer job or internship. How could you have handled yourself better during that session? What did you do well?

Interview Day Etiquette

Dress

Wear comfortable clothes, but look neat and well groomed. Guys don't need to wear a suit. Pants with a dress shirt or sweater are fine. Girls may choose a dress, suit, or well-coordinated skirt and top. Wear dress shoes instead of sneakers, and leave your baseball cap in the car. Don't wear jeans or denim.

Introductions

Make sure you get to the interview office with plenty of time to spare. Make eye contact as you greet the interviewer. Have a firm handshake. Introduce those who have accompanied you. Let them ask any questions they may have. They should not, however, participate in the actual interview.

Body Language and Demeanor

It's natural to be somewhat nervous during an interview, no matter how well you have prepared. The interviewer will not count that against you. Do your best, however, not to slouch, fidget, or cross your arms tightly. The interviewer might interpret this body language as a lack of confidence. Speak clearly and maintain eye contact. Try to "read" the interviewer's reaction to what you're saying and adjust your remarks accordingly.

The Interview Process

Each interviewer and interview is different. Some interviews are structured. The interviewer will have a list of questions and choose those most relevant to you. But a good interviewer will give you plenty of leeway in the conversation, too. That means you'll have to be prepared to ask questions as well as answer them.

Each interview is different. Some colleges use a group session with admissions staff and current students.

Courtesy of Ryan Smith/Corbis Images

College Interview DOs and DON'Ts

Interview DOs

1. Do take the interview process seriously.

2. Do be prepared for the interview. Research the school prior to arriving on campus—look at its website.

3. Do dress appropriately—you never get a second chance to make a first impression.

4. Do arrive on time.

5. Do bring a résumé of your activities and leadership projects to give to the admissions officer.

6. Do bring a list of questions you would like to ask during the interview.

7. Do be ready to actively engage in a conversation.

8. Do be yourself—the admissions staff is trying to get to know who you are and how you will fit into the school.

9. Do enjoy the interview.

10. Do say thank you to the interviewer and send a thank-you note.

Asking Questions

Don't interrupt your interviewer or try to take the lead in the conversation. But do take an active role in it. This will help you steer the conversation in the direction you want. You'll be able to get answers to any questions that the materials you've read haven't answered. Your ability to participate in the interview is also an indication of your interest and initiative.

If you want to ask good questions, do your homework. Read the college catalog and website carefully, and don't ask questions that these sources answer. Instead, use such information sources as a springboard for in-depth questions. For example, suppose you're thinking about majoring in chemistry. Ask questions such as, "I noticed that Dr. Laura Brown is head of the chemistry department. Is she doing any research, and are students involved in it?" Another good question might be, "Where have some recent chemistry graduates found employment?"

Interview DON'Ts

1. Don't say you came to the interview because your parent(s) made you.

2. Don't mumble or speak unclearly—this is your opportunity to convey information that might not be asked again on the application.

3. Don't give one-word answers, even if you are shy.

4. Don't be afraid to talk about yourself or your accomplishments.

5. Don't forget that this is your opportunity to make a great impression.

6. Don't be afraid that you might give the wrong answers—there are no wrong answers and the admissions staff is only trying to get to know you and your interests.

7. Don't make excuses for poor performance.

8. Don't be arrogant or obnoxious, even if you are nervous.

9. Don't forget to ask questions—this is your interview with a school, not just the school's interview with you. Get everything out of the interview that you need to make your decision about the school.

10. Don't use profanity or inappropriate language.

11. Don't chew gum during your interview.

Answering Questions

Although you will want to have questions to ask, chances are you will spend most of the time during the interview answering questions. Be prepared to do some hard thinking. The interviewer does not want to grill you or make you feel uncomfortable; he or she does, however, want to see how you think and how you express yourself.

The interviewer will want to find out how you respond to predictable questions, as well as how you think on your feet. He or she will want to make sure that you can speak intelligently, not only about your grades, career plans, and test scores, but also about a variety of other topics. Don't be too quick to start a response. Think through your response so you don't appear nervous and remember to communicate confidence.

Typical interview questions include the following:

- Which courses have you enjoyed most in high school?
- Do you think your grades reflect your potential?
- Other than your studies, which school activities have been important to you and why?
- How did you spend last summer?
- Have you had a mentor? Who is it? How has this person influenced you?
- What has been your toughest challenge in life and how did you overcome it?
- What was your proudest achievement?
- What would you add to campus life at this college?
- Which other colleges are you considering?

The interviewer may even throw in some questions about topics of the day or ask your opinion on an important world issue. Answer these questions as knowledgeably as you can, but don't express any radical, hotheaded opinions. Support your ideas with facts.

The interviewer might ask you about the best book you've ever read. Don't try to bluff it. Don't pick an impressive title unless you can speak about the book in an intelligent way. Pick a book you know well.

Above all, don't get flustered if you get an unexpected question and find yourself tongue-tied. Simply say you'd like some time to think about the question and ask if you can send in a written answer later. If you don't know something, don't pretend that you do.

Before you end the conversation, ask the college to mail you any other helpful information, such as an activities calendar.

Interview Follow-Up

Make notes about the interview, and within a day or so of returning home, send a thank-you note to your interviewer. Mention a few highlights of the interview. Stress how much you are interested in the school. Without overdoing it, emphasize why you think you would be an asset to the campus. If you forgot to mention something about yourself during the interview, say it in your thank-you note. If you promised to write an answer to an interview question, include this also. File away any business cards with contact information that the interviewer and other admission staff offer.

There is a lot to remember when it comes to college interviews. Figure 4.1 covers some of the main things.

BEFORE

☑ Research colleges through brochures, course catalogs, and the Web.

☑ Make an appointment.

☑ Get directions to the campus and admissions office.

☑ Practice answering the following sample questions.

DURING

Be prepared to answer…

☑ Why do you want to attend this school?

☑ What do you think will be your major? Why?

☑ How would you describe yourself to a stranger?

☑ What is your greatest accomplishment?

☑ What is the most significant contribution you've made to your school or community?

☑ What do you see yourself doing in the future? In five years? In 10 years?

☑ What is your favorite book? Who's your favorite author?

☑ Tell me about your family.

☑ What extracurricular activities are important to you?

☑ What is your strongest/weakest point?

☑ If you could have lunch with one special person (dead or alive) who would it be? What would be your first question?

☑ Who are your heroes and why?

☑ How would you spend $1 million in 24 hours?

ASK

Ask at least three questions that can't be answered in the school's brochures …

☑ Why would you recommend this school?

☑ How would you describe college life at this school?

☑ Do you have any advice for me?

FIGURE 4.1

College Interview Checklist

Campus Visits

Most colleges strongly encourage applicants to visit their campuses during the search process. Nothing beats seeing a college campus for yourself and talking with the faculty and students there. Many colleges will arrange for prospective students to visit overnight. You should plan to visit colleges before applying, if possible. That way, if you find after visiting that a college doesn't appeal to you, you can cross it off your list. If you wish, you can schedule your interview during your campus visit.

Planning the Visit

Once you have finalized your list of possible colleges, start planning an itinerary, or *travel schedule*, that leaves time to explore each school, as well as time to get from one to the other.

Set up appointments. Call the admissions office at least three weeks before your planned trip. Try to find a mutually convenient time for an interview. If you have a choice, it is better to have the interview toward the end of your visit rather than at the beginning. By that time, you will be more familiar with the campus and have better questions to ask. Also, ask about campus tours. If one is occurring during your visit, sign up. Finally, ask whether you need to bring anything with you to the interview. Plan to bring your family on your trip. Although it's ultimately up to you to select the college that you will attend, family members' input can help you make the decision. They know you best, and they can help you sort through your choices. Seeing the campus will help them decide what college they think is best for you, and their opinions should factor into this important decision.

Nothing beats seeing a campus for yourself. If you can, bring your family along and get their input.

Courtesy of Ed Kashi/Corbis Images

What to Do on Campus

Try to begin your visit by taking the official campus tour. Then get a campus map and go off on your own to places that interest you most. Go inside the buildings and look around. Sit in on classes, if allowed. Talk to professors and students. Classrooms and labs are important, but don't overlook the student union. Talk to students there. Try to see what they think of the school. Ask them what advice they'd give an incoming freshman.

In addition, you might want to:

- Read the bulletin boards for events and other activities.

- Stop by the bookstore. Are the textbooks exciting? What other items do they have on sale?

- Tour the library and the computer and science labs. Do they look modern and well-equipped? Well staffed? Are they busy? Are students actively engaged?

- Spend time in the cafeteria. Eat at least one meal. How is the food? What are the choices? If you are a vegetarian, are there choices for you?

- Visit entertainment areas, such as the stadium, auditorium, theater, art center, or dance studio. Are they spacious and well maintained?

- Read the student newspaper. Look at accounts of recent campus news and activities. Also, read the editorials and letters to the editor. Do you care about the same issues as the current students?

Throughout the visit, take notes. Take photographs, too, if you want. Once you've seen several campuses, you can use the photos to jog your memory.

Questions to Ask When Visiting a Campus

You should prepare for your campus visit as carefully as you do for your interview. While on campus, you should seek answers to the following questions, among others:

- What is the student/faculty ratio? The average class size? The retention rate?

- Are most classes taught by professors or by teaching assistants? (A teaching assistant is *a graduate student who is specializing in the course topic.* The college pays teaching assistants to teach introductory courses while they are studying for their graduate degrees.)

- What housing options are available? If you live in a dorm, can you choose your roommate?

- Are there fraternities and sororities on campus? What other student activities are there?

- Are the student facilities, such as the library, health center, and gym adequate?

- What student employment is available on and off campus?

- Do you need a car? Do many students bring cars? Is adequate parking available?

Alternatives to a Campus Visit

If you can't visit one or all of the colleges on your list, make especially good use of the colleges' websites and written materials. Pick up information at college fairs. Find out from your guidance counselor whether a representative from the college will be making a recruitment visit to your high school. In addition, many colleges produce their own videos, CDs, and DVDs. Ask about such materials in your high school guidance office or school library.

✔ CHECKPOINTS

Lesson 4 Review

Using complete sentences, answer the following questions on a sheet of paper.

1. Give some examples of the types of essay questions colleges will ask on their application forms.

2. List two overall guidelines for writing a good essay.

3. Why is an interview a good idea for both you and the college to which you're applying?

4. What are three things you should definitely do, and three things you should not do during a college interview?

5. What are the main things you should look for when visiting a college campus?

6. Why is it a good idea to have your family take part in college visits?

APPLYING ESSAY, INTERVIEW, AND CAMPUS VISIT SKILLS

7. Imagine that a college essay question is, "What are your career goals, and why does this college fit into them?" Outline the main points you will include in the essay. Then draft the essay itself, using the points in this lesson.

8. Practice a college interview with a friend or fellow student. Take turns being the interviewer and the student. Ask each other some tough questions.

CHAPTER 5

Courtesy of Dwight Cendrowsky/Alamy

Charting Your Course

"Each of you will experience your education uniquely—charting and ordering and dwelling in the land of your own intellect and sensibility, discovering powers you had only dreamed of and mysteries you had not imagined and reaches you had not thought that you could reach."

— A. Bartlett Giamatti, former President, Yale University

Quick Write

_____

_____

Write a paragraph on what you think will be the three biggest challenges in adjusting to college life.

Learn About

- aspects of campus life
- what is expected of you as a student
- making healthy lifestyle choices
- the importance of personal accountability

"College is not mandatory. There is no truancy from it. It does not follow an all-day schedule...What will you choose to do with your mind? What will you allow to have influence over it? When will you let it be at rest, at peace?"

Dr. Kip Robisch, English teacher and writer, keynote speech at University High School of Indiana Commencement, 2011

Aspects of Campus Life

If you go to college, you'll face some of the biggest challenges you have ever experienced. You may be living away from home for the first time. You will have to make new friends. You'll face greater academic demands than you did in high school. You'll be exposed to activities, lifestyles, and temptations that you may not have encountered before.

Perhaps most important, you will have to make many decisions for yourself. This may sound ideal because you have probably wanted more independence for a long time.

College life is one of decisions—decisions about how to live, learn, make friends, and avoid distractions to academic progress.

Courtesy of Peter Finger/Corbis Images

But there's a catch: You will also have to face the consequences of your decisions. Your parents, guardian, or a favorite teacher won't be there to cushion the blow if you make mistakes. You'll be on your own. Many college students get into trouble because they love the freedom of college life but don't realize that freedom carries responsibilities.

In this lesson, you'll learn about some of the decisions you'll have to make in your freshman year and throughout your college career. The more you know about the options, the better prepared you'll be to make good decisions.

Campus Organizations

Among the decisions you will make in college is what to do other than study. Colleges offer a variety of organizations and activities in which you can become involved. Participating in them can bring you new experiences, broaden your perspective, and teach you skills that you'll find helpful when you enter the workplace.

Here are some of the organizations and activities typically available on campus. For information on specific groups or activities at the college or colleges you're interested in, check each institution's catalog or website.

Academic Organizations

An academic organization is *a group that helps members learn about an academic subject and meet other people with a similar interest.* These organizations are similar to the math club or other groups in high school. College will offer a broader choice of organizations and a wider range of experiences than high school can offer.

Vocabulary

- academic organization
- professional organization
- political organization
- religious organization
- social organization
- fraternity
- sorority
- rush
- hazing
- recreational organization
- intramural athletics
- service organization
- international organization
- academic success center
- academic adviser
- on-campus housing
- residential adviser
- off-campus housing
- plagiarism
- credit
- academic probation
- drop/add
- stress
- burnout
- accountability

"As the full service professional society for Biomedical Engineering and Bioengineering, our goal is 'to promote the increase of biomedical engineering knowledge and its utilization.' Student members in BMES have many opportunities to learn about engineering and to meet fellow students with similar interests, including presentations on current information in research topics, academic programs, and career options; bioengineering projects for Engineering Open House; and numerous volunteer/outreach opportunities as well as social events."

Other academic organizations on your campus may range from international groups such as a German club or an Asian studies society, to science groups such as a horticulture club or a women-in-science group, or cultural organizations such as the American Academic & Cultural Exchange. They may invite guest speakers, host educational events for the entire campus, and produce publications you can read and write for. Some even sponsor tours that include travel to other countries. Joining such an organization is a great way to deepen an existing interest or explore a new one.

Professional Organizations

A professional organization is one that *helps its members learn about careers in a particular field*. These organizations will often overlap with an academic counterpart. For example, accounting is both an academic subject and a profession. The difference is that the professional organization focuses exclusively on careers in accounting.

Political and Religious Organizations

If you are interested in politics, you will probably find on your campus an appropriate political organization, or *group of people with similar political interests*. This may range from a traditional group such as Young Republicans or Young Democrats to an activist group focused on controversial issues, such as climate change or immigration.

A religious organization *unites students with a similar religious faith or interest*. There are many such groups, like Korean Catholic students' ministry, International Christian Fellowship, Episcopal Campus Ministry, Hindu Students Council, Jews in Greek Life, Muslim Student Association, and more. It's not uncommon for a large university to have 50 or more such organizations.

Social Organizations

A social organization *focuses on bringing a group of people together for social activities*. It may be a group with a specific interest, such as ballroom dancing or skiing. Or it might be a fraternity, *a men's student organization for scholastic, professional, or extracurricular activities, and having a name consisting of Greek letters*, or a sorority, *a women's student organization formed chiefly for social or extracurricular purposes, and having a name consisting of Greek letters*. There is also another type of fraternity that allows only male members for social purposes; they may have secret rites, and will have a name consisting of Greek letters. Unlike other social organizations, which are open to all students, fraternities and sororities choose their members. This happens on a regular basis during rush, which is *a drive each semester by sororities or fraternities to recruit new members*. During rush, members get to know you. They then determine, by vote, whether to invite you to join.

Fraternities and sororities offer opportunities to have fun, make friends, and do good things for the college and community. Many have their own "houses" where many of the members live. Fraternities and sororities play major roles in social life on some campuses. Many are national organizations; they establish *chapters* at campuses throughout the country. Some also have alumni groups.

Joining a national fraternity or sorority can open opportunities to meet your fraternity or sorority "brothers" or "sisters" in other cities throughout your life. But fraternities and sororities don't always have the best of reputations. Some are known for giving wild parties. Though most commonly associated with sororities and fraternities, hazing can occur in any student organization. Hazing is *any act that inflicts extreme physical, emotional, or psychological pressure or injury on an individual or that purposely demeans, degrades, or disgraces an individual*. Fraternities and sororities also charge annual or monthly fees and may require members to purchase pins, blazers, and other items. Fraternities and sororities can provide wonderful experiences. However, they have some drawbacks. Consider everything membership entails before you decide to participate in rush.

Lambda Kappa Sigma (LKS)

Lambda Kappa Sigma (LKS) is an international, professional pharmacy fraternity with the Alpha Chapter at the University of Massachusetts.

Purpose

"Open to undergraduate and graduate pharmacy students and practicing pharmacists, the fraternity is dedicated to developing the intellectual, leadership, and professional skills needed to maximize their potential…LKS educational programs enhance professional development in the field of pharmacy, with an emphasis placed on Women's Health Issues."

Functions

"LKS promotes academic growth. Scholarship opportunities are available through the LKS Educational Grant Program. Annual awards recognize excellence in academics, community service, leadership and professional achievement. LKS promotes social growth through active participation in campus activities and fraternity programs."

Logo courtesy of Robert J. Beyers II/Shutterstock

Intramural sports are healthy, competitive activities that support a learning environment.

Courtesy of Rich Pedroncelli/Corbis Images

Recreational Organizations and Intramural Athletics

If you like to be physically active, you'll certainly find a recreational organization, *a group focused on a specific activity*, that you can join. Recreational organizations can be based on anything from a sport (fencing, tae kwon do, squash) to the arts (dance and theater companies, comedy groups) to hobbies (photography, cars). If you enjoy competitive athletics but are not skilled enough to join a college varsity team, most schools offer a program in intramural athletics, which is *sports competition between teams within the college*, such as a dormitory or fraternity team. Intramurals are a great way to expand your base of friends on campus, to divert your attention (for a while) from the pressures of the classroom, and, of course, to help keep the "freshman 15" off the body. The topic of "freshman 15" will be covered in more detail later in the lesson.

Service Organizations

A service organization is one that *performs social or educational services for the community*. Most campus social organizations also perform community service as part of their larger mission. For example, a fraternity may sponsor a car wash, or a sorority may give proceeds from a dance to a charity. A service organization is different from these because, as the name implies, its sole purpose is to serve. Service organizations can range from groups whose members provide tutoring or recreational opportunities for disadvantaged children to groups such as the campus American Red Cross club, which works with adults and families. Some campus service organizations are local; others have a national affiliation. Being part of such a group can provide some of the most satisfying activities at college.

International Organizations

An international organization is *a group composed of people from a certain nation or part of the world or of students who have a special interest in such a place*. Depending on the diversity of the student body at your college, you could find international groups formed around countries from Australia to Zambia. Topics of discussion at these groups' meetings might include anything from international trade to international health to diplomacy. As we become more of a global society, joining an international organization while attending college may create more career opportunities after graduation.

College can be a confusing place. Deciding which campus organization(s) to join might be challenging because of the number of options available. But you may face other decisions at college that will be even more difficult because they will affect your future in a big way. Fortunately, most colleges offer resources to help you overcome these difficulties. For new students, these resources provide real support when you need it, so let's review some of the resources available to you.

Campus Resources

Academic Success Centers

An academic success center *provides one-on-one or group study sessions, tutoring, specialized instruction, and self-paced tutorials.* These centers can help if you start to fall behind in a certain subject. Maybe you want to understand a class better or you need to enhance your study skills. At most colleges, your tuition fee will cover the cost for these services. Some of these academic success centers may include:

- Computer labs
- Writing centers
- Math centers
- Tutoring centers
- Language labs
- Academic advising

Colleges encourage students to use these centers, because they want all students to succeed. Many campuses also provide online resources for study, including assistance from tutors.

Libraries

One of the great benefits of college is access to books in the college library. Large universities often have several libraries. The University of Virginia, for example, has 11 libraries. These include a main library and smaller, specialized libraries in fields such as chemistry, mathematics, astronomy, and fine arts. In these libraries, you will find highly skilled, specially educated librarians who can help you find books and gain access to online information or other resources.

Besides the wealth of information they contain, college libraries are great places to study.

Courtesy of Monkey Business Images/Shutterstock

Libraries are also great places to study, undisturbed by music, loud talking, or other distractions. Many college/university libraries are now available online, providing 24/7 access to books, journal articles, magazines, and other reference materials needed for research.

Academic Advisers

Your academic adviser, *the person who helps you make decisions about your collegiate education*, is one of the most important people you'll meet at college. A good adviser can help you choose classes, organize your schedule, find resources, or suggest ways to get the most out of your college experience. Although your adviser may also teach one or more of the courses you take, it's possible that you will see your adviser only when you register for classes each semester. Some colleges provide academic advising in their academic success centers.

On most campuses, the college assigns an adviser to each student; a few colleges, however, allow students to select their own advisers. Once you've chosen your college, find out your adviser's name as soon as you can. When you get there, make an appointment, and stop by to get acquainted. Usually these relationships work out well; most advisers are knowledgeable faculty members as well as experienced counselors.

But personal compatibility and comfort are also important. If you find that you and your adviser are not compatible, you can go to the dean of students, who holds primary responsibility for student affairs, and request a reassignment.

Support, Health, Career, Safety, and Other Services

College is not just a place for intellectual challenges. Many students face social, personal, physical, career, and spiritual challenges as well. Recognizing that students will sometimes need extra help, colleges provide a number of special services.

Support Services for Special-Needs Students

International students, minority students, those with disabilities, or others with special needs can usually find sources for help in adjusting to campus life. These might range from individual counseling to group sessions. College support services can also provide academic accommodations necessary to meet individual learning disabilities.

Health Services

Most students receive health services through the campus health center. Physical and mental health services you receive from the campus center should remain confidential. In other words, the center will not share any health-related information with other campus offices, or with organizations and individuals off campus unless you provide consent. If you are particularly concerned about confidentiality, ask about the health center's privacy policies.

Career Services

Most colleges offer career advisement to students or help them identify summer jobs or work-study programs, as well as full-time employment following graduation. Staff members of these offices sometimes help students set up job interviews. At large universities, corporate interviewers will conduct interviews right at the career center. Companies looking to hire may also participate in some form of college-sponsored "career day" or other large event where students may meet company representatives and drop off resumes or do on-the-spot interviews.

Campus Safety and Security Services

All campuses have some type of security or police service provided to protect students and other members of the campus community. For example, if you are working at the library late at night, the campus police or after-hours escort might walk you to your car. They will make sure that drinking doesn't become a problem for drivers, pedestrians, or anyone else. They also provide crowd control services during sports events or concerts.

Other College Resources

- *Child care center*—Offers day care for students' young children
- *Registrar*—Oversees the office where students register for courses
- *Student newspaper*—Source of news and information about campus events and issues
- *Student government*—Student-elected body that discusses and helps resolve campus issues and serves as a liaison to the college administration
- *Student radio station*—Provides information and entertainment, as well as practical experience for students who are interested in media careers
- *College website*—Provides up-to-date information on campus news and policies
- *Recreation centers*—Physical activity is a key component of a healthy lifestyle. Incorporating exercise and recreation into your daily routine can increase your energy and improve your confidence.

What Is Expected of You as a Student

A campus is a community. Like all communities, campuses have rules and regulations. Members of the campus community must be aware of these rules and policies and follow them. It's your responsibility as a student to learn about them. Unlike in high school, no parent, guardian, or teacher will be there to make sure you follow all the rules, meet all the deadlines, and fulfill all the requirements you will face as a college student.

Residential Policies

Some colleges require that all their students live on campus; others do not. Some campuses require freshmen or sophomores to live on campus but permit upperclassmen to live off campus. On-campus housing *includes dormitories or residence halls owned and operated by the college.* If you live in such a facility, you will be subject to its policies. You'll have a residential adviser, *an adult or upperclassman who lives in your dormitory and helps you solve living problems.*

You will probably have one or more roommates. In your first semester, the school usually assigns you a roommate. After that, you can choose both roommates and rooms. (For tips on how to get along with your roommate, see "Coping With Roommates" later in this lesson.)

Many colleges now have co-ed dorms, meaning that men and women live in the same building. In some cases they share the same floor and even share bathrooms. If you do not want to live in a dorm with the opposite sex, find out what options your college offers and request a situation that is comfortable for you. Most colleges also offer "quiet" dorms or floors, in which students agree not to engage in rowdy behavior so that residents can concentrate on studying.

As a first-year student, you may have the opportunity to choose a dormitory, or even a room in a dormitory. But you must sign up by a deadline. If you've visited the campus and have your heart set on living in a certain building, don't miss out by forgetting the deadline for registration.

Off-campus housing *includes apartments, houses, or rooms in someone else's home located off the college campus.* Many of these are located next to or near the campus. If you plan to live quite a distance off campus, however, you may need a car, bike, or take public transportation you can easily access. Some large colleges and universities offer bus service for students living off campus.

Academic Policies

Every college has written academic policies. It is up to you to become familiar with the policies and procedures of your college. You can find them in the college catalog or on the school's website.

Academic policies cover a wide variety of matters, including how many semesters you have to live on campus to graduate, deadlines for adding or dropping a course, and how many courses you have to take during a semester to be considered a full-time student. They also cover social issues, such as the use of illegal drugs or alcohol. And they cover academic problems such as dishonesty and plagiarism. Plagiarism is *passing off someone else's work as your own*. Plagiarism is considered a violation of academic integrity and in some cases can lead to dismissal from the college or university.

A college instructor teaching a class outdoors.
Courtesy of Art Vandalay/Getty Images

In order to graduate, you must earn a certain number of credits and fulfill the requirements of your major. A credit is *a point that the college assigns to a certain course*. Every student must earn a certain number of credits to graduate. Colleges have different systems of credits. Most systems are based on the number of hours a class meets per week. For example, if your English class meets every Tuesday and Thursday, an hour each time, the class would probably be worth two credits. But this can vary. When you meet with your academic adviser, be sure to clarify the college's credit system. Then each time you register, make sure you are collecting enough credits to graduate on schedule. If not, you may have to remain in college for another term or two to earn the required number of credits to graduate and earn a degree.

Colleges will also require that you maintain a minimum grade point average (GPA) to graduate. If you consistently get poor grades, you may not be able to graduate— or graduate on time. If your grades are very poor, the college may place you on academic probation; this *means your grades have fallen below the minimum needed GPA to graduate*. If you still do not raise your grades enough during this probation period, the school may refuse to let you return to take any further classes.

Deadlines

Colleges set deadlines to ensure that things run smoothly. They are strict about enforcing them. These deadlines cover both residential and academic policies.

Registration for Classes

While you are still in your first semester, you will have to register for second-semester classes. The school will give a deadline. Don't miss it! If you want to register for a class that has 35 spaces, and 45 people want to take that course, the registrar will accept only the first 35 students who sign up. If that course is required for your major, you may be in trouble. Don't jeopardize your chance of completing all your required courses because you missed a registration deadline. Remember, the school does not offer all courses every semester.

Drop/Add

What if you start a class and then decide that you don't like it? Maybe the course covers material that you're already familiar with. Maybe it's too challenging. Maybe the professor or teacher does not meet your expectations. Or maybe you have more course work than you can handle. To cover these possibilities, a college may have a drop/add option. Under drop/add, *a student can attend a course for a week or two before deciding whether to take it or to drop it and substitute another course in its place.* This is a significant opportunity. Colleges offer many courses—far too many for a single student to take in four years. It's a waste of time and money to take a course that's uninteresting, redundant, or over your head. Use the drop/add option if you feel it's appropriate.

Make sure you have an alternate course in mind when you use drop/add. Some students don't think through this process. They just drop a course without adding another. This may put them behind in acquiring the credits needed to graduate on time, or forces them to make up for the lost credits by having to attend a summer session. It may also cause you to fall below the required number of courses to be considered a full-time student. This may affect your ability to receive scholarship or tuition assistance funding.

Exams

Colleges post final-exam schedules each term. The exam may not be held in the room where your class met; it may also be scheduled on a different day of the week or time. Double-check the schedule, and then be there on time. Scheduling makeup exams is difficult.

Making Healthy Lifestyle Choices

In college, a healthy lifestyle, like a healthy GPA, requires making some choices. Staying physically fit keeps you alert for your classes. You'll also need to deal with interpersonal relationships, such as getting along with roommates.

Stay Healthy

College will put many demands on you—you cannot afford the time to be sick! So don't take good health for granted. You cannot make the most of your college experience if your body is not functioning well.

Eat Well

Eating a well-balanced diet can be hard once you're on your own. Constant snacking is a temptation for some people, because at college you are always studying or running somewhere. People talk about the "Freshman 15," meaning the 10–15 pounds that the typical freshman puts on because of all the snack food he or she consumes. Try to eat three well-balanced meals every day. It will help you stay alert and energetic. Do not depend on caffeine from coffee or energy drinks to get through the down times—caffeine is addictive. Keep your intakes of salt, fat, and sugar at moderate levels. For expert information about nutrition and eating right, visit *www.foodpyramid.com*.

Exercise Regularly

If you are used to working out, keep doing so. Find a regular time to go to the gym, and write it down in your schedule. Working out can also help you keep your weight down. Table 5.1 shows various activities and how many calories they burn in one hour of activity, based on the person's weight.

As a general goal, you should aim for at least 60 minutes of physical activity every day. The number of calories you burn may vary widely depending on the exercise, intensity level, and your individual situation.

If you haven't usually worked out in a gym, this might be a good time to start. However, you don't need a gym workout to keep physically fit. If you walk to class each day, especially if you are on a large campus, that's probably enough. Bicycling, running, swimming, or just getting on a treadmill are also great ways to exercise.

Independent physical activity is an important asset that stimulates brain function in an academic environment.

Courtesy of Erik Isakson/Corbis Images

LESSON 1   Adjusting to College Life

Table 5.1 Physical Activities and Calories Burned

ACTIVITY (1-HOUR DURATION)	WEIGHT OF PERSON AND CALORIES BURNED		
	160 lbs. (73 kg.)	200 lbs. (91 kg.)	240 lbs. (109 kg.)
Aerobics, low impact	365	455	545
Basketball game	584	728	872
Bicycling, < 10 mph, leisure	292	364	436
Bowling	219	273	327
Canoeing	256	319	382
Football, touch or flag	584	728	872
Hiking	438	546	654
Ice skating	511	637	763
Resistance (weight) training	365	455	545
Running, 5 mph	606	755	905
Skiing, cross-country	496	619	741
Softball or baseball	365	455	545
Stair treadmill	657	819	981
Swimming, laps	423	528	632
Volleyball	292	364	436
Walking, 2 mph	204	255	305

Adapted from Ainsworth, B. E., et. al., 2011, *Compendium of Physical Activities: A Second Update of Codes and MET V1*; 43:1575.

Tobacco, Alcohol, and Illegal Drugs

If you do not smoke now, don't let the stresses of college be the reason for starting. Although partying and alcohol are part of life on most college campuses, do not feel you have to join in the drinking. You can have a great time without it.

Drinking alcohol is a bad idea. First, underage drinking is illegal. Second, excessive drinking is a health risk. Finally, getting drunk can cause you, at best, to do things that will embarrass you the next day. At worst, it can cause you to do things that put your life, or maybe someone else's, at risk. Alcohol abuse is a major factor in campus sexual assaults and rapes. According to one study, as many as 1,400 college student deaths a year are linked to alcohol.

As for illegal drugs, the answer is simple: Don't use them, ever! If you think you need drugs to get through college, you need to seek professional medical assistance, and you probably are not ready for college!

Relationship Problems: Coping with Roommates

One of the biggest challenges for college students is relationships, and one of the first and most important relationship challenges involves roommates. Think about it: For many years, you have probably lived with the same people—your family. They may not be perfect, but you know their quirks. You have adjusted to them, and they have adjusted to you.

Suddenly, you have to live with a stranger whose habits, likes, and dislikes may be quite different from your own. A roommate may want to listen to music when you want to sleep, entertain visitors when you want to study, or sleep when you finally have a chance to relax and talk.

As noted above, your college will select your first roommate. It will make this decision based on information you provide regarding your likes and dislikes. So the first step in finding a compatible roommate is to give this information frankly and in enough detail so it will not be misinterpreted. Don't try to be cool—just be honest. If, hoping to sound impressive, you say you are a bodybuilder because you lifted weights once a year ago, you might end up with someone who seems to live in the gym.

If the college sends you your roommate's name ahead of time, make contact in person or over the phone. If you do not seem compatible, ask for a change. It is better to do it early rather than waiting until school starts, when the pressures of college life will be on top of you. You don't want to have to pack up and move to another room once classes have started.

Here are some other tips for good relations with roommates:

1. *Wait until all your roommates arrive before dividing up space*—Claiming space because you were there first is not a good way to start a relationship.

2. *Respect pet peeves*—If a roommate hates to see toothpaste in the sink, be courteous and don't leave messes. Little things can strengthen or destroy relationships.

3. *Air grievances politely*—If your roommate does something that annoys you, bring it up in a nice way. He or she may not even be aware of what's bothering you.

4. *Don't buy things jointly*—If you need a toaster oven for your room, one of you should buy and own it. Don't split the cost. This will make it easier to divide possessions at the end of the year.

5. *Be careful about rooming with friends from high school*—unless you know your lifestyles are compatible. You could ruin a perfectly good friendship.

6. *Divide housekeeping tasks fairly*—Develop and agree on a schedule for cleaning, cooking, and other chores.

7. *Work out a study and sleeping schedule that everyone in the room can live with*—If necessary, do your studying in a quiet place such as a library rather than in your room.

Managing Stress and Preventing Burnout

Adjusting to college life is exciting, but it can also be difficult—no doubt about it. You need to protect your mental as well as physical health during your college experience. Here are some ideas on how to prevent two common, related threats to a college student's well-being: stress and burnout.

Stress

Stress is *a mentally or an emotionally upsetting condition that occurs in response to outside influences*. Stress can have both physical and psychological effects.

For many college students, the greatest source of physical stress is fatigue. You will have a lot to do at college. You may have to stay up all night at times during a term to study for an exam or to write a paper. You may also stay up late for parties or other social events. You may travel home some weekends. You may not eat as well as you should, and this reduces your energy level.

Psychological stress comes from being away from home, feeling pressured to accomplish a lot in a little time, preparing for exams and writing papers, and dealing with social pressures.

Other sources of stress might include family emergencies, financial problems, difficulties with a boyfriend or girlfriend, or problems with a job. Though not related to school, they can complicate your already stressful college life.

The first step in dealing with stress is to identify exactly what's causing it. For example, if relationship problems are causing the stress, what is the real source? Is it your roommate? Or is your boyfriend or girlfriend making you irritable, and you're just taking it out on your roommate? Is the source of stress an overly demanding professor? On the other hand, is it the ineffective use of time management and poor study habits?

Burnout

One common result of stress in college is burnout, *the feeling of being worn out and unable to carry on usual activities*. A person with burnout often forces himself or herself to keep going to the point of physical and emotional exhaustion. Symptoms of burnout include irritability, anxiety, feelings of hopelessness, and lack of motivation and enthusiasm. You may feel burnout if you believe that you've put more into something than you have received in return, whether it is a course, a job, or a relationship. In its most severe forms, burnout can lead to depression and suicide attempts.

Taking some preventive measures will reduce your risk of burnout. For example, it might not be wise to be a full-time student while holding a full-time job. That's a big load for anyone to carry. Don't take more courses, or harder courses, than you can handle. Set high expectations for yourself, but be realistic.

Tips for Managing Stress and Preventing Burnout

1. Maintain a balance among family, work, and play.

2. Find satisfying activities that take your mind off your schoolwork for a while—for example, join a campus service organization, play a sport, create art, play a musical instrument, or pursue a hobby.

3. Explore religion as a source of spiritual strength.

4. Don't be reluctant to seek help—go to family members or trusted friends first. If that doesn't work, seek professional assistance from the health or counseling center.

5. Ask yourself these questions each day:

   • Have I had fun? This could be something as simple as enjoying a good meal or a great joke.

   • Have I done something hard but worthwhile? If you haven't, you may be letting the hard things pile up—if you have to do all the hard things at once, your stress level will grow.

   • Have I helped someone? Doing something for someone else will give you a feeling of satisfaction.

   • Have I done something physically strenuous? Get some exercise every day—on a busy day; a quick walk around the block should do it.

   • Have I been close with someone? Spend time with someone you care about, even if it's only a short phone call.

   • Have I been in touch with nature? Don't just glance at the sunset or notice the wind—stop somewhere to appreciate the beauty around you, if only for a short time.

Fight stress and burnout by planning to spend time with people you care about.
Courtesy of Stockbroker/Alamy

A small amount of anxiety is normal. It's even beneficial. For example, if you are totally relaxed before a test, you may not perform as well as you otherwise would. On the other hand, too much anxiety is disruptive. It interferes with your concentration. The campus health center will have one or more experts to help you deal with stress, depression, and burnout.

There is also help online provided by the National Institutes of Health at *http://www.nlm.nih.gov/medlineplus/tutorials/managingstress/htm/index.htm* and the American Academy of Family Physicians at *http://familydoctor.org/familydoctor/en/prevention-wellness/emotional-wellbeing/mental-health/stress-how-to-cope-better-with-lifes-challenges.printerview.all.html*.

The Importance of Personal Accountability

When it comes to meeting deadlines, following campus policies, being academically honest, or maintaining a healthy lifestyle, personal accountability is key. Accountability is *being answerable for the outcomes of your words and actions*. No one expects small children to be accountable; they're too young. Adolescence involves a growing sense of accountability. Being an adult, however, means being fully accountable, accepting responsibility and consequences of an action.

The importance of being accountable is a hard lesson for many students to learn. If you sign up for a course and then skip classes or don't study enough, you will do poorly on exams. You might even fail. You are responsible for that failure. Don't expect your professor to be sympathetic to your excuses. You may have been able to talk your way out of trouble in high school, but that strategy won't work in college.

Other adults in positions of authority on campus will also expect you to be accountable. For example, your academic adviser will expect you to prepare for meetings. You'll need to become familiar with the course offerings for the next term, know the requirements for graduation, and come to your appointment with a list of courses you want to take. Your residential adviser will expect you to be accountable for your actions in the dorm. If you have a scholarship, the organization giving you the scholarship will hold you accountable for any requirements connected with it, such as maintaining a certain GPA.

Think about all the decisions you will make at college regarding courses you will take, friends you'll make, organizations you may join, and how you will spend your free time and study time. All these decisions will have consequences. Enjoy your college experience by making mature decisions, and enjoying the results of your effort.

CHECKPOINTS

Lesson 1 Review

Using complete sentences, answer the following questions on a sheet of paper.

1. What are three types of campus organizations? What are their functions?

2. List three types of resources on campus available to help and protect students.

3. What residential options can you expect to have at college?

4. Why should you have a good relationship with your academic adviser?

5. List some of the deadlines you must be aware of at college.

6. Explain ways to maintain your physical and mental health in college.

7. Name five things you should do to have a good relationship with your college roommate.

8. What are some questions that you should ask yourself every day to make sure you are not becoming a victim of stress or burnout?

APPLYING COLLEGE LIVING SKILLS

9. Reread the paragraph you wrote under Quick Write on what you think will be the biggest challenges in adjusting to college. Now that you've studied this lesson, would you change any of the challenges you listed? If so, which ones?

10. Go to the website of a college that you think you would like to attend. Find a list of campus organizations. Which ones do you think sound interesting?

Quick Write

_____

_____

Pick three subjects you can imagine majoring in at college. Why do you think those majors fit you? What careers will they lead to?

Learn About

- how college majors relate to personal interests and desires
- basic areas of college study
- careers associated with possible majors
- a six-step process for selecting a college major

""If you don't try something complex, you are forever doing something trivial."

Anonymous

How College Majors Relate to Personal Interests and Desires

At some point early in your college years, you will have to choose a major—your primary subject of study and academic specialty. You won't need to make this important decision right away. At most schools, students can wait until their junior year to declare a major. That gives them time to get used to college course work and to think more about their career interests and preferences.

Selecting the right major is an important decision—almost as important as selecting the right college. Therefore, it's a good idea to start weighing the options as early as possible. Your major should be a subject that interests you so much that you want to learn more and more about it—not only while you're in college but throughout your life.

Maybe you had a high school course that opened your eyes to the fascinating complexities of physics. Or perhaps a relative who's an actor has turned you on to the arts. Your favorite book, a biography of a US President, might have sparked an interest in political science. Or perhaps Wall Street and the world of high finance fascinate you, and you want to study business and economics. But it's also possible that you don't know where your career interests lie. You haven't taken time to think about it. Or you may have so many interests that you're not ready to narrow them down to one or two. As college approaches, how do you choose?

A good place to start is to listen to people who know you well. Your parents, guardian, or other relatives will probably have some ideas on what you should major in. Your high school guidance counselor may also be able to guide you. And when you get to college, you'll have a faculty adviser who will help you choose the right major. You won't have to do it alone.

Listen to all these people, and ask them lots of questions. But remember also: This is your decision. You're the one who has to live your life.

That's why, when it's time to choose a major, you need to think seriously about what kind of person you are. You need to know yourself. You can approach this task in several ways.

For example, in Chapter 3, Lesson 2, "Self-Discovery," you discovered that you have a preferred learning style, which helps people determine their interests in different subject areas. You learned that where you direct your energy, how you process information, how you make decisions, and how you organize your life help determine your personality.

Vocabulary

- major
- minor
- elective
- core requirements
- prerequisites

An interest in chemistry and lab work can lead you to careers in a variety of scientific fields.

Courtesy of Tom Grill/Corbis Images

You also learned that learning styles and personal interests are often associated with specific careers.

If, for example, you enjoy leading and speaking, you would probably do well in a major that can lead to a career in business, management, or the armed forces. A major in business or economics, or perhaps in history or a foreign language would prepare you for these careers. If you're a "creator," an artistic person, you may lean toward a career in the arts or teaching, and might consider majoring in art, education, English, or music.

You can also approach the decision about a major based on your personal interests. You may have discovered after completing the interest inventory from Chapter 3, Lesson 2 that you are mechanically inclined. Maybe you should major in mechanical engineering. Do you love to draw? If so, a major in architecture or art history might be right. If you are an athlete and want to coach or play professionally, you will probably want to major in physical education.

Don't be too narrow in your approach to choosing a major. What if you love art but want to work in business? There's no reason why you can't study both business and art. It just might take a little longer. For a great career in business, you could decide to get a master's degree after you've earned your undergraduate degree. This may require enrolling in a business school or college that offers an advanced degree in business. If you do this, you won't need to take a full load of business courses. You could earn an undergraduate degree in art. Your academic major, *a subject or field of study representing a student's primary interest and which includes a large share of classes*, would be in art. The remainder of your classes would be in business—what you'll focus on in business or graduate school. As an art major, you will acquire knowledge and skills that you enjoy and can use throughout your life. You will have a broad-based education that will serve you well as a businessperson, because you'll be able to talk knowledgeably with all kinds of people. You may even find unusual ways to combine business and art— for example, by becoming an art dealer or the head of an art studio.

Choosing a Minor

So how would you prepare for graduate work in business while majoring in art? The best way is by choosing a minor, or *a secondary focus for your academic studies*, in business. A minor in business does not require as many courses as a major does, but it will give you a good understanding of marketing, finance, and other subjects essential for business. A minor can also help prepare you for a second career.

For example, you may major in physical education because you're aiming for a career as a coach. But what if you want to switch careers after working in the sports field for 10 years or so? A minor in social work, business, religious studies, or any number of other subjects could help you prepare for a second career after your coaching days are over.

When you major in a subject, you will need to complete a certain number of required courses in your field. For example, as a studio art major, you might have to take courses in such topics as art history, drawing, graphic design, illustration, and digital media. Someone majoring in business might be required to take courses in accounting, economics, statistics, and leadership, as well as finance and marketing.

Your college minor allows you to focus on a second area that interests you.
Courtesy of Jose Luis Pelaez, Inc./Corbis Images

Together, these required courses may account for more than half the courses you'll take during your four years of college. This is why you should declare a major by your sophomore and no later than your junior year. If you wait longer, you might not have time to complete all the required courses by the time you graduate.

A course that is not required is called an elective, *a course you choose, or elect, to take*. Electives round out, or complement, your major. For example, if you're majoring in French, you might want to take an elective class in Spanish to increase your understanding of European languages. If you're majoring in US history, you might want to take an elective class in Native American Art. Or you might want to major in political science and take an elective French class; this would ensure you have language skills that could help you in a career in international affairs.

As you ponder these options, don't forget the main point: You want to be excited about learning. Your major and your minor should be subjects that you want to take that will help you pursue a career in the field of your choice.

Basic Areas of College Study

Every college offers a different selection of majors. The number of choices depends primarily on the size of the college. A large university may offer more than 150 majors; a small college may offer only a few dozen.

Whatever size school you choose, your choice of majors will fall into one of four basic categories: technical and engineering; arts and humanities; social sciences and human sciences; and science. These categories are listed in Table 5.2. Under each category are possible majors and examples of the typical interests of students who major in these fields. (Some majors fall into more than one category.)

These lists are far from complete. They simply give you an idea of the kinds of majors, interests, and skills that fall under the four basic categories of study.

Careers Associated With Possible Majors

Every major prepares students for one or more careers. A major in architecture would naturally lead to a career as an architect, and a major in fashion design could lead to a career as a fashion designer.

But don't take these associations too literally. A major in architecture could also lead you to a career in city planning, landscape design, or business (for example, managing an architecture firm). Or you could teach architecture. If you majored in fashion design, you might find employment with a New York design house, be a buyer for a retail-clothing chain, become a model, or help women in a developing country learn how to design clothes for export. You could even start your own clothing-design business. It all depends on where your interests and abilities lie.

Table 5.3 lists careers that fall under each of the four categories of majors. This list, like the lists above, is not complete. For example, if you like learning about technical and scientific subjects, but prefer studying English to math and physics; you may find a career in technical writing a possible goal. You and your guidance counselor may be able to think of more from the information gathered from your preferred learning styles or completed interest inventory.

Table 5.2 Basic Areas of College Study

Category	Sample Majors	Examples of Interests or Skills of Students Majoring in This Area
Technical and Engineering	• Agricultural technology • Architecture • Aviation management • Civil engineering • Computer science • Electrical engineering • Environmental studies • Medical technology	• Repairing electrical appliances or electronic equipment • Building houses • Developing computer hardware • Working on cars • Preserving the environment • Solving mechanical problems
Arts and Humanities	• Advertising • Art history • English • Foreign languages • History • Music • Religious studies	• Playing in an orchestra or band • Drawing • Writing poetry or short stories • Acting • Taking photographs • Learning languages
Social Sciences and Human Services	• Anthropology • Business • Child development • Communication • Criminology • Economics • Education • Human resource management • Journalism • Psychology	• Working in parks or recreation facilities • Tutoring or mentoring • Helping people solve their personal problems • Working in a religious setting • Helping people who have disabilities • Supervising a project or team
Science	• Astronomy • Biology • Computer science • Forestry • Geology • Nutrition • Statistics	• Doing lab experiments • Designing models • Programming computers • Solving mathematical problems • Playing chess

Reprinted from *Selecting a College Major: Exploration and Decision Making*, edited by Virginia N. Gordon and Susan J. Sears (2010), by permission of Pearson Education.

Table 5.3 Occupations by Area of College Major

Technical and Engineering

- Agricultural educator
- Animal breeder or trainer
- Aviator
- Computer software engineer
- Computer data systems analyst
- Construction engineer
- Dental technologist
- Electrical engineer
- Electronics technician
- Environmental designer
- Fish and wildlife manager
- Fitness trainer
- Forest ranger
- Geologist
- Industrial arts teacher
- Industrial engineer
- Mechanical engineer
- Oceanographer
- Scientific photographer

Arts and Humanities

- Actor
- Architect
- Art teacher
- Artist
- Cartoonist
- Dance therapist
- Digital graphic designer
- Editor
- English teacher
- Film editor
- Graphic designer
- Historian
- Interior designer
- Interpreter
- Musician
- Orchestra conductor
- Writer

Social Sciences and Human Services

- Athletic director or coach
- Athletic trainer
- Chef
- Clergy member
- Clinical psychologist
- Criminologist
- Dental hygienist
- Detective
- Dietitian
- Family counselor
- Geographer
- Historian
- Librarian
- Motion picture director
- Nurse
- Park naturalist
- Police officer
- Social worker
- Speech or hearing pathologist
- Teacher or professor

Science

- Aeronautical engineer
- Airplane pilot
- Astronomer
- Biochemist
- Biomedical engineer
- Chemist
- City and regional planner
- Computer scientist
- Dentist
- Geologist
- Horticulturist
- Marine biologist
- Mathematician
- Metallurgist
- Optometrist
- Pharmacist
- Physician or surgeon
- Sociologist
- Statistician
- Veterinarian

Reprinted from *Selecting a College Major: Exploration and Decision Making*, edited by Virginia N. Gordon and Susan J. Sears (2010), by permission of Pearson Education.

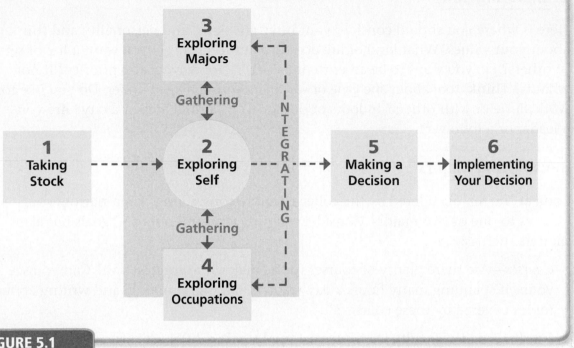

FIGURE 5.1

A Model for Choosing a College Major

Reprinted from *Selecting a College Major: Exploration and Decision Making*, edited by Virginia N. Gordon and Susan J. Sears (2010), by permission of Pearson Education.

A Six-Step Process for Selecting a College Major

Figure 5.1 illustrates the six steps involved in choosing a college major. It provides a handy way of organizing your thoughts about some of the issues and decisions covered in this lesson and in previous lessons about college and careers. Following these steps should help you come up with a major—and possibly a minor—that will be right for you. You might also be able to adapt this six-step approach for use when you face other major life decisions.

1. Taking Stock

Start the decision-making process by figuring out what you know, what you don't, and what further knowledge you need. Ask yourself questions such as:

- Do I know which career I want to pursue?
- Do I know which major will best prepare me for that career, or do I need to do some research?
- Am I undecided about my career but sure of where my interests lie and which major I will enjoy?
- Am I unsure about everything at this point?

Remember, if you responded "yes" to the last question, don't worry. Few high school students are sure about their college majors.

2. Exploring Self

Here is where you should consider your interests, skills, and personality and think about your values. What kind of life do you want to lead? Do you want a life of service to others? Do you want to be an entrepreneur? Is money your top priority? If not, what is? Think, too, about the type of work environment you prefer. Do you like to work alone or with others? Indoors or outdoors? In a rural area or a city? Are you a leader or a follower?

3. Exploring Majors

Look at the majors offered by the colleges you're considering. Then narrow your choices to one or two majors. Consider not only your interests and goals but also matters such as:

- *Courses*—Are there plenty of courses in the major that interest you? Can you see yourself spending many hours a day reading, talking, thinking, and writing about topics covered by these courses?

- *Faculty*—Are the faculty in this major good teachers? (You can often find reviews of college faculty on the Internet, but be careful not to be influenced by biased comments without supporting specifics.) Are they knowledgeable? Where did they receive their degrees? Have they published articles or books in their areas of expertise? Do the professors teach most of the classes, or do they rely on teaching assistants? Do faculty spend time advising and mentoring students? Have they actually worked in their professional areas, or have they always worked in an academic environment?

- *Students*—Are the students in this major interesting? Are they people you feel at ease with?

- *Class size*—How big are classes? Are there enough students in this major so that you will feel comfortable, but not so many that you'll feel lost if it becomes necessary to get help or individualized assistance?

- *Graduates*—Have recent graduates who've majored in this area gone on to interesting careers? Will it be easy to find a job, or to get into a good graduate school after graduation?

- *Requirements*—What are the core requirements, or *required classes for majoring in this area*? For example, what kind of grade point average does this major require? What prerequisites, or *courses required to enter a certain field of study*, do you need? Can you meet them? How heavy is the course load? Will you be able to juggle the required courses with electives and any job or family responsibilities you might have?

It's not possible to answer all these questions fully in advance. But they're things you should think about. When you're talking with your guidance counselor, interviewing with college admissions officers, making campus visits, and doing your research, ask questions about topics such as these.

4. Exploring Careers

Once you've narrowed your choice of majors, examine the careers that these majors might lead to. You might select a major directly related to a career that you have already decided to pursue. Such majors include, for example, physical therapy, electrical engineering, or elementary education. Or you can choose a major that provides a general background that will prepare you to enter a variety of professions. Such majors include history, English, or philosophy, which can lead to a career as a researcher, writer, or lawyer.

5. Making a Decision

By this point, you should be ready to commit yourself to one of your alternatives. As you do so, remember that there is no perfect choice. Every decision will require trade-offs. An engineering major may be more academically demanding than some other majors, but it may give you greater possibilities for earnings upon graduation as well as more opportunities for advancement. A physical education major may be easier, but the chances for earning lots of money, as well as the variety of job choices and opportunities for growth, may be limited.

Questions to Ask Yourself When Choosing a Major

Once you've identified your probable major, test it against the following questions. If you can answer "yes" to these questions, this major may be the one for you:

- Does this major match my skills and interests?
- Are the courses interesting?
- Have I done reasonably well in similar courses in high school?
- Are careers related to this major interesting and within my reach?
- Am I comfortable in the work environments of careers associated with this major?
- Are the careers associated with this major consistent with my values?
- Do I meet the academic and other prerequisites for this major?
- Do I think I can do the work?
- Do I have the time to fulfill all the requirements?
- Do I feel good about my choice?

If you prefer being outdoors to working in an office, take that into account when choosing your major.

Courtesy of Gaetano/Corbis Images

6. Implementing Your Decision

Once you've decided on a major, contact your faculty adviser and start the formal process of committing to the major. This will involve registering in the department of your major (for example, chemistry department, philosophy department, education department), meeting with an adviser in that department, and signing up for courses.

But remember, your decision isn't set in stone. You can change it, assuming you still have time to complete the requirements for another major. And even if switching majors means you have to stay in school an extra term or year, it might be worth it in the long run.

After you make and implement your decision, continue to think about it. Does it feel right? As you take more and more courses, are you still excited about this major? Are your grades as good as you thought they'd be? Can you still see yourself in a career that this major will prepare you for? If so, you are on your way. If not, start over. Reexamine your interests and ambitions.

If, after careful thought and consultation with adults, you find a better fit, don't be afraid to make a change. Base each new decision on the self-knowledge and experience you have already gained.

✔ CHECKPOINTS

Lesson 2 Review

Using complete sentences, answer the following questions on a sheet of paper.

1. Write down the top three multiple intelligences from the Multiple Intelligences Survey you took in Chapter 3, Lesson 2. Based on these, list three majors that should fit you well.

2. From the skills and interest inventory tool you completed, write down three interests areas in which you scored high. Then list a college major that would fit each of those interests.

3. Write down three careers that you might like to pursue. List three possible majors that would prepare you for each of those careers. Now compare this list with the lists you made in response to Questions 1 and 2. Are the majors you chose the same or at least similar? Why or why not?

4. What are the six steps in the process of choosing a college major?

APPLYING SKILLS IN CHOOSING A MAJOR

5. List the three majors that are the most interesting to you at this point. Then go to the websites of five colleges on your priority list. Do they offer the majors you're considering? If so, find out the prerequisites for a major in those areas, what kinds of courses the college offers in your major areas, the size of the departments offering the majors, the backgrounds of the faculty (for example, which schools they attended and when, and what they have published), and where alumni who've majored in that field are employed. This information will help you select a college as well as a major.

Planning Your Schedule

Quick Write

_____

_____

Do you sometimes have trouble getting things done on time? Do you put off certain tasks? Make a list of the kinds of work you tend to put off, and the reasons you put it off.

Learn About

- the importance of time management
- procrastination and how to beat it
- managing your college schedule

"Don't say you don't have enough time. You have exactly the same number of hours per day that were given to Helen Keller, Pasteur, Michelangelo, Mother Teresa, Leonardo da Vinci, Thomas Jefferson, and Albert Einstein."

H. Jackson Brown, Jr., American author of best-selling book, *Life's Little Instruction Book*

The Importance of Time Management

When you get to college, you'll enter a completely new world—a world in which you will have more control of your time than ever before. This freedom and independence will probably feel thrilling; however, to succeed in this new environment with this new freedom, you will also have to exercise your skills at time management, or *keeping control of your time in a way that best enables you to achieve your goals according to your priorities.*

Take a moment to think about these questions: Do you make the best use of every minute? Do you meet your deadlines? Or do you postpone some tasks until it's almost too late, and then work in a frenzy to get them done? Have you ever planned ahead enough to ask a teacher for an extension on a deadline for a major assignment?

Time-management skills are important for everyone—not just college students. You can learn and practice time management while you're still in high school. Time management includes setting priorities, planning, fighting procrastination, eliminating distractions, and eliminating activities that don't help you meet your goals.

When you manage your time well, you reach those goals; you get things done. You also maintain order in your life and reduce stress. On the other hand, when you don't manage your time well, you frequently feel stressed and under pressure; you bounce from activity to activity feeling unprepared and constantly trying to catch up; you don't accomplish tasks as well as you could; and you waste time. Many people do not realize that managing time will help create time for things you *want* to do as well as things you *have* to do. Using time-management skills can make your life a lot easier.

Setting Priorities

You may think people succeed because they're rich, talented, or just lucky. Those things do help. However, one of the most significant reasons for many people's success is much simpler: They know how to make good use of their time. They know how to set priorities. Priority is *the value a person places on an activity, a goal, or another demand on time or energy*. A high priority is *something that you consider more important than other things*. You can't do everything. There's just not enough time. So you have to make choices about what to do, or what to do first. Successful people know their priorities, and they manage their time with an eye toward achieving them.

Your priorities should reflect your goals—the things that are most important to you. For example, getting good grades is a goal for most college students, but meeting people and enjoying new experiences are important, too. Sometimes these priorities will go hand-in-hand—for instance, you might make some friends through working on a group project or by joining a productive study group. However, quite often your academic priorities and your social priorities will not fit together, and you will need to make choices about how to spend your time. To be a successful college student, you'll need to manage your time in a way that reflects your academic priorities and helps you meet your goals.

In college, you can expect to spend far less time *in class* than you do in high school but far more time studying *out of class*. The average undergraduate student takes four to five courses per semester. Most courses meet for three hours a week, either twice a week for an hour and 15 minutes or three times a week for 50 minutes. A few classes meet for just two hours a week,

Vocabulary

- time management
- priority
- high priority
- procrastinate
- multitasking
- distractions

and some (especially science and engineering courses with labs) meet four or five hours a week. So instead of heading off to school five days a week at 7:00 a.m. and staying there until around 3:00 p.m., you'll spend only a few hours in class each day, often with two to four hours in between classes. You may even have days with no class at all. If you are taking courses online, you'll determine when you go to class, and, to a great degree, how long you spend in the online classroom.

At first, you may feel as though you have lots of time on your hands. But don't think you're in for the easy life. The reason you are in class fewer hours in college is to give you more time to study the material outside of class. Nearly all college experts advise college students to spend at least two hours studying for every hour spent in average classes. For more challenging classes, plan on three hours per class hour; for the toughest classes, plan on four.

For example, suppose you sign up for four average courses, and one hard course during the first term of your freshman year. One course meets two hours a week, three meet three hours a week, and one meets four hours a week, for an average of three hours a week, equating to 15 hours total. This is a common course load for freshmen who plan to complete college in four years. Table 5.4 illustrates the amount of studying you should expect to do to succeed in these courses.

As the table shows, even though you would spend only 15 hours a week in class (far less than you probably spend in high school), you will need to study outside of class 33 hours a week, for a total of 48 hours per week. And that is just your weekly work. You will need to make additional time along the way for large projects, term papers, and exams. This change in the ratio of in-class hours to out-of-class studying is one of the major differences between high school and college academic life. There are no study halls in college, and you won't have your parents or guardian around to ask whether you've done your homework. That volume and consistency of studying on your own will require self-discipline.

Table 5.4 Hours in Class Versus Hours Studying

Difficulty	Hours in Class/Week (#credits)		Hours Studying/Week		Total Hours/Week
Average	3	+	6 (3 hrs. × 2)	=	9
Average	3	+	6 (3 hrs × 2)	=	9
Average	2	+	4 (2 hrs. × 2)	=	6
Average	4	+	8 (4 hrs. × 2)	=	12
More Challenging	3	+	9 (3 hrs.× 3)	=	12
TOTALS	15	+	33	=	48

Managing your time, however, doesn't mean giving up fun. A well-balanced schedule includes time for play as well as for work. Too much of one and not enough of the other can make for a boring life. A healthy combination of the two will prove more rewarding than all partying and play.

Time management isn't just for college students, however. It's a skill you can use even now in high school, and it will be a priceless skill throughout life. This lesson provides some well-tested tips on how to use your time well.

Part of preparing for college is learning how to manage time properly, balancing learning with your social activities.

Courtesy of Alix Minde/Corbis Images

Procrastination and How to Beat It

Did you ever wait until the last minute to write a paper and then work on it all night? And did you swear that the next time you'd start earlier? Did it work? If you're like most people, you didn't learn from that unhappy experience. You repeated your mistake—if not the next time, then soon thereafter. One of the most significant obstacles to good time management is the tendency to procrastinate, *to put off doing something, especially out of habitual carelessness or laziness.*

Many people think that using time well means working all the time. But what do you really mean by "working"? Are you watching TV while reading your history assignment? If so, you're not concentrating fully on your assignment. You're not learning effectively. What's more, you're probably not enjoying the TV show as much as you would if you didn't have a book on your lap. You're truly wasting time—spending it and getting nothing in return.

Alternatively, you might be working well, but working on the wrong thing. For example, if you're working on your art project, which is due next week, rather than your English paper, which is due tomorrow, you are not setting proper academic priorities or managing your time well.

Why People Procrastinate

Why do people procrastinate? There are many reasons:

- *Superhuman expectations*—You put more on your calendar than you can possibly accomplish, hoping that by sheer willpower you'll get it all done. When you discover that you can't do it all, you eliminate the things that are the hardest—but those may be the most important.

- *An incorrect view of your ability*—You come up with all kinds of reasons why you just aren't good enough. For example, you tell yourself that smart people don't have to study, and everybody is smart but you—so why even try? In fact, everyone has to study. People may *seem* smart because they are disciplined and manage their time well. People are not born with calculus formulas in their heads. Most who excel have learned to use their time well and to study effectively.

- *Fear of failing*—Perhaps you've done poorly in a difficult subject in the past. You're scared that's going to happen again, so you give up without trying.

- *Emotional blocks*—You know that it's already past time to start working on your science project, but you don't know how to start. You feel guilty because you have wasted so much time. You feel defeated before you even begin. "I might as well just play some video games for an hour or so," you say. "They will get me relaxed, and then I can start." Soon other distractions come along. Before you know it, you are really behind. It's a vicious cycle: Delay leads to greater delay.

It might be helpful to think of time management not as a way to get more work done but as a way to make more time for fun. If you get your work done on time, you will have more "free time" that truly is free. You won't be out at a movie with friends thinking in the back of your mind, "Man, I really should be working on that paper." That's no fun.

How to Beat Procrastination

Procrastination is such a widespread problem that many experts have made entire careers advising people how to beat this dangerous habit. These experts agree that the first step in using your time better is *to become aware of how you use it now*. They recommend an experiment in which you keep track of your time in 15-minute blocks over an entire week. This process shows you how much time you really spend watching TV, playing games, texting, surfing the Internet, or talking on the phone. You may be surprised at how much time you waste. Once you have tracked your use of time for a whole week, you can begin to recognize areas where you tend to procrastinate or waste time in other ways, and you can begin to make changes to your studying, working, and recreating habits.

To fight procrastination, try these strategies:

- *Look at each task in terms of your long-range goals*—Will getting an A on this test help raise your grade point average (GPA) and increase the chances you'll get into the college at the top of your list? If you keep your long-term goals in mind, you'll be more likely to focus on short-term tasks.

- *Think positive thoughts*—When you're ready to study, push negative thoughts out of your mind. Tell yourself that you are growing and becoming more competent. Look your fears in the face. If you procrastinate because you're afraid you'll fail, be honest about it. Make up your mind you are going to overcome this fear by studying and preparing every day.

- *Set a regular time for study*—Work when you're most alert. That's when you'll be most productive. Some people work better in the mornings; others work better in the evenings. Determine your personal best time to study, and build your schedule around it. Once you've done so, tell your friends about your schedule. Give them a certain time when they can call—say, between 8 p.m. and 9 p.m. You'll then be able to enjoy phone conversations without being distracted from your studies, and you'll also be able to study without feeling you are missing out on time talking with friends.

- *Set a regular place for study*—Having a suitable place to study is essential. It might be the library or your room. It might be a coffee house, as long as you find a quiet place in the corner and resist the temptation to join some friends that drop in. In choosing a place, don't kid yourself—unless you are very unusual, you can't study best in front of the TV or while texting with friends.

- *Allow time for having fun, for downtime, and even for sleeping*—Don't get involved in too many outside activities, but don't turn into a bookworm, either. You'll have many options for worthwhile, productive activities on campus. However, not all of them will contribute to your long-term goals or highest priorities. Think carefully before you decide to join a club, a music group, or a team. Each choice will have pros and cons. How much time will it take? Will it help you grow and learn? Does it fit with your other commitments and goals?

"No" is a powerful word. Use it. But at the same time, give yourself time to explore new activities. If something ends up taking too much time, find a way to bow out gracefully.

Don't over-program your life. Spend some time every day doing what you want to do. This principle includes exercise: Physical fitness is essential (see Chapter 5, Lesson 1 for more about the importance of physical fitness). Set aside time for friends and family. Don't overlook time for spiritual development. And don't manage your schedule to the point that you lose sight of the important things in life.

Give yourself time to sleep, too. You can't get into a habit of staying up all night—whether to party or to study—and still expect to do your best.

LESSON 3 Planning Your Schedule

- *Break up big tasks into small ones, and set a time limit for each task*—If you have to write a paper, can you work on one segment tonight and another one tomorrow? If you finish a small segment each day, a term paper becomes nothing more than a series of small tasks.

  Next, decide how much time it should take to do each part. Push yourself to complete each part of the job in that time limit. Try to work more efficiently.

- *Jump in*—Sit down in your study area, take a deep breath, and plunge into your studies. You might not work at 100-percent efficiency from the beginning, but you will have made a start. Good students have a lot in common with athletes: Both need a warm-up period before they can function at their best.

- *Juggle tasks*—Your overall goal should be to organize your time so that you don't miss a deadline and are well prepared for the next. However, you should allow some leeway. Be creative in your approach to studying, and choose the method that best fits you.

  Some students, for example, have a "do it now" policy. They do simple tasks as soon as they receive them. They get them out of the way and off their "to-do" lists. Other students like to tackle the hardest task first. They find that doing so gives them a psychological boost.

  Another strategy is to practice multitasking, or *doing more than one thing at a time*. What things can you do simultaneously? For example, can you read a chapter in your biology text while you're waiting to use the printer in the library or riding on the bus? (As noted before, multitasking does not include counter-productive efforts to do multiple tasks, such as studying and watching TV at the same time.)

- *Be good to yourself*—Promise yourself small and large rewards for your accomplishments. Perhaps you've just spent two hours looking for articles on the Internet for a research paper. You've found what you need. Before you plunge into writing your paper, watch a TV program, go for a walk or a jog to collect your thoughts. Talk to a friend for a few minutes. Answer your e-mail.

  Also, think ahead to the rewards you will get when you finally complete a difficult task. You'll be able go to a movie or hang out with friends guilt-free, because you've finished your work. In addition, you'll be one step closer to successfully completing the course.

Try out these new study habits for 21 days. Focus on the ones that you think will be most helpful to you. By then, you'll be on the way to overcoming the habit of procrastination. If you're still having trouble, talk to your adviser or a professor about it. Show him or her what you have done, and ask if you're on the right track.

Most colleges realize that time management is a problem for new college students, so they give freshmen help. Visit your school's Learning Center or Academic Center (different schools give them different names) for tools and help with time management and study skills. Some colleges include information on time management in required

Some Common Distractions

Eliminating distractions, such as *activities, relationships, or thoughts that draw your attention or interest away from what you should be doing at the moment*, is an important part of managing your time. College students experience many distractions from studying such as the following:

- Phone calls
- Socializing, including social networking
- Watching television
- Spending too much time on the computer sending e-mails and instant messages
- Playing video or computer games.

If you avoid these activities when you are supposed to be studying, you can complete your assignments, feel less pressured, and still make time to have fun.

orientation classes for freshmen. George Mason University in Fairfax, Virginia, offers tips to students at *http://www.healthyexpectations.gmu.edu/rsrc_tm.htm*. You can find more information online, including time-management tips from other colleges, by typing "time management in college" into a search engine.

Managing Your College Schedule

College presents many challenges for students. The first few months of the freshman year can be particularly difficult—many students find it hard to manage their time. They become stressed out or even depressed. Their grades start to suffer.

Managing your time while in college begins with setting up your class schedule. You do this when you register for classes for the following semester. Among other things, you must consider which days each class meets, which building it meets in, where you will be immediately before the class, and how long it will take you to get there. If you're a student at a small college, this planning may not be such a problem. But at a large university, it can take 30 minutes or more to get from one location to another. You may have to take a bus, ride a bike, or even drive. And if you're living off campus, it can take even longer.

Managing your time in college begins with setting up your class schedule, and then fitting your other activities around it.

Courtesy of Scott Speakes/Corbis Images

After setting up your class schedule, fitting your other activities around your schedule will require using effective time management skills for you to be successful.

For example, say you schedule yourself for an English class that meets in the southwest corner of campus. You also want to take an anthropology course that meets at the other end of campus 10 minutes after your English class ends. But after considering the distance and checking the campus bus schedule, you realize you won't be able to make that class. Therefore, you may need to find another course that meets at a time that's more convenient for you. Or perhaps you decide to schedule the anthropology course for the time you wanted and find another section of the English class.

Another factor is the time of day classes meet: If you're an early riser, you may want to schedule your classes in the mornings. However, if you're a night owl, it might not be wise to schedule early morning classes that you won't be able to get up for.

Also consider whether you are the kind of person who likes to spread out your workload—your weekly studying—or the kind who prefers to get a lot in a large chunk of time. This preference might influence whether you spread out your class schedule and study hours or not. Some students also like to group their courses so they have a day or two off per week for studying—or working a part-time job. If you do so, however, be sure you have the self-discipline to use those large blocks of time productively.

You should also think about the number of credits and the balance of more difficult versus easier courses you take each semester. Don't schedule all your hard courses in the same semester if you can help it—try to spread them out over several semesters. Remember that those difficult courses will require more study time.

Once you have your class schedule worked out, you need to think about fitting in your other activities. To manage your time wisely, make out a schedule in advance, using the following five tips.

Five Tips for Managing Your College Schedule

1. Set Specific Academic and Personal Goals

If you know where you're going, it's a lot easier to determine what you need to do to get there. So write down your goals. For example, goals for your freshman year might be to:

- Earn at least a 3.25 GPA
- Make the college volleyball team
- Make two new friends
- Write for the school newspaper
- Decide on a major
- Get a summer internship

Look at your list at least weekly. Add or change short term goals as appropriate, but make sure they're realistic. Determine whether your activities are helping you meet your goals or interfering.

2. Create a Term Calendar That Lists Major Campus Events

Important things can be overlooked when you're focused on everyday demands. Don't forget the big picture. Get a term calendar and write down one-time things such as orientation week, homecoming and parents' weekends, vacations and term breaks, visits by guest speakers, and recruitment visits by employers. Keep the calendar handy and refer to it often.

3. Create a Weekly Schedule of Your Classes, Labs, Meetings, and Other Activities

In addition to a term calendar, get a weekly calendar that lets you enter activities by the hour. Your computer or phone probably has a calendar program that is easy to use. However, you might try using a planner book or just creating your own chart on paper. Write in all your classes and other regular activities, such as science and language labs, review sessions, or workouts. If you have a part-time job, put those hours in. Don't forget to set aside time do your laundry and clean your room. Schedule a regular time to relax—to read for pleasure, or go to a movie. Also, write in one-time activities as they come up. These might include a special meeting of your chemistry study group, a session with your faculty adviser, or coffee with a friend. Carry your weekly schedule with you all the time.

4. Decide on Specific Times to Work on Each Course

Block out regular times for study, and don't let other things on your agenda get in their way. Specify which courses you will study for at which times. For example, if you have sociology and art history classes on Tuesdays and Thursdays, plan to study for them on Mondays and Wednesdays. But don't forget: If you also do a little each day on those courses, you won't have to cram it all into two days.

5. Make a To-Do List for Each Day

Write down the things you *must* accomplish each day, followed by the things you'd *like* to get done if you can. Use a piece of paper, a 3-by-5 card, a notes app on your phone or computer, or whatever will be most convenient for you. Take it out several times a day and look at it—especially when you're thinking about what you should do next. No matter how well you plan your week in advance, you'll always have last-minute things to do—for example, making a quick trip to the store, stopping by your professor's office to ask a question, or meeting a friend from home who's in town for a day or two. These spur-of-the-moment activities can eat up your time. Set aside a few minutes every evening to enter these activities on your calendar and to-do list. You may be surprised at how much more efficiently you can complete different tasks with this little bit of planning each day.

A Sample Weekly College Schedule

Figure 5.2 shows a sample weekly calendar for a college student. It will give you an idea of the kinds of activities you'll need to include in your own schedule. Using your time well in college might be harder than it is in high school for several reasons.

The course work will be more challenging, your life will have less structure, and you'll have greater independence. At first, you may have trouble adjusting. However, if you learn to manage your time well in high school, you'll have taken a big step toward using it well in college. So don't procrastinate—start managing your time right now!

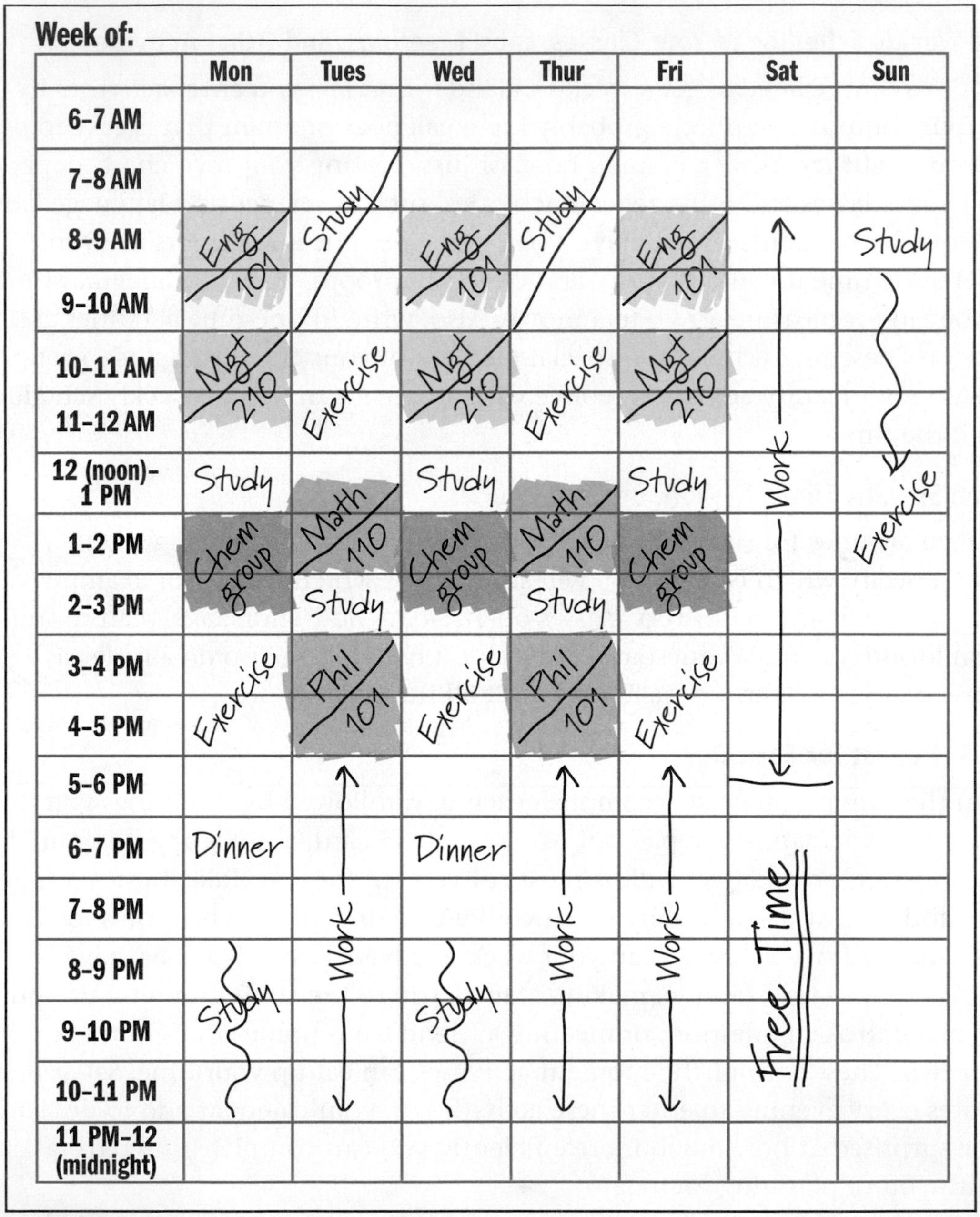

FIGURE 5.2

A Weekly College Calendar

Reprinted from *Cornerstone: Building on Your Best,* Concise Fourth Edition, edited by Robert M. Sherfield, Rhonda J. Montgomery, and Patricia G. Moody. (2005), by permission of Pearson Education.

✔ CHECKPOINTS

Lesson 3 Review

1. List some things involved in time management.

2. What are some benefits of managing your time well? What are some consequences of poor time management?

3. Is working all the time the same as managing time well? Why or why not?

4. Give two reasons why people procrastinate. Do these reasons apply to you?

5. Give three strategies for preventing procrastination that you think could work for you. Why do you think these might be successful?

6. List three activities in a college schedule.

7. What are some challenges in scheduling your college courses?

APPLYING SCHEDULING SKILLS

8. Think about how you'll plan your schedule when you get to college. Get a blank calendar for one week. Imagine five courses you will take in your first semester. Sketch out a possible schedule.

Courtesy of Brocreative/Shutterstock

Applying for Jobs

"The secret of getting ahead is getting started. The secret of getting started is breaking your complex overwhelming tasks into small manageable tasks, and then starting on the first one."

Mark Twain, American author and humorist

The Job Search Process

Write a few sentences about how you would look for a job. How will you go about finding openings? How will you convince a prospective employer that you are the best person for the job?

Learn About

- identifying your personal job preferences
- selling your skills to an employer
- how to organize a job search

"If you don't know where you are going, you'll end up someplace else."

Yogi Berra, New York Yankees' Hall of Fame catcher

Identifying Your Personal Job Preferences

Finding a job is not just a matter of searching the want or classified ads, *advertisements for job openings, services, or items for sale*. It's not a matter of making a few phone calls, or having a successful interview. Getting a good job requires more than a great résumé. Important as job ads, interviews, and résumés are, there is one thing that is even more important—knowing your own personal job preferences. In an earlier lesson, you learned about finding your passion for a career. To get the job or career that's right for you, you need to know yourself well. That's why, as you learned in Chapter 3, finding a good job begins with appraising

Finding a good job begins with appraising who you are, what's important to you, and where you are going.
Courtesy of Kayte Deioma/PhotoEdit

who you are, including how you learn, what areas interest you, and where you want to go with your career and life.

Self-analysis doesn't come easily. Most people resist looking long and hard at themselves. They give little thought to questions such as, "What kind of person am I?" "What kind of people do I best interact with?" and "Based on my values, what are the most important things I want in a job?"

To find the job that is best for you, you need to know the answers to these questions. One way to find these answers is to do an inventory of your personal job preferences. In this context, an inventory is *an evaluation or survey*. Doing a personal job-preferences inventory involves analyzing and recording several things about yourself. These include your interests, needs, and wants; your abilities and skills; your values; and your goals.

Vocabulary

- want/classified ads
- inventory
- needs
- wants
- skill
- intrapersonal values
- interpersonal values
- benchmark
- benefit statement
- informational interview
- entry-level
- network

Interests, Needs, and Wants

You should base your inventory on an understanding of what you are interested in, what you need, and what you want in a job.

Interests

To identify your interests, you should ask yourself some probing questions. Use the techniques for self-discovery you learned in Chapter 3, Lesson 2. Write down the answers.

- What do I do really well? In what areas am I most competent? Don't focus just on classes—take into account all your activities.

- What things do I find most enjoyable or rewarding? Again, draw on ideas from any area of your life.

- What do people often compliment me on? What has been my greatest accomplishment? What unique abilities (for example, playing the piano, repairing a car, organizing an event) and personal traits (for example, honesty, compassion, and intelligence) made those accomplishments possible?

The answers to these questions will not lead to a particular job. For example, people may compliment you on your fashion sense, but this does not necessarily mean you should become a model or fashion designer. Your answers to these questions will, however, reveal what you are best at. And chances are you're good at something because it interests you. By helping you identify your interests, these questions will give you a start toward knowing where to focus your job-search effort.

Needs

As you learned in the very first lesson on financial planning, needs are *things that you must have to sustain your livelihood*. Food and shelter are the two most important ones. Your job-related needs may not be a matter of life and death; they are, however, things that you need to be satisfied and content. Ask yourself about your needs in the following areas:

- *Salary*—How much money will you need to pay your bills, have a decent life style, and add to your savings? Using the skills you developed in Chapter 1, Lesson 1, "Creating a Budget," figure out how much you'll need to earn.

- *Benefits*—Do you need a job that offers health insurance and a paid vacation as well as holidays?

- *Work environment*—Some people need a quiet work environment. Others would fall asleep in such an environment; they need one that is more active.

- *Schedule*—Some people are able to work only during the days. Others don't mind, or even prefer, the night shift. Some people can travel and some cannot.

- *Challenge*—Some people need a job that is continually challenging. Others find their challenges elsewhere. They'd rather focus their creativity on such things as family or hobbies.

- *Opportunity for advancement*—Are you ambitious? Or, are you happy just to do a job well, without worrying about advancement?

Wants

You also learned in financial planning the balance you strike between needs and wants. Wants are *things that you do not have to have, but would like to have, or own*. For example, many people want the highest possible salary, but some people are happy with less money. For them, a high salary is not a need.

Go through the list above. Ask yourself if you have some wants in those areas. Consider, for example, any wants that might fit under the "Schedule" category. Maybe you enjoy helping those who are physically challenged, like coaching for the Special Olympics. You don't *need* to do this— but you enjoy it and find it rewarding. If a job offers the possibility of flexible hours, you might be able to continue your coaching duties. You would not make flexible hours a job requirement, but if a job offered this possibility, you might consider it a plus.

Table 6.1 Needs or Wants?

Personal preferences	• Popularity and fame • Wealth • Respect • Time with family • Time to pursue private interests
Job/career preferences	• Status and recognition • Top salary • Friendly coworkers • Fair boss • Pleasant work environment • Responsibility and challenge • Opportunity to advance • Good benefits
Leisure-time preferences	• Watch TV • Participate in sports • Write poetry or stories • Do yard work • Do crafts and artwork • Read • Go to movies, plays, or sports events • Travel
Long-range wants and needs	• More education and training • New activities and interests • Reaching a top position • Marriage and children • A home • A great car • Continued good health

Everybody is different: One person's need, such as health insurance, may be another person's want. To a third person, health insurance may not matter—for example, a married man who has coverage under his wife's policy.

Look at each item on Table 6.1: Is it a need, a want, or is it irrelevant? Keep these factors in mind as your job search gets under way. You'll probably never find a job that offers you everything you want. But understanding what's most important for you can help you weigh your options. Using this list, write down your 10 most important needs and your five most important wants. Keep the list handy as you search for jobs.

Abilities and Skills

A skill is *the ability to do something that you have acquired through training or experience.* Abilities are inborn; skills are developed. For most people, abilities and skills are linked. If you have an ability to do something, you are likely to want to become skilled in it. For example, you might have good hand-eye coordination, which gives you the ability to hit a moving ball with a baseball bat. But you will not be a good baseball player until you get the training and experience to turn that ability into a skill—to the point that people will be able to count on you to hit a baseball out of the park.

Similarly, you may have been born with an ability to draw or to take apart machines and put them back together easily. That ability, however, will not be enough to earn a living. You will need additional art or engineering training before you are able to get a job. Once you have the job, you will need ongoing training to turn those abilities into skills that can build a career.

As you begin the job-search process, you must have a clear idea of your abilities and skills. The ones that are the most developed are those you will sell to employers. List specific work-related skills that you have gained on any past jobs or in other activities, including volunteer work. Examples can be operating a computer or teaching. Also list abilities that you can turn into skills with education and training. These may include an ability to write interesting stories, to persuade people to do things, or to do math quickly in your head.

Values

The organization you work for—its leaders, goals, philosophy, and employees—should reflect your values and beliefs. Otherwise, you will be unhappy. For example, if you believe that nicotine is a major threat to health and that people should not smoke, would you be happy working for a tobacco company? A workplace where people believe in the product or service they offer is more productive than a workplace where workers do not share company values. Identifying your values is a personal matter. Friends and family are not the authorities on who you are or what you should believe. You are the authority on you! When it comes to deciding on values that relate to jobs and careers, you may find it helpful to think of them in three broad categories: *things and processes*; *intrapersonal values*, and *interpersonal values*.

Things and Processes

These refer to your values at work in terms of what you have and what you do. The choices you may find valuable to consider in this category are:

- A clean, quiet workplace versus a crowded, bustling workplace
- Strict regulations or those that are more flexible
- Top money and benefits versus average compensation
- Casual or traditional dress
- A slow-paced or a fast-paced work environment

Intrapersonal Values

Intrapersonal values refer to *values you feel inside you*. Examples of things you and others may find valuable in the workplace are:

- Respect and honesty from bosses and peers
- Working with details
- Varied assignments
- A sense of achievement
- Power and status
- Education and training opportunities

Interpersonal Values

Interpersonal values refer to *values among people*. Workplace choices that relate to this value include:

- Working in teams or working independently
- Interacting with customers versus interacting only with coworkers
- Communicating face-to-face or via letters or email
- Leading a group or working independently

Goals

Now that you have defined your needs, wants, and values, you're ready to set some job or career goals. Your goals will help you focus your job-search process. They will also be your benchmark, or *standard by which to judge your progress*. They will help you decide whether your job search is on track.

You learned in Chapter 5, Lesson 3, "Planning Your Schedule," that time-management skills are an important ingredient of success. The ability to set goals is equally important. For example, researchers at Yale University asked seniors, "Have you set goals? Have you written them down? Do you have a plan to accomplish them?" Only 3 percent of the class answered "yes." When the researchers surveyed these alumni 20 years later, they found some interesting results: The 3 percent of graduates who said that they had set goals were more likely to be happily married, successful, have satisfying family lives, and be in better health than their classmates who had not set goals.

Elements of a Goal Statement

A goal statement should answer three questions:

1. What is going to happen?
2. When is it going to happen?
3. How is it going to happen?

Suppose you have decided you want to be the chief software engineer for a computer company. That's the first question, and you have answered it:

The second question, when it will happen, may be harder to answer. You obviously cannot become a chief software engineer by next week. You'll need to take deliberate steps to get there. From Chapter 1, you learned about setting short, intermediate, and long-term goals in finance. Just as with financial goals, the key is setting short-term, intermediate-term, and long-term career goals. *Short-term goals* are things that you hope to accomplish within the next year. *Intermediate-term goals* are things you want to accomplish within one to five years. *Long-term goals* are things you want to accomplish beyond five years. You'll need to set realistic types of goals. Setting goals will not only tell you when you will reach certain stages of progress but also tell you *how*. In other words, it will answer the third question.

For example, your long-term goal may be to be a chief software engineer, but that does not tell you how you'll get there. It doesn't tell you what you need to do to accomplish that goal. That's where short-term goals come in. If you want to be a chief software engineer, you may want to get a summer internship with a computer company (*how*). By the end of the summer you will have taken one more step toward your long-term goal (*when*).

Another short-term goal might be to read at least one computer magazine a month (*how*), starting next month (*when*). A third short-term goal might be to join the high school computer club tomorrow. Building on these short-term goals, your intermediate-term goal may be getting accepted into a college that offers a top-flight computer program. Short-term goals will feed into intermediate-term goals that will ultimately lead to your long-term goal.

Seven Steps for Writing a Goal Statement

Here are seven steps that will help you write a good goal statement:

1. *State your goal specifically and completely*—The more detailed your goal, the better you will be able to do what needs to be done to reach it.

2. *Set dates*—Setting dates will help you avoid procrastination.

3. *Make your goals realistic but challenging*—Use goals as an opportunity to test your limits. A goal must motivate you. If you have low goals, you will have low achievements.

4. *Make your goals measurable*—Use each short-term goal as a benchmark. If your intermediate-term goal is to get into a top college, define five things you need to do to reach that goal. Then track your progress. Celebrate your successes. Analyze the reasons for your failures and learn from them.

5. *Base your goals on your values*—If a goal is not yours, you will not be committed to it. Listen to what your parents or guardian, teachers, and advisers have to say. But write your goals to please yourself, not them.

6. *Identify internal roadblocks*—You will come up against many barriers on the road to a successful career. Make sure that none of them is self-imposed. The most damaging internal roadblock is your attitude—perhaps the belief that you are not good or smart enough. Keep positive. There is great truth in the old saying, "Attitude is everything."

7. *Have fun!*—Keep a sense of humor. If reaching your goals is all work and no play, you may feel overwhelmed and give up.

Summing It Up

Once you have listed your interests, needs, and wants, your skills and abilities, your values, and your goals, you have the raw material needed to launch a job search. Now it's time to bring all these things together and to organize them in a way that will help you present yourself to employers in the best light.

Drawing on your notes and everything you have learned about yourself so far, make a list that contains the following four sections:

1. *Personal qualities and characteristics that can be useful in a job*—such as dependability, enthusiasm, honesty, a high energy level, tact, cooperativeness, punctuality, or a sense of humor

2. *Skills that you have developed in a job or another activity outside school*—such as computer maintenance and repair, accounting, or the ability to work with children. Don't forget abstract skills such as leadership, the ability to learn quickly, organizational ability, and problem-solving.

3. *Work-related skills and abilities that you have been trained or educated for, but haven't necessarily performed in a job*—such as operating a cash register, building a cabinet, or writing a newspaper or online article

4. *Personal, educational, and job accomplishments*—examples might be a high grade point average, a scholarship, a sports honor, or an award for community service

Writing down goals and reviewing accomplishments, then practicing them orally, can raise confidence at a job interview.

Courtesy of EDHAR/Shutterstock

Sample Benefit Statements

SKILL: I am a detail-oriented person.

PROOF: When I was working for United Aviation and the US Marine Corps, I followed step-by-step procedures, schematics, drawings, and prints. I troubleshot and pinpointed problems on systems using schematics. I fabricated parts to the customer's drawings.

BENEFIT TO AN EMPLOYER: I can follow instructions to the detail, thereby saving time by doing things correctly the first time. This is a benefit to any employer, as not following instructions and having to do things over is costly in terms of profit and time.

SKILL: I have excellent time-management skills.

PROOF: While attending Riverdale High School, I worked 20 hours a week as an intern for CommNet Cellular directly for the senior systems engineer. I was still able to maintain a 3.8 overall GPA and earn a varsity letter in cross-country and track.

BENEFIT TO AN EMPLOYER: This ability will allow me to complete more projects in a timely manner, thereby offering you a more productive workforce and an increase in profits due to your not having to pay overtime.

Selling Your Skills to an Employer

If you've ever tried to sell something, you know that to be successful you need two things: You need to know everything about the product you are selling, and you need to know what your customer is looking for.

When you're looking for a job, your task is to sell yourself to a prospective employer. The same principles apply: Know your product (that is, yourself) and know your customer (the employer).

To sell yourself to an employer, it's not enough to make general statements about how good you are or how much you want the job. You must back up your statements with evidence. An effective way to present yourself is to prepare a benefit statement, or *a well-thought-out statement of your skills and abilities, with examples that illustrate them.* You will need a slightly different benefit statement for each job you apply for—but you can base each individual statement on a single, comprehensive statement.

SKILL: Leadership is one of my strongest qualities.

PROOF: One of my responsibilities at Gotham City Cellular was to implement digital technology as an overlay to our analog system. This required coordinating and managing multiple departments to ensure that everything was done. The project was completed one and a half months ahead of schedule.

BENEFIT TO AN EMPLOYER: All progressive companies need leadership, and employers want to be satisfied that when they delegate responsibility for a project to someone, that person will be able to coordinate all departments, stimulate cooperative teamwork, and complete the project on time. I can do this.

SKILL: One of my greatest strengths is excellent communication skills. I can express myself clearly, both orally and in writing.

PROOF: At Quality Insurance, where I worked for five years, I was responsible for dealing directly with customers who were filing claims. I was able to assist them, over the phone and in person, in an effective manner by listening carefully and then transcribing the information correctly for the claims adjustors. This saved time and kept the customers happy because the company quickly identified and handled their claims.

BENEFIT TO AN EMPLOYER: I believe you would find this skill very useful in your business because listening to the customer and identifying what he or she needs is critical to new business and repeat business.

A benefit statement has three parts:

1. A statement of your skills, abilities, and knowledge

2. Examples of when and where you demonstrated or learned those skills, abilities, and knowledge

3. How and why your skills, abilities, and knowledge will benefit the employer.

success TIP ★

Make your benefit statement specific. Give facts, figures, and evidence of your knowledge or experience. Remember, the bottom line for all organizations is to save money and time.

Organizations that operate for a profit, such as corporations, want to make money and eliminate unnecessary expenses. How can you convince your prospective employer that you can help the organization do those things?

To construct a benefit statement, you should know your "buyer." This means you need to research the position you are applying for and the company that's offering it. Read the job description carefully; study the company's website. What skills does the job demand? What kind of education and experience should the successful applicant have? Once you know these things, put together your own benefit statement for this job. Make sure it shows how you meet all or most of the requirements.

How to Organize a Job Search

As your job search gets under way, you'll need to discover where the best jobs are and determine the company's requirements for the job you're going after. Begin by putting together a list of employers you would like to work for. You should include a wide scope of potential employers, including small businesses, large corporations, government agencies, nonprofit organizations, and educational institutions. You might start at a local library or your school guidance office. You can find books on organizations classified by industry, size, and location. The Internet can be a good source, as can local newspapers and magazines.

Informational Interview

Build a list of names and contact information for every organization you think could be a possibility. Once you have compiled the list, you are ready for the next step in organizing your search: the informational interview or *a conversation with someone working in the field you are interested in.*

One great way to find out if your skills and abilities match those of your targeted job is to talk to people working in your field of interest. This will help you learn more about the requirements of the position you are seeking, or others like it. You'll also learn about trends in the field.

An informational interview can eliminate surprises in an actual job interview. It can help you learn to ask questions, as well as to answer them intelligently. Moreover, an informational interview can help you develop employment leads, and may even lead to a job offer.

Here are several tips for conducting an informational interview:

1. Choose the top five organizations from your list of potential employers. Not all organizations will have someone available to talk with you, so start with the top five and work your way down.

2. Try to talk with the person in charge of the department that does the type of work you want to do. The person who answers the phone will often be a receptionist or secretary. Part of that person's job is to screen callers, so you need to get past that person. Be firm but polite. Say that this is not an employment call, but an information call. Stress that you are not looking for work at this time. You simply want to learn more about the field and would appreciate speaking with someone who has that information.

3. When you reach the person you want to speak with, state your name and the purpose of your call. Emphasize that you need his or her expertise. Ask for 15 to 20 minutes of time. If possible, arrange a personal interview; don't settle for a phone conversation.

4. *Prepare your questions.* Your objective is to find out all you can about the requirements and characteristics of the job you are looking for as well as the industry. Write down questions you want to ask. Below are a few examples. If answers to some of these questions appear in the company's website, build on that information to ask an in-depth question of your own.

- What is unique about this company? How is it different from others in its field?
- Who are the company's competitors? (This could give you clues as to other places to go for job possibilities.)
- What skills, abilities, and personal qualities are you looking for in entry-level, or *beginning* workers?
- What are the main duties and responsibilities of entry-level positions?
- What are the opportunities for training in the job?
- What is the salary range for entry-level positions? What are the advancement opportunities?
- Could the interviewer suggest any other people to talk to? Could you use the interviewer's name as a reference?

5. Treat this interview as seriously as you would a job interview. In a face-to-face interview, dress professionally and be on time. Listen carefully and make eye contact. Keep to the allotted time unless the person you're interviewing offers more. When the interview is over, thank the person.

6. Write a thank-you note after the interview, whether the interview was over the phone or in person. Let the person know that you appreciate the time he or she took from a busy day and how much it has helped you. If other people helped you arrange the interview, send notes to them as well.

Your Objective

Once you have conducted your informational interviews, you should be clearer than ever about your objective in your job search. In the next lesson you will learn how to write a job objective. It is an important part of your résumé, and will help to keep you focused in your job search.

Networking

Of all the resources available to you in your search for employment, *human resources* will provide the greatest return. Human resources are the people you already know and those you meet in the course of a job search. Human resources can also make your job search more enjoyable.

As you learned in Chapter 3, Lesson 1, meeting people and making contacts in your job search is called *networking*. *The group of people you meet and maintain contact with* is called a network. A resourceful job hunter spends a good deal of time networking, because people who provide advice and information often offer the quickest and surest means of obtaining leads that result in employment. Experts who study the job market say that a majority of people get their jobs through networking.

Creating Your Network

The following types of people should be in your network:

- *Family, friends, and acquaintances*—This group includes not only people you know directly but also friends of your parents, friends of neighbors, and friends of friends. As employers and employees themselves, these people know which jobs are open and whom you should talk to about the openings. They might be able to tell you about a job before it's advertised. Family members, friends, and acquaintances may answer your questions directly or put you in touch with someone who can. This can open the door to a meeting with someone who can provide information on a specific career or company. This is also a good way to learn about the training necessary for a certain position, the prospects for advancement, and what the person likes and dislikes about the work.

- *People working in your field*—People working in your field can offer information about their jobs as well as other jobs available in their companies. Talking with them can enable you to clarify and reaffirm your interest in a particular type of work. You can find these individuals through the organizations they work for. As an example, maybe you want to be a computer programmer. You could call almost any bank, insurance company, brokerage firm, or other business likely to have a computer information system and ask for the information technology (IT) department or the computer department. The person who answers will probably be not only knowledgeable about the position you want, but also able to recommend the name of someone you might talk to. You won't always get a positive response—sometimes people are just too busy to talk—but if you are persistent, you will likely find someone who is willing to help you.

If you would prefer to have the name of an individual to talk to before speaking to the department itself, do a bit of research online on the organization, or ask the receptionist. Explain what you are doing, and he or she may recommend a particular individual to talk with. In either case, the person you talk to is likely to feel flattered that you have asked for help. Most people are willing to share thoughts and ideas. Just be well prepared, let them know that you won't take a lot of their time, and thank them before closing.

• *Other job hunters*—In your search for employment, you'll meet many other job hunters. You may meet them at the companies you are interviewing with, at employment agencies, or at other locations. Introduce yourself and share your experiences with them. Although your career interests might be quite different from theirs, they may be able to provide you with information relevant to your job search and give you the names of individuals you might contact. Other job hunters may also be able to suggest job-hunting techniques you haven't considered. Once you're serious about your job search, virtually anyone can turn into a member of your network. For example, you may get some names during your informational interviews. Put them on your networking list. Don't forget former employers with whom you had a good experience. They can provide names of employers they know. Your teachers may also be good sources.

Letters of Introduction

Besides giving you leads, some members of your network may be willing to write letters of introduction or serve as references for you. A reference would give you an opportunity to arrange an interview with a potential employer who might not otherwise be willing to talk with you.

Maintaining Your Network

Once you develop a contact network, you'll need to devote time to maintaining it. Keep in touch with everyone on your list. This does not mean bugging them until they want you to go away. It means keeping them informed of your progress, asking for their help, and giving them help when they need it. Your contact network will expand many times over with each new person you meet. You'll see a ripple effect. The more people you know, the more people you will meet who may be able to help you in your job search.

Finding Lists of Job Openings

The most likely places to find lists of job openings are on the Internet. Do an online search for the organization or company where you would like to work, open their Human Resources or "Job Openings" page to see what is available.

Classified/Want ads used to be the most important place to find job leads—today, more employers are using online services to find workers.

Courtesy of (left) Minerva Studio/Shutterstock; (right) Elena Elisseeva/Shutterstock

Classified Ads

Classified ads, also known as *want ads*, used to be the dominant method for listing jobs, mostly found in your local newspaper and in magazines published by trade and professional organizations. They're simple to find. Because many newspapers have reduced their size and staffs, the want or classified ads sections are not as important as in years past. Now, many newspapers post job listings and other want or classified ads online rather than pay the large costs of publishing ads in the print editions. You should use both sources for finding jobs, especially in the local community.

Depending on the community in which you live, hundreds of people may apply for just one job listed either in the local newspaper or online. In this case, the employer can be very selective. You may not get an interview— in some cases, the employer may not even respond to your application. But do not let that discourage you.

A key is to use many sources for job leads, and when you do find a job that interests you, always read the ads or job postings thoroughly. Follow the exact directions written in the ad, and provide the specific information requested, no more or less. If the ad says "No phone calls," don't call.

The Internet

More and more job listings are appearing online. If you want to work for a specific organization, go to its website. Find the link titled "Jobs," "Careers," or "Employment" and click there. If you don't see these categories, enter those words in the website's search engine. If you still don't find the information you want, call the main number (usually listed under "Contact Us") and ask the person who answers how you can get a list of job openings.

The Internet also has a number of job databases. Some of them are supported by ads and are free to job hunters; others charge a fee. On a job website, you might find thousands of openings. Narrow your search by defining specifically what you want. For example, if you are looking for an office assistant job, you can specify "office assistant" and then "entry-level." You will get a list of jobs matching those criteria. You can also specify locations in the country, size of organization, or other preferences.

Popular online job sites include:

- LinkedIn: *www.LinkedIn.com*
- America's Job Bank: *www.ajb.dni.us*
- CareerBuilder: *www.careerbuilder.com*
- Hotjobs.com: *www.hotjobs.yahoo.com*
- Monster.com: *www.monster.com*
- For US government jobs, visit the free website *www.usajobs.gov*

Most job databases offer you the opportunity to post information. The information you provide is compiled to form a *job profile*. A job profile posted by someone looking for a job might include:

- Name
- Email address
- Type of job sought
- Experience
- Training and education you have achieved
- Other wants or needs (such as where in the country or overseas you want to work, the level of responsibilities you are seeking, and the type of organization you want to work for)

One online career site that is growing in popularity and reputation is LinkedIn. Not only do you have the opportunity to find jobs through LinkedIn, there is a large networking component. You can make connections with others in your field of interest, or even make personal connections with trusted friends or peers who may help recommend you for certain positions. Employers, especially among professional occupations, often look for possible job candidates through LinkedIn, using their own network connections to find the right job candidates to review and interview.

If you do place a résumé or general information about yourself with an online service to attract an employer, be as careful as you would be with other social media like Facebook. Do not enter any information that could be compromised. And if you receive an email or a call from a job recruiter, check the credentials of the individual or the firm the recruiter represents before you respond.

Remember: Networking is the single best source of job information. Talking directly to people will always yield better information than a website or want ads.

Internet job databases list thousands of job openings, and most allow you to post information about yourself.

Courtesy of Paul Schlemmer/Shutterstock

CHAPTER 6 Applying for Jobs

✔ CHECKPOINTS

Lesson 1 Review

Using complete sentences, answer the following questions on a sheet of paper.

1. What are the four elements of a personal job-preference inventory?

2. What is the difference between an interest, a need, and a want? Why should you know each of those things about yourself?

3. Why are your skills and abilities important to your job search?

4. Name five of your values when it comes to work and describe why each one is important to you.

5. What are five steps you should follow when writing a goal statement? What is your long-term goal?

6. Why is an information interview a valuable tool for a job seeker? How can you prepare for such an interview?

7. How can you start to build a job network? List three people you can contact today.

8. Name three job websites.

9. Name three organizations that you would like to work for. How will you find out what jobs they have open? How will you apply?

APPLYING JOB-SEARCH SKILLS

10. Choose a job that you would like to get and an organization that you would like to work for; construct a benefit statement that you could use to sell yourself to that employer.

11. Select an online job database of several organizations you would like to work for; go online and find five openings for the kind of job you would like to get.

Quick Write

Make a list of the things that you've done that would make you a valuable employee. Include work, education, and outside activities. You've just taken the first step in preparing your résumé!

Learn About

- the purpose of a résumé
- types of résumés
- six tips for writing a great résumé
- preparing a personal résumé
- cover letters
- portfolios

"I find that the harder I work, the more luck I seem to have."

Thomas Jefferson, 3rd President of the United States

The Purpose of a Résumé

When you apply for a job, the person in charge of hiring will probably not know much about you. To make a good hiring decision, he or she will have to learn a lot about you very quickly. What is your background? What are your skills? What experience do you have? How are you different from other people applying for the job?

Your résumé gives a potential employer a lot of information about you quickly and efficiently.

Courtesy of Jeff Greenberg/PhotoEdit

How will the employer find out these important things quickly and efficiently? His or her first step will usually be to look at your résumé, or *brief summary of your work experience and qualifications*. (When the word *résumé* refers to a job document, it is pronounced "REZ-oo-may.") Everyone who applies for a job should have a résumé.

The main purpose of a résumé is to get a job interview with the company you submit it to. But a good résumé has a life far beyond that original purpose. For example, employers sometimes forward résumés they've received to their counterparts at other companies who are hiring. If you have impressed a company with your résumé, but they can't use you at this time, the person who reviews the résumés might send it on to someone else.

And between interviews, you may post your résumé on career websites such as those listed in Chapter 6, Lesson 1, "The Job Search Process." As you found out in the previous lesson, job searching can be a long process. Therefore, it never hurts to have as many irons in the fire as possible.

A good résumé has other purposes. For example, you might want to do some volunteer work in the community. The organization for which you want to do this work may ask for a résumé so it can review your qualifications. Or you might decide to apply for an internship or other job-related experience that has a tight deadline. If you've got your résumé ready, you're a step ahead of the game.

Vocabulary

- résumé
- chronological résumé
- functional résumé
- hybrid résumé
- targeted résumé
- electronic résumé
- action verbs
- job objective
- summary of qualifications
- keyword
- cover letter
- portfolio

Types of Résumés

There are five basic résumé formats:

1. Chronological Résumé

A chronological résumé *lists your jobs, education, and other relevant accomplishments in reverse chronological order* (Figure 6.1). It begins with your current or most recent job and schooling, and works backward. This is the most common résumé type and is the easiest to write. Use it if you have followed a clear progression of jobs and education and if there are no big gaps in your record that this approach would reveal.

2. Functional Résumé

A functional résumé *arranges your information under skill headings, without focusing on dates* (Figure 6.2). The headings will depend on your particular experience and skills. Examples of such headings might be "Administration," "Sales," or "Computer." Specific examples and results that you can provide are especially important (this is true for all styles of resumes). You might want to use a functional résumé if there are gaps in your chronological record. When they look at a chronological résumé, some interviewers question gaps of time during which you've been unemployed. Even though you had a valid reason for a gap—perhaps you had to care for a sick relative or were in school full time—it is a potentially distracting item in your résumé. In such a case, a functional résumé that does not give dates may be more effective.

3. Hybrid Résumé

A hybrid résumé is *a combination of the chronological and functional formats* (Figure 6.3). As in the functional résumé, you list skills you can offer an employer, and as in the chronological résumé, you list your work experience in reverse chronological order. In a hybrid résumé, however, you list the number of years that you worked in a particular job rather than the dates.

4. Targeted Résumé

A targeted résumé *includes the title of the actual job or career you are seeking*. You can write such a résumé in the same form as you would write a chronological, functional, or hybrid résumé. A targeted résumé, however, presents your qualifications in terms of the specific job you are applying for. This format is especially effective when you are interested in a particular job and need a separate résumé for it.

5. Electronic Résumé

An electronic résumé is *one prepared specifically for online use*. It provides keywords that computers can recognize, and you write it in plain text format. You can write an electronic résumé as a chronological, functional, hybrid, or targeted résumé.

JOHN E. JONES

11567 East 17th Street, Spokane, Washington 01435
(609) 555-4587 (Please leave message)
johnjones95@aol.com

SUMMARY OF QUALIFICATIONS

Ten years' experience as a Surveyor. Proficiency, knowledge, and strengths in the following areas: Surveying, Field Engineering, Mapping, Drafting, Blueprinting, Supervision, Training, Customer Relations. Roads/Bridges: Commercial & Residential.

SUMMARY OF EXPERIENCE

Currently work as an independent contractor doing surveying and drafting for some firms in the Spokane area. Contracts include boundaries, commercial, heavy construction, and topographic jobs.

2009–2012   **Avery Structures, Inc.**, Spokane, WA
Survey Party Chief on large construction jobs. Directed all surveying and drafting.

2003–2009   **Centennial Engineering**, Seattle, WA
Party Chief for survey team in the construction of bridges and roads. Managed team responsible for calculations and drafting on all phases of the jobs.

2000–2003   **J.R. Developers**, Tacoma, WA
Party Chief completing all survey work on the subdivisions.

1998–2000   **Al Messahaq/ARAMCO**, Saudi Arabia
Party Chief on all project work in Geodetic Control, roads and highways, in addition to plant layout.

EDUCATION

ITT Technical Institute, Spokane, Washington, 2003
2000 Hours in Map Drafting

Spokane School of Surveying and Mapping, Seattle, Washington, 1997
Certificate for 1600-hour program in Surveying and Mapping.

REFERENCES

Will be provided upon request.

FIGURE 6.1

Chronological Résumé

Reprinted from *The Job Searcher's Handbook*, edited by Carolyn R. Robbins (2006), by permission of Pearson Education

JOHN E. JONES

11567 East 17th Street, Spokane, Washington 01435
(609) 555-4587 (Please leave message)
johnjones95@aol.com

OBJECTIVE

A position in Computer Operations with progressively expanding responsibilities leading to an appointment to Systems Analyst.

EDUCATION

Spokane Technical Institute, Spokane, Washington
672-hour course in Computer Programming & Operations. State Certified. Graduated with honors. GPA: 3.67

Washington State University, Seattle, Washington
Completed 15 semester hours in Computer Science, including mastering Fortran.

Seattle School of Surveying and Mapping, Seattle, Washington
Certificate, 1600-hour program in Surveying and Mapping.

ITT Technical Institute, Spokane, Washington
Map Drafting (2000 hours).

PROFESSIONAL EXPERIENCE

Computer Computations/Data Processing
Involved in all aspects of data retrieval from computations to design to the finished product in the land surveying industry.

Mathematical
Performed daily algebraic and trigonometric calculations.

Teamwork
Worked cooperatively and effectively in fast-paced, demanding environment with all members of surveying crew, and interacted with various executive key personnel.

EMPLOYMENT HISTORY

Party Chief for the following companies:

- **Avery Structures, Inc.**, Spokane, Washington
- **Centennial Engineering**, Seattle, Washington
- **J.R. Developers**, Tacoma, Washington
- **Al Messahaq/ARAMCO**, Saudi Arabia

FIGURE 6.2

Functional Résumé

Reprinted from *The Job Searcher's Handbook*, edited by Carolyn R. Robbins (2006), by permission of Pearson Education

JOHN E. JONES

11567 East 17th Street, Spokane, Washington 01435
(609) 555-4587 (Please leave message)
johnjones95@aol.com

OBJECTIVE

A position in Data Processing, preferably in Computer Operations or Programming.
Five-Year Career Goal: Systems Analysis Management

SUMMARY OF QUALIFICATIONS

Computer Science, Operations & Programming—*Two years*. Computer Programming with emphasis in the following languages, software and operating systems: BASIC, Fortran, COBOL, MS-DOS, Excel, dBase III, SPF/PC, IBM, OS/VS, JCL and CICS.

Computer Computations/Data Processing—*Eight years*. Involved in all aspects of data retrieval from computations to design.

Mathematical—*Five Years*. Performed daily algebraic and trigonometric calculations.

Teamwork—*Eight Years*. Effectively and cooperatively worked in a fast-paced, demanding environment with all members of a surveying crew, and interacted with various executive key personnel.

Additional Qualifications—Demonstrated ability to "debug" programs written by others. Developed training and instructional materials for software packages. Designed, set up and operated PC-based database for record-keeping.

EDUCATION

Spokane Technical Institute, Spokane, Washington, 2005
672-hour course in Computer Programming & Operations. State certified. Graduated with Honors. GPA: 3.67

Washington State University, Seattle, Washington, 2004

Completed 15 semester hours in Computer Science which included courses in Computer Networking.

Seattle School of Surveying and Mapping, Seattle, Washington, 2001
Certificate for 1600-hour program.

EMPLOYMENT BACKGROUND

Party Chief for the following companies:

- **Avery Structures, Inc.**, Spokane, Washington, 2009–2012
- **Centennial Engineering**, Seattle, Washington, 2003–2009
- **J.R. Developers**, Tacoma, Washington, 2000–2003
- **Al Messahaq/ARAMCO**, Saudi Arabia, 1998–2000

REFERENCES

Professional references will be provided upon request.

FIGURE 6.3

Hybrid Résumé

Reprinted from *The Job Searcher's Handbook*, edited by Carolyn R. Robbins (2006), by permission of Pearson Education

Six Tips for Writing a Great Résumé

Your résumé is an advertisement for you. In it, you tell prospective employers who you are, what you've done, and what you can do. Your résumé's appearance is very important. You want to deliver your message in a clear, concise, and readable form, free of grammar and spelling errors.

So you should put a good deal of thought into your résumé. Before you start writing, read over these tips. Then keep them in mind as you do your first draft.

1. Use Action Verbs

Use action verbs, *verbs that give your résumé power and direction.* Your résumé should be lively. It should portray you as a dynamic person who has done many good things and can bring lots of value to an organization. For this reason, you should use action verbs when describing your accomplishments in a print résumé. (You'll have to use nouns in an electronic résumé because of technical requirements, as explained below.) Table 6.2 contains two summaries of accomplishments related to the same job, an office assistant. Both these people are seeking to move up to an office manager job. Which candidate does a better job of summarizing his or her qualifications? An employer would be more likely to see the person who wrote Résumé 2—who uses the action verbs "responded," "assisted," "selected," "purchased," and "advised" to describe performance—as able to respond to demands, make important decisions, and advise people. This person would clearly be a valuable employee.

Table 6.2 Using Action Verbs in Résumés

Résumé 1	• Telephone answering • Picking out office supplies and buying them • Advising new employees
Résumé 2	• Responded to calls from customers and suppliers and assisted them in finding information • Selected and purchased office supplies • Advised new employees on office policies, computer installation, and security procedures

2. Give Facts, Figures, Results, and Numbers

You'll never impress an employer with vague phrases such as, "I am a great problem solver and a hard worker"—*unless* you follow up with proof to support them. Tell the prospective employer where and when you obtained your skills, and where and how long you used them. If you say you're "detail oriented," give an example of a situation in which you used that talent and describe its outcome. Numbers work well on résumés. For example, if you made a financial difference for a previous employer— you may have found a way to save $500 on office supplies—say so. Employers love it when employees find new ways to save or earn money.

3. Give Your Résumé a Personality

Make your résumé reflect the things that are unique about you. Don't be afraid to deviate from the norm or to be innovative, but do it carefully. If you are applying for a job in the arts field, creativity might be acceptable; it might even be expected. But a job in the computer field might demand something more traditional. Always use good taste. If you're striving for originality and are unsure about whether a certain strategy works, have a friend—or better yet an adult working in the field—review it.

4. Be Honest

Preparing a résumé is not an exercise in fiction writing. It's now easier than ever to verify facts, and more and more employers are checking résumés for accuracy.

5. Keep It Positive

Don't put anything that could be interpreted as criticism, conflict, or hostility on your résumé—especially criticism of a previous employer. Also, be careful not to include any information that could stereotype you. For example, if you're interested in guns, don't say it. It might alarm some employers.

success TIP ★

Avoid exaggerated language in your résumé and cover letter. Phrases like "vast knowledge" and "world-class professional" can damage an entry-level job applicant's credibility.

6. Keep It Concise

A résumé for a high school student should usually be just one page long. As you grow older and get more experience, you can expand it as needed.

Preparing a Personal Résumé

Preparing a résumé is not difficult. It just takes time and organization. Like any other piece of writing, it's easier when you follow a process to plan and organize. Here are the basic steps:

Gather Your Information

You begin by gathering your background information. List everything you think could interest an employer. This might include information on:

- Full-time or part-time jobs
- Education, including relevant courses you have taken and your grade point average (GPA) if it is above 3.0
- Volunteer work
- Hobbies and free-time activities
- Awards and honors
- Anything else that might be interesting to an employer, such as places you have traveled or languages that you speak besides English.

Here is where you can use the *benefits statement* that you prepared in Chapter 6, Lesson 1, "The Job Search Process." It will provide the basic information you need to draft your résumé.

Organize Your Information

Next, you organize your information, based on the type of job you are going to apply for. Keep in mind that your résumé is not your life history. Employers may discard a résumé if it is too long or contains irrelevant information. For example, if you are applying for a job in a computer company, the fact that you got an A in a computer-programming course would be relevant, and you should include it on your résumé. But if you're applying to be an assistant to an animal trainer, a programming course is probably irrelevant, regardless of your grade.

Write the First Draft

Once you've compiled your information and decided on the résumé style that best suits your job objective, you're ready to write the first draft.

Here are the basic sections of a résumé and what to include in each section. Most résumés will have all these sections, usually in the order presented. You do have some leeway, however. For example, if you're just entering the job market and have little work experience, the education section should precede the work-experience section. Once you're an experienced worker, your job experience is probably more important than your formal training, so you could move back the education section.

Job Objective

The job objective is *a brief statement that describes the type of position you are seeking.* It always appears at the beginning of the résumé, immediately after your name and address. This section is very important—it's the employer's first opportunity to get to know you. If it appears that you didn't take the time to construct a coherent job objective or, worse yet, that you don't know what you want to do, the employer may read no further.

As you write your objective, keep one idea in mind: "What is my career goal?" The objective should consist of one or two short sentences and should mention your long-term employment goals. You can use the *goal statement* that you prepared in the last lesson to help you decide what to say.

However, be careful about making your objective too specific. For example, don't say you are seeking a specific job title or that you want to work only for a specific company. A general title, such as "editor," is fine. A title such as "associate editor for community news" is too specific. You never know where your résumé will end up, and you don't want to rule out any possibilities.

Summary of Qualifications

The summary of qualifications is *a brief overview of your skills, experience, and knowledge.* For the reader's convenience, place the summary near the top of the first page. The order in which you present your qualifications is important. Put the ones that are most relevant to the job first.

Education

The education section includes all the relevant training and education you have received—whether it was formal education in a school or college, on-the-job training, or training you received elsewhere. Include any education that is relevant to the skills or knowledge needed for the job you're seeking. But don't forget education that gave you broader skills, such as ability to communicate, handle conflict and stress, take initiative, and think strategically. These are essential in today's workplace.

List the names of the institutions you attended, starting with the most recent one, along with the city and state they are located in. If you have a high school education, list relevant courses. Include your GPA if it's above 3.0. (If you go to college, you'll include your major and any other relevant courses.) Unless you're doing a functional résumé, give the dates when you attended high school or college.

Employment History

The employment history section lists all the jobs you've had—full-time, part-time, student, and co-op jobs, as well as internships. On a chronological résumé, you'll list these jobs in order, starting with your current or most recent job. Include dates of employment, expressed in months and years. Give the name of the organization and the city and state. You do not need to provide the address and phone number. For each job, briefly describe the duties you performed and the responsibilities you held. Tell what you accomplished in the job, in measurable terms if possible. For example, if you painted houses one summer, say how many houses you painted, especially if the number is impressive. Give the outcomes of your work: If you worked in sales, for example, say how much money you made for your employer. If it isn't clear from the name, say in a few words what the company does. Do not include reasons for leaving a job or your salary there.

Related Professional Experience

Include this section if you have done volunteer work that pertains to the job. For example, if you led a Boy or Girl Scout troop on a camping expedition, and the job you are applying for requires leadership skills or working with youth, tell prospective employers about your Scouting experience.

Other

This is the place for information on such topics as fluency in a second language, awards, and travel. You should document your level of fluency when possible, and be sure not to overstate your capabilities, as employers will often ask you to demonstrate these abilities in the interview phase.

References and Letters of Recommendation

You don't need to include references on a résumé. If an interviewer decides that you are a serious candidate, at that point he or she will ask for references. People who serve as references should be former employers, teachers, counselors, or others who know you well. If you list only family members as references, it may raise a red flag to prospective employers. Some people have letters of reference or commendation from former employers or teachers, testifying to their skill level or good character. If you have such letters, you could include them with your résumé. An option is to bring copies of the letters to the job interview and to give them to the interviewer at that time.

What To Omit

Do not include *personal information* on your résumé. This includes, for example, your age, marital status, any children you might have, religion, race, or state of health. Antidiscrimination laws prohibit employers from asking about these issues. ***Do not*** put your Social Security number on your résumé or give it when applying for a job. Give it only if you are hired.

Revising and Proofreading

You'll need to write several drafts before your résumé really starts to shape up. If possible, let some time pass between each draft. You'll probably think of things to add or other ways to improve it.

This is time well spent. Employers may receive dozens of résumés in response to a single job ad. They will throw out any that are messy or confusing, or have grammar errors and misspellings. Do not rely on the spell checker alone; it could prove to be embarrassing. Remember, your résumé is your first introduction to the employer. You must present your qualifications in a professional manner. If your résumé is not well prepared, you will probably not have a chance even to land an interview, much less get the job.

Proofread your résumé carefully, using a current collegiate dictionary and a grammar handbook. Scrutinize every word for spelling and grammar mistakes. Don't guess about correct spelling, grammar, and punctuation. Even only one or two errors in correctness can land a résumé in the "hold" box, or worse. When you're satisfied, have at least three other people read your résumé for content as well as correctness.

Preparing the Final Copy

You've already given great thought to what your résumé says. Now it's time to focus on how it looks.

- *Use an appealing format and layout*—The résumé should look neat, balanced, and not crowded. Single-space the text; use double or triple spaces between sections. The font size should be 11 point or 12 point; and margins should be between one and one-and-a-half inches. You may vary fonts to make the résumé attractive, but don't overdo it. Use no more than three fonts, and make sure they are readable. Highlight important points by CAPITALIZING, **bolding**, or underscoring them, but do not overdo highlighting, either. The three sample résumés in this lesson are examples of what prospective employers expect.

- *Number and identify pages*—If your résumé is more than one page long, place a heading in the top left corner of all following pages that includes your name and the page number.

- *Forget the title*—A title such as "Résumé" is unnecessary. Your reader knows what the document is.

- Use standard 8.5-by-11-inch white, ivory, or light-gray paper.

- Print your résumé using a letter-quality printer with dark ink. If you make photocopies, make sure they are bright and clear.

- If you mail your résumé, put it in a 9-by-12-inch or 10-by-13-inch envelope. If you fold it to fit in a smaller envelope, the résumé will not look neat and crisp.

Completing an Electronic Résumé

Most of the guidelines for a print résumé also apply to an electronic résumé. An electronic résumé, however, has some unique requirements that affect its content and format.

Content

The most important element of an electronic résumé is the use of keywords. A keyword is *a specific word that a computer looks for when searching a database*. In the case of résumés, the employer's computer will look for words that correspond to the job requirements. Keywords are usually noun forms. For example, on your paper résumé you may write, "Answered telephones for busy office." On your electronic résumé, write "Telephone receptionist."

Format

You must usually save an electronic résumé as a text-only file. This means that your résumé can contain virtually no formatting. You may not be able to use boldface, underlined, or italic type; document borders; or document headers or footers that may help to make a print résumé look attractive. Moreover, don't center your headings; use only flush-left text instead. If you must emphasize something, use all caps. Put your name at the top, along with the title of the job you are seeking (if you're sending the résumé in response to a specific job). Put your address, e-mail address, and phone number at the bottom of the last page.

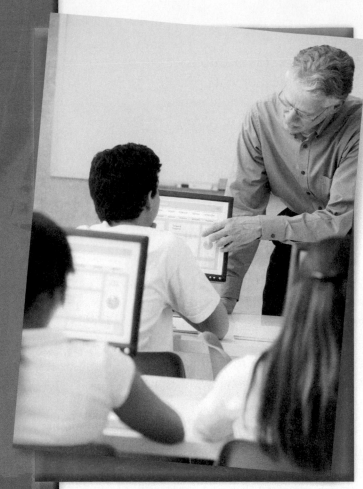

Whether you're preparing a paper résumé or an electronic one, review and proofread it carefully, using standard references. Remember, this is your first introduction to a potential employer.

Courtesy of Corbis Super RF/Alamy

success TIP ★

For a cover letter that will engage your reader, show that you've researched the organization and the position you seek. Readers are favorably inclined towards applicants who have taken the extra time to get to know their prospective employer.

Cover Letters

Once your résumé is complete, you must take a final step—writing a cover letter.

A cover letter *gives prospective employers further information about you that is not in your résumé.* It points out items in your résumé that show why you could be of value to the organization. It helps generate interest in you and gives you an opportunity to sell yourself. For these reasons, you must draft your cover letter thoughtfully. A cover letter is attached to your résumé. It identifies the position you're applying for and explains why you're suitable for it. You should always provide a cover letter to your résumé, including electronic résumés.

You should structure your cover letter along the following lines:

- *The opening*—Address this to a specific person. If you don't have a name, address the letter to the head of the department who would be in charge of the position you're applying for.

- *The first paragraph*—Begin by explaining why you're writing. State the position you're applying for or the position you qualify for. If someone referred you to the employer, tell the reader who that was. Explain in one sentence why the company or organization is attractive to you.

- *The second and third paragraphs*—State your qualifications for the position in these paragraphs. Remember that your purpose is to prompt the reader to select you for an interview. So relate your qualifications to the organization's needs. This means you must do some research into the company or organization before you apply for the job.

- *The closing paragraph*—Thank the reader for taking the time to review your qualifications, but not for anything he or she hasn't done yet, such as granting you an appointment. *Always ask for an interview*, and explain how the reader may contact you.

Don't send a generic cover letter. You should carefully adapt and personalize each cover letter for each prospective employer. Figure 6.4 gives an example of a good cover letter.

7854 East Martin Luther King Blvd.
Aurora, Colorado 80010

May 15, 2012

Mr. Dennis Kelly
MAC Tools Corporation
1757 Hoyt Street
Lakewoord, Colorado 80215

Dear Mr. Kelly:

I have recently earned my Associate's degree in Occupation Sciences of Automotive Technology from the Westwood College of Technology (formerly Denver Institute of Technology) graduating with a GPA of 4.0. This accelerated education, in addition to years of great interest in the field of automotive technology, makes me eager to be placed in a position with your company.

The attached résumé summarizes my experience and education for you. Westwood College offers, to all graduates, the opportunity to receive lifetime training, so I can keep current with new material and procedures. This benefit will be an asset to your company because I will have ongoing retraining in my field at no cost to you.

As for my other qualifications, I have completed EDGE training that has taught me diagnostic procedures for automotive repair. I am ASE certified and have a clean, no-ticket driving record. I have most of the tools needed to begin my career and am in the process of purchasing more diagnostic equipment.

I believe you will consider me for a position with MAC Tools Corporation when you review the enclosed résumé and see that I match the qualifications that you ask of your automotive technicians. I look forward to meeting with you and becoming part of your team. You can contact me at the number below between 5 and 10 p.m. weekdays and all day on the weekends. I have voice messaging and pick up my messages regularly. Please do not contact my present employer as he is not aware of my decision to leave, and I want to give two weeks' notice at the appropriate time.

Sincerely,

Harold Blake

Harold Blake
(303) 555-1221
blake56@yahoo.com

Enclosed: Résumé

FIGURE 6.4

Sample Cover Letter

Reprinted from *The Job Searcher's Handbook*, edited by Carolyn R. Robbins (2006), by permission of Pearson Education

Portfolios

A portfolio is *an instrument that gives employers a comprehensive picture of an applicant—* including experience, education, and skills, and most importantly, concrete evidence of that applicant's background. A portfolio is a powerful tool for a job seeker. It is more than a résumé and a cover letter because it allows you to include items that can't accompany your cover letter or résumé.

In the past, a portfolio was used more by those in creative fields such as graphic arts, education, entertainment, architecture, and so on. Today, it is a practice that job seekers use in many different occupations. A major reason for this: *portfolios can be maintained electronically, and accessed online, without the inconvenience of having to carry them around physically.*

Although photos are rarely included in résumés, they should be added to your portfolio, along with video and audio items, but only if they show you in a favorable light. Caution: get a second opinion to be certain they are evidence of your best capabilities.

Here are some suggestions for types of items you might wish to include in your portfolio, to demonstrate who you are and what you can provide to the organization you seek to join.

1. *Education and Relevant Training*—All transcripts, certificates of training, degrees, and licenses. All conferences and/or workshops, including the program material that was covered.

2. *Past Work Experience*—Job descriptions with itemized duties, lists of transferable and functional skills, samples of your work, and favorable employer evaluations and reviews.

3. *Achievements*—Awards, letters of recommendation and commendation, merit documents, and innovative, original creations.

4. *Participation in Clubs, Teams, Societies, and Associations*—Photos, news articles, certificates, merit badges, positions you have held.

5. *Volunteer Programs, Community Service Projects*—Any community service program where you volunteered your time and/or expertise.

6. *Publications*—This can be an opportunity to demonstrate many abilities, especially written communications skills. It can include any manuscript, essay, or publication from school assignments, to news articles, and so on.

Once you have written and gathered all of the samples, information, photos, and lists you want to include, you are ready to put your portfolio together in a professional manner.

If it is a physical portfolio, enclose it in a quality binder with a title page, a table of contents, and possibly some section dividers for easy access. Keep the documents clean, neat, and fresh. The title page is placed at the beginning, and immediately after that, you should include your goals statement (where you see yourself in three to five years).

If it is an online or CD portfolio, scan in all documents and photos carefully so they are attractive and legible, and consider including video and audio items as well.

✔ CHECKPOINTS

Lesson 2 Review

Using complete sentences, answer the following questions on a sheet of paper.

1. Why is it important to have a good résumé?

2. What are the basic résumé styles? What are the main differences among them?

3. Why is it important to use active verbs on a print résumé? Why should you not emphasize verbs on an electronic résumé?

4. Explain the purpose and importance of a job objective.

5. List some additional pointers that will make your printed résumé effective.

6. What is different about the electronic résumé?

7. What is a benefit of developing a portfolio? How is an electronic portfolio more appropriate than a traditional one in the 21st Century?

APPLYING RÉSUMÉ-PREPARATION SKILLS

8. Prepare a résumé for yourself in two different styles.

9. Pick a job with a company you think you might be interested in working for some day, and write a draft cover letter to go along with the résumés you have prepared.

Building Interviewing Skills

Quick Write

_____

_____

Imagine you are an employer looking to fill an open position. Make a list of the qualities you would look for in a job applicant.

Learn About

- the interview process
- interview do's and don'ts
- types of interviews
- basic interview questions
- how employers evaluate interviewees

"By failing to prepare you are preparing to fail."

Benjamin Franklin

The Interview Process

Of all the phases of job searching, most people find the interview the most difficult and stressful. And no wonder: The impression you make during that brief period is the most critical part of your job search. It will determine whether you are hired.

What can you do to minimize the anxiety and the sweaty palms? With a job interview, as with almost any other part of life, preparation makes all the difference. Knowing how the interview process works, and understanding what to do and not to do, will make you feel more secure. Knowing how employers evaluate interviews can also help.

The interview process is not complicated. You see a job that appeals to you, decide to apply, and submit your résumé along with the company application form or any other required paperwork. Then you wait. Meanwhile, the company reviews all the résumés it has received and selects those that look most promising. This process generally takes a few weeks, but it may take longer, depending on the size of the company and the number of résumés it receives.

If your résumé is among those selected, someone from the organization will call or e-mail you to schedule an interview. In some cases, you may interview with someone in the human resources department, *the department that handles hiring, benefits, and other issues concerning employees.* In other cases, you may have an interview with the person who would be your boss or your boss's boss. Sometimes you'll talk with a combination of these people. And if the company decides after the first interview that it likes you, it may ask you to come back another day for more interviews.

Interview Do's and Don'ts

As noted in Chapter 4, Lesson 4, a successful interview takes preparation. You must do your research, dress and act appropriately, and know how to answer and ask questions well.

How to Prepare

The first step in preparation is to research the company you are seeking to join and its industry sector, or *general field in which the company provides a product or service.* If your interview is with a computer company, find out as much as you can about what is happening in the computer industry today. This will help you ask good questions.

- *Become as familiar as you can with what the company does— its history, goals, mission, and people*—Go to the organization's website. It should contain most of what you need to know. You can also enter the organization's name into a search engine and find out what people are writing about it.

- *Discover as much as you can about the people you will speak with during your interview*—Some company websites give a short biography of each of the company's top executives. Or you can ask the person who schedules your interview to send you bios of the people you'll meet.

- *Know the job requirements well*—The interviewer won't be impressed if you don't even understand the position you're applying for. Practice for the interview by role-playing. Get together with a friend or relative and have him or her pretend to be your interviewer. Tell these people to ask tough questions about your background, goals, and knowledge of the company and industry. Chances are your role-play interviewer will be harder on you than the real one. But if you practice, the questions that arise during the actual interview will be less likely to throw you off balance.

Vocabulary

- human resources department
- industry sector
- body language
- group interview
- peer
- rapport
- unstructured interview
- structured interview
- stress interview
- behavioral interview

- *Know how to get to the interview site*—If you arrive late at your interview, you'll be in big trouble. Being late to the interview tells the employer just one thing: You'll probably be late to work, too. So be sure you know how to get to the interview, where to park, and any rules for visitors, such as getting a security badge to enter the building. Conduct a dry run beforehand if you think it will help. Be sure to account for variations in traffic, especially during rush hours.

- *Try to find out the salary range*—If you can't, don't bring up salary in the interview. It will seem like you are more interested in money than the job. But do come to the interview knowing the lowest salary you can afford to accept and how much others with your background earn. You can get this information from friends, your school counselor, or on websites such as *www.salary.com*.

- *Bring along a copy of your résumé*—together with a list of your references, transcripts, or extra copies of any other material the interviewer might need.

How to Dress

First impressions count. During the interview, you want to give the message that you expect to be taken seriously. Your clothes can help convey that message. Your interviewer will notice the amount of care you take in your dress. He or she will assume you'll take the same amount of care with your work. Don't let anyone think you'll be a sloppy employee.

While there are various standards of dress for different kinds of jobs, a conservative approach is the safest route. Do a little investigating to learn what to wear to the interview so you will look as though you "fit in" with the company.

Learn what to wear by:

- Calling the human resource office where you are interviewing
- Visiting the organization's office to see if there is a dress code
- Watching people arriving and leaving work

It's a good idea to match your interview outfit to the position. If you are applying for a job working on a warehouse floor, you will look out of place wearing a formal suit. However, you will still be expected to present a professional appearance at the interview.

Here are some useful general guidelines:

- *Look neat and clean*—Other than that, the exact type of clothing you'll wear depends on the job you're seeking. If you're applying for an office job or a job in which you'll meet the public, formal dress (suit and tie for young men, suit or dress for young women) is best. If you're applying for a job in a repair shop, by contrast, you can dress more casually.

- *Dress conservatively*—Don't try to make a fashion statement. Wear a neutral color—for example, dark blue is better than black or white. If you do choose black, wear a bright scarf or tie to offset it. Studies have shown that business executives dislike greens and yellows least of all the colors.

- *Watch out for the style of your clothing as well as for color*—If you're a woman, don't wear a low-cut top or one that exposes your midsection. Men should never show up for an interview with sagging trousers; it may be fashionable, but is frowned on in the work place. Men should also avoid casual sportswear and wear socks that are the same color as their trousers. Whether you're a man or woman, don't wear sandals, flip-flops, or sneakers.

- *Be careful with the extras*—If you wear jewelry, avoid anything that dangles or glitters excessively. If you're a young man who usually wears an earring, leave it at home unless you are sure it will be appropriate. Also recognize that—especially in conservative office environments—visible piercings and tattoos will limit your chances for a successful interview. Natural hair color will also be more acceptable during an interview; avoid extreme colors or styling fads.

- *Go easy on makeup and cologne*—This is an interview, not a party!

Dressing carefully conveys the message that you want a potential employer to take you seriously.

Courtesy of grafica/Shutterstock

success TIP

Be aware that over 90 percent of the decisions on who to bring back for a second interview are made during the first two minutes after meeting a job applicant. This is why how you look is very important. There is never a second chance to make a good first impression. If you go to an interview dressed properly, you will have a sense of confidence and others will relate positively to your self-assurance.

During the Interview

Your behavior during the interview also conveys a lasting impression about you. Follow these tips to present yourself at your best:

- *Arrive early*—Get to the site at least 15 minutes ahead of time. Go to the restroom for a final check of your clothes, hair, and makeup.

- *Don't take notes unless the interviewer asks you to.*

- *Remember the interviewer's name*—Make sure you know how to pronounce it correctly and use it during the interview. Refer to the person as "Mr." or "Ms." unless the interviewer invites you to use his or her first name or another title.

- *Shake hands firmly, whether the interviewer is male or female*—If your hands tend to perspire, run them under cold water for a few minutes before the interview.

- *Do not smoke, chew gum, or drink anything during the interview*—If you are offered something to drink, politely turn it down. Even handling a cup or glass can be distracting, and spilling something could really disrupt the image you want to create.

In your interview, be clear about your career direction and goals. Sell yourself.

Courtesy of P. Winbladh/Corbis Images

- *Wait for the interviewer to offer you a chair before you sit down.*

- *Answer all questions truthfully and appropriately*—Put your best foot forward. Talk about things that put you in the best light possible, and never lie—don't even exaggerate.

- *Keep positive*—Do not badmouth your school or teachers and never criticize a past employer.

- *Be enthusiastic and confident*—But don't boast.

- *Be aware of your body language.*

- *Be clear about your career direction and goals*—Have in mind the points you want to make about how well you can do this job and be sure you make them. Sell yourself.

Body Language—The Silent Communication That Comes Through Loud and Clear

Your body language and your dress leave an immediate and lasting impression about you.

Courtesy of Digital Vision/Getty Images

Body language is *the nonverbal message that your facial expressions, physical stance, and gestures convey to a listener*. Experts estimate that as much as 65 percent of communication is nonverbal. During your interview, pay particular attention to the following:

1. *Facial expressions*—Eye contact is important. If you avert your eyes, the interviewer may interpret this as a lack of self-confidence or even dishonesty. Avoid touching your face or hair during the interview. It can indicate nervousness. Your mouth is a major silent communicator. Smiling appropriately is great. However, if you constantly smile or purse your lips, the interviewer may interpret this negatively. A good rule of thumb: If in doubt, do what your interviewer is doing.

2. *Body gestures*—Crossed arms can indicate defensiveness or dissatisfaction. Keep your hands in your lap. If you tilt your head too far up, people think you feel superior. If you tilt it too far down, you give a message of inferiority. Sitting too straight can make you seem inflexible, but slouching makes you appear lazy. Don't lean on the desk or get too close to the interviewer.

3. *Hand gestures*—Gesture naturally. Avoid clenched hands; this can reveal anxiety. Never put your hands in your pockets or point your index finger at the interviewer. Avoid straightening your clothing, because the interviewer may view this as a sign you're unsure of yourself.

☑ I have prepared a list of appropriate questions to ask the interviewer.

☑ I have brought a list of references.

☑ I have reviewed my benefit statements and am prepared to sell myself to get the job.

☑ I have done research on the company.

☑ I am well groomed and appropriately dressed:

- My hair is cut, washed, and combed.
- I have bathed and used deodorant.
- My makeup, jewelry, and perfume or after-shave lotion are not excessive.
- My fingernails are trimmed and clean and I have brushed my teeth.
- My shoes are clean, neat, and unscuffed.
- I have shaved, if needed (males).

☑ I will be myself, whatever the circumstances of the interview.

☑ I will take extra copies of my résumé, transcript, portfolio, and any other print materials that the interviewer may request.

☑ I have a pen or pencil to fill out the company application form, should this be necessary.

☑ I will smile, be positive, and present myself in the best possible light.

FIGURE 6.5

Interview Day Checklist

Reprinted from *The Job Searcher's Handbook*, edited by Carolyn R. Robbins (2006), by permission of Pearson Education

Ending the Interview

You will know the interview is ending when the interviewer asks if you have any questions. Ask your questions. Then reiterate the main points that make you a strong candidate. Ask the interviewer when he or she thinks the company will make its decision. Emphasize how much you would like the job, and thank the interviewer for spending time with you.

Follow-Up

As soon as you get home, make notes about your impressions. List any points you forgot to mention or questions you forgot to ask. Within two days of the interview, send a follow-up letter or note (by US mail preferably, but e-mail is acceptable). Mention the points or questions that have come up since the interview ended. Stress again that you want the job and explain why you are qualified. Send separate notes to everyone who interviewed you.

Types of Interviews

Interviews can take many formats, from a face-to face interview to a videotaped session to a lunch or telephone interview. Here are the most common types of interviews you will experience:

Group or Committee Interviews

In a group interview, *several people will ask you questions*. These interviewers may include a potential peer, or *coworker at your level*. In some cases, you may be one of several applicants interviewed simultaneously. In that case, you may find yourself interacting with other applicants as well as with your interviewer(s). The objective of this interview approach is to determine how well you function in a group. Another variety of the group interview is a *committee* or *panel* interview, in which several people will interview you alone at once.

In any of these situations, you should:

- Make eye contact with, and speak to, each individual
- Try to establish rapport, or *a relationship or connection*, with everyone in the group
- Never interrupt anyone
- Think before you reply to a question, but don't pause too long
- Keep your answers short and direct.

Unstructured Interviews

The unstructured interview is *an informal session during which the interviewer will expect you to do most of the talking*. He or she will ask broad questions that you could answer in any number of ways. Employers like these kinds of interviews because they yield information about a candidate's opinions and reactions.

An unstructured interview can give you a great opportunity to sell yourself. You can bring up what you want to, as long as it relates to the question. The risk is that you might talk yourself right out of the job if you stray from the subject or say anything controversial. Stay focused: Talk about your ability to fill the position, your qualifications, and what you can do for the company. Don't get sidetracked into talking about irrelevant topics or personal trivia.

Structured Interviews

The structured interview is *a set of questions that the employer asks all candidates*. The questions are usually based on the job description. The drawback to this type of interview is that it does not allow you full opportunity to exhibit your personality, communication skills, or other attributes. You must stick to the canned questions the interviewer asks.

Stress Interviews

The stress interview *deliberately creates an environment that puts you under pressure so that the employer can see how you behave in tense situations*. This kind of interview is relatively rare. If you're applying for a job that may have a lot of stress, however, the employer may use it.

If you find yourself in a stress interview, stay calm. The interviewer may deliberately and frequently interrupt you, remain silent for long periods, or ask intimidating questions. Don't take the questions personally. Answer them as well as you can, and remember that the interviewer is testing you to see if you can handle stress.

Behavioral Interviews

A behavioral interview is *an interview during which the interviewer asks you to give examples of situations in which you demonstrated particular behaviors or skills*. Employers are using behavioral interviews more and more because they find they can often predict a potential employee's future conduct based on his or her past behavior.

During a behavioral interview, someone will ask you to describe in detail a particular event, project, or experience; how you dealt with it; and what the outcome was. Some questions might be:

- Describe a time when you faced a problem that tested your coping skills. What did you do?
- Give an example of a situation in which you had to make a quick decision.
- What is one of your important goals? How are you doing in meeting it?
- Describe the most creative work-related project you have completed.
- Give me an example of when you had to show good leadership.

The key to answering these questions is to be specific and honest. Don't describe how you should have behaved; describe how you *did* behave. If you later decided you should have behaved differently, explain why. The employer will be impressed to see that you learned from the experience. In preparing for this type of interview, it's helpful to review your experience and have a few stories ready to tell. That way you don't hesitate or draw a blank when the interviewer asks you to relate one.

Other Types of Interviews

If you are applying for a job in another city, a prospective employer may ask you to do a *videotaped interview*. If you face a camera instead of a person, speak slowly and clearly and show enthusiasm. Body language is especially important on camera—the camera sees you somewhat differently than the human eye does.

A prospective employer may need to interview you by phone. Don't worry: Preparing for a *telephone interview* is just like preparing for a face-to-face interview.

In today's workplace, *live video interviews* are becoming popular, because they are as convenient as telephone interviews, but allow you and the interviewer to interact visually. In this type of interview, you should always prepare as you would for a face-to-face interview. Here are some tips for live video interviews:

- Ask if you can arrive early to take some time to become familiar with the equipment.
- Use the picture-in-picture feature so you can see how you appear to the interviewer.
- Make eye contact. If you don't, the camera will be focused on the top of your head.

During a *lunch interview*, you may be tempted to relax too much. Remember, this is still an interview. Order something that you can handle and eat easily, without too much mess. This probably isn't the time for lobster or spaghetti with tomato sauce! Also, don't order the most expensive items on the menu; doing so might indicate to the interviewer that you are not cost-conscious.

Basic Interview Questions

Some standard questions pop up during virtually any interview, regardless of type. You'll also want to have a set of questions to ask at any interview. Here are some questions you'll probably have to answer at one point or other and some questions you may want to ask.

Questions Interviewers Ask

- *Tell me about yourself*—The interviewer does not want to know about your hobbies, your boyfriend or girlfriend, or your favorite TV show. He or she wants to know what you think is important about yourself with respect to the job you've applied for. Take this opportunity to present your best qualities and to explain how much you are interested in the company. Focus on the company's needs, not yours.

- *What do you see yourself doing in five years?*—The interviewer wants to see if you plan or live day-to-day. To answer this question impressively, your career goals should relate to those of the company. This is also a good opportunity to ask about the career path for the position you are interviewing for.

- *What is your greatest weakness (or strength)?*—The question is about your work behavior. The interviewer wants to find out how well you know yourself. If you need to talk about a weakness, focus on one that you are correcting, and tell the interviewer how you are doing that. This will show that you are mature. Everyone has weaknesses, but not everyone admits them or is working to correct them.

- *Why should we hire you?*—Think about this question beforehand and have a few good reasons ready. Make your reasons specific: Match your skills with those of the job.

- *What salary do you expect?*—Many employers want to know if your salary expectations match what they are willing to pay. If possible, avoid salary negotiations until you actually have a job offer. If the interviewer presses you, give a salary range rather than a specific figure. For example, say, "I understand that positions of this type generally pay between $25,000 and $28,000. That range would be acceptable."

- *Why do you want to work for us?*—Do your research, and then give an honest answer about why you like the organization.

Questions You May Want to Ask

- What would a typical workday be like if I had this position?
- What is the expected career path in your organization for a person in this position?
- Do you have a formal training program? Can you describe it?
- How do you evaluate your employees? How often?
- From your experience, what would you say are the organization's greatest strengths?

Questions You Should Not Ask

- *What happened to the person who had this job before?*—Answering this question could make the interviewer uncomfortable. Perhaps the employee moved on to a competing company. Or maybe the company asked the employee to leave because of poor performance. Frame this question in a positive way: Ask if the position is newly created or is an existing position that has become vacant.

- *Will I have to work overtime?*—This might make the interviewer think that you don't want to work too hard.

- *How much job security do you offer?*—Today's job market doesn't offer a great deal of security. Asking this question will only make you seem insecure.

- *When will I get my first raise?*—This question is inappropriate until you have been hired.

- *What benefits does the company offer?*—This question is not appropriate for the first interview, but you will want to find out the benefits of the job before you accept an offer.

Being able to anticipate questions that interviewers ask will make you more confident in any type of interview.

Courtesy of Adrian Weinbrecht/Getty Images

How Employers Evaluate Interviewees

During and after the interview, your potential employer will be evaluating you. What is he or she looking for? There is no standard evaluation or rating form that all employers use. Each company evaluates applicants differently. How you dress and speak, your mannerisms, and the validity and content of your answers to questions will all influence the evaluation. The employer will probably evaluate you in three basic areas: *character*, *commitment*, and *competence*.

Character

Employers want to be sure you are a person with a positive personality and good habits. In evaluating your character, they will look at your:

- Attitude
- Appearance
- Ability to communicate orally and in writing
- Ability to work collaboratively
- Self-confidence and poise
- School or work attendance record
- Community or extracurricular activities
- Leadership potential

Commitment

Employers also want to be sure you really want to work for them, will show up for work, and won't leave them in a few months—after they've invested time and effort in training you for the job. When employers look for commitment, they are looking for:

- Enthusiasm for the job and the company
- Goals and self-motivation
- Willingness to do what your employer asks

Competence

Finally, potential employers need to be sure you can do the work and do it well. In evaluating your competence, they'll look at your:

- Job-related skills and ability to perform the job
- Grades on courses and tests
- Educational qualifications for the job

It's important to understand that the person who gets the job is not always the person with the best skills, education, and experience. An employer wants someone who fits with the organization and its culture. Your interpersonal skills are very important, and that's one thing the interviewer will look for. Can you take criticism? Are you a good team player? Are you flexible? Can you communicate well?

Your personality is also important—especially qualities such as creativity, warmth, diplomacy, and self-confidence. In the end, people hire people they like. After all, they have to work with you every day.

✔ CHECKPOINTS

Lesson 3 Review

Using complete sentences, answer the following questions on a sheet of paper.

1. What are several things you should do to make sure your interview goes well?

2. Imagine that you have an interview next week at a major bank in your city. Describe what you will wear to the interview. List some types of clothing you should not wear.

3. List some body language you should avoid during an interview.

4. List and explain the different types of interviews.

5. Why are more and more employers using behavioral interviews?

6. Give one question you are afraid an employer might ask you. Decide how you would respond to the question. Write down your answer.

7. List some questions you should ask during an interview.

8. List some questions you should not ask during an interview.

9. What are the three basic areas that an employer will evaluate you on? Give examples of each area and explain its importance.

APPLYING INTERVIEWING SKILLS

10. Imagine that you've been asked to interview for a job you have your heart set on. Ask a friend or relative to do a role-play. Dress as if you were going to a real interview. Tell your interviewer to ask you the hardest questions he or she can. If you have a video camera, tape the interview. Play it back and analyze how you answered the questions. Pay attention to your body language.

CHAPTER 7

Courtesy of: (left) *PJF/Alamy*; (top) *gosphotodesign/Shutterstock*; (right) *MBI/Alamy*

Working for the Federal Government

Chapter Outline

"[One] who does not have what it takes to perform military service is not likely to have what it takes to make a living."

John F. Kennedy, 35th President of the United States

"Some people live an entire lifetime and wonder if they have ever made a difference in the world, but the Marines don't have that problem."

Ronald Reagan, 40th President of the United States

Branches of the US Military

When planning for your career, the options are endless. Service in our nation's armed forces is one of those options. The US military includes four peacetime service branches.

- The Air Force is the military's primary air and space arm. It defends the nation's air, space, and cyberspace, *the online world of computer networks, especially the Internet*, at home and overseas. It transports troops and equipment, and conducts air superiority warfare. Air Force bases support and maintain bombers, fighters, helicopters, in-flight refueling tankers, and reconnaissance aircraft.

- The Army is the nation's major ground fighting force. It uses infantry, armor, and artillery to conduct sustained combat operations. Army units move into an area to control, secure, and then help the local populace transition back to peacetime. The Army has the largest helicopter wing of all the services. This is for troop movements, air combat support operations and medical support. The Army also guards US installations worldwide.

- The Navy makes the seas safe for travel and trade. During wartime, it can bring to a fight a sizable attack force with many warships. Or it can launch strategic missile strikes from submarines and other vessels. The Navy's aircraft carriers protect fleets, or sometimes go on the offensive. The Navy also performs search-and-rescue missions, and delivers supplies to forces around the world.

- The Marine Corps is the United States' rapid-reaction force. Marines are trained as naval infantry. They are skilled in amphibious operations to assault an enemy shoreline from the seas. Often, Marines are involved in the most challenging situations in fighting for, and holding, land for incoming heavier land forces and air operations. Marines also provide security for the nation's embassies around the world.

America's fifth military service is the US Coast Guard. It is not a branch of the armed forces during peacetime. The Coast Guard's peacetime mission is conducted under the Department of Homeland Security (DHS). Under DHS, the Coast Guard protects our nation's coastlines, ports, and waterways. Its mission includes maritime safety and law enforcement. The Coast Guard is also widely known for its rescue operations.

However, in wartime, the Coast Guard, under Presidential order, becomes a fifth branch, serving under the US Navy, and would take on missions as directed by the Navy.

This lesson contains basic information about military career options. It describes how to join, what to expect about military life, and the benefits.

The US military in uniform is America's largest employer. More than 1.4 million people are on full-time active duty today. These men and women have varied skills, knowledge, and talents. They work in more than 4,000 career specialties, *positions that are distinctive, or peculiar to a military career.* That's a wide range of career options.

Air Force

The Air Force has about 333,000 men and women on full-time active duty. They work in interesting careers. They fly aircraft. They maintain and support the world's most technically advanced air and space vehicles. These include long-range bombers, supersonic fighters, reconnaissance aircraft, and many others. Their skills are in demand in the commercial world, *also referred to as the private sector.* As you may know, the private sector consists of *businesses that are part of the nation's economy run by private individuals or groups, usually for profit.*

Vocabulary

- cyberspace
- specialties
- commercial world
- private sector
- term of enlistment
- civilian
- civilian equivalents
- enlisted personnel
- junior enlisted personnel
- noncommissioned officers (NCOs)
- senior NCOs
- Armed Services Vocational Aptitude Battery (ASVAB)
- Armed Forces Qualification Test (AFQT) score
- security investigation
- basic training
- warrant officers
- commissioned officers
- cadet

Army

The active duty Army has more than 550,000 soldiers. They provide the Army's combat power, support, and services. Army career opportunities are quite varied. Jobs can be challenging with the Army's many overseas missions. However, these jobs prepare soldiers well for later civilian careers.

Navy

The Navy's 326,000 sailors work in all kinds of sea, land, and air-based career fields. The Navy has a large number of sailors who support battle groups with many ship and shipboard aircraft operations and maintenance. These jobs all require technical skill. Sailors also support living in the veritable small cities that comprise aircraft carriers at sea. And they have similar duties at land-based naval bases around the world.

Marines

The Marines are 202,000 strong. Most Marines are directly involved in light, mobile combat operations; others support units in hundreds of job specialties. They all require skill and a high level of discipline and dedication because of the nature of the Marine mission.

You can see that the range of possibilities for a service career covers a wide variety of jobs.

If you want to join the armed forces, you have two basic options. First, you can enter military service after high school. With this option, you'll quickly start to gain job skills during your training and will add valuable work experience throughout your time in service. Or you can go to college first, and then enter the military with the opportunity to prepare for a career as an officer. These options also have different requirements for your term of enlistment, or *the number of years you agree to remain in the military before you have the option to leave or sign up for another term.*

Reasons for Choosing a Military Career

Military careers are challenging. They require hard work and intelligence. The work offers great responsibility. It requires you to be strong—in mind, body, and spirit.

Military careers often appeal to people who are adventurous. Military service is also often a family tradition that is passed from one generation to the next. For many, the military experience is a chance to learn a skill for later in life. There are thousands of occupational specialties from which to choose. Many of them are very similar to civilian jobs.

In return for your service, the military will give you a chance to learn one or more job skills. You will gain work experience you can take back to the private sector as a civilian. A civilian is *a person who is not on active duty in the armed forces.*

What Military Life Is Like

To help you make a smart decision about a military career, here are some basic facts:

- *Earnings*—Pay itself starts fairly low in the military. However, it increases quickly as you are promoted and as your time in service. People serving in some positions receive extra pay for hazardous duty, specialized training, or foreign duty. In addition to salary, you'll receive clothing and housing allowances. You also receive medical and dental care. These benefits make earnings comparable to those offered by many civilian employers.

Military work requires you to be strong in mind, body, and spirit.

Courtesy of (clockwise from top left) MSgt Scott Reed, US Air Force Photo Archives; Oleg Zabielin/Shutterstock; AP Images; Petty Officer 1st Class Jennifer Villalovos/Defense Video & Imagery Distribution System

LESSON 1 Military Careers

- *Working conditions*—Many military personnel do much of their work outdoors, but others work entirely indoors. In either case, be prepared for plenty of exercise. In the military, physical fitness is part of the job. All military service members are deployed in many locations around the country and the world, in climates ranging from extreme cold to desert environments.

- *Hours*—The hours vary with the job. The mission comes first. You may have to work more than eight hours a day, and at times exceed a normal workweek.

- *Age*—You must be at least 18 years old (or 17 if a parent or guardian consents) to join the military.

- *Physical Requirements*—You must be in good physical shape and meet established weight standards.

- *Motivation*—In the military, you'll be serving your country. That's probably the most important attraction, along with college benefits for most young people who choose a military career.

Many Air Force enlisted jobs require highly skilled airmen such as Inflight Refueling Technicians..
Courtesy of the US Air Force

Military life offers many other advantages. The job security is great. While you are in the service, the military will meet most of your basic needs. You will have benefits like health care for you, your spouse, and children; low-cost life insurance; 30 days of vacation with pay each year; and the option to shop on the base, where prices tend to be lower than in civilian stores. Military bases also offer a variety of recreational facilities. In addition, you get to travel and see different countries. Finally, you can retire with benefits after only 20 years of service.

If you are18 when you enter the military, you could retire and begin a new career at age 38. Civilian employers will highly value your military training and experience. They will also welcome your discipline and leadership skills.

How Military Training and Experience Can Be Used in Civilian Jobs

Military service offers chances to gain many different skills. Once you've gained them, you'll have more career options. Many military positions have civilian equivalents, *jobs that are the same or similar to those in the civilian workplace*. These offer the chance to take your skills into a successful career elsewhere. In fact, nearly 80 percent of the military's career specialties have civilian job equivalents.

Air Force career options include jobs operating and maintaining aircraft. Airmen also work in strategic operations centers. Others work at air bases in communications; air traffic control; flight operations; or air transport logistics. Airmen also are office managers, vehicle mechanics, and computer specialists. As base security police and firefighters, they are first-responders. Like their civilian colleagues, they must react quickly to accidents or security problems.

The proportion of combat troops is fairly small among the Army's more than half a million soldiers. Some 80,000–90,000 new soldiers are needed each year. The Army has jobs in administration; logistics; food preparation; supply; and transportation of all kinds. Soldiers fix all types of weapons and equipment. They also serve in emergency medical treatment jobs. Many are in field computer and communications jobs. In the combat arms component of the Army, soldiers gain a background in their technical specialties, but also teamwork and leadership training that is unparalleled outside of the military. Most of these skills are needed in the private sector. A well-trained soldier has a chance for success in uniform and in civilian life.

Navy jobs also give sailors a chance to build skills for successful careers in and out of the service. Sailors serve in a variety of jobs aboard ship and on shore. They are navigators, pilots, flight officers, mechanics, and radio operators. Others work in intelligence or computer networks. Navy personnel operate and repair nearly 300 combat ships, submarines and support vessels, and over 4,000 aircraft.

The Marine Corps may be a small, mobile combat force, but it offers many career choices. Marines serve in about 300 specialties. They include construction; communications; logistics; maintenance and repair; security; computers; and field medical specialties. Marine training is intense. The Marine approach to all duties is highly regarded by civilian employers. They know that, as with all former service members, they'll get a motivated person ready to take on all challenges.

One of the most valued skills you will learn in the military is how to work with others.
Courtesy of Larry Steagall/AP Images

success TIP ★

When you consider a career, think of the military as a training ground for your future.

Entering the Military as an Enlisted Member

The majority of the military consists of enlisted personnel. Enlisted personnel are *generally young men and women who enter the armed forces with a high school diploma or equivalent*. They make up 85 percent of military personnel. They do most of the hands-on work. They perform much of the combat and support work that involves details and specialized skills.

In 1973, the draft was eliminated. Now, all of the military services rely on volunteers to fill thousands of enlisted jobs that come open each year. Enlisted ranks follow a career path, as outlined below:

- Junior enlisted personnel *enter at the lowest ranks, and focus much of their time on learning skills*. After training, they gain increases in responsibility and rank. But generally, they have little authority.

- Noncommissioned officers (NCOs) *have advanced leadership and technical skills. They often serve as specialists and supervisors.*

- Senior NCOs are *highly skilled and experienced. They carry significant authority and responsibility at the top enlisted ranks as leaders and managers.*

If you enlist, you will move up the ranks as you develop new technical and leadership skills.

Requirements for Entering the Service as an Enlisted Member

Armed Services Vocational Aptitude Battery (ASVAB)

Each of the services requires minimum scores on the Armed Services Vocational Aptitude Battery (ASVAB), which is *the entrance test to enlist in the US Military*. The ASVAB has two main purposes:

1. It determines whether you have the mental aptitude to enlist in the military branch of your choice.

2. The results help the service(s) determine which military job(s) you have the mental aptitude to perform.

The most important score from the ASVAB is the Armed Forces Qualification Test (AFQT) score, *used to determine if someone is eligible to enlist in the military*. The AFQT is made up of four subtests from the ASVAB. These include Paragraph Comprehension (PC), Word Knowledge (WK), Math Knowledge (MK), and Arithmetic Reasoning (AR). All enlistees must obtain a minimum score on the AFQT (see Tables 7.1 and 7.2).

Table 7.1 Enlistment Requirements by Service

US AIR FORCE	• Be between the ages of 17–27* • Have no more than two dependents • Minimum AFQT Score: 36 • ASVAB score determines available specialties
US ARMY	• Be between the ages of 17–34.* • Have no more than two dependents • Minimum AFQT Score: 31 • ASVAB score determines available specialties
US COAST GUARD	• Be between the ages of 17–39* • Have no more than two dependents • Minimum AFQT Score: 40 • ASVAB score determines available specialties • Have a willingness to serve on or around the water
US MARINES	• Meet exacting physical, mental, and moral standards • Be between the ages of 17–29* • Minimum AFQT Score: 32 • ASVAB score determines available specialties
US NAVY	• Be between the ages of 17–34* • Minimum AFQT Score: 35 • ASVAB score determines available specialties • Have a willingness to serve on or around the water

*Age limits vary based on active-duty, prior service or reserve status. 17-year-old applicants require parental consent.

Source: MILITARY.COM

The ASVAB is the most widely used multiple-aptitude test battery in the world. The ASVAB measures your strengths, weaknesses, and potential for future success. The ASVAB also provides you with career information for various civilian and military occupations; as such, it is a guide for planning whether you choose to go to college, vocational school, or into the military.

For each service, there are slightly different enlistment requirements (Table 7.1). Women are eligible to enlist in almost all fields, including combat-related specialties. Because some specialties are still restricted, interested women should contact a specific service's recruiter for details.

Table 7.2 Minimum Scores Required for Enlistment on the Armed Forces Qualification Test (AFQT)

Branch	MINIMUM AFQT	
	TIER I	TIER II
	≥ HS Diploma	= GED
US ARMY	31	50
US NAVY	35	50
US AIR FORCE	36	65
US MARINES	32	50
US COAST GUARD	45	50
US ARMY NATIONAL GUARD*	31	50
US AIR NATIONAL GUARD*	31	50

*The AFQT's minimum required scores for persons with a high school diploma (as of May 2012) are significantly lower than for those with a GED equivalent.

Source: MILITARY.COM

If you enlist, a security investigation will reveal any trouble you may have had with the law.

Courtesy of Mikael Karlsson/Alamy

If you graduated from high school, or obtained a GED equivalent, Table 7.2 shows what score each service requires.

Security Investigations

If you enlist, you will go through a preliminary security investigation. This *reveals information on any past arrests or questioning by law enforcement officers*. Military members must maintain high standards of behavior. They may have to handle classified information and equipment. You may need a more complete security check if your job requires it.

Delayed Entry Program

If you want to enter the military but wish to delay your entry until a more convenient time, you may often do so. Under the Delayed Entry Program, you can enlist before you graduate from high school, or in some cases, college, and report for training after you graduate. After you enlist, you can put off starting your training for up to 365 days. You will not have to do any active duty military activities. Also, you will not receive pay or benefits during the waiting period. You agree to enter active duty on a certain date, and if qualified, you will start your initial training at that point. One benefit of using the delayed entry program is that the job you want may not be available right now. However, if you are willing to wait a period of time prior to entering the military, an opening may become available in a job you really want.

Military Occupational Groups for Enlisted Personnel

Most military enlistees may choose jobs from the occupational groups listed in Table 7.3, which are common to all of the military services. But as you can see, there are skills also specific to each service.

What do you want to do? The military offers many rewarding careers within all the services. While you may think you want to work in one particular service branch, you should keep an open mind and know that many of the same jobs are offered within multiple branches.

Educational Opportunities for Enlisted Members by Service

Post–9/11 GI Bill

The Post–9/11 GI Bill was signed into law in 2009. It is the most comprehensive education benefit since the first GI Bill of 1944. If you serve at least 90 continuous days on active duty, you can qualify. If you decide to go into the National Guard or the Reserves, you can qualify if you have more than 90 days of active duty in any period starting after 9/11. Since all veterans benefits are legislated by Congress, benefits are subject to change.

The current Post–9/11 GI Bill pays all public school in-state tuition and fees. The full benefits are significant:

- Tuition and fees paid up to the highest such public in-state fees in each state
- Tuition and fees paid for online courses same as in-resident fees
- Living stipend that would be equivalent to the basic housing allowance for an E-5 with dependents (for that Zip Code)
- Up to $1,000 per year for books and supplies

Table 7.3 Occupations by Area for Each Military Service

US ARMY

Over 200 MOSs* for active duty personnel in such fields as:
- Administrative Services
- Combat Operations
- Electronic Maintenance
- Engineering and Construction
- Health Care
- Intelligence and Electronic Communications
- Mechanical Maintenance
- Media, Public and Civil Affairs

US NAVY

Over 100 careers in such fields as:
- Arts and Photography
- Aviation
- Business Management
- Computers
- Construction
- Education
- Electronics
- Engineering
- Finance and Accounting
- Information Technology
- Intelligence, Law Enforcement
- Legal
- Medical and Dental
- Music
- News and Media
- Special Operations
- Transportation and Logistics
- World Languages

US AIR FORCE

Over 300 AFSCs† in 35 career fields, including:
- Administration
- Avionics
- Base Operation
- Communications
- Electronics
- Engineering
- Flying/Navigation
- Information Technology
- Intelligence
- Medical
- Professional
- Special Forces
- Weapons Systems

US MARINE CORPS

Over 150 careers in such fields as:
- Avionics
- Data/Communications
- Electronics and Aircraft Maintenance
- Engineering
- Intelligence
- Legal Services
- Logistics
- Personnel & Administration
- Public Affairs
- Transport

US COAST GUARD

Over 20 jobs for enlisted personnel in:
- Administration
- Aviation
- Deck and Ordnance
- Engineering
- Port Security
- Science

*Military Occupational Specialties   †Air Force Specialty Codes
Source: MILITARY.COM

Basically, full benefits are paid for those who serve a minimum of three years on active duty. You can get a portion of the benefits for serving less time on active duty. Some colleges will contribute additional money to qualified service members under the Yellow Ribbon Program. The schools that participate, and the amounts they will contribute can be found at the Department of Veterans Affairs website. See: *http://www.gibill.va.gov/gi_bill info/CH33/YRP/YRP_List_2010.htm*.

These GI Bill benefits are payable for up to 15 years following an honorable discharge or retirement from service.

The Army, Navy, and Marine Corps College Fund Program

Called the GI Bill Kicker, the Army, Marine Corps and Navy all offer an additional amount of money that can be added to the Post–9/11 GI Bill. However, each service branch determines who qualifies for the College Fund and the amount received. These programs are usually offered when you first join the military.

To qualify, you must have a high school diploma and also be enrolled in the Post–9/11 GI Bill. Depending on test scores and your military occupation, there may be additional limits. Talk to a recruiter to find out if you are eligible, then ask for an application.

The Air Force doesn't have a College Fund Program, but it does have its own unique community college program.

Community College of the Air Force

The Community College of the Air Force (CCAF) is the largest multi-campus, two-year college in the world. It has more than 355,000 students. CCAF offers an associate of applied science degree for Air Force specialties. It combines credit for off-duty formal education with credit for training in Air Force skills. All active-duty Air Force enlisted persons are eligible for admission to CCAF after they pass the ASVAB and complete basic training. Basic training is *the period during which an enlistee enters the service and learns basic military skills.*

Tuition Assistance Programs

If you are in the service and want to continue your education, Tuition Assistance Programs are available. They allow you a chance to enroll in courses at accredited colleges, universities, junior colleges, and vocational-technical schools.

Each service has its own requirements, but all can help with tuition for almost any kind of degree or certificate. The monetary benefit, if you are on full-time active duty, is the same—up to 100 percent of the cost of tuition, or expenses up to $250 per credit, or up to $4,500 total per fiscal year.

Each service has different requirements for assistance; this can include the time you must have remaining on active duty, or the total number of credit hours you can complete. For example, under the Coast Guard's College Student Pre-Commissioning Initiative, you must attend a school from a specific list.

In the Selected Reserves and National Guard, tuition assistance benefits will also vary.

Servicemembers Opportunity Colleges (SOC)

Servicemembers Opportunity Colleges (SOC) is a flexible way to gain an education while serving. Family members can benefit as well. Hundreds of thousands of people are enrolled in SOC each year. Courses can be taken in the classroom or at a distance by computer or correspondence.

SOC offers college degrees through an association with accredited colleges, universities, and technical institutes. Two-year, four-year, and graduate-level programs are available. A subgroup of SOC offers associate and bachelor's degree programs to Army, Navy, Marine, and Coast Guard servicemembers and their families.

SOC offers servicemembers a personal degree plan. It also offers college credit for military experience, military training courses, and for national tests (see below). Member schools acknowledge and transfer credits. This makes it possible to continue your studies when you move to new duty stations. You can see more details at: *http://www.soc.aascu.org/*.

Loan Repayment Programs

The Army, Navy, and Air Force offer loan repayment programs. These programs help enlisted members pay off college loans accrued prior to their active service. Each service's program has unique requirements, but they are all designed as enlistment incentives to help recent college attendees manage education debt.

- *Army*—Active-duty soldiers can qualify to have their loan(s) repaid at the rate of one-third of the loan for each year of full-time duty served (up to $65,000). The Army even helps soldiers pay off approved Perkins, Stafford or other Department of Education–guaranteed student loans.

- *Navy*—For active-duty Navy personnel, a $65,000-maximum Loan Repayment Program is also available. To qualify, you must have a high school diploma; a loan guaranteed under the Higher Education Act of 1965; and had no prior military service.

- *Air Force*—The College Loan Repayment Program (CLRP) is a program created for those considering duty with the Air Force who have taken some college courses and have accumulated debt. Participants can qualify when signing the enlistment contract. Under CLRP, the repayment maximum is $10,000 per recruit.

For additional information about college loan repayment programs contact the service's recruiter. There may be additional restrictions to accepting loan repayment.

Educational Testing Programs

Military enlistees may also earn college credits by passing certain tests. Testing is a fast and inexpensive method of obtaining college credit.

College-Level Examination Program (CLEP)

The CLEP consists of a series of general examinations that test a person's college-level knowledge. You can gain this knowledge through courses or

Military members study to get ready to take tests for college credit.
Courtesy of Lisa Billings/AP Images

through independent study, cultural pursuits, travel, or other avenues. The 90-minute CLEP exams are funded by the Department of Defense. You could save hundreds, even thousands, of dollars toward your degree. You can take them at over 1,700 locations across the country. They are also given at on-base testing centers worldwide. College credits for successful scores are valid at 2,900 colleges and universities.

The CLEP general tests cover five topics:

1. English Composition
2. Social Science, History
3. Natural Sciences
4. Humanities
5. Mathematics

There are more specific "subject exams" that are computer-based and timed. For each one a servicemember passes, he or she usually gets three college-credit hours.

According to the College Board, each college and university has its own CLEP evaluation system that it uses to determine how much credit to give you for your knowledge. Some colleges offer up to 30 hours of credit to enlisted members who pass the tests.

DANTES Subject Standardized Test (DSST)

Passing a DSST exam also earns servicemembers college credit. There is no time limit and the test is paper-based.

Excelsior College Exams (ECE)

Excelsior College is a "virtual university" that counts many military personnel among its worldwide graduates. Excelsior College Exams are accepted for college credit by hundreds of colleges and universities.

Also, as of August 1, 2011, servicemembers can receive reimbursement for some licensing and certification exams, as well as for fees related to the SAT, LSAT, ACT, and other college and graduate school entrance tests.

Serving in the Military as a Warrant Officer

A second career path open through military service is that of a warrant officer. Warrant officers are *highly skilled officers who work in a single-track specialty throughout their military service*. Warrant officers serve in the Army, Navy, Marine Corps, and Coast Guard. The Air Force ended its warrant officer program in 1959. A warrant officer (grade W-1 to CW-5) is rated as an officer above the senior-most enlisted ranks, as well as officer cadets and candidates, but below all commissioned officer grades.

Warrant officers serve as the military's technical experts, covering virtually all fields where in-depth knowledge is needed. They provide specialized skills and guidance to commanders and organizations. Unlike commissioned officers, whose careers offer increased levels of command and staff positions, warrant officers remain single-specialty officers with career tracks within their fields.

You must be a high school graduate and a US citizen to apply for a warrant officer position. Most specialties also require applicants to have already served five years or more in the military (one exception is Army aviation). Therefore, becoming a warrant officer for most high school graduates is a long-term rather than an immediate goal.

However, this career path is an attractive one allowing you an extended career path as a highly respected specialist.

Entering the Military as a Member of the Officer Corps

Military Education and Commissioning Programs

The military has several options for combining education with a commission. Commissioned officers are *personnel who enter the armed forces with a four-year college degree or higher, and who compete to enter and earn a commission from the President after confirmation by Congress*. They fill key leadership, managerial, professional, and technical jobs. They include combat and support branch officers, doctors, nurses, lawyers, engineers, and pilots. Commissioned officers make up 15 percent of armed forces personnel.

One option for getting a commission is competing to get into one of the military service academies. You'll learn more about the service academies later in this lesson.

The Army, Navy, Marine Corps, and Air Force also have bachelor's degree programs through SROTC (Senior Reserve Officer Training Corps). After achieving a degree through SROTC, each graduate is required to serve a military commitment.

All services have an Officer Candidate School or Officer Training School (Air Force). They accept college graduates who did not complete Senior ROTC courses or attend a service academy. OCS/OTS programs also train individuals with special skills such as chaplains, doctors, nurses, or lawyers for direct commissions. These programs will also be covered in more detail later in this lesson.

Commissioned officers are those with the rank of second lieutenant and above. Military officers in the Air Force, Army, and Marine Corps with the rank of second lieutenant, first lieutenant, and captain are called *company-grade officers*. In the Navy, those with the rank of ensign, lieutenant junior grade and lieutenant are called *junior-grade officers*.

Air Force, Marine, and Army majors, lieutenant colonels, and colonels are called *field-grade officers*. In the Navy, the equivalent ranks of lieutenant commander, commander and captain are called *mid-grade officers*. An officer who ranks above colonel is a *general officer*. In the Navy/Coast Guard, those above the rank of Captain are *flag officers*.

How to Become a Commissioned Officer

To be a commissioned officer, you must be a US citizen and have at least a bachelor's degree from an accredited college. You must achieve the minimum entry score on an officer qualification test administered by each service branch. Additionally, to earn a commission as an officer you must successfully complete an officer-commissioning program through a service academy, SROTC, or an officer candidate (training) program. Some positions require a graduate degree or specific courses. In addition, you must be physically fit and of high moral character. You must be in good health and pass a medical exam. Certain diseases or conditions may exclude persons from enlisting or commissioning.

There are four main paths to becoming a commissioned officer: the service academies, Senior Reserve Officer Training Corps (SROTC), Officer Candidate or Officer Training School (OCS/OTS), and direct appointment.

The Service Academies

The United States has four service academies:

- United States Military Academy at West Point, New York (Army)
- United States Naval Academy at Annapolis, Maryland (Navy and Marine Corps)
- United States Air Force Academy at Colorado Springs, Colorado
- United States Coast Guard Academy at New London, Connecticut

Service academies are very competitive. Only those applicants with high qualifications are admitted.

Courtesy of (clockwise from top left) Michael Kaplan/Defense Video & Imagery Distribution System; Dave Bartruff/Corbis Images; Jack Sauer/AP Images; Mayre Beltran/AP Images

Competition for entry into the academies is keen. Only the highest-qualified candidates are accepted. To be eligible for admission to any of the academies, you must be at least 17 years old, a citizen of the United States, of good moral character, and academically and physically qualified.

In addition, candidates for the Army, Navy, and Air Force Academies must be nominated—usually by a US senator or representative, but sometimes by the Vice President or the President. The process for obtaining a congressional nomination is not political, and candidates do not have to know their senator or representative personally to secure a nomination. To request a nomination, you can call or write a senator or representative's office (from your state or territory) to ask for information.

Each member of Congress and the Vice President can nominate up to five nominees attending a service academy at any time. Additional nomination slots are available for children of career military personnel, children of disabled veterans or veterans who were killed in action, or children of Medal of Honor recipients.

The Coast Guard Academy does not require a nomination from a Congressional member or the President or Vice President. Admittance is based solely on personal merit. Applications for the Coast Guard Academy are now only accepted online.

The Army, Navy, and Air Force Academies all accept between 1,000–1,500 new student/cadets per year. The Coast Guard takes in only a little over 400 per year.

The academies offer four-year programs of study leading to a bachelor of science degree. Students receive free tuition, room, board, medical and dental care, and a monthly allowance. Graduates receive a commission as a military officer. After graduation, they must serve on active duty for at least five years. Depending on the type of specialty training you receive after graduation, your commitment to serve may be longer.

Senior Reserve Officer Training Corps (SROTC)

Undergraduate students may receive training to become officers under the Senior Reserve Officer Training Corps (SROTC) Program. SROTC programs for the Army, Navy, Air Force, and Marine Corps are available in more than 1,400 colleges and universities nationwide.

SROTC programs recruit, educate, and commission officer candidates through college campus programs. Cadets normally enroll in the first two years of SROTC classes at the same time and in the same manner as they enroll in other college courses. A cadet is *a SROTC candidate or military academy appointee.* Depending on the service and option they select, SROTC students train for two, three, or four years. Many receive scholarships for tuition, books, fees, and uniforms. They also get a monthly allowance, or stipend. In addition to their military and college course work, SROTC cadets perform leadership-building activities and drills for a number of hours each week. At some point, cadets take part in military training for several weeks during the summer. Graduating SROTC candidates receive commissions as military officers. They then go on active duty or become members of Reserve or National Guard units.

SROTC instructors are normally active-duty military officers (although there are some Reserve instructors, depending on the university). Most have a master's degree and usually hold the academic rank of assistant professor.

ROTC candidates climb ropes on an obstacle course at Oregon State University, Corvallis, Oregon.

Courtesy of Bohemian Nomad Picturemakers/Corbis Images

Table 7.4 Officer Candidate/Officer Training Schools, by Service

School	Duration	Rank upon Graduation	Location	More info.
Army Officer Candidate School	12 weeks	Second Lieutenant	Fort Benning Fort Benning, Ga.	*Army OCS*
Marine Corps Officer Candidates School	10 weeks	Second Lieutenant	Marine Corps Base Quantico, Va.	*Marine Corps OCS*
Navy Officer Candidate School	12 weeks	Ensign	Naval Station Newport, RI.	*Navy OCS*
Air Force Officer Training School	12 weeks	Second Lieutenant	Maxwell-Gunter Air Force Base Montgomery, Al.	*Air Force OTS*
Coast Guard Officer Candidate School	17 weeks	Ensign	Coast Guard Academy New London, Ct.	*Coast Guard OCS*

Source: *http://www.todaysmilitary.com/before-serving-in-the-military/officer-candidate-school*

Officer Candidate/Officer Training Programs

Officer Candidate School (OCS), or Officer Training School (OTS) in the Air Force, for those interested in becoming officers, have similar training programs for enlisted servicemembers who go through Basic Training. The types of people who attend OCS/OTS usually are:

- Graduates from a traditional four-year college or university
- Enlisted servicemembers (often called "Prior Service") who are making the transition between enlisted ranks and officer roles
- Those who hold direct commissions, and are going through either an officer basic course or other form of an officer training school.

While duration and type of training varies among the Services, all teach military subjects, leadership skills and physical training. The goal is to prepare these recruits and newly commissioned officers for the challenges of officer life, from managing others to understanding military culture and law. You can learn more about specific programs and classes by visiting the service-specific websites listed in Table 7.4.

Direct Appointments

Professionals in medicine, law, biomedical engineering, and religion who are fully qualified in their fields may apply to receive direct appointments as military officers. After entering military service, they can begin practicing their professions with a minimum of military training. Their appointments last two years, although some are longer. Some scholarship programs are available to assist students in these fields in return for several years of service.

CHECKPOINTS

Lesson 1 Review

Using complete sentences, answer the following questions on a sheet of paper.

1. Name the military services that make up the nation's armed forces in wartime. Describe them.

2. Name three military skills from any service that you could transfer into a civilian career.

3. Name and describe two major military educational programs from which you may benefit while serving in the military.

4. Describe the differences between an enlisted servicemember and an officer.

5. What is the name of the test administered by the armed forces to decide eligibility for enlistment and show aptitude for training?

6. List six military occupational groups from any service, that are available to enlisted personnel.

7. Describe and distinguish between the various levels of rank among enlisted servicemembers.

8. Name and describe the four main pathways to becoming a commissioned officer.

9. List the four service academies and write a brief description of each academy.

10. What are the basic requirements for you to receive an appointment to any service academy? Which service academy does not require a Congressional recommendation?

APPLYING CAREER SKILLS

11. Assume that you decide to enlist in the military after you graduate from high school or college. Write a letter to a relative that explains why you chose to take this step, which service, and why that service? Make your letter at least three paragraphs long.

Careers in Aerospace

"No matter where you are from, with hard work and dedication, by learning math, science and engineering, you too might travel to the stars."

G. Wayne Clough, Secretary of the Smithsonian Institution

Aerospace as a Career Direction

Careers in aerospace are in demand, partly because of the appeal of the field, *an area of a profession*. Aerospace careers are challenging and rewarding. The aerospace field will continue to grow and need skilled workers, engineers, and scientists. If you decide to enter one of these careers, you will be of great service to your country and the world. Working in commercial aviation, you will help transport people and many of the world's products. You'll also probably have opportunities for travel not available in other career fields.

The aerospace industry employs tens of thousands of people in general, commercial, and military aviation.

Courtesy of Ilja Mašík/Shutterstock

What Does "Aerospace" Mean?

Aerospace *combines "aero," from "aeronautics," or flight within Earth's atmosphere, and "space," or flight beyond the atmosphere.*

It's sometimes hard to make a distinction between these two types of flight. One reason is that scientists haven't agreed on where the earth's atmosphere ends and space begins.

That's why the word *aerospace* is a handy way to refer to either type of flight. It refers to general, commercial, and military aircraft. It also covers spacecraft, satellites, and space probes.

If you pursue a career in aerospace, you will need a full range of skills, education, and training. The time invested will be worth it. If you enter this field, you can design, build, pilot, or maintain aerospace vehicles. Aerospace engineers, flight operations specialists, astronauts, pilots, machinists, and flight attendants are among the many people employed in the hundreds of careers available in aerospace. So are aircraft maintenance and other technicians, and air traffic controllers.

How Do You Know if You Want an Aerospace Career?

One way to decide if a career in aerospace is right for you is to examine your abilities and interests. Reflect back to your interests established with the Holland inventory and career exploration from Chapter 3, Lesson 2. Think about your favorite courses as well as your hobbies.

Consider the opening quotation in this lesson. When you gaze into the night sky, do you wonder about travel to the planets and stars? Do you wonder about extraterrestrial life, *life originating, existing, or occurring outside the earth or its atmosphere*? What about what makes an airplane fly? Or what could make it fly more quietly or safely?

Vocabulary

- field
- aerospace
- extraterrestrial life
- scientists
- scientific research
- basic research
- applied research
- industry
- engineers
- technician
- technologist
- National Aeronautics and Space Administration (NASA)
- Federal Aviation Administration (FAA)
- astrophysics
- heliophysics
- machinists

On a more practical level, do you like to solve problems and puzzles? Do you like to create or build? Do you enjoy working with computers? Do you enjoy math and science? Do you get good grades? And are you prepared to study hard?

If you answered "yes" to most of these questions, an aerospace career could be within your reach.

Scientists

One way to get into aerospace is to be a scientist. Scientists are *those who seek answers to expand knowledge through discovery about why things happen the way they do*. They are always asking questions because they are fascinated by nature, earth, and the universe. Scientists focus on theories and concepts, especially the physical qualities or properties of things. More simply, their scientific research is *a process of discovery*.

There are two major kinds of research: *basic* and *applied*. Sometimes research is a combination of the two approaches.

Scientists often conduct basic research. This is *pure research that typically has no specific initial goals*. Scientists are trying to develop theories that explain events. They base their theories on the discoveries of other scientists and their own findings. Applied research is *focused on using previous findings to solve a practical problem or to develop a product*. Scientists advance knowledge by sharing their findings with other scientists.

Most scientists do their research in schools or universities, and many teach as well. Others work in industry, *a group of productive or profit-making enterprises*, or for the government.

Engineers

Engineers are *professionals who use the results of applied research, mathematics, and other well-established principles to change ideas and theories into realities*. Engineers do things like design skyscrapers, race cars, jumbo jets, and space vehicles. Engineers are practical thinkers. They use science and math to solve problems. They take the results of scientists' research to make products that people use every day. Engineering is the link between scientific discovery and practical use.

Computers, television, and satellites depend on engineers. Without engineers we would probably not have many of the things we take for granted today; houses, cars, bridges, roads, television, and airplanes are a few examples.

Engineering is the second-largest profession in the United States. Among the professions, only teaching employs more people.

Technicians and Technologists

A technician is *someone who translates the technical plans created by engineers into useful products and services*. Technicians are experts at detail. They work closely with scientists and engineers. On an aerospace team, technicians use their skills to operate wind tunnels, construct test equipment, build models, and support many types of research. To prepare for their work, technicians must complete either a two-year technical training program or significant on-the-job training.

A technologist *does work similar to that of a technician, but at a higher level*. Technologists are graduates of four-year programs in engineering technology. Both technicians and technologists play critical supporting roles in all areas of science and engineering. They work in all phases of the aerospace industry, from theory through construction, testing, and operations. Thousands of career opportunities today require a technical education.

Salaries in Aerospace

The aerospace industry needs top-notch people. To get them, it offers good salaries. Table 7.5 lists salaries of some typical careers in the industry. These figures were current as of 2012.

Table 7.5 Aviation Jobs and Salary Ranges

Career/Industry Group	Minimum Salary	Average Salary	Maximum Salary
Air Traffic Controllers	$37,282.00	$108,040.00	$132,108.00
Airframe and Powerplant Mechanic	$18,000.00	$ 49,570.69	$ 93,400.00
Avionics Specialist	$35,698.00	$ 66,658.00	$100,000.00
Computer Specialist	$30,350.00	$ 62,358.00	$ 80,000.00
Dispatcher	$43,240.00	$ 59,170.00	$ 75,100.00
Aerospace Engineer	$40,000.00	$ 80,416.67	$200,000.00
Flight Crew (Flight Attendant)	$24,000.00	$ 47,000.00	$ 70,000.00
Ground-Ramp Workers	$23,000.00	$ 33,000.00	$ 45,000.00
Airport Management Official	$31,200.00	$ 73,352.32	$160,000.00
Airport Office Administrator	$32,150.00	$ 40,450.00	$ 48,750.00
Pilot	$24,000.00	$ 77,625.00	$130,000.00
Sales/Marketing	$35,000.00	$ 58,000.00	$100,000.00

Sources: 2012 aviation salary data provided by Avjobs, Inc. at *http://www.avjobs.com/salaries-wages-pay/salaried-aviation-pay.asp*; additional information from *http://www.bls.gov/ooh/transportation-and-material-moving/air-traffic-controllers.htm*

Major Organizations in the Aerospace Sector

Two main federal agencies support the US aerospace industry. They are the National Aeronautics and Space Administration (NASA), *the government agency responsible for the US space program and general aerospace research*; and the Federal Aviation Administration (FAA), *the government agency responsible for the safety of civil aviation*.

National Aeronautics and Space Administration (NASA)

NASA is responsible for the US space program and general aerospace research. It conducts research into both civilian and military aerospace systems. NASA's main office is in Washington, D.C., but conducts research around the world. NASA has supported *basic* and *applied* research that has improved aerospace and our everyday lives.

Humans have always been fascinated by space. But it wasn't until the 1950s that scientists and engineers were able to tackle some basic questions about space exploration. What's out there? How do we get there? What will we find? What can we learn from exploring space that will make life better here on earth?

In the late 1950s, the Soviet Union launched *Sputnik*, the first space satellite. This was the beginning of space exploration. Hoping to help the United States gain the lead in the "space race," President Dwight D. Eisenhower established NASA in 1958.

Through the Mercury and Gemini projects, NASA developed the technology and skills for further explorations. President John F. Kennedy would proclaim that the United States would put a man on the moon, and indeed, on 20 July 1969, US astronauts Neil Armstrong and Buzz Aldrin became the first men to walk on the moon.

An astronaut working on a NASA space shuttle in orbit around Earth.

Courtesy of NASA/Alamy

In the 1970s, NASA focused on developing a way to give the United States ready access to space. The outcome of this work was the space shuttle. NASA launched its first space shuttle in 1981. By 2011 when manned space shuttle missions ended, NASA had recorded 166 successful manned space flights. Two crews, however—aboard the shuttles *Challenger* and *Columbia*— were lost. In 2000, the United States and Russia established a permanent human presence in space aboard the international space station.

Meanwhile, NASA's planetary research program continues. In 1997, the Advanced Composition Explorer (ACE) became the first in a fleet of spacecraft to explore Mars. NASA also launched Terra and Aqua, satellites that orbit Earth. The data sent back from these satellites are helping us understand life on Earth.

You can view all of NASA's current missions in space at: *http://www.nasa.gov/ missions/current/index.html*.

NASA's Mars rover *Curiosity*'s mission is to assess whether Mars is, or ever was, able to support life.
Courtesy of NASA/JPL-Caltech/MSSS/Rex Feat/AP Images

NASA Mission Directorates

NASA conducts its work in these main areas:

- *Aeronautics Research*—Works to solve things like air traffic congestion, safety, and environmental impacts. Studies are ongoing in new aircraft technologies.
- *Human Exploration and Operations*—Includes the International Space Station, and robotics.
- *Science*—Explores the Earth and the planets. Studies are done in astrophysics, *the study of how Earth works and how the universe began and evolved*. Other studies are in heliophysics, *understanding the Sun and how it interacts with Earth and other parts of the solar system*.

Working for NASA

NASA offers careers for scientists, engineers, technicians, technologists, computer programmers, personnel specialists, accountants, writers, maintenance workers, and many others. At its website, *www.nasajobs.nasa.gov*, you can review employment opportunities with NASA. You can also find opportunities for student internships and summer employment.

For many young people interested in careers at NASA, the ultimate goal is to be an astronaut. Former astronaut Dr. Sally K. Ride, the first American woman in space, has these suggestions:

The most important steps that I followed were studying math and science in school. I was always interested in physics and astronomy and chemistry, and I continued to study those subjects through high school and college and into graduate school. That's what prepared me for being an astronaut. It actually gave me the qualifications to be selected to be an astronaut. I think the advice that I would give to any kids who want to be astronauts is to make sure that they realize that NASA is looking for people with a whole variety of backgrounds...So find something that you really like and then pursue it as far as you can, and NASA is apt to be interested in that profession.

Lesley Janosik works in an exciting field as a materials research engineer. Her reason for working at NASA?

"I chose NASA because it provides a unique environment that allows me to pursue new challenges. My work impacts material selection and component design. NASA has allowed me to continue to grow and improve professionally to achieve my own personal goals. I have been able to further my education through formal courses. I've also had the opportunity to meet and work with some wonderful people, and have formed many close relationships."

Lesley Janosik
Materials Research Engineer
Glenn Research Center
Pennsylvania State University
Joined NASA in 1991
Courtesy of NASA/Johnson Space Center

Being responsible for a pilot's life support equipment, Bob McElwain has an important job, where his two-year degree was put to good use.

"I have had a somewhat unique path to NASA," says McElwain. "When I was starting out, college really wasn't an option. But because I loved the thought of being around aircraft, I joined the Air Force, where I earned my associates degree in Survival and Rescue. I spent 26 years in the military, then joined private industry for three years, and finally joined NASA.

At NASA, I feel I'm a part of aviation history. I get involved in all the flight projects (and) my biggest responsibility is training aircrews how to eject from a disabled aircraft, (employ) parachuting procedures, and survival techniques. I know my work could make a difference in an emergency situation."

Bob McElwain
Life Support Technician
Dryden Flight Research Center
Joined NASA in 1994
Courtesy of NASA/Johnson Space Center

Federal Aviation Administration (FAA)

The FAA is the government agency responsible for the safety of civil aviation. The FAA was formed in 1958. The FAA promotes safety in civilian aviation and new aviation technology. It also regulates air traffic control and navigation, aviation noise, and commercial space transportation.

What Does the FAA Do?

The FAA conducts work in many areas, such as:

- *Safety Regulation*—Enforcing regulations and minimum standards in manufacturing, operating, and maintaining aircraft; and certifying civilian pilots and airports that serve air carriers.
- *Airspace and Air Traffic Management*—Operating a network of airport towers, air traffic control centers, and flight service stations; and also developing air traffic rules, assigning the use of airspace, and controlling air traffic.
- *Air Navigation Facilities*—Maintaining, operating, and ensuring the quality of air navigation facilities.
- *Civil Aviation Overseas*—Promoting aviation safety and encouraging civil aviation overseas; and exchanging aeronautical information with foreign governments.
- *Commercial Space Transportation*—Regulating and encouraging the US commercial space transportation industry.
- *Research, Engineering, and Development*—Developing better aircraft, engines, and equipment; and conducting aeromedical research, or medical research that deals specifically with the aerospace field.

The nation's air traffic controllers work for the Federal Aviation Administration.
Courtesy of Chad Slattery/Getty Images

Commercial Aerospace Organizations

Most inventions and discoveries start out being the result of a pure love for science. The Wright Brothers, no doubt, were thinking in those terms as they sought to fly. If they were to see now where aerospace has progressed in the first 100 years, they would certainly be amazed.

The advance from experimental flight to commercial air travel was bound to happen. Rapid growth of the aerospace industry came into being not long after the Wright Brothers' first flight at Kitty Hawk, North Carolina.

As commercial aviation grew, so did military aviation. During both of the two world wars, American companies shifted from making commercial aircraft into making the bombers, fighters, and other aircraft necessary to win those conflicts.

Today, about 500,000 people work in aerospace. They are in scientific and technical jobs across the nation. Another 700,000 people work in related areas as machinists, or *workers who make, assemble, or repair machinery*, engineers, and in other fields.

Aerospace companies like Boeing, Lockheed-Martin, and Northrop Grumman lead the nation in developing advanced new air- and spacecraft. But they also do other jobs.

Boeing

If you visit Boeing's "Careers" area of its website at *http://www.boeing.com/careers*, you'll learn that Boeing is the world's largest manufacturer of commercial jetliners and military aircraft combined. Boeing designs and manufactures planes, helicopters, satellites, space launch vehicles and advanced information and communication systems. Boeing is also NASA's prime contractor for the International Space Station. If you dream about about working for a company with a global presence, Boeing has customers in more than 90 countries around the world.

Boeing has over 170,000 employees. More than 140,000 have college degrees—including nearly 35,000 advanced degrees—in virtually every business and technical field from approximately 2,700 colleges and universities worldwide.

Lockheed Martin

Lockheed Martin is another large aerospace company. A global security and aerospace company that employs over 120,000 people, Lockheed Martin is principally engaged in research, design, and development of new technologies such as the F-22 advanced fighter and the C-17 cargo plane, and is the leading provider of computer security solutions to the Federal government.

A High School Field Trip Launches a Career

Brittany Bailey
Lockheed Martin
Aeronautics engineer
Courtesy of Lockheed Martin

Brittany Bailey, a Lockheed Martin Aeronautics engineer, found her career path on a field trip. She explains:

"I first realized that I wanted to become an engineer as a junior in my high school chemistry class. My teacher was actively involved with the local chapter of the National Society of Black Engineers and established a junior chapter at Tri-Cities High School. I was on a field trip for my chemistry class and we made a visit to the robotics lab at Georgia Tech. Ms. Tarver was all about exposing her students to as much science and math as we could handle. As a 16-year-old, I would do anything to go on a field trip, so of course I joined the junior chapter at my school. Little did I know I would find something that truly interests me and would ultimately become my career.

After completing my bachelor's degree in Computer Science at Tennessee State University, I came to work for Lockheed Martin Aeronautics Company where I am a software engineer. As an engineer, my goal is to make my user's life easier, whether that user is the mission planner of an F-35 or the maintainer of the F-22.

As a software engineer, I am able to take someone's conceptual decision of a system and apply my problem solving skills to turn this design into reality. To think that all of this came about by a field trip with my chemistry teacher still amazes me. I often wonder what my career path would have been if my teacher didn't push me or if I didn't have parents that always encouraged me and never let me settle.

All things happen for a reason and I am truly proud to say that I am an engineer."

"Little Did I Know an Interesting Field Trip Would Ultimately Become My Career," by Brittany Bailey, reprinted from *http://www.lockheedmartin.com*, by permission of Lockheed Martin

The company develops advanced technologies in:

- *Aeronautics*—Tactical aircraft, airlift, and aeronautical research and development
- *Electronic Systems*—Missiles and fire control, naval systems, simulation and training
- *Information Systems & Global Solutions (IS&GS)*—Government and commercial information technologies and command, control, communications, computers and intelligence (C4I) systems
- *Space Systems*—Space launch, commercial satellites, government satellites, and strategic missiles.

Northrop Grumman

Northrop Grumman is another of the big aerospace companies. Like Lockheed Martin, it has many missions in addition to aerospace such as electronics, information systems, and technical services. Its main aerospace contributions to defense include:

- Global Hawk, Fire Scout and UCAS-D unmanned aircraft systems
- B-2 stealth bomber
- E-2D Advanced Hawkeye
- Joint STARS targeting and battle management system.

Northrop Grumman also supports civilian aviation through navigation technology, airspace management, and commercial aircraft protection systems.

Aerospace Jobs Related to Flight

If you look across these and other aerospace companies, you'll find many jobs directly related to flight. There are also many more jobs available in a large group of industries that do supporting roles. They employ many people with different skills. Some of these are in:

- *Rotorcraft (helicopters)*—Emergency medical services (EMS); offshore oil and gas exploration; and law enforcement. Employment, production and demand are expected to expand in this industry.
- *General Aviation*—US manufacturers produce products like: piston aircraft; turboprops; jets; balloons; dirigibles; and experimental aircraft.
- *Engines*—There are major engine manufacturers for both civil and military aircraft. Other industries include maintenance, repair, and overhaul.
- *Unmanned Aircraft (UA)*—There has been a rapid growth of military and civilian unmanned operations.
- *Airport Infrastructure/Aviation Security*—These needs are driving demand for jobs across the aerospace industry.
- *Alternative Aviation Fuels*—There have been successful test flights using biofuels from substances such as algae. Commercial production in this field is expected soon, and new jobs will be available.
- *Supply Chain*—Aerospace includes many jobs in connected industries. Maintenance and repair, and overhaul are among those. Jobs in composites, metalworking, avionics, and testing equipment are also growing.

As the Department of Commerce's website states, "Foreign firms are attracted to the US aerospace market because it is the largest in the world and has a skilled and hospitable workforce, extensive distribution systems, diverse offerings, and strong support at the local and national level for policy and promotion." According to a recent study, aerospace supports more jobs through exports than any other industry. Aerospace, then is a "superhighway" career path offering a great variety of choices.

CHAPTER 7 Working for the Federal Government

Educational Requirements for Careers in Aerospace

Engineers, Scientists, and Mathematicians

To be a scientist or an engineer you will need from four to seven years of college education. A four-year bachelor's degree is essential. After that may come a master's degree, which usually takes about two years. You will need an additional two to four years to earn a doctorate.

If you want a starting position as an engineer, a mathematician, or scientist, you'll need a bachelor's degree. (A master's or doctoral degree in related fields is highly desirable.) To prepare for a career in aerospace, you should look at electrical, mechanical, or aerospace engineering. Bachelor's degrees that provide a foundation for aerospace careers include: physics; chemistry; geology; meteorology; mathematics; psychology; and biology.

Other Career Fields

Some careers in aerospace require no more than a high school diploma. On-the-job training is most likely available for these jobs. No matter how well educated you are when you start out, almost any career in aerospace will demand lifelong learning. The field is competitive and constantly changing. You'll need to update your skills and knowledge throughout your career—by going back to school or through on-the-job training.

Career Options in the Aerospace Industry

The aerospace industry needs people with a wide range of knowledge and skills. For example, it must have pilots, aircraft maintenance technicians, and air traffic controllers. It must have flight dispatchers, reservationists, technicians, and safety inspectors.

You may be surprised to learn, however, that the industry also needs medical doctors, lawyers, analysts, accountants, and marketing personnel. It needs machinists, sheet metal workers, welders, and carpenters. Unskilled employees such as drivers, receptionists, and building maintenance workers are needed as well. Regardless of your education or training, you can find a place among the many positions in aerospace.

Table 7.6 lists the titles of some of the major aerospace careers.

Table 7.6 Aerospace Career Titles

Pilots or Crew Members	• Pilot astronaut • Mission specialist	• Payload specialist
Physical Scientists	• Astronomer • Chemist • Geologist	• Meteorologist • Physicist • Oceanographer
Life Scientists	• Biologist • Medical doctor • Physiologist	• Nutritionist • Psychologist
Social Scientists	• Economist • Sociologist	
Mathematicians	• Computer scientist • Mathematician	• Systems analyst • Statistician
Engineers (specialists)	• Aerospace/astronautics • Chemical • Civil • Biomedical • Computer • Electrical • Industrial • Environmental	• Materials • Mechanical • Nuclear • Petroleum • Plastics • Safety • Systems
Technicians (specialists)	• Electrical/electronics • Engineering • Aerospace model • Aircraft • Avionics	• Fabrication • Materials • Pattern making and molding
Technical Communicators	• Writer • Artist • Editor • Education specialist	• Public relations specialist • Audiovisual specialist • Photographer
Other Fields	• Quality control inspector • Ground radio operator	

Aerospace Engineer

Aerospace engineers develop new technologies for use in aviation, defense systems, and space exploration. They design, develop, and test aircraft, spacecraft, and missiles. They also supervise manufacturing of these products. Aerospace engineers specialize in areas such as: design; guidance; navigation and control; instrumentation and communication; or production methods. They may also specialize in a particular type of vehicle, such as fighter jets, helicopters, or missiles and rockets. They may operate within the Earth's atmosphere as well as in space. For this reason, the terms aerospace and aeronautics are interchangeable. Aerospace engineers who work with aircraft are considered aeronautical engineers. Those working specifically with spacecraft are astronautical engineers.

Working Conditions

Most aerospace engineers work a standard 40-hour week. At times, deadlines or design standards may bring extra demands. When this happens, engineers may work long hours and experience considerable stress.

Most aerospace engineers work in offices. Some outdoors work may be required. For example, an engineer may travel to a test site to perform product tests such as firing a rocket engine.

Other Engineering Specialties

Aerospace engineering may not appeal to you. Still, you may want to work in the aerospace industry. In that case, consider *electrical engineering*. Many of the people who work in aerospace have an electrical engineering background. That's because electronic components are essential parts of satellites and aircraft. Another option is *mechanical engineering*. This will lead to you working on mechanical components, such as the landing gear of airplanes or shuttles.

Aviation Safety Inspector

Aviation safety inspectors enforce regulations concerning civil aviation safety. This includes how well aircraft fly, and the competence of pilots, mechanics, and other personnel. They are also responsible for the safety of aviation facilities and equipment. These jobs require knowledge and skill in the operation, maintenance, or manufacture of aircraft and their systems.

Working Conditions

These jobs require considerable travel. Inspections, consultations, and investigations must often be done at the scenes of accidents.

Requirements and Experience

Because safety inspectors need a broad range of knowledge, they often come to this career after working in other areas of aerospace. Some are former pilots or crew members. They can also be experienced air traffic controllers, mechanics, machinists, or electronics technicians. You need a four-year college degree for this position.

Air Traffic Control (ATC) Specialist

Air traffic controllers give pilots instructions for taxiing and takeoff as well as weather advice. They use radar or manual procedures to keep track of aircraft in flight. They must quickly be able to recall registration numbers of aircraft under their control. ATC specialists need to know all aircraft types and speeds, positions in the air, and the location of navigational aids or landmarks.

Working Conditions

Because they work with radar equipment, air traffic controllers often work in semidarkness. They never see the aircraft they control except as "blips" on the radar scope. Total concentration is required at all times, so the work can be stressful and exhausting. Night and weekend shifts are common.

Requirements and Experience

To be an air traffic controller, you must have experience in administrative and technical work. You may be able to substitute a four-year college degree for the general experience requirement.

Aircraft Manufacturing Technician

If you are a technician, your knowledge should include how to apply information in various scientific fields. Your title may be something like: senior documentation analyst; software programmer; contracts administrator; or technical illustrator.

Working Conditions

Technicians work in research departments, labs, or engineering departments. Some outdoor work may be necessary.

Requirements and Experience

You will need at least a two-year degree in science or engineering. Or you may want to get a degree from a college or university, community college, technical institute, or a diploma or certificate from a technical or vocational school. You may qualify for some technician jobs by completing on-the-job training. You can also get experience while on active duty with the military.

Aircraft Mechanic

Aviation maintenance mechanics keep airplanes and their equipment working safely and efficiently. An aircraft mechanic may be licensed or unlicensed. The licensed mechanic may receive a mechanic or repairman certificate from the FAA. A person with a mechanic certificate can work only on the specific parts of the aircraft for which he or she is rated. Similarly, a mechanic with a repairman certificate can work only on those parts of the aircraft that the certificate specifically allows. If you have an interest in electronics, you may choose to specialize in avionics. This includes: aircraft navigation and communication radios; weather radar systems; autopilots; and other electronic devices. This field is becoming more interesting and challenging as the technology expands.

Licensed aircraft mechanics receive certification from the FAA.
Courtesy of Wolfgang Kumm/Getty Images

Working Conditions

Depending on the type of work they do, aircraft mechanics and technicians work in hangars, on the flight line, or in repair shops. They use hand and power tools along with test equipment. They often work under pressure to maintain flight schedules.

Requirements and Experience

An aircraft mechanic should have an above-average mechanical ability and a desire to do hands-on work. He or she should also have an interest in aviation, and appreciation of the importance of doing a job carefully and thoroughly. Having a high school diploma is not required to become an apprentice aircraft mechanic. However, employers give preference to high school or vocational school graduates.

Aviation Safety Specialist

Aviation safety specialists inspect airports and flight schools to make sure they comply with federal and state regulations. They confer with airport and local governmental officials about complying with state and federal laws and regulations.

Working Conditions

Some positions require travel to visit the airports and flight schools you are inspecting. Or you may have to meet with local, state, and federal government officials.

Requirements and Experience

To work as an aviation specialist, you'll need a bachelor's degree from a four-year college. Also required is a pilot's license and two years of professional experience as a pilot, air traffic controller, or certified flight instructor.

Avionics Technician

Avionics technicians repair and maintain components used for: aircraft navigation and radio communications; weather radar systems; and instruments and computers that control flight, engine, and other primary functions. Technicians now spend more time repairing electronic systems, such as computerized controls. They are sometimes required to analyze and develop solutions to complex problems.

Working Conditions

Avionics technicians usually work indoors in aircraft factories or hangars. When hangars are full or repairs must be done quickly, however, they may have to work outside, sometimes in inclement weather. They often work under time pressure to maintain flight schedules.

Requirements and Education

A few people become aviation mechanics and technicians through on-the-job training, but most learn their job at a trade school or in the military. There are about 170 trade schools certified by the FAA that award two-year and four-year degrees. The degrees are awarded in avionics, aviation technology, or aviation maintenance management. Additional licenses, such as a radiotelephone license issued by the US Federal Communications Commission (FCC), may also be required.

An avionics technician works on an aircraft control console. There is no room for error in aircraft maintenance, and technicians spend years studying to earn airframe and powerplant certifications so they can work on aircraft.

Courtesy of Antony Souter/Alamy

Jobs at airports include airline ticket agents and customer service agents.

Courtesy of Joshua Lott/Getty Images

Jobs at Airports

Many different jobs are available at commercial airports. These include airline ticket agents, customer service agents, baggage handlers, and security personnel. Airports also employ a variety of building maintenance and repair workers. Many airport jobs require only a high school education, while others will require a two- or four-year college degree.

The best way to select your program is to decide which area of aerospace most interests you. Are you a research-and-development person, or would you be more suited to design and manufacture? Apply to the programs that most closely match your interests.

Preparing for a Career in Aerospace

If you carry a grade point average of 3.0 or better (on a 4.0 scale), it will increase your chances of getting a job within the aerospace industry. Your studies should focus on core subjects such as science, mathematics, and English.

To further explore your interests in aerospace you should pursue high school programs such as the Junior Reserve Officer Training Corps (JROTC). After-school extracurricular activities such as the Civil Air Patrol are excellent character-building life experiences and should also be part of your career plan. Get involved in after-school sports and clubs.

Look for opportunities to explore career choices through co-op or internship programs, summer jobs, career days, or volunteer work. Visit the National Air and Space Museum; Kennedy Space Center; Intrepid Sea, Air and Space Museum; San Diego Air and Space Museum; or the California Science Center.

Finally, read! Learn as much as you can about the aerospace field. Public libraries and the Internet are good sources of information. Read books about key events in the history of aerospace. Include in your reading some science fiction, such as stories about interplanetary travel, living and working in space, or the colonization of the moon and Mars. These help you gain the proper perspective about whether these books are "good science" or "bad science." This is part of the process of critical thinking. Read magazines about the latest aerospace developments and the most recent discoveries in the solar system.

✔ CHECKPOINTS

Lesson 2 Review

Using complete sentences, answer the following questions on a sheet of paper.

1. What are the roles of engineers, scientists, and technicians in the aerospace field? Define each role and show how it differs from the other two.

2. Explain the roles of NASA and the FAA and why each was created.

3. What are three of the major missions of commercial aerospace companies?

4. What education will you need beyond high school if you are interested in a career as an aerospace scientist or engineer?

5. What are three areas that you might want to major in if you decide to pursue a career in aerospace?

6. List some aerospace careers that require no college but do require specialized training.

APPLYING CAREER SKILLS

7. Pick one of the careers in aerospace that you wrote down under "Quick Write" at the beginning of this lesson. Imagine that you are planning an entire career. Write a summary, no longer than one page, that describes what education and what continued learning or training you would need to reach the highest level of responsibility in that field.

Careers in Public Service

Quick Write

_____

_____

Write a short paragraph about two benefits you think having a career in public service might provide to your community

Learn About

- types of public service careers
- careers available in public service
- options for criminal justice careers
- careers in fire science and technology
- careers in Homeland Security

"Ours is a time with no shortage of pressing issues. Our country and world need thoughtful, dedicated people to help find and implement new solutions to stubborn problems. As a result we need many of you to choose careers in public service and in other arenas in which you can help make a real difference."

General David Petraeus, Commencement Address, Dickinson College, 20 May 2012

Types of Public Service Careers

A career in the military or the government is often called public service. Public service is generally considered _employment within a government or nonprofit organization that is for the benefit of the community._ But as you will learn in this lesson, there is a little more to it.

Careers in public service are as varied as they are in any job sector. Often, they are more satisfying. Public service jobs are near your home in your town or county. If you think about your community, there are jobs all around you that help the public. There are police, firefighters, and emergency medical teams that are crucial to community safety. But there are also those who work in nonprofits. These are _institutions not organized to make a profit that operate to promote social welfare._ Health, social, and environment organizations are a few examples. Museums, local schools, colleges, and churches all offer benefits to a community.

Many jobs in profit-making companies also benefit the public. In health care, for example, many work in sales or general management. These jobs don't serve the public directly because they focus on making their companies money. On the other hand, many parts of the health care industry do serve the public daily. Doctors and dentists, physical therapists, and many others work in their communities to improve the quality of peoples' lives and health. Many of these professionals make very good salaries. But they also have studied for a long time to achieve advanced degrees to practice their crafts.

If you go to college, you may decide to use your own degree and training to help make a difference to the world on a major social, environmental, or health issue.

There are also many careers in public service that don't require an advanced education. However, they can be very satisfying, in much the same way as military service. It's making a contribution right in your community. And like a military career, public service brings a sense of patriotism with it. Many find this idea attractive, although few in these fields get rich by working in them.

So what kinds of jobs might you find in public service or a nonprofit if you have a high school diploma? With proper training, you could be a dispatcher with the police or fire department. That's an important job because a dispatcher plays a major role in helping first-responders get to a crime or fire scene quickly. A dispatcher needs to be able to communicate well. He or she must have a sense of urgency and compassion with a caller in need. At the same time, information a dispatcher gets from a caller must be timely and accurate to assure a quick response to an emergency.

You could be a volunteer coordinator with a local nonprofit environmental group. You could work with a group that rescues endangered or abused animals. You could be in agriculture with an organization that assists small farmers. You could work on a church staff to help organize religious activities that benefit your local community.

Vocabulary

- public service
- nonprofits
- philanthropic
- foundation
- endowments
- community foundation
- corporate foundation
- independent foundation
- criminal justice
- forensics
- paralegal
- polygraph test
- first responders
- homeland security
- analysts
- "homegrown" terrorism
- cybersecurity

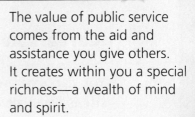

success TIP

The value of public service comes from the aid and assistance you give others. It creates within you a special richness—a wealth of mind and spirit.

Importance of Public Service in American Society

In 2010, the United States had almost 108 million people working in private sector jobs. Compare that to 22.5 million people working in federal, state, and local governments. That's about 21 percent of the total. If you count nonprofit workers, such as in health care, environmental, or public safety, the number in public service grows by 11 percent more. Public service, then, represents almost a third of all American jobs.

Employees in the public sector also have more years of education on average than in the private sector. In 2010, more than half of the workers in federal, state, and local governments had a bachelor's degree or more. Only 34 percent of private sector workers had that much education.

Salaries in public service can be good, too. Some are almost equal in pay to private industry, depending on your education. But many nonprofits tend to pay lower wages. That's because jobs in these organizations often depend on donations or gifts. These groups are often called philanthropic, meaning they *benefit people through charitable aid or donations*. People who work for these organizations often do so because of the causes they represent. The satisfaction comes from being associated with a cause that benefits the local community or society at large.

Another form of nonprofit is a foundation. This is a *public or private organization that acquires money from a range of contributors to support one or more causes*. These monies are endowments, or *gifts, usually for specific community or global causes*. The causes can range from research on a cure for cancer or malaria to promoting the arts and education. A foundation is chartered for such a purpose or mission for tax purposes.

There are several kinds of foundations. A community foundation r*aises funds from donors and may support local programs through grants*. A corporate foundation is usually *a separate entity of a corporation that makes charitable grants*. Usually this kind of foundation gets money from only one source. An independent foundation *is normally philanthropic, with funds coming from a single individual or family*. Foundations often collaborate with other nonprofits to support a mutual cause.

Careers Available in Public Service

You can explore many kinds of careers in public service on the Internet. One useful site is *www.careersinpublicservice.org*. This website is a combined effort of three large public service groups. It's a single source for you to find education and training opportunities in public service. They also promote the ideals of public service in the community.

Table 7.7 Annual Wages of Some Selected Public Sector and Private Sector Employees, 2009

Profession	Average Annual Wage:
Federal Government Workers	$67,756
State Police	$61,000
Local Firefighters	$60,572
State Govt. Workers	$48,742
State Legislative Workers	$48,129
Local Government Workers	$43,140
Local Schools	$41,113
Private Sector Certified Public Accountant (CPA)	$71,216
Federal Government CPA	$67,531
Local Govt. CPA	$64,050
Government (all types)	$47,552
Private (total sector)	$45,155

Source: Bureau of Labor Statistics, 2009

Table 7.7 lists selected public service careers and the salaries you might expect to make.

What Are Nonprofit Jobs Like?

In nonprofits, jobs are a bit different from those in government public service. For example, you may work on many different health issues at a local, state or federal health agency. At a nonprofit, you may focus on one special issue. Maybe it's clean air, lung cancer, heart disease, nuclear power, child abuse, international relief, or homelessness. A focus on one issue can make you feel more like you are making a real contribution, rather than jumping from one issue to the next, sometimes several at once. Yet, some people enjoy the multiple challenges that government service, for example, can present.

Red Cross volunteers come to the aid of those in need during catastrophic events.

Courtesy of Tom Hood/AP Images

Nonprofits and public service jobs in government differ in how they are managed. In a nonprofit, you may do many different tasks, even though they are focused on one major issue. You may also have more individual authority. In government, you may be limited in your authority and flexibility to do things.

If you like the idea of working to solve one major problem, a good way to get involved is with a related nonprofit. Fund raising or volunteering is usually the best way for you to work toward a career. These activities make you appreciate how money is raised and used by these organizations.

The outlook for nonprofit careers continues to be good. That's because nonprofit institutions offer assistance when federal and state governments cut funding for social programs. This has been the case recently. The weak economy in 2010, and cuts in government funding limited the number of services it could provide on many levels. One example would be the Bill and Melinda Gates Foundation; they provide billions of dollars to global health, schools, and development programs.

Options for Criminal Justice Careers

> "Injustice anywhere is a threat to justice everywhere."
>
> Martin Luther King, Jr., civil rights leader

Military careers, as you learned in an earlier lesson, require hard work and dedication. But they offer the benefit of having great responsibility.

There are many civilian careers in public service that also require strength of mind, body, and character. Jobs within criminal justice require these qualities. These jobs are often attractive to young people because they offer a chance to do service for the communities in which they live.

Criminal justice is *a system of institutions and practices aimed at: maintaining social control; deterring crime; upholding the law; and giving fair punishments to offenders.* But as you probably see it in your community, it is a simple concept—maintaining law and order.

You need special skills to pursue a career in criminal justice. Among those are:

- An ability to communicate well with peers and the public
- Clear thinking under physical and mental stress
- A capability to handle details
- A strong sense of leadership and personal discipline

Table 7.8 Position or Job Titles Found Within Criminal Justice

- Criminal lawyer/judge
- Criminologist
- US Marshal
- Federal Bureau of Investigation (FBI) agent
- Police detective
- Drug Enforcement Administration (DEA) agent
- Central Intelligence Agency (CIA) agent
- Bureau of Alcohol, Tobacco, Firearms, and Explosives (ATF) agent
- Customs and Border Protection (CBP) agent
- Internal Revenue Service (IRS) agent
- Postal Service Investigator

- Cybersecurity professional
- Crime scene investigator
- Coroner
- Social worker
- Police officer (civilian or military)
- Correctional officer
- Airline security
- Security guard
- Bailiff
- Youth advocate
- Probation and parole officer
- Court clerk
- Court reporter
- Paralegal

Education Requirements and Work Environments Within Criminal Justice

Careers in criminal justice can focus on many things: social justice; crime solving and prevention; and the law. The amount of education you would need to work in these fields varies. Work settings vary widely as well. Jobs may be at the federal, state, and local levels. They may be at prisons, courtrooms, police forces, or investigative services. You could be working on the streets with the police, or in and around prison grounds. You might be doing security at airports. Or you could be in an office environment. The private sector also offers similar kinds of jobs. Table 7.8 lists a sampling of the many jobs and positions found within the criminal justice field.

Law enforcement professionals often work security details for major events.

Courtesy of Terry Renna/AP Images

Jobs in Criminal Justice Requiring College Education

If you are aiming high, then an advanced degree will allow you many career options. You could achieve a doctorate in criminal justice. This PhD would be a great way to get to an upper-level administration, research, or teaching job. You could become an administrator for a state or federal agency. You might choose to teach as a criminal justice professor for a college or university. You could also be a chief criminologist or head of a large investigative service.

Another advanced degree is a Juris Doctor (JD) degree. This is a law degree for those who want a career in the court system. This kind of degree will allow you to meet the requirements to become a defense attorney, a judge, or a prosecutor.

A medical degree (MD) would allow you to be in a law enforcement agency as a medical examiner.

If you want to have a career that pays well that doesn't require a PhD, then a master's degree is available in several areas. There is a Master of Science in Criminal Justice (MSCJ), or Criminology (MSC), or a Master of Arts in Criminology. These degrees will lead you to management, supervisory, research, and teaching jobs. They will help you become a criminal justice instructor at a community college, a crime prevention specialist, or a warden.

Another popular field is the Master of Science in Forensic Science. This degree will help you enter a career as a ballistics expert, or a specialist in forensics, which is *the application of scientific knowledge and methodology to legal problems and criminal investigations.*

Forensic scientists have become very important in helping police solve crimes.

Courtesy of corepics/Shutterstock

With a bachelor's degree, you'll be able to work in federal, state or local law enforcement. You can also be hired at a mid-level position in the court system. It will also prepare you to be: a criminologist; a corrections officer; a federal agent; a parole officer; or a private detective. A Bachelor of Science in Forensic Science will also allow you to work in a forensics lab. You could become a crime scene examiner or a criminal laboratory analyst. Experts in criminal justice say, however, that it may be just as important to have a bachelor's degree in biology, chemistry, or physics for these jobs.

Other jobs do not require a four-year degree, but at least some college. You can be a bailiff, local or state police officer, paralegal, or security guard. An associate's degree is usually enough for these jobs. An associate's degree in paralegal or legal studies will help you get an entry-level position in the court system as a paralegal, *a person trained to undertake legal work but not qualified as a lawyer.* Another popular field is in cybersecurity, whether it's in a cybercrimes unit or other part of a law enforcement agency. For this, you'll probably need a minimum of an associate's degree in computer forensics.

Jobs in Criminal Justice Not Requiring a College Education

According to the US Department of Justice, only one percent of local police departments require new officer recruits to have a bachelor's degree. Just eight percent require an associate's degree and six percent require some college. There is also little or no college required for entry-level positions such as detention officers, bailiffs, airport security, game wardens, and corrections personnel. Some states don't even require such officers to have a high school diploma. But that doesn't mean you can jump into a job right after high school. Almost every criminal justice agency requires you to be 21 at the time you're hired. What that means is it may be better to stay in school and study criminal justice for a couple of years at a college and possibly earn an Associate Degree. This will give you an educational advantage over other applicants, and later, better opportunities for promotion.

The Criminal Justice Hiring Process

The hiring of criminal justice professionals and law enforcement officers varies widely. Jobs requiring more education will require more of you, as you'll have to go through a multiple-level application process.

If you want to become a police officer, for example, the initial application may ask for very little detail. You may only have to produce evidence that you are minimally qualified with a high school diploma. And you will need to be at least 19, or 21 years old. This will depend on the jurisdiction where you are applying.

In some states, you may also need to have a minimum number of college credit hours. Some agencies may require military experience. In Florida, for example, you must also show two years' worth of experience in which day-to-day contact with the public was a part of your job—in customer assistance, waiting tables, or a cashier.

It gets more complicated after this first stage. You may have to do a second, more detailed application. Then you'll go through a background security check, an oral interview, and even a polygraph test, *a test using an instrument to determine if a person is telling the truth.*

Qualities That Are Important as a Security Guard

The US Department of Labor's Bureau of Labor Statistics lists the following as important qualities of persons working in physical security:

- *Communications*—Security guards must be able to speak clearly. This includes communicating with the public, with suspected offenders, and with other law enforcement officers.

- *Decision-making*—Guards must be able to quickly assess and take the best course of action when a dangerous situation arises.

- *Honesty*—Guards must be honest because they are trusted to protect confidential information or expensive equipment.

- *Being Observant*—Guards have to remain alert and be particularly aware of their surroundings in order to quickly recognize anything out of the ordinary.

- *Physical strength*—Guards must be strong enough to deal with offenders and to handle emergency situations.

See: *http://www.bls.gov/ooh/protective-service/security-guards.htm#tab-4*

You will also have to pass a physical fitness evaluation. As a police officer, you may be chasing someone on foot, or getting into a physical struggle with one or more individuals. You will need to be able to hold your own, physically. You'll also receive a medical exam to ensure you are physically capable of performing the job.

You will probably have to pass a psychological exam, as well. The purpose of this is only to determine whether you have the kind of personality traits that can cope with stressful situations.

Private security positions also have a wide range of hiring procedures. This will depend on the level of pay, and amount of property value for which you will be responsible. But in general, you'll need at least a high school diploma and, probably, a state license.

If you are applying for a position that does not require being armed, then a high school diploma may be all you need to be hired as a security employee. But most jobs that require carrying a sidearm will require more.

Fifty-three percent of all security guards are hired through private investigative and security service companies. These kinds of jobs can be very mundane and boring. You may be sitting long periods at a security desk. In other security jobs, you may be on the move constantly, covering a lot of ground to do surveillance of facilities.

Work schedules are as varied as the jobs themselves, and can go around the clock, and in various shifts.

For armed security personnel, the hiring company may want to see that you have had some college coursework in criminal justice beyond your high school diploma.

You will need a license from a local or state authority allowing you to carry a firearm. Also, like with federal, state, or local law enforcement agencies, you will have to go through a background check. You will also be checked for a criminal record. Fingerprint checks are also common.

According to the Bureau of Labor Statistics (BLS), some employers prefer to hire security guards with as much as a police science or criminal justice degree. Some colleges do offer programs and courses that focus specifically on security guard work.

Training

Different criminal justice jobs can require different kinds of training. Many jobs requiring college degrees will be supplemented by organizational or other formal training.

If you are thinking of becoming a law enforcement officer, you can assume that training will be difficult.

If you become a law enforcement officer, you will need to be in good physical condition. Exercise should become a regular part of your routine before you even enter a police officer training program. It usually helps if you find a time of day that you put aside every day for exercise or aerobic activity. Early morning workouts get your brain working and help increase your stamina. Everyone is different; you should determine your best time of day for exercise.

A good exercise routine should also include a proper amount of rest for muscle groups to recover and strengthen.

Physical fitness is an important aspect of police academy training.

Courtesy of Enigma/Alamy

LESSON 3   Careers in Public Service

Many new police officers undergo a specialized training program that teaches them:

- *Ethics*—To determine if the new officer has the proper ethical attitude
- *Mental agility*—To see if an applicant is mentally prepared for the duties required of a law officer
- *Procedural training*—To make sure applicants can handle the day-to-day details of being a police officer
- *Firearms training*—Law enforcement officers need to qualify with a small arms weapon, and most spend some regular amount of time at the firing range to keep their skill levels high

Law enforcement situations often require quick decisions. They must be ethically and procedurally correct. They must also take into account public safety.

If you become enrolled in a police academy, training may be as much on the streets as in the classroom. Real-life situations are important to learn for a new officer.

are you AWARE ?

A major security organization is ASIS International. For information on security careers, see: *http://www.asisonline.org/*.

The amount of training security guards receive can be very different, also. Often they get training in emergency procedures and detention of suspects. Training in communications is important. Many employers give newly hired guards formal instruction before they start the job. Others provide only on-the-job training. An increasing number of states are making ongoing training a legal requirement for keeping a license. Median annual wages for selected security careers are shown in Figure 7.1.

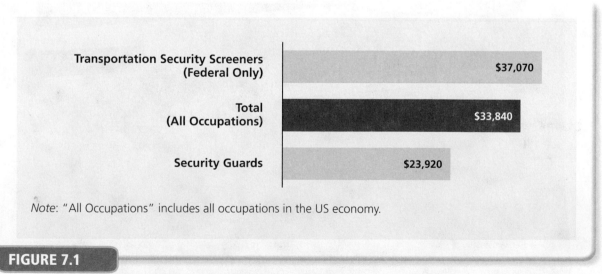

Note: "All Occupations" includes all occupations in the US economy.

FIGURE 7.1

Median Annual Wages for Seleced Security Careers, May 2010
Source: US Bureau of Labor Statistics, Occupational Employment Statistics

Careers in Fire Science and Technology

Maybe you aren't aware that the job of firefighting is much more than handling a hose and going into burning buildings to save people. The truth is, firefighting has an entire range of scientific study. Development of new technologies is also a big part of the field.

Every decade brings with it new methods to fight fires. If you watch the news on television, you can see how science and technology are used to deal with large wildfires and forest fires. This is also true for local firefighters, who are always employing new kinds of equipment and protective clothing to do their jobs better and more safely.

Firefighting is demanding and sometimes dangerous. But it can also be very satisfying in terms of saving lives and property. A firefighter may have to get very close to flames, intense heat, and smoke to save valuable structures and their interiors. Another may perform search and rescue, pulling people from a burning structure. On a highway or street, a firefighter may have to pry trapped persons from a burning or badly damaged vehicle in an accident.

Firefighters are also required to know and use emergency medical procedures. That's because they are often the first to arrive to treat persons who may have suffered a heart attack, stroke, or other physical injury. They will step in quickly after an explosion, car accident, or even a terrorist attack.

The events of September 11, 2001 (9/11) put a great deal of attention on firefighters' and police officers' roles in New York. Afterward, they became known across the nation as first responders, *personnel certified to provide urgent medical care and other emergency procedures before more highly trained medical personnel arrive on the scene.* Since 9/11, the term has become part of our daily language to describe with respect all professionals in public safety.

Firefighting at a higher level is a science. Firefighting must respond to changes in building and structural materials, and changing conditions. Firefighters employ new techniques based on science that help them become more effective in fighting fires.

One example of this is at the US Naval Research Laboratory. There, US Navy scientists and engineers have been using high expansion foam to protect large-volume, mission-critical spaces. These include hangar bays, well decks, and structures where expensive vehicles and aircraft are stored. Expansion foam is also used in smaller compartments to save these spaces from being inundated with large amounts of water. The use of foam is effective against these compartmental fires, and requires less water.

Civilian fire science has led to a new kind of fluid that stops hot particles from reaching kindling temperature to start flames. This fluid also protects the environment by not damaging the ozone layer.

The US Fire Administration (USFA) is part of the Department of Homeland Security. It works on new scientific developments that can be turned into new and effective firefighting technologies.

These are some of the projects USFA is undertaking in science and technology:

- **Beam and Vaulted Ceiling Fire Tests—**
  Investigation of Sprinkler Activation under Sloped Ceilings
- **Benefit-Cost Analysis of Residential Fire Sprinkler Systems**
- **Characterizing the Effectiveness of Automatic Sprinklers for College Dormitory Fires**
- **Evaluation of Structural Ventilation Techniques**
- **Applying Technology to Reduce Escape Times from Fires**
- **Study of Municipal Water Supply Systems**

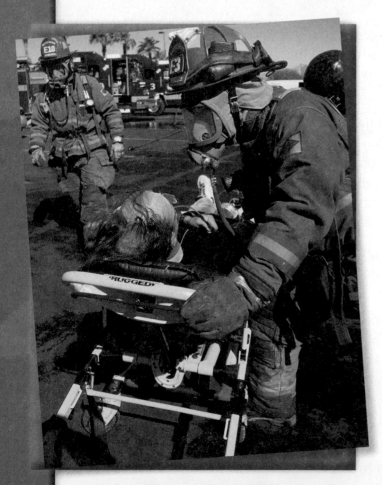

As first responders, today's firefighters must complete a more rigorous amount of training and testing then ever before.

Courtesy of Mark E. Gibson/Corbis Images

Firefighters are testing new kinds of hoses, chemicals, and other materials all the time. New equipment and materials help meet the goals to: stop fires more quickly; save more lives; and prevent loss of large structures.

Technology has also improved in: data collecting: computing: and chemical engineering. Firefighters now use thermal imaging to spot wild fires. They employ computer programs to predict how fires move by using current weather information.

City fire departments are constantly updating equipment and techniques. Firefighters at airports, race tracks, and other scenes where fires are possible work tirelessly to update their methods.

Fire Science and Technology Occupations

You have now seen that you can be a professional in firefighting science and technology or management. Or you can be on the front lines, doing the actual hard, but satisfying, physical work of fighting fires on the scene.

Most firefighters have a keen awareness of the service they do for the public. They understand that the pay is low, balanced against the potential dangers involved. But they also share a comradery in their commitment to serving the public. Many firefighters volunteer to go thousands of miles to help out communities in need of disaster assistance. They did so during the ravaging Colorado wildfires of 2012. Firefighters from all over the country also responded to perform rescue and assistance after Hurricane Katrina struck the Gulf Coast in 2005. Table 7.9 lists some of the common jobs in firefighting and prevention, as described by the Bureau of Labor Statistics.

Table 7.9 Jobs in Firefighting and Prevention

Fire-Prevention and Protection Engineers

They study the causes of fires. They determine fire protection methods. They design or recommend new materials or equipment. Their goal is to assist organizations in safeguarding life and property against fire, explosion, or related hazards. You can earn a median income of more than $75,400 per year.

Fire Inspectors

They inspect buildings and equipment to detect fire hazards. They also enforce state and local regulations. Salaries are more than $53,000 per year, on average.

Fire Investigators

They conduct investigations to determine the causes of fires and explosions. Salaries are on a par with fire inspectors.

Municipal Fire Fighting and Prevention Supervisors

They supervise the firefighters who control and extinguish municipal fires, and their rescue efforts. Salaries are more than $69,000 per year.

Forest Fire Fighting and Prevention Supervisors

They supervise firefighters who control and suppress fires in forests or vacant public land. Salaries are on a par with municipal supervisors.

Forest Fire Inspectors and Prevention Specialists

They enforce fire regulations and inspect forest for fire hazards. They also recommend forest fire prevention or control measures. Often, they report forest fires and weather conditions for authorities. Their average income is about $33,700 per year.

Municipal Firefighters

They control and extinguish fires. They protect life and property and conduct rescue efforts. Salaries are a little above $45,000 on average.

Forest Firefighters

They fight to stop fires in forests or vacant public land. Salaries are about the same as for municipal firefighters.

Fire, Police and Ambulance Dispatchers

These are key people who operate communications equipment at emergency response centers. They receive emergency reports from the public and relay information to authorities who are responding to the scene. They may maintain contact with a caller until responders arrive. These are not high-paying jobs, at a little under $36,000 per year. However, they carry a high level of responsibility.

Emergency Medical Technicians and Paramedics

They are the first to assess injuries and administer medical care at the scene of an emergency. They rescue persons trapped in cars or other structures. They transport the injured or sick persons to nearby hospitals. Yet these first responders' average pay is less than $31,000 per year.

Source: US Bureau of Labor Statistics

Hiring Practices in Fire Science and Technology Occupations

Almost two out of three firefighters have some college, but no degree. A typical program in firefighting leads to an associate's degree.

If you apply for a firefighter job, you need to be at least 18 years old and have a valid driver's license. A high school diploma is required, and increasingly, some college education. Some colleges offer certificate programs or degrees in fire engineering or fire science. You will also have to pass written and physical tests. There will be a series of interviews. In addition, you will need to have an emergency medical technician (EMT) certification. Some states require mandatory firefighter training and certification. You will have to pass a medical exam and drug screening in order to be hired. After being hired, you may have to go through random drug screening.

In addition to participating in local training, some firefighters attend federal training sessions sponsored by the National Fire Academy.

Courtesy of Adam Berry/Getty Images

Training

You will get extensive training as a new firefighter. First, there will be several weeks of training at a fire academy run by a local fire department or by the state. Classroom instruction and practical training will cover fire-fighting and fire-prevention techniques. You will study local building codes and emergency medical procedures. You will also learn how to fight fires with standard equipment. That means training with axes, chain saws, fire extinguishers, and ladders.

Some fire departments have accredited apprenticeship programs that last up to four years. These programs combine formal instruction with on-the-job-training, supervised by experienced firefighters.

The topics covered include:

- Anti-arson techniques
- Disaster preparedness
- Hazardous materials control
- Public fire safety and education

You can advance within the firefighting profession—to engineer, then lieutenant, or captain. If you want to get to the level of battalion chief, assistant chief, deputy chief, and chief, you may need a bachelor's degree. It should be in fire science, public administration, or a related field.

The National Fire Academy offers a certification as executive fire officer. You will need at least an associate's degree to be eligible.

---

success TIP ★

In considering a career path in firefighting, recognize the qualities that will make you an effective firefighter. You need to quickly evaluate a situation and make decisions. You must communicate clearly to relay conditions to other first-responders. You must have courage to face danger. You need stamina to stay alert and continue working at a disaster scene for long periods. You also need physical strength to move equipment and debris, and if necessary, carry victims to safety. Most importantly, you need a sense of teamwork to work together with others to minimize physical damage and injuries to civilians and your fellow firefighters.

Careers in Homeland Security

Your memories of the terrorist attacks on the United States on September 11, 2001 may be vague and dim. Your parents or other relatives may have reacted to the attacks of that day with fear. Almost 3,000 people lost their lives that day in New York, at the Pentagon, and in Pennsylvania.

From the events of that day, we started hearing and using a new term in our language—*homeland security*. The United States has always protected its borders, mostly with its military. But on the day we call 9/11, we realized that our country could be attacked in a different way. It changed the way we now think about how to protect the nation.

A new federal department was formed, the Department of Homeland Security (DHS). It was created to organize how the government would protect many of our public facilities, population centers, and borders against a terror attack.

Here is how the President's advisors initially defined homeland security:

"Homeland security is a concerted national effort to prevent terrorist attacks within the United States, reduce America's vulnerability to terrorism, and minimize the damage, and recover from attacks that do occur." *

---

*Source: National Strategy for Homeland Security, 2002

But there were many things to consider about this new way of protecting the nation. And as time passed, homeland security became more widely defined. Homeland security took on new missions. We wanted to secure our borders and airspace, for example. We wanted to protect human life from harm by any terror threat. We wanted to secure our ports and coastlines. We wanted to protect infrastructure like oil refineries, nuclear power plants, and the electric power grid. We wanted to protect food production and water quality. We wanted to protect the medicines we make. We also needed to protect major computer systems in all of our major banks, military operations, and other systems that could be disrupted.

Homeland Security Occupations

From this birth of a new government department has come a major homeland security industry. It is largely within government at this time. However, as the years go by, more effort by private business will be needed, and corporations will be investing millions of dollars for added security.

The Department of Homeland Security has become the center of many organizations once considered independent. Now they are focused on a joint mission. Table 7.10 from the Bureau of Labor Statistics lists just some of the kinds of occupations that now exist in the general area of homeland security. These are all public service jobs, with the goal to help people and communities. Some jobs under homeland security overlap with jobs we discussed earlier in this lesson, like firefighting, law enforcement, and security.

Peacetime Coast Guard operations are under the direction of the US Department of Homeland Security.

Courtesy of Purcell Pictures, Inc./Alamy

The DHS occupations found in Table 7.10 are not intended to be all-inclusive. Over time, some jobs change. Some jobs found within one division of DHS but may also be found elsewhere in the government. Most of the listed jobs below require a college degree.

Even within the military, there are civilian jobs available that are the equivalent to those in homeland security. Some were created as a result of the shootings at Fort Hood, Texas, in 2009, focusing additional security assets on protecting stateside military bases.

You should consult the DHS website and search "jobs" or a particular job type. You can also search "career opportunities" or "job opportunities" to see how widely these jobs will be found across DHS. You may also find similar opportunities within state employment services by searching for the field in which you are interested.

Table 7.10 US Department of Homeland Security (DHS)— Selected Occupations

Citizenship and Immigration Services

- Asylum officer
- Immigration officer

Customs and Border Protection

- Border Patrol agent
- Import specialist

Federal Emergency Management Agency (FEMA)

- Federal coordinating officer
- Program specialist (fire; national security; response, recovery, preparedness, and mitigation)
- Emergency planning
- Emergency management

Federal Law Enforcement Training Center

- Law enforcement specialist (instruction)

Immigration and Customs Enforcement

- Detention and deportation officer
- Police officer
- Immigration enforcement agent
- Security specialist

Information Analysis and Infrastructure Protection Directorate

- Protective security advisor
- Intelligence operations specialist
- Information technology (IT) specialist in information security
- Security specialist
- Telecommunications specialist

Office of the Inspector General

- Attorney
- Auditor

Science and Technology Directorate

- Biological scientist
- Chemist
- Computer scientist
- Engineer
- Physicist

Secretarial Offices

- Human resources specialist
- Policy analyst

Transportation and Security Administration

- Criminal investigator
- Intelligence operations specialist
- Program and management analyst
- Transportation security screener

US Coast Guard

- Contract specialist engineer

US Secret Service

- Criminal investigator

Source: US Bureau of Labor Statistics—www.bls.gov

Hiring in the general field of security—federal, state, local and private—went up just 5 percent between 2000 and 2010. Federal homeland security hiring grew quickly. But it was almost offset by a decline in private security guards. There were also cuts in local and state police officers.

Private sector jobs, though slow to grow in number, are there. Commercial businesses and *nonprofits* need help in physical security. However, protecting employees, customers, and electronic assets against terrorism threats has become more important.

Many companies and organizations now want emergency planners. Emergency planners develop policies and procedures to handle all types of emergencies. After the shootings at Virginia Tech in 2007, colleges began hiring such planners.

New products and services in security are being developed. Sales professionals are being hired to get those products into those markets. Nonprofits are hiring planning experts to meet terrorist threats that affect industries they represent. In education, people who teach and conduct research on homeland security are being hired.

You learned in Chapter 3 of the rapid growth in cybersecurity jobs. The government and private companies are now hiring analysts, *workers who analyze situations and recommend solutions*. Many are trained with government-supported grants. They become experts in preventing cyber-crimes. Some focus on antivirus techniques and mobile code analysis. If you are computer-savvy, businesses will hire you to help find "holes" in software security. A former DHS director recently predicted an increasing role for private firms in fighting "homegrown" terrorism, *terrorism caused by persons native to, or citizens of, a region or country*. He said that the jobs in the next 10 years will grow at the local level and in the private sector. Meanwhile, additional people will be needed on the legal side of cybersecurity, *the branch of computer technology known as information security as applied to computers and networks*. Others will be hired to develop cybersecurity standards.

The private sector hasn't hired as quickly as government for another reason. The number of people trained to the level needed for those positions hasn't been achieved. There aren't enough professionals to go around, leaving many job vacancies.

Working in cybersecurity sometimes means thinking like a detective. Some people working in the field started their careers in law enforcement. Others came out of science. Many have been trained while serving in the military. People can enter from a number of different career fields.

However, as one expert puts it, cybersecurity is less about "getting the bad guy," and more about investigation. Locating a breach, preventing it from getting worse or happening at all is where the need is. Cybersecurity can combine the thrill of an investigation with the satisfaction of knowing you are benefiting your organization and the nation.

Hiring in Homeland Security

The nature of homeland security work means meeting certain criteria not generally required of other workers. For example, if you apply for a job in homeland security, most positions require security clearances or background checks. When seeking employment at DHS, you may wait longer to be hired than with other jobs.

You saw many similar hiring requirements in the section about criminal justice. You must have many of the same qualities, be physically, mentally and ethically fit. You must also be a US citizen. But the good news is, opportunities exist all across the job spectrum, no matter what your interests, skills, and background may be.

Training

You will find that the higher the focus is on terrorism, the more likely it is you will receive formal training. Many local programs have on-the-job training programs that are usually geared to the community they serve.

Federally Supported Homeland Security Training Resources

- **Center for Domestic Preparedness (CDP)**—The CDP provides hands-on training to state and local emergency responders. The focus is on incidents involving weapons of mass destruction (WMDs). The center is located at the former home of the US Army Chemical School at Fort McClellan, Alabama. The center conducts live chemical agent training for civilian emergency responders.

- **New Mexico Institute of Mining and Technology (Energetic Materials and Research Testing Center) (EMRTC)**—This center conducts live explosive training and field exercises. Classroom instruction is also conducted. Training includes explosives and firearms, live explosives, and incendiary devices.

- **Louisiana State University (LSU) National Center for Biomedical Research and Training (NCBRT)**—This center trains emergency responders throughout the United States. It has more than 25 courses certified through DHS. The center also has introduced 10 complementary online courses allowing students flexibility to study at locations and times that are convenient.

- **Texas Engineering Extension Service (TEEX), National Emergency Response and Rescue Training Center (NERRTC)**—This center delivers a set of courses to prepare state and local officials for the threat posed by weapons of mass destruction. Technical assistance is available to state and local jurisdictions in developing WMD assessment plans.

- **US Department of Energy's Nevada Test Site—Counter Terrorism Operations Support (CTOS)**—This center focuses on preventing, mitigating, or responding to radiological or nuclear weapons.

- **Security and Emergency Response Training Center (SERTC), (Transportation Technological Center Inc.) Pueblo, CO**—This hazardous materials (HAZMAT) training center focuses on emergency response for surface transportation.

- **National Disaster Preparedness Training Center (NDPTC)—University of Hawaii**—This center develops and delivers training and educational programs on natural hazards; coastal communities; and the special needs of islands and territories.

DHS has its training developed through The National Domestic Preparedness Consortium (NDPC). The programs are delivered to state and local emergency response units.

Considering a Career in Public Service

You will have many choices upcoming in your life. When you consider a possible career, remember that government employment is not the only road to making a contribution to your country or to society. There are public service careers in nonprofits, associations, the private sector, and at colleges. You can have a productive career that contributes directly to the public good.

Public service careers can provide good pay and benefits, and many choices of where to work. And there are opportunities for further training and education. Think of what you might contribute in a career toward managing global climate change, supplying food to the needy, or clean water to developing countries.

Think about how you might help secure the United States and other countries against terrorism. You may want to help redevelop older urban areas that have lost their manufacturing plants. You may want to help end global diseases or providing quality education and health care to children living in poverty.

There are full and satisfying careers to be had today, and more will be available in the near future, to serve the people with whom you share a piece of our planet.

Lesson 3 Review

Using complete sentences, answer the following questions on a sheet of paper.

1. Why can a public service career be considered patriotic?

2. What are two reasons why someone would choose to work in public service rather than in a for-profit corporation?

3. When an organization is called philanthropic, what does that mean?

4. What are four special skills you need to pursue a career in criminal justice?

5. If you wanted to have a career in forensics, what would you choose to do in the field, and what education level would you need to achieve such a position?

6. Name three important requirements in order to be hired for most criminal justice jobs. Why are these important?

7. Why do firefighters need to know emergency medical procedures?

8. Explain the differences between the homeland security responsibilities of a border patrol agent and a local sheriff's police force officer?

9. Name two kinds of technical and personal skills needed by someone working in cybersecurity.

APPLYING JOB-SEARCH SKILLS

10. Name three community problems that a public service career could address. Explain what qualities you would need to work effectively in an organization that will address one of these problems.

Developing Your Career Skills

Chapter Outline

LESSON 1

Planning Your Professional Development

LESSON 2

Learning to Work With Others

LESSON 3

Seeking Feedback and Promotions

LESSON 4

Your Civic Responsibilities

> "Don't be afraid to give your best to what seemingly are small jobs. Every time you conquer one it makes you that much stronger. If you do the little jobs well, the big ones tend to take care of themselves."
>
> Dale Carnegie, self-improvement expert

Planning Your Professional Development

_____

_____

What do you think are the three most important factors in developing your career? Write them down on a sheet of paper, then consider how you will achieve them.

Learn About

- how to plan your professional development
- preparing a career portfolio
- organizational and personal values that contribute to success

"I've missed more than 9000 shots in my career. I've lost almost 300 games. I've been trusted 26 times to take the game-winning shot and missed. I've failed over and over and over again in my life. And that is why I succeed."

Michael Jordan, Hall of Fame basketball player and owner of the Charlotte Bobcats

How to Plan Your Professional Development

Your career is one of the most important parts of your life. Unless you are independently wealthy, you'll depend on it to earn a living. If you choose the right career, it will also give you great personal and professional satisfaction.

Professional development *includes all the activities necessary to have a successful career.* Professional development is a personal activity. No one can set your goals or plan your career for you.

Planning your career development means answering the following questions: What field do I want to work in? How high in that career do I want to advance? What steps must I take to qualify for the promotions I will need to achieve my goals?

For example, you may want a career in sales. Some sales representatives enjoy their work so much that they prefer to remain in that role. Others aspire to become sales managers, supervising the work of several sales representatives. Or, if they work for a large organization, they may want to become zone sales managers, regional sales managers, or sales vice presidents.

Your employer may offer training programs that will allow you to acquire new skills that you'll need in your current job and for future advancement. The company may provide opportunities to move on to higher-level jobs. Many large companies have also invested money in formal training programs in order to keep employees from moving to another company, especially a competitor.

With smaller companies, however, formal training isn't always available. In fact, more often than not, you are in charge of your own professional development. In your grandparents' day, an employee often spent his or her whole working life with one organization. That organization took care of professional development for its employees. Today, most people work for several organizations over the course of a lifetime. They should not depend on their employers to help them grow their careers. Therefore, if you want to advance within an organization, it must come from your own efforts. You will have to do a lot of your own research to find good opportunities for professional development.

Vocabulary

- professional development
- career ladder
- career portfolio
- courtesy
- compassion
- dependability
- perseverance
- work ethic
- honesty
- integrity
- loyalty
- mutual trust
- competitiveness
- patience
- organizational values
- equity
- risk taking
- teamwork
- visionary leadership

Planning your professional development includes identifying the knowledge, skills, and attitudes you need for success.

Courtesy of Yuri Arcurs/Shutterstock

LESSON 1   Planning Your Professional Development

Knowledge, Skills, and Attitudes for Your Career

Planning your professional development includes two main activities:

1. *Identifying* the knowledge, skills, and attitudes you need for success in your career

2. *Developing* that knowledge and those skills and attitudes.

Suppose your goal is to be a corporate executive. First, you have to identify the knowledge, skills, and attitudes you will need to do well in that career. Some of these might be:

Knowledge	Skills	Attitudes
How to sell things	Sales and marketing	Concern for pleasing customers
How to manage money	Financial planning	Conscientious money-handling
How to manage people	Management/leadership	Commitment to professional growth of subordinates
How to manage a company	Organizational ability	Desire to promote company welfare

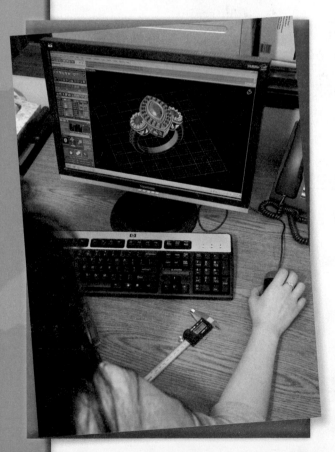

You will need to develop new knowledge and skills throughout your career.

Courtesy of Bloomberg/Getty Images

To rise to the top in business, you'll eventually need to know more, acquire more skills, and cultivate other attitudes. But this list is a good starting point. You can make a similar list for any other career that you want to pursue.

How do you develop the knowledge, skills, and attitudes you need? You begin by becoming educated. You complete high school with a good grade point average. You learn as much as you can in subjects like history, English, math, and science. These will help you in any job or career.

If you go to college, you will extend your education by majoring in a subject that coincides with your career ambitions. Graduate school choices should enable you to further deepen your knowledge, skills, and attitudes.

If your career goal is to be a journalist, for example, you will study subjects that will give you the *knowledge* necessary to write about many subjects. In your classes, you will perform exercises and write articles that will help you acquire the *skills* to write news stories the way a professional journalist does.

You might do an internship to get on-the-job experience. You will also bring certain *attitudes*, such as curiosity, inquisitiveness, objectivity, and love of language to stories you write about that will help make you a good journalist. College will help you refine those attitudes to the point where they become second nature. You'll be able to express them constantly in your work, giving your articles a distinctive writing style.

High school, college, and graduate school are only the start of your professional development. Developing new knowledge, skills, and attitudes will continue throughout your career. The organization you work for may give you the opportunity to enroll in a training program to improve your skills. It may pay tuition fees that will enable you to attend an adult education program in a community college or even enroll in classes at a university. It may offer you a chance to take part in career-testing programs to identify attitudes that you must develop to be successful. Some organizations may offer a career ladder, *a series of jobs that, over time, will take you higher and higher in the organization.*

You will want to take advantage of as many of these career-developing opportunities as possible. Self-learning, however, is just as important. Self-education opportunities are everywhere, once you start looking.

Improve Your Knowledge

Keep up with your areas of interest by reading books, magazines, and journals to improve your knowledge—or even by watching quality television programs. Attend lectures by well-known people in your field. Take advantage of opportunities to travel and meet "as many different kinds of people as you can." You can also write articles for professional journals. Writing is one of the best ways to learn about a subject, because in order to explain it to others you have to know it well yourself.

Expand Your Skills

Practice and expand your skills by doing volunteer work. For example, if you are in the computer field, volunteer to help a community nonprofit organization maintain its computers. Teach computer skills at a local senior citizens' home. You'll have the satisfaction of helping others while improving your skills.

Develop Good Attitudes

Attitudes may seem more abstract than skills. But those, too, take work. A positive "can do" attitude will help you become a better person—and a better professional. You can develop good attitudes on the job, in a volunteer program, when you are out with your friends, or at home with your family. Make it a conscientious effort to look for the opportunity behind every challenge.

success TIP ★

A key to a good attitude is to treat setbacks as learning experiences and move beyond them. Strive to see the glass as half full, instead of half empty.

Preparing a Career Portfolio

As you move forward in your career or profession, people will often ask you about your background and accomplishments. The request may come from your boss if he or she is writing your annual evaluation. It may come when you are interviewing for a new job.

An effective way to be able to answer these questions is to first put them in writing. Writing down your accomplishments, then picking from the best ones to communicate orally when asked, will allow you to feel confident when you talk about those things.

As you have learned, a résumé can be one tool for doing this. Another, more detailed tool, is a career portfolio. A career portfolio is *a folder or notebook that contains information on you and your achievements over time*. It provides examples of your work and evidence of your accomplishments, your educational development, and your career growth.

Reasons for a Career Portfolio

Creating and maintaining a career portfolio has many advantages. A portfolio will:

- Serve as an ongoing record of your completed work
- Allow you to track your improvement and growth over time and to identify you strengths and career-growth needs
- Make it easier to apply to schools and for jobs
- Document your accomplishments as you move from one school or one job to another

You may think you have little to put in a career portfolio at this time. Don't sell yourself short. If you have been participating in school and community activities, begin to document them now, and review and expand your portfolio with a line or two every time you complete a new activity. Soon, your portfolio will be impressively strong.

Elements of a Career Portfolio

A career portfolio contains different elements, depending on its purpose. A college-application portfolio contains different materials from a job-application portfolio. If you are applying for a scholarship based on academic accomplishment, your portfolio should contain information on grades and other evidence of academic success. If you are applying for a scholarship based on community service, the portfolio should contain evidence of your work with neighborhood organizations. Although most portfolios are in print, sometimes your file will need to be electronic (for example, if you are applying for a job as a webmaster or web content developer).

Regardless of their purpose, most portfolios have these common elements:

- A cover page
- A cover letter (addressed and tailored to the person who will be doing the hiring or placement)
- A table of contents
- A personal statement (a one-page summary of goals that relate to the job you are seeking or the school you would like to attend)
- Your résumé
- Letters of reference
- Transcripts, diplomas, and certificates
- A list of awards you've received
- Samples of your schoolwork and job accomplishments
- Names and contact information of people who have agreed to serve as your references

Assembling Your Portfolio

After you gather all of the materials listed above, select those that are most appropriate for the purpose at hand.

You'll need a slightly different combination of materials for each portfolio, and you will tailor the cover letter and table of contents accordingly.

Don't let your portfolio get too bulky. You don't want to overwhelm the reader. But do make sure that you include any needed support materials. If you received an award, for example, you should briefly explain its purpose. Also include explanations of the circumstances under which you wrote or produced any work samples.

Put your materials in logical order. If you're responding to a scholarship application, for example, put your materials in the order they appear on the application. Make your portfolio as neat and professional-looking as possible. Organize the contents so that they're easy to find. For example, if you include a great deal of information, consider dividing into sections with tabs.

Start a file folder for storing work you have accomplished for your portfolio. Keep the original and copies. Mark the original in some way so you don't inadvertently put it in the portfolio and send it away. In a separate section of your portfolio, keep contact information on people in your professional network, such as fellow classmates, teammates, parents' friends, and other people you meet at church, at social activities, in business, or while traveling. Keep this information separate, because it is for your own use only. You should not share it with others.

Questions to Ask When Preparing a Portfolio

- *Purpose*—Why am I creating this portfolio? Is it for a particular school or academic program? A job? A scholarship? A promotion?

- *Audience*—Who will read this portfolio? My boss? A prospective employer? A scholarship committee? Community members?

- *Format*—How should I present this information? In a notebook? A folder? Electronically?

- *Required materials*—Have I included all the required documents?

- *Other information*—Do I need multiple copies of the portfolio? Who should I contact if I have questions?

A potential employer may want to have a portfolio of your work in advance in order to discuss your achievements during a phone interview, or in person.

Courtesy of Stephen Coburn/Shutterstock

success TIP ★

Go beyond getting simple references for a portfolio. You have learned in an earlier lesson about the value of joining a community organization. Participate in one of these, or find an internship related to your career goals. Volunteer to do things, and take a leadership role when possible. If you are complimented on your work, then ask the head of the group to write you a letter of reference. Such letters add significant value to your portfolio, and keep you ready for new opportunities when they come your way.

Once you've assembled your portfolio, give it to a few friends or adults. Ask them for feedback and change the portfolio accordingly.

Updating Your Portfolio

Review the information in your portfolio at least three times a year. Remove anything that is outdated, such as phone numbers or e-mail addresses. Add anything new, such as a reference from the supervisor of an internship you've just completed.

Keep your portfolio growing. To do this, look for opportunities to participate in activities in which you excel, and then document your experiences. Get references from teachers when you've done well in their classes. The same goes for bosses.

Organizational and Personal Values That Contribute to Success

In previous lessons you learned about the importance of personal values. Your values are a big part of who you are. They help determine how you handle difficult situations, how you make decisions, and how you relate to others. Good personal values are a key to your success in life.

Personal Values in the Workplace

The values of a workplace start with each individual's personal values. How do you measure up in these areas?

A Positive Attitude

A positive attitude is a fundamental requirement in any work setting—in a classroom, on an assembly line, at a construction site, or in an office. If you want to succeed, you must keep a positive attitude toward yourself, your coworkers, your boss, and even your boss's boss. This isn't always easy. It can be especially hard when you feel your team member in a class exercise or a coworker, for example, isn't pulling his or her share of the load, or when you think your boss is unfair.

Being a complainer is never the solution. The most popular and productive people in any work environment are usually those with the best attitudes. These people inject humor into work. They bolster team spirit. This makes everyone happier and more productive. An upbeat attitude is contagious. Being negative all the time, on the other hand, will turn people off. It will eventually affect your success on the job.

Courtesy and Enthusiasm

Being courteous is more than saying "Please" and "Thank you." It's more than being polite. Courtesy is *consideration and cooperation in dealing with others.* Being courteous means always being helpful to other people—customers, coworkers, subordinates, supervisors, and anyone else you deal with.

Enthusiasm ties in both with a positive attitude and courtesy. Each of these traits can create success or spell failure for an organization. Can you remember a time when a worker in a store, a bank, or another business was not courteous to you or seemed bored? Did you feel like going back? How about a phone conversation with a customer service representative who did not know how to deal with your problem? Courtesy and enthusiasm, like a positive attitude, are contagious. You should practice them wherever you are or go, and you will build a successful career.

Your organization and coworkers will judge you based on how you treat people.

Courtesy of Ocean/Corbis Images

Compassion and Caring

Compassion is *a feeling for and understanding of another person's situation.* To show compassion is to put yourself in the other person's shoes. How does this person feel? Your organization and your coworkers will judge you based on how you treat people. When employees treat one another poorly, they create poor morale. Poor morale leads to poor performance.

Dependability and Reliability

Dependability is *the quality of being dependable or reliable.* It means showing up on time, to be sure, but it's more than that. A dependable person will be trusted. Employers can count on people who are dependable and reliable to get the job done well and to get it done on time—even in tough times. Whether you are a boss or an employee, you always want to be dependable and reliable.

Perseverance

Perseverance is *the quality of sticking to something until you achieve it.* It's persistence. A person who perseveres learns from mistakes. Perseverance is one of the most important factors in personal success, whether it's finishing a project due in science class, or making the school track team when most of your friends thought you did not have a chance. It's about not quitting. No one achieves success without a lot of hard work. And no organization gets to the top without employees who keep working hard to reach their goals, and those of the organization.

> "Opportunities are usually disguised as hard work, so most people don't recognize them."
>
> Ann Landers,
> American advice columnist

Personal and Organizational Values

Successful individuals and successful organizations share many of the same values. Among them are the following:

Work Ethics

Ethics are the basic values or standards that govern people and organizations. Showing a good work ethic means *taking into consideration the effects of your decisions and actions on all people connected with your organization—employees, customers, owners, suppliers, and competitors.*

Ethics come into play when you have to make a difficult decision. When you face a decision at work, ask yourself three questions:

1. Is it legal? Will I be violating either civil law or company policy?

2. Is it fair and balanced to all concerned in the short term as well as the long term? Does it promote win-win relationships?

3. How will it make me feel about myself? Will this decision make me proud? Will I feel good if a newspaper publishes my decision? Will I feel good if my family knows about it?

Making the decision, although challenging, is just the first step. The most difficult part of being ethical is *doing* what is right, not simply deciding what is right.

Honesty and Integrity

Honesty is *the practice of being truthful, trustworthy, and sincere; it is refraining from lying, cheating, or stealing*. Honesty strengthens an organization. Even when the truth hurts, it is best in the long run to be open and honest.

Integrity is *commitment to a code of values or beliefs that results in a unified, positive attitude and approach to life*. It is a sense of wholeness in your actions and beliefs. A person with integrity "walks the talk."

Honesty and integrity in making business decisions have significant long-term effects. A lack of honesty and integrity, by contrast, eventually drives away customers and demoralizes employees.

Loyalty

Loyalty is *being faithful to someone or something*. Loyalty is a two-way street. If you tell an organization or a supervisor you will do something, you must follow through and do it. If you do not, you are being disloyal. Likewise, if an organization makes you a promise, it must follow through on that promise.

In today's work environment, where people may change jobs many times, loyalty is often in short supply. Being loyal helps make personal and organizational relationships successful.

Mutual Trust and Respect

Mutual trust *develops when people and organizations know that they can rely on one another to do the right thing*. Trusting someone does not mean that you necessarily agree with that person. It simply means that you know where he or she stands. You know that such people mean what they say. As a result, you respect them. Trust and respect don't happen overnight: You must earn them over time. Personal and organizational trust are based on dependability, faith, and ongoing communication.

Competitiveness

Have you competed in a sports event, a spelling bee, a debate, or any other type of contest? If so, you know what competition means. Competitiveness is *the act of striving against others to achieve an objective*. In sports, the objective is simple: winning a game or a championship. In the workplace, the objective is sometimes more complex, but the purpose of competition is the same—winning, beating a competitor to a new product or source of customers. Competitiveness is essential in a business environment. Your employer will value you if you can help the organization do well against the competition.

Patience

In a work environment, you may often be under pressure to get things done as quickly as possible. That won't always happen. Delays and problems will come up, despite your efforts. When they do, you'll have to be patient. Patience is *the ability to bear difficulty, delay, frustration, or pain without complaint*. People who are patient have a calming effect on those around them. Once people calm down, everyone can focus on getting an essential task done.

Patient people have a calming effect on those around them.
Courtesy of Yuri Arcurs/Shutterstock

Organizational Values

From a career perspective, some values apply more to organizations as a whole than to their individual employees. Organizational values include *the combined personal values of the people in an organization and the values of the organization itself*. Strong organizational values such as the following can make the difference between a good organization and a great one.

Equity

People want to work for an organization that has equity. Equity is *equal justice or fairness*. For example, an organization that pays its employees fairly based on skill and experience practices equity. It promotes people according to accepted practices that it sets forth in writing. Leaders of an equitable organization don't play favorites.

Risk Taking

Risk taking is *taking chances*. An organization usually needs to take risks if it wants to get ahead—otherwise it can get stuck in a rut or in outdated ways of doing things. It should not, however, take foolish risks. An organization that is a healthy risk taker is an exciting place to work. Its employees are stimulating people because they, too, have adventurous spirits.

Teamwork is as important in the workplace as it is on the basketball court or football field.
Courtesy of Monkey Business Images/Shutterstock

Teamwork and Cooperation

Teamwork is *working together to identify and solve group-related problems and to achieve goals*. A spirit of cooperation stands out in organizations whose employees excel at teamwork. Teamwork is as important in the workplace as it is on the basketball court or football field.

Visionary Leadership

Visionary leadership is *leadership exercised by people who have a clear sense of where they are guiding their organizations and who can persuade others to follow them*. Visionary leaders see into the future. Most people find it satisfying to work for an organization with visionary leaders because they feel they are participating in an important effort.

Using complete sentences, answer the following questions on a sheet of paper.

1. What are the three basic areas of your life that you must identify and develop to have a successful career?

2. What are three reasons to have a career portfolio?

3. Name five things to include in a career portfolio.

4. What are three personal values that will help you be successful in the workplace? Do you have those values? If not, how can you develop them?

5. What are three values that are common to successful people and to successful organizations?

6. What are three organizational values that any successful organization should have?

7. Name three people you consider "visionary" leaders, and explain what qualities they have.

APPLYING PROFESSIONAL DEVELOPMENT SKILLS

8. Pick a career you might like to pursue. Make a list of the knowledge, skills, and attitudes you think will be needed to succeed in that career. Then list ways that you will develop them.

9. Prepare your own career portfolio based on information from this lesson; create individual sections that reflect your accomplishments in different areas.

LESSON 2

Learning to Work With Others

Quick Write

_____

_____

Think of a recent experience as a team or group member. Was it always easy to communicate your point of view? Write a paragraph about the experience, including how you resolved any communication problems.

Learn About

- the communication process
- verbal and nonverbal communication
- barriers to effective communication
- communications within organizations
- collaboration and teamwork

"Coming together is a beginning. Keeping together is progress. Working together is success."

Henry Ford, American industrialist and founder of the Ford Motor Company

The Communication Process

Whenever you work with other people—at school, work, or any social activity—you have to communicate. Communication is _creating or sending of information, thoughts, and feelings from one person to another._

As the definition implies, communication has two sides. It includes _sending_ messages in speech, writing, or another medium, such as music or video. It also includes _receiving_ messages through listening, reading, or watching, and, most importantly, understanding those messages. The ultimate test of successful communication is understanding. If your listener understands your message, you have succeeded. If not, you have failed to communicate.

Words are a primary vehicle for communication. So when two people speak the same language and use the same vocabulary, communication should be easy, right? Well, not always. Words can have different meanings for different people. That's because people base the meanings of words not only on dictionary definitions but also on personal experience, and to some extent, local culture. For example, if you say to Brad and Cyndi, "I'll meet you at the club tonight," Brad might be happy, because he enjoys clubs. He's spent many happy evenings with friends in clubs. But Cyndi might be afraid because she was once in a club when there was a fire. The word _club_ has a different subjective meaning, or _personal significance,_ to each of your friends.

Subjective meanings vary even more for abstract words such as _democracy_ and _freedom._ To the average American, _democracy_ has a positive subjective meaning. It refers to a form of government in which the people elect their rulers. To someone from a country ruled by a dictator, however, *democracy* may imply chaos and lack of leadership. This is because he or she has never seen a democracy in action.

To discover if your listener has understood you, or to let a speaker know that you don't understand what he or she is saying, you either ask for or provide feedback. Feedback is *the receiver's response to the sender's message*. If you express ideas well and the person listens well but doesn't give you any feedback, you still have no idea whether you communicated successfully. Feedback closes the communication loop.

Recall that feedback is not always oral. Body language can be one of the most effective forms of feedback. A nod of the head signifies agreement and understanding; a frown might indicate confusion or displeasure. Eye contact usually means the listener is with you; if a listener avoids eye contact, you might be having a communication problem. Finally, one of the most effective forms of feedback is silence. Silence can speak volumes—it often indicates a failure of communication.

Vocabulary

- communication
- subjective meaning
- feedback
- verbal communication
- nonverbal communication
- distortion
- stereotyping
- filtering
- semantics
- defensiveness
- informal communication
- grapevine
- formal communication
- horizontal communication
- vertical communication
- intermediary
- collaboration

Body language—including gestures—can be an effective form of feedback when communicating.

Courtesy of Poznyakov/Shutterstock

COSTELLO: Look Abbott, if you're the coach, you must know all the players.

ABBOTT: I certainly do.

COSTELLO: Well you know I've never met the guys. So you'll have to tell me their names, and then I'll know who's playing on the team.

ABBOTT: Well, let's see, we have on the bags, Who's on first, What's on second, I Don't Know is on third…

COSTELLO: That's what I want to find out.

ABBOTT: I say Who's on first, What's on second, I Don't Know's on third.

COSTELLO: Are you the manager?

ABBOTT: Yes.

COSTELLO: And you don't know the fellows' names?

ABBOTT: Well I should.

COSTELLO: Well then who's on first?

ABBOTT: Yes.

COSTELLO: I mean the fellow's name.

ABBOTT: Who.

COSTELLO: The guy on first.

ABBOTT: Who.

COSTELLO: The first baseman.

ABBOTT: Who.

COSTELLO: I'm asking YOU who's on first.

ABBOTT: That's the man's name.

COSTELLO: That's who's name?

ABBOTT: Yes.

COSTELLO: Well go ahead and tell me.

ABBOTT: That's it.

COSTELLO: That's who?

Verbal and Nonverbal Communication

There are two types of communication: *verbal* and *nonverbal*. Verbal communication refers to *written as well as spoken words*. In this lesson, however, *verbal communication* refers to spoken words, consisting of two actions: *speaking* and *listening*.

Speaking

When speaking, you must pay particular attention to three things: the tone of your voice, your emotions, and self-disclosure. For example, when you shout, your *tone of voice* makes you sound angry or upset, even if you are not. But a whisper can convey anger, too.

Because voice tone can be misleading, you also must be careful of your *emotions*. Your emotions convey silent messages that you may not be aware of. For example, if you don't trust a person, your verbal communication will usually convey that mistrust, whether you whisper, shout, or speak in a normal tone. If you are afraid of someone, your verbal communication will reflect that fear.

ABBOTT: Yes.

Pause

COSTELLO: All I'm trying to find out is what's the guy's name on first base.

ABBOTT: No. What is on second base.

COSTELLO: I'm not asking you who's on second.

ABBOTT: Who's on first.

COSTELLO: I'm only asking you, who's the guy on first base?

ABBOTT: That's right.

COSTELLO: What's the guy's name on first base?

ABBOTT: No. What is on second.

COSTELLO: I'm not asking you who's on second.

ABBOTT: Who's on first.

COSTELLO: I don't know.

ABBOTT: He's on third, we're not talking about him.

COSTELLO: Now how did I get on third base?

ABBOTT: You mentioned his name.

COSTELLO: If I mentioned the third baseman's name, who did I say is playing third?

ABBOTT: No. Who's playing first.

COSTELLO: What's on first?

ABBOTT: What's on second.

COSTELLO: I don't know.

ABBOTT: He's on third.

COSTELLO: He's on third and I don't give a darn!

ABBOTT: What?

COSTELLO: I said I don't give a darn!

ABBOTT: Oh, that's our shortstop.

"Who's on First," used with permission and copyright TCA Television Corp., Hi Neighbor and Diana K. Abbott-Colton.

Be aware also of the power of *self-disclosure*. To communicate well, you must disclose yourself to others. You must let the other person see your fears, likes and dislikes, beliefs, and perceptions. But too much disclosure can be risky, especially in the workplace, where competitors as well as friends surround you. While some people will appreciate your honesty, others might take advantage of what they learn and use it against you. Think about who your listener is, and use self-disclosure accordingly.

Listening

Contrary to what many people think, listening is an active, not a passive, activity. *Active listening* is genuine, two-way communication. It's giving undivided attention to a speaker in a genuine effort to understand the speaker's point of view. Listening consists of four actions:

1. *Hearing*—Receiving the physical sound through your ears
2. *Understanding*—Interpreting and comprehending the message
3. *Remembering*—Retaining what you've heard
4. *Acting*—Responding by action or inaction.

It is not enough to hear. You must also understand, remember, and act.

Some people think they are communicating when all they're doing is talking. To communicate, however, you must have an active listener. If you tend to talk a lot, ask yourself whether people are actively listening or tuning you out. If they don't volunteer feedback, seek it out. Test their understanding. It will let you know how well you are communicating.

True listening is a form of paying attention. When you pay attention to someone, you focus on what he or she is saying and block out distractions such as background noise and competing thoughts. This isn't always easy—in fact, studies show that people often only really listen to about 25 percent of what others say. If you tend to dominate a conversation, force yourself to talk less and listen more. Then structure your response based on what you've heard.

Physiological barriers, such as being tired, not having enough exercise, or eating poorly can affect how well you listen in either a formal setting or in conversation.

Courtesy of Radius Images/Corbis Images

One barrier to active listening is the fact that most people can understand information much more quickly than a speaker can provide it. As a result, a listener's mind might wander many times during an average conversation. Think about the last time you listened to someone. Did your mind wander? Was it because the person wasn't speaking fast enough? Seemed too unemotional? What was the reason?

There are other barriers to keep you from listening effectively, like being preoccupied with other thoughts; multitasking, trying to shift from one thought or action to another almost simultaneously; pretending to listen when you would rather not; information overload, a flood of information that your brain can't process or segment properly; and physiological distractions, like being tired, sick, hungry, or any number of factors that distract you from listening properly.

Finally, fear and anger create barriers to good listening. If people are upset before they even begin to listen, or get angry soon after someone begins to talk, they won't hear much. Communication will suffer because they may offer improper responses, having heard only part of the other person's message.

Six Rules for Effective Listening

1. *Don't evaluate what you're hearing*—Suspend snap judgments. Take everything in. Evaluate the speaker's ideas later.

2. *Don't anticipate*—Sometimes you may think you know what someone is going to say before he or she even says it. More often than not, you'll be wrong. Don't try to second-guess the speaker.

3. *Take notes to boost your recall, but don't go overboard*—People forget one-third to one-half of what they hear within eight hours. For this reason, taking notes can be helpful. If you focus too much on note taking, however, your listening will suffer. Find the right balance.

Active listening takes energy and requires concentration, but it pays off in better understanding—and better personal and professional relationships.
Courtesy of STOCK4B-RF/Corbis Images

4. *Listen for themes and facts*—Listen for the speaker's major themes as well as for important facts. Remember, the person is communicating ideas, not just words. Listen for the ideas.

5. *Don't fake paying attention*—Concentration actually uses less energy than pretending. Acting is difficult!

6. *Review*—If you're listening to a speech, periodically review in your mind the main points you've heard so far. Pretend you're going to summarize the speech to a friend later in the day. What key points would you mention?

Nonverbal Communication

Nonverbal communication is *communication without words*. It's more common than you might think. Studies show that 70 percent of all communication is nonverbal. Body language is the primary means of nonverbal communication. As you learned in the lesson on interviewing, body language includes things such as posture, eye contact, gestures, and distance from the other person. Stay aware of what you are doing with your body when you are communicating. When in doubt about body language, mirror the other person. If the other person is folding his or her arms, do the same. It may help the other person feel more comfortable with you, too.

Barriers to Effective Communication

Communication experts call the barriers to communication *noise*. Some of the most common forms of noise are *distortion, semantics, defensiveness, external noise,* and *mistrust*.

Distortion

Distortion is *a distraction that interferes with communication*. For example, you may try your best to listen to your history teacher, but you're distracted because you are worrying about your upcoming math exam. Other types of distortion include stereotyping, or *holding a concept that is based on oversimplified assumptions or opinions, rather than on facts*, and filtering, or *hearing only what you want to hear*.

Semantics

Semantics refers to *achieving a desired effect on an audience especially through the use of words with novel or dual meanings*. Consider, for example, the many dictionary meanings of an ordinary word such as *hardball*. Add to these the subjective meanings that a word such as *hardball* has, such as another term used for baseball or someone difficult to deal with and you can see how communication barriers might arise. If you want to talk about hardball, make sure your listener understands the word in the same way as you do. If you're not sure, define it up front and even ask for feedback if you think it's needed. Make sure the listener understands how you intend to use the word. And never guess about definitions; use a current collegiate dictionary to ensure you are using a standard meaning.

Defensiveness

success TIP ★

Judge others fairly, do not try to control them, show concern for others' feelings, and listen to others' points of view.

When people feel threatened by communication, they may become defensive. Defensiveness is *an effort to justify oneself*. For example, if you feel a person is judging you wrongly, you may feel threatened. You become less likely to trust, or understand, what he or she says. You may become defensive if you think someone is trying to control or manipulate you, or if you think the other person has no concern for your welfare or feelings. Just as you want other people to be supportive in their communication with you, you should support them.

External Noise

External noise in the environment is a barrier to communication. Noise doesn't have to be loud: While a jackhammer outside your window may certainly be a distraction, whispering can also be. External noise affects people differently—some people study best when music is playing; others find any kind of music a distraction.

Mistrust

Mistrust between two people or among group members can also create a barrier to communication. If you don't trust your boss, for example, he or she will have a hard time communicating instructions to you in a way you will understand and respond to. In an organization, trust comes from openness, constant feedback, freedom to act with integrity, and shared goals and values. One moment of dishonesty or lack of support for another person can ruin weeks, or even years, of efforts to build trust.

Communications Within Organizations

When you interact with others in an organization, you use many types of communication. The type of communication you use depends on the situation in which communication takes place, the positions of the people participating in the communication, and the nature of the information to be shared.

Informal and Formal Communication

Informal communication refers to *social interactions among people who work together or are associated with one another in some other way*. Informal communication happens when people gossip, tell stories, spread information, and participate in the grapevine, or *the informal channel of communication among people in an organization*. The grapevine can include both personal information—who just had a baby or who got fired— and business-related information, such as rumors about a new company product. Its reliability isn't guaranteed and it can have positive or negative effects on the organization.

Formal communication is *a structured, stable method of communication among people*. Speeches, memos, written instructions, e-mail, and official Web communications are examples of formal communication. All official communication in an organization flows through this channel.

Horizontal and Vertical Communication

You can also define communication within an organization based on the direction in which it moves. For example, horizontal communication is *communication among people at the same level in an organization, no matter what department they are in*.

If you are an entry-level worker in the finance department of a bank and you communicate with an entry-level worker in the marketing department, you are conducting horizontal communication. This kind of communication increases the organization's flexibility, helps with problem solving, and allows information sharing among the organization's various parts. Its primary drawback can be simply that there is too much of it.

Vertical communication is *that which takes place between people at different levels within the same department*. The communication between you and your boss is vertical communication. The communication between your boss and his or her boss is also vertical communication. In most organizations, information often flows fairly well from top to bottom; the challenge is usually to increase the amount of information that flows from bottom to top.

To increase this information flow from bottom to top, some organizations have unions, and the representative who helps try to improve the information flow upward in order to achieve some action, such as safety improvements in a factory or plant, is a *union steward*.

Think about your high school, or collegiate and professional sports teams that have *captains*. These are team leaders that communicate to the manager or coach certain needs of the players or about injuries that may affect a player's ability to do his job when the player may otherwise feel too prideful or embarrassed to tell the coach themselves. In this way, a captain is an intermediary, *someone who shares communication between two or more individuals*. He or she is the one who is considered best suited to communicate both horizontally and vertically to improve the team's chances of winning.

Written Versus Oral Communication

You may think that written instructions for many things you do in class are unimportant. Well, much of what you do is to prepare you for the workplace. Written communication is essential in the workplace. If the leaders of an organization want to put into place a new policy, for example, they should always communicate it in writing. The written document will ensure that everyone gets the same message. The company may later supplement the written message by oral communication. For example, it may schedule informal sessions during which employees may ask questions about the new policy.

Sometimes you must express one-on-one business communications in writing. For example, if your boss tells you that you will get a 10 percent raise next month, you may want to ask him or her to put it in writing to ensure that both of you remember the oral commitment.

Written communication, especially e-mail, is more likely to cause misunderstanding than oral communication. Be especially careful about communicating anything negative in emails. If you're like most people, you write e-mail or text messages and send them off quickly. Haste alone increases the possibility of miscommunication. The main problem with email or text messages, however, is that the receiver can easily share them with others. To save yourself potential trouble and embarrassment, follow this basic rule of e-mail protocol: Never say something in an e-mail or text message that you would not want the whole world to read.

Three Benchmarks for Ethical Communication

To ensure that you are being ethical in your communication, ask yourself three questions:

1. Is my message truthful, honest, and fair?

2. Am I communicating as clearly as I can? Misunderstanding can be an inadvertent source of unethical actions. Be sure everything is clear from the start.

3. If I am saying something negative (for example, if I'm a supervisor who must reprimand an employee), am I communicating in a way that protects the other person's dignity and sustains the relationship? A good rule of thumb when communicating something negative is to condemn the action but never the person.

In some cases, communicating verbally is much better than communicating in writing. Some issues or topics are so sensitive that it is best not to write them down. For example, if you must criticize a fellow employee, always do so face-to-face. It's much harder to be harsh in a face-to-face meeting, and seeing someone eye-to-eye usually softens harsh feelings. Using body language and verbal communication will also convey your support of the person. It also lets you read the other person's body language and verbal style to adjust your words accordingly.

Ethics in Organizational Communication

Ethics plays a central role in the communication process, especially in an organization. You cannot collaborate with others and work as a team if you cannot trust one another to tell the truth and do what is right. You may have read about ethical breakdowns in a few large US corporations in the past few years. Executives were dishonest in their communication with employees, stockholders, the public, and the government. As a result, stockholders and employees lost billions of dollars, companies failed, and the guilty parties often paid huge fines or went to jail. Ethical behavior—especially ethical communication—is essential on the job, at school, and in all other areas of your life.

Collaboration and Teamwork

Collaboration is *working with others in a team or group*. Effective collaboration leads to innovation, quality improvement, and the sharing of knowledge. You've probably realized by now that people can't collaborate if they can't communicate. But different people have different communication styles. These styles quickly become evident when a team or group begins to collaborate on a project. How should team members overcome differences in communication and work styles?

People must communicate to collaborate. To communicate effectively, you must understand people's different communication styles.

Courtesy of Corbis Flirt/Alamy

When two or more people with different personalities try to communicate, they must use their speaking and listening skills to communicate and collaborate effectively. Some personalities prefer to be brief and concise. They like to state opinions directly. On the other hand, some colleagues may prefer not to be so direct. They might like a more relaxed, indirect style of communication. In fact, they may take offense at a direct approach.

So what do you prefer? This is where your communication skills come in. Pay attention to what you are communicating verbally and nonverbally. Choose your words and tone carefully. Practice active listening. Get feedback. Pay attention to your body language as well as the other person's. Can you see why communication is one of the most important aspects of working in an organization?

Teamwork and Communication

The opportunity to be a member of a team is one of the most rewarding parts of working in an organization. A four-person team can usually accomplish much more than those same four people could accomplish working individually. This is because a good team gives every member a chance to contribute his or her unique skills to a project.

Think of a doctor. Doctors are highly trained professionals, yet they can't do it all alone. For this reason, they work in teams that consist of nurses, anesthesiologists, paramedics, midwives, interns, pharmacists, and others. Teamwork is essential not only in health care, but also in business, education, and the military— just about everywhere.

Characteristics of an Effective Team

- *Purpose*—Members share an understanding of why the team exists— they are invested in accomplishing its mission and goals

- *Priorities*—Members know what needs doing, when, and who should do it

- *Roles*—Members know their roles—the team leader assigns tasks to the people best qualified to do them

- *Decisions*—Team members understand who holds authority and decision-making responsibility

- *Conflict*—Team members deal with disagreements openly—they understand that overcoming conflict is essential to team effectiveness and personal growth

- *Personal Traits*—Members feel their personalities are appreciated and that they contribute to the welfare of the group

- *Norms*—The group sets and adheres to well-defined performance standards

- *Effectiveness*—Team meetings are efficient and productive—members enjoy working together

- *Success*—Members share a sense of pride and accomplishment when the team achieves its goals

- *Training*—Team members receive ongoing feedback and opportunities for updating their skills.

When a group shares a goal and is able to think and act as one, it's a satisfying and productive experience for the individuals and the organization. But working in teams can also be frustrating. When you have to work with people who are not your personality type, who have a different cultural background, or who have different ideas about how to attain the team's goals, you have to be careful about what you say and how you say it. Some people think that good team members have to be good friends. That's not necessarily true. Good team members do, however, have to be good communicators. Good collaborators know how to take personality, cultural, and philosophical differences among team members and make those differences work for the team's benefit.

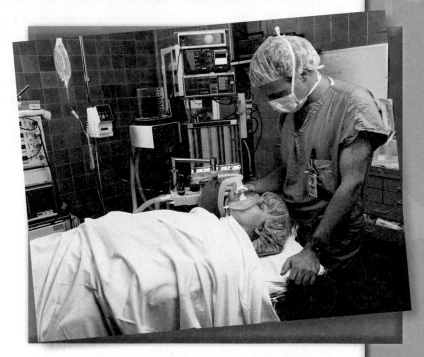

In the health-care field, doctors work in teams that consist of nurses, anesthesiologists, pharmacists, and many others.

Courtesy of Julian Calder/Corbis Images

Take the batting order of a baseball team, for example. Not everyone is a home-run hitter. Some are good at hitting singles and doubles. Others strike out very seldom and have a knack for drawing walks. The manager takes these various skills and sets up the players to bat in the order that will best benefit the team. He wants the first, second, and third hitters to get on base so the fourth batter— the home-run or "clean-up" hitter—can drive them in and score more runs. Successful teams in other walks of life similarly find ways to best use each team member.

To be a good team member and collaborator, you should do the following:

- Participate fully—contribute ideas and solutions
- Recognize and respect differences in others
- Value the ideas and contributions of others
- Listen and share information
- Ask questions and get clarification
- Keep your commitments
- Be flexible and respect the partnership created by the team
- Have fun and care about the team and the outcomes
- Work for a climate of trust and open, honest communication.

Different Approaches to Life and Work

Remember that different people at the workplace will have different approaches to life and work. These approaches aren't necessarily wrong—they're just different. Some have their origin in personality; others are based on an individual's personal philosophy. People in different circumstances will also balance different priorities, such as spouse, work, family, education, and religious faith, in different ways. Others will complete a task quite differently from you. The key point is not to ignore these differences or get upset by them. It's to figure out how to make the most of what each individual brings to the workplace.

✔ CHECKPOINTS

Lesson 2 Review

Using complete sentences, answer the following questions on a sheet of paper.

1. What are three barriers to communication? What can you do to overcome each of them?

2. Explain the importance of ethical communication.

3. What is active listening? Why is it important?

4. What challenges would you expect when communicating and collaborating with someone whose personality was exactly the opposite of your own? What would you do to solve these challenges?

5. Suppose you work with someone who grew up in another country, but who speaks English well. How would you go about learning to communicate and collaborate better with that person?

APPLYING COLLABORATION SKILLS

6. Think about a time when you disagreed with someone— a friend, family member, or teammate. Write a one-page paper on the communication and collaboration difficulties you faced, and how you might better overcome such difficulties in the future.

Seeking Feedback and Promotions

Quick Write

_____

_____

Has someone ever praised you for your work on the job or in school? Has someone ever criticized you? Pick one incident—a time when you were praised or criticized—and write a paragraph about it. Was this kind of feedback helpful?

Learn About

- seeking and receiving feedback in the workplace
- strategies for earning a promotion
- developing a career-path strategy

"Feedback is the breakfast of champions."

Ken Blanchard, American author and expert on the subject of management

Seeking and Receiving Feedback in the Workplace

You've learned that giving and receiving feedback is part of the communication process. Feedback may involve asking a question, repeating information for understanding, or providing other input in response to someone else's words or actions. It can be verbal or nonverbal.

Feedback is important in any communication or environment; it has become more essential to success in the workplace. Feedback can come from your boss or your coworkers. In some jobs, it comes from customers.

Feedback is a good source of motivation. It lets you know whether you're doing good work. It can reassure you.

Feedback can come from your boss, coworkers, or customers.

Courtesy of Monkey Business Images/Shutterstock

It can also provide suggestions for improvement. You need other people's feedback, and they need yours. If well used, feedback leads to improvements that can benefit individuals and organizations.

Feedback can be informal or formal. Informal feedback occurs daily in the course of business operations. If you don't get the feedback you think you need to do your job well, you should seek it out—from your boss or others. In many workplaces, formal feedback occurs on a scheduled basis. It's often tied to a supervisor's evaluation of an employee's work.

Seeking Feedback

Suppose you put a lot of time and effort into a project at work or school. You spent several days doing research and writing a draft. You polished the draft to make sure it was the best you could do. You presented it to your boss or teacher, and all he or she said was "Thanks." That's the last you heard about it. That individual didn't give you any feedback. As a result, you don't know for sure whether your work was good or bad. You don't have any tips for how to do it better the next time.

Unfortunately, lack of feedback is common in the workplace and school. It's usually not intentional. Sometimes those in charge are so busy that they just forget. Or they may assume that as long as they don't criticize your work, you automatically understand that they approve of it.

What's the solution to this communication gap? It's simple: If your boss or teacher doesn't give feedback, ask for it. As you hand in a report or schoolwork, say to your boss or teacher, "Could you please let me know if this is what you need or are looking for? And how could I make it better?" Such questions will show that individual that you want to improve. That alone will be impressive. In addition, when you ask the question, it helps your boss or teacher remember that you value feedback. You may soon start to receive it.

Vocabulary

- performance appraisal
- 360-degree feedback
- halo/horn effect
- promotion
- benefits
- merit promotion
- ability promotion
- career-path strategy

success TIP

Feedback is most useful when based on clear standards for performance. A key to success in a new job is to review and make sure you understand the standards. If you have any concerns about meeting them, you should ask for further guidance and training.

Feedback From the Job

Feedback can come from just about anyone in an organization. For example, if you are new to a job, seek out experienced people whom you can trust to evaluate your performance. Their feedback can be just as helpful as your supervisor's remarks.

Also be aware that feedback isn't only a vertical, top-down activity. Feedback should flow horizontally as well. Team members should evaluate each other as well as the team itself. You should ask for feedback from your colleagues, coworkers, and fellow team members. Ask them to be honest about your strengths and weaknesses. Give them feedback, too.

Finally, if you deal with customers, always ask them how you and the company are doing. People appreciate requests for their opinions. It shows them that you care about doing a good job.

Receiving Feedback

Getting feedback—both formal and informal—is important in just about every situation in life. In school, you get feedback from teachers. You might meet with them periodically and ask them how you are doing and how you can improve. The school also provides a formal feedback system – grading and report cards. Outside the classroom, you may ask friends or family to read your papers and give you comments. If you're an athlete, your ultimate feedback is winning or losing a game or receiving a trophy. You even face feedback in dating. If someone likes you, you know you are doing well!

Informal feedback helps organizations and their employees improve continually. It allows supervisors, employees, and team members to be aware of their day-to-day performance. Additionally, organizations also need a more regular, structured means of providing feedback. They do this through a variety of evaluation processes.

The Performance Appraisal

One common type of formal feedback in an organization is a performance appraisal, or *a systematic review of how well an individual employee has performed during a specified period.* Some companies refer to this as a performance review or a performance evaluation. A performance appraisal is often based on written standards or expectations that the employee and supervisor have discussed in advance. If you're a new employee, you may receive a copy of these standards at the time the organization hires you. A performance appraisal is intended as a tool for growth. It is often part of a long-range plan for an employee's professional development.

Electronic Feedback

In today's workplaces, feedback is often in the form of e-mail messages. Feedback is especially useful when it is in writing. Written feedback provides evidence to justify additional training, promotions, and other actions. To help track your progress in your job and career, set up a file folder on your computer for feedback you have received from bosses and colleagues. Save any messages and other documents containing praise and suggestions for improvement, and periodically review them. Also, bring these email messages to any performance appraisal meetings you may have with your supervisor. By doing so, you can confidently make corrections and capitalize on your successes to ensure you're on track with your career goals.

If your organization gives performance appraisals, your boss will probably schedule one with you once or twice a year. It will be a one-on-one session in which just you and your boss will take part. Your supervisor may use the results of your appraisal to decide whether to give you a permanent position, salary increase or a promotion. If necessary, a boss can also use the appraisal to initiate disciplinary action.

You should look forward to these private sessions with your boss. They'll give both of you a chance to review your progress, your problems, and your contribution to your group's work. They'll let you know whether your work is meeting the company's standards, values, and goals. They'll identify your strengths as well as your weaknesses. A good appraisal will also offer specific suggestions on how to overcome your weaknesses. If your organization doesn't give formal performance appraisals, you should ask your boss for an informal one at least yearly.

To get the most out of a performance appraisal, prepare for it. Think about what you've accomplished since your last appraisal or since you joined the organization. Think about what strengths you've shown, what weaknesses you have uncovered, or even what mistakes you have made. Some supervisors will ask you to write a memo highlighting what you think are your accomplishments during the evaluation period. Many companies are also requesting employees to establish goals for themselves in the areas of education, promotion, career, or organizational. These goals indicate to your supervisor your desire for self-improvement and to meet organizational goals. Make notes and bring them to the meeting. If you've identified weaknesses and mistakes, show what you are doing to correct them. Most organizations will tolerate mistakes, at least the first time, if you show that you understand the error and have taken steps to ensure it won't happen again.

Getting feedback—whether a formal award or an informal comment—is important in almost every facet of life.

Courtesy of Yellow Dog Productions/Getty Images

360-Degree Feedback

Another type of formal feedback in organizations is 360-degree feedback, which is *a performance appraisal that comes from all levels around the employee—from a boss, coworkers, and subordinates, as well as the employee himself or herself.* The "360 degrees" refers to the degrees in a circle, and like a circle, this appraisal is complete. It gives everyone an opportunity to provide input. Such 360-degree feedback lets you learn how people see you from many angles. It can be even more helpful than a performance appraisal, which evaluates you from only one perspective—your supervisor's.

If you aren't getting feedback, seek it out. It can make the difference between doing only a fair job and achieving real success.

Responding to Feedback

Responding to feedback can be difficult. If the feedback is positive, you'll naturally be proud. However, don't assume this means there's no room for improvement. Instead, ask your supervisor what you could do to improve your work even more. Moreover, never let a positive appraisal be an excuse for coasting. The workplace is competitive. You need to continue to do your best every day. If the feedback is negative, don't get defensive. Don't respond with a sentence that begins with the words, "But I...." That's a sure indication that a defensive statement is about to emerge. Learn from what the person giving the feedback tells you. Ask polite questions that help you understand the remarks and see things from the other person's point of view. Above all, don't reply to the reviewer in anger. Go away and think about what the reviewer has said so you can come up with a calm and useful response.

When assessing whether you've received fair feedback, watch out for the halo/horn effect. The halo/horn effect is *the tendency to rate a person high on all performance factors or low on all of them because of an impression the evaluator may have of that individual.*

The *halo* effect can also stem from a reviewer's tendency to rate someone based on experience rather than on recent observations. For example, if you've always received great appraisals but have begun to get lazy recently, the reviewer may give you a good rating solely based on past performance. On the other hand, if you've done only fair work in the past but have recently made a real commitment to do well, the reviewer may give you a mediocre rating because he or she is basing the review on your previous efforts; this is known as the *horn* effect.

Whether feedback is positive or negative, remember that people sometimes do have biases that can interfere with an objective appraisal of someone else's work. It's a fact of life that people will not always judge you fairly. The bottom line: Always be aware of your strengths and weaknesses, no matter what others say. In the light of this self-knowledge, listen carefully to others. And always give and receive feedback graciously.

Strategies for Earning a Promotion

If you've worked for an organization for a while and done a good job, you may be eligible for a promotion, or *a new job at a higher level*. This new position will enable you to use the skills and knowledge you've developed in your current job and give you opportunities to develop new skills. A promotion will usually give you a higher salary and more impressive title.

A promotion may also increase your benefits, or *compensation you receive from your employer in addition to your salary*. Benefits can include a number of things: health insurance, more paid vacation days, participation in a company retirement—savings plan, life insurance, or a company car, just to name some of the most common. Many employers offer these kinds of benefits as a way of building good employer—employee relations. These employers value their employees and want them to stay loyal to the company or organization. For some employees, such benefits—especially health insurance—can be the single determining factor in deciding whether to stay with one organization or to accept a job with another.

But promotions have disadvantages as well as advantages. A promotion will mean more responsibility and higher expectations. You might have to work longer hours. You may have to supervise people for the first time, or your supervisory responsibilities may increase. If you think management isn't one of your strengths, you may be uncomfortable in that role.

Some people turn down promotions if they think the disadvantages outweigh the advantages. For example, if you value your free time and feel that a new job will require you to give up too many personal activities, think twice about accepting a promotion. But if the new job is an important step in reaching your career goal, you'll probably jump at the opportunity to grow and to learn.

Types of Promotions

There are two kinds of promotions: merit promotions and ability promotions.

A merit promotion is *based on your performance in your current job*. Merit promotions are like rewards. You get more money and a higher position because you've done well in your present post.

An ability promotion is *based on your potential to do a new job, rather than how you did in your old one*. You might think of an ability promotion as a challenge. It rests on someone's belief that you are able to handle broader responsibilities.

Both types of promotions result from someone else's estimation of your abilities. Ultimately, however, you are the person who will do the job, and you need to be comfortable in it. Before accepting a promotion, be sure you understand what you are getting into and that you can do what the new job requires. You don't want to be a victim of the "Peter principle." This principle, popularized by Dr. Laurence J. Peter, states that employees of an organization are eventually promoted to their highest level of competence. After this point, further promotions raise them to a level at which they are no longer competent. When this happens, the organization, as well as its employees, may suffer. The person is not comfortable in the job because he or she can't do it well. You may like challenges and feel ready to move to a higher level, and find new opportunities exciting. The key is self-knowledge. You must be aware of your strengths and weaknesses. You must have the self-confidence to accept these opportunities, but you should not try to exceed your limits.

One more thing to keep in mind about promotions: If you receive a promotion, you might find that your coworkers resent your success. Some may feel that they, not you, deserved the promotion. Handle this initial resentment with an attitude that is accepting of other perspectives. Be sensitive to other people's feelings, and never brag or boast.

How to Get a Promotion: Some Tips

As you've seen, promotions provide opportunities and challenges. As a result, some people have mixed feelings about promotions. They are happy to receive an offer of a promotion, but they don't necessarily seek it out. Other people seek promotions. If you decide it's time for a promotion, you should do several things:

1. *Seek more responsibility in your current job*—Prove that you deserve a promotion. Pave the way by taking on more responsibility whenever you can. Volunteer to tackle new and difficult projects, and complete them successfully.

2. *Document the good things you've done in your current job*—Keep a list of projects you've successfully completed, money you have saved or earned for the company, suggestions you've made that increase productivity, and any other accomplishments or attitudes that make you a valuable employee. Share this list with your boss during your performance appraisals and at other times as appropriate. Convince your boss that if you've done this much in a lower position, you could do much more in a higher one.

3. *Understand the responsibilities of the new job and do the needed preparation*— Many jobs look enticing from the outside. But when you find out what they involve, you may realize you are not prepared. For example, if you are a beginning journalist, you might ask your editor for the city hall beat.

You want to write about the mayor and other city officials. But think about the knowledge and experience that this assignment would entail. Do you understand how city government works? Are you confident enough to ask the important questions that the public wants to know? Can you write on a tight deadline without making mistakes? Make sure you're ready for the job. Otherwise, your boss will not take your request seriously. Even worse, you might get the job and fail.

4. *Be prepared to explain why you are a good match for the new position—* Why should your boss promote you, and not someone else, to this position? In a competitive situation, you must convince your boss that you are the best one to fill it. Outline your strengths and explain how they meet the requirements of the job you're seeking.

5. *Be able to explain why promoting you will help the organization—*Your boss is not going to promote you just because you want more money or a more impressive title. You'll get a promotion if the organization believes you will be more valuable in your new position than you are in your current one. Be able to persuade your boss that this is true.

6. *Know where you want to go with your career and how a promotion fits with your ambitions—*If you're sure of your career goal and can help your boss understand how this new position is in line with that goal, your boss will be likely to promote you. If you're uncertain about your career goal, your boss may question your ability to advance. An organization wants strong, confident leaders who know where they're headed.

7. *Develop a good relationship with your employer—*Employee-employer relationships are essential to achieving promotions. This means establishing good relations not only with your boss, but also with other high-ranking people in the organization—your boss's boss, people in the human resources department, and other managers. If your boss is considering you for promotion, he or she may ask such people what they think of you. If you've developed good relationships with many people in the organization, they'll be likely to recommend you for promotion. Don't become so immersed in your work that you forget to build relationships.

If you've developed good relationships with many people in your organization, they'll be likely to recommend you for recognition and promotion.
Courtesy of wavebreakmedia/Shutterstock

Developing a Career-Path Strategy

From Chapter 3, we learned that a *career path* is the route a person follows in pursuing his or her career goals. Suppose, for example, that you want to become the branch manager of a bank. Figure 8.1 shows several career paths that you might pursue to get to reach this position. The diagram shows many bank positions, and the arrows indicate where each position could lead. The positions shown in the diagram don't have to be in the same organization. You could be a teller in one bank, then move on to be a loan analyst and assistant branch manager in another, and then gain a position as the branch manager at a third bank.

To achieve your career goal, you must have a career-path strategy, or *a plan for how you will make progress in your career.* A career-path strategy will help ensure that you reach your goal as quickly and efficiently as possible.

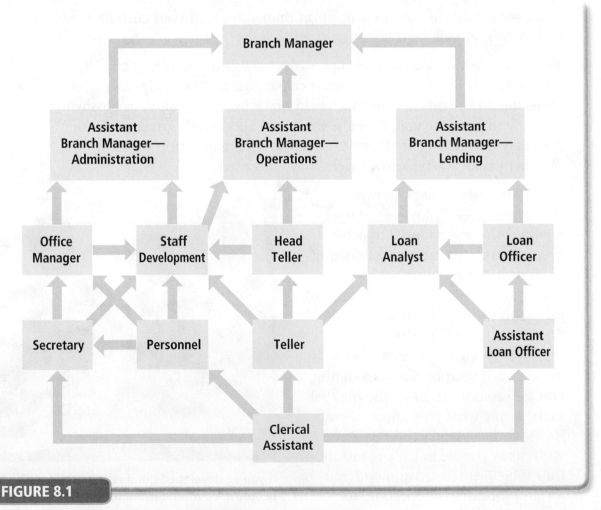

FIGURE 8.1

Potential Career Paths in a Bank Branch Office

Reprinted from *The Human Challenge: Managing Yourself and Others in Organizations*, edited by Mary L. Tucker, Anne M. McCarthy, and Douglas A. Benton (2002), by permission of Pearson Education

A career-path strategy should be a written document that sets forth everything you'll need to do to gain the knowledge, skills, and competence to function well in the career you've selected. Your school or employer can help, but it's ultimately up to you to develop your career-path strategy. You must take the initiative in planning your career. If you know what career path you want to pursue, you can start to outline a strategy now. You can also do this during college or when you begin working. The sooner you start, the better. Begin your career-path strategy by writing down your ultimate goal: for example, to be the manager of a branch bank. Then outline the types of positions you want to hold and the organizations (by name or by type) that you want to work for as you progress toward your goal. Set a time frame for your short-term goals. For example, you may want to be a bank teller for two years and then become a head teller.

However, what if a head teller position isn't available in your bank at the time you feel you're ready to move up to that job? You could wait until a position became open at your bank, but that might take a long time. To keep your career path on track, you may want to consider opportunities at other banks that you would like to work for. Then when you're ready for a promotion, investigate openings at these banks. In the meantime, look for opportunities to get to know important people in other banks, so they won't feel you're a stranger when you apply for a job. In fact, if you network successfully, one of these people might even call you and ask if you're interested in a new job. It's a good idea to look 5, 10, and even 20 years down the road when developing your career-path strategy.

When you write your career-path strategy, include the educational qualifications you'll need—such as degrees or certifications—and the training each job requires. What are the best schools in your field? If your goal is to be a branch manager, choose a college that has a good program in business and finance. You may want to go to graduate business school as soon as you get your bachelor's degree. Another option is to work in your field for a few years between college and graduate school. In that case, you could work as a teller after college, move on to a head teller position, and then go to graduate school. After graduate school, you could apply to be an assistant branch manager, which is the next step on your career path. As soon as you enter the workplace, be sure to take advantage of any training programs your employer offers.

Think about informal, as well as formal, opportunities for learning. Ask yourself, "What other experience do I need to reach my career goals?" To be a branch bank manager, you may want to write articles for publications in the banking field. You may want to learn about the newest software in the banking field. For other career goals, you might need to learn another language or travel to certain countries or regions of the world. It also might be helpful to become active in professional associations and to attend their local and national meetings. This kind of networking is essential throughout your professional life.

Steps in Career Advancement

1. Learn how to learn
2. Learn from your job
3. Perform your job well
4. Know your potential next job
5. Try to understand your next job
6. Find a mentor and develop a network
7. Keep track of your career accomplishments
8. Make clear career choices.

From *The Human Challenge: Managing Yourself and Others in Organizations*, edited by Mary L. Tucker, Anne M. McCarthy, and Douglas A. Benton (2002), by permission of Pearson Education

Ultimately, you should strive to become an expert or authority in your field—someone others look to for answers and expertise, and who speaks and writes about the field. Following the guidelines we have provided in this lesson, you should be able to develop a strategy for success. A career-path strategy is an excellent way to ensure you'll achieve your professional goals.

✔ CHECKPOINTS

Lesson 3 Review

Using complete sentences, answer the following questions on a sheet of paper.

1. Why is feedback so important in workplace communication?

2. Is it a good idea to ask your boss for feedback? Why or why not?

3. Name one of the two formal appraisal systems described in this lesson and explain how it works.

4. What do you need to watch out for when receiving feedback?

5. What are four things that you should do when seeking a promotion?

6. Explain why many employers offer additional benefits to employees.

APPLYING FEEDBACK AND PROMOTION SKILLS

7. At this point in your life, what career do you think you will pursue? Outline a career-path strategy that would enable you to reach that goal.

Your Civic Responsibilities

Quick Write

_____

_____

What qualities of America today set it apart from other countries? What do you think are the most important responsibilities Americans have toward one another and toward the nation as a whole?

Learn About

- society and civic responsibility
- registering to vote
- the Selective Service System (Draft)
- jury duty
- the value of volunteering and community involvement
- planning a volunteer event

"Ask not what your country can do for you. Ask what you can do for your country."

John F. Kennedy, 35th President of the United States

Society and Civic Responsibility

If you visit India, do you become an Indian citizen? If a young man from the United States takes a vacation to South Korea, will he be required to serve two years in the military as their male citizens are? The answer to both questions is no, of course, but why not? Why aren't you defined socially or culturally by where you are physically standing on the earth or sleeping at night?

Have you ever thought about what makes a country a country, or a city a city? Is it the borders on the map? The language spoken? Is it the shape of the town square? The laws? The president, king, or mayor? All of these things are parts of a nation or a city, but they do not *make* it what it is. Do you know the answer? The *people themselves* make a society—nation, state, county, city, town—what it is. Whether you are aware of it or not, you are part of a community, *a group of people united by common government, location, interest, or activity.* Communities, including nations, states, and cities, are made possible because a certain group of people have agreed to live near one another, depend on one another, buy and sell things together, and abide by laws, *rules of conduct or action formally recognized as binding or enforced.* Other communities arise as people unite behind a cause or common activity—like going to the same school. The members of a defined group do not have to agree on everything, but they do share things in common with one another that they do not share with other communities. At this time in life, you may belong to several different communities.

As you move from high school to your college and adult years, you become increasingly connected to the society around you. You will begin to fulfill more and more civic responsibilities, *legal or social obligations to your community.* As early as age 18, you must fulfill some civic responsibilities, like registering for selective service, which we cover later in this lesson. Other responsibilities are optional, such as voting in elections, but essential for our society to succeed.

This lesson discusses five aspects of your civic responsibility, all of which apply to you by the time you are 18: registering to vote; registering for selective service; jury duty; involvement in your community; and planning a volunteer event. All of these are good ways for you to begin exercising your responsibility to the communities you belong to and fulfilling your duty to American society as you as you enter adulthood.

Registering to Vote

As you know, one of the foundations of our society is that our leaders, from the President and Congress to mayors and school board members, are chosen by its citizens. This selection takes place through elections in which every citizen 18 years and older may vote for the candidates of his or her choice.

However, a person cannot just walk into a voting booth anywhere on Election Day and cast a vote. If this were the case, some people would vote more than once, giving an unfair advantage to one candidate. This requires a process to ensure that each person gets an equal vote and that people vote only for their own state and local officials, so that someone from Maryland cannot cross the state line to Virginia and vote for a new Virginia governor. Elections are different from the popularity contests on Internet sites such as Facebook in which people from all over the world can "like" a person, business, or site as many times as they want.

Vocabulary

- community
- laws
- civic responsibilities
- primary election
- polling stations
- absentee ballot
- draft
- Selective Service System
- conscription
- deferment
- jury
- summons
- exemption
- deferral

Registering in Your State

A number of national and state websites provide information about the voting process. The US Election Assistance Commission's (EAC) website provides official, non-biased answers to questions about elections. The site is found at *http://www.eac.gov/voter_resources/register_to_vote.aspx*. The EAC site also has links to each state's election board website so you can find out specific requirements for your state.

Registering to vote is not complicated, but the process, requirements, and deadlines vary slightly from state to state. In general, the process will look something like this:

1. You obtain a registration form on which you put your name, address, and some additional personal information. Your state election office provides the form online (see the link above), or you can go to your state's Secretary of the State's office and fill out the form in person.

2. You fill out and submit the form in person or via mail. *Be sure to submit your form by your state's deadline.* This will probably be at least a month before the election. If you wish to vote in your state's primary election, *the preliminary election for choosing the representative candidates from each political party*, find out early in the year about deadlines. Some states have their primaries nine or ten months before the main election. You cannot currently submit the form online, though some sites may help you do a portion of the process that way. You will probably need to submit an original (not a scan, fax, or photocopy) of your signature.

3. Once your state processes the form, you receive a confirmation with information about where to vote in the next election.

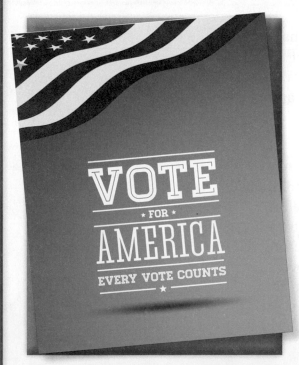

Voting is one of our most important civic duties.

Courtesy of Grounder/Shutterstock

When it comes time to actually vote, you will normally do so at one of many polling stations, or *official locations for casting votes*, in your area.

If you are serving in the military and are stationed out of your state of legal residence, or a civilian living away from home at the time of an election, you can register and vote via mail. To do so you use an absentee ballot, *a voting form sent by mail by voters who cannot visit a polling station in their community on election day.* Your state election website and the EAC website will also provide the information and forms you need to do so. If you plan to vote with an absentee ballot, get started early! You will need to register well in advance in order for your state to send you the ballot in time for you to vote and mail it in—all of which may take even longer if you are living overseas.

Each Vote Matters

You may feel that your one vote among millions of others' votes cannot possibly make a difference. Consider this: if everyone felt that way and decided not to vote, we couldn't have an election. Your vote may be just one among many, but you owe it to your country, yourself, and those whose views you share (those whom your vote supports) to make your preference heard. Many elections, especially for state and local leaders, are won and lost by closer margins than you might think.

And even if your candidate doesn't win, the person who does will get a clearer idea of how many people disagree with him or her by knowing who voted for other candidates. Officials are elected to serve everyone, not just those who voted for them; seeing how many people voted for someone else can guide their future decisions.

> **success TIP** ★
>
> To be an informed voter, don't just listen to the campaign ads, media coverage, and gossip. Do some online research of your own to find out who the candidates are, and especially what they stand for. Your voting experience will be far more rewarding if you vote for candidates you really believe will do the job well.

Don't Give Up Your Rights!

Unlike the Draft and Jury Duty, registering to vote is not required. You won't go to jail or get a fine if you don't register. However, in failing to register, you deprive *yourself* of one of the most prized rights of people in free countries: the right to vote. If you do not register, you cannot vote. Soldiers and civilians alike gave their lives during the Revolutionary War to earn the freedom to make our own laws and elect our own lawmakers and leaders. In fact, one of the major roles of the military today is to help secure and preserve the same freedom for other countries. So remember that even though registering to vote—and then actually voting!—are not required by law; they are part of your civic responsibility as a US citizen.

The Selective Service System (Draft)

You may have heard of the military draft, *action by the US Government for selecting eligible males to serve in the military.* While the federal government has not used the draft for 40 years, it keeps a record of all eligible young men in the event of a national crisis that requires more people than the volunteer active and reserve armed forces can supply. *The agency that keeps these records and executes the draft if it is ever needed* is called the Selective Service System. By law, all men who are citizens or residents must register within 30 days after they turn 18. Men are eligible for the draft until they reach the age of 26.

This World War II recruiting poster was aimed at getting young recruits for the US Army Air Force.

Courtesy of K..J. Historical/Corbis Images

You will probably receive a notice in the mail informing you of this requirement. Even if you are not told directly, however, *you must still register.* Registering does *not* mean you will automatically be drafted. Some countries, like South Korea, Israel, and Mexico require all young men to serve in the military for a year or two. This is called conscription, *the compulsory or mandatory enlistment of people in some sort of national service, most often military service.* The US Government prefers to make the military an all-volunteer force; therefore, it views the option to draft people as a last resort for troops needed in a crisis. In fact, no one has been drafted into the US military since 1973.

History of the Draft

The United States Congress declared, in accordance with our traditional military policy expressed in the National Defense Act of 1916, it is essential that in a free society our strength must always be assured. President Franklin D. Roosevelt created the Selective Service System in 1940 to face the prospect of another World War. However, the requirement for men to serve in the armed forces goes back even further. In the Civil War, some men were required to serve. Drafting men, as we know it today, took place for most of the major 20th century conflicts. In World War I, 2.8 million men were drafted; in World War II, the total was over 10 million. The US also drafted 1.5 million men for the Korean Conflict and 2 million for the Vietnam War.

How Do I Register?

There are several ways you can register for the draft:

- *Online*—at the Selective Service System website: *www.sss.gov*. For most men, this method will be the easiest.

- *At the post office*—Forms are available at the post office, and you can fill one out and mail it right there. Just bring enough money for a stamp!

- *On the Federal Student Financial Aid (FAFSA) form*—If you are applying for financial aid, you can check box #22 on this form, and you will automatically be registered with Selective Service when the form is processed.

- *At your high school*—Many schools have a teacher or staff member assigned to help men register. Check your school's website or ask in the administrative office to find out whether your school offers this service.

What If I Don't Register?

If you do not register for the draft, you may face serious consequences, including:

- A fine of up to $250,000
- Up to five years in prison
- Disqualification from receiving the federal student loans or grants described in Chapter 4, Lesson 1
- Difficulty receiving other kinds of federal aid later in life.
- Difficulty getting a security clearance to work for the government or to work as a contractor for the government

Are There Any Exceptions?

There are very few exceptions to the requirement to register. The Selective Service website given above includes a list of categories of men who do not need to register.

If you join the active military or attend one of the service academies, you do not need to register. However, if you enter an ROTC program or plan to join the military a few years after high school, *you must still register*. Also, if you leave the military before you turn 26, no matter how or when you entered, you must register.

Those who do not need to register are those in the US on a visa, such as a student or work visa. However, immigrants must register if they are between 18 and 25 even if they do not yet have their citizenship.

If you have a disability that you think might disqualify you from service, *you must still register*. If you were to get drafted, the government would then evaluate you to see if you qualify for service. Even if you are 100 percent sure you could not serve due to a disability, register as required so you do not disqualify yourself from government benefits later on.

How the Government Decides Who Is Drafted

If the US government decides to draft people due to a national crisis, it will choose from those registered using a random lottery based on year of birth. A draft held today would use a lottery system under which a man would spend only one year in first priority for the draft—either the calendar year he turned 20 or the year his *deferment* ended. Deferment is *the official postponement of military service*. For each year after that, he would be placed in a lower priority group and his liability for the draft would lessen accordingly. In this way, the closer a young man gets to his 26th birthday, the less chance there is that he will be drafted.

After the selection, each person would then be evaluated for physical, mental, and moral fitness for duty before being issued reporting orders. You can read a more detailed description of the draft process at the Selective Service System website listed above.

Why Do Women Not Have to Register With Selective Service?

You may wonder why, in a time when women serve in almost all aspects of the armed forces, they are not required to register for the draft. The law as it is currently written requires only men to register. The government considered changing it several years ago but concluded that it was not necessary to do so.

Jury Duty

Another civic responsibility of all US citizens is Jury Duty. Even if you have never sat in on a trial, perhaps in a book or film you have seen the group of twelve people near the front, the jury, listening to the arguments presented by lawyers. You may be familiar with the aspect of the court system involving a jury, *a group of adult citizens who listen to the evidence in a court case and decides which side is in the right*, the plaintiff (the person or group making the accusation) or the defendant (the person or group defending themselves against the accusation). Have you ever wondered who those jury members are or how they were placed in such a position of responsibility?

One of the most fundamental values of American society is that everyone has a right to a fair trial if accused of a crime. The requirement that a jury of regular citizens determine the outcome of a trial is part of that goal to make trials fair. A jury is made up of ordinary people chosen from their local area to serve on that particular trial. These people have regular jobs, but if chosen, they are required to serve on the jury to provide the fairest perspective possible on the evidence from the common person's point of view.

However, there's a problem: Even regular citizens have different opinions or biases, and not all will serve equally, especially on certain issues. The government recognizes this natural human tendency; therefore, in another step toward fairness, the system allows the defense and prosecuting attorneys and the judge for a given trial to select the jurors from a larger group of potential jurors. Therefore, in order to provide a large enough group for the court to select from, many more people are called in as potential jurors than are needed for trials that week. Most people called for jury duty do not actually end up serving as jurors on a trial.

Unlike voting and the draft, you do not actually have to register for jury duty. By being registered as a resident of your state and county (through getting a driver's license, paying state and local taxes, or registering to vote), you place your name in a long list of residents who are eligible to serve on a jury in your area. Jurors are selected randomly to be available for a short period of time, typically a week, for trials in their area that come up while they are on duty.

You may receive a jury duty summons, *a legal document requiring you to appear at the court on a specific time and date*. Under circumstances when you cannot reasonably fulfill it, the system allows you to request an exemption, *release from the requirement*, or a deferral, *a delay of your duty to a later time*. Military service allows you to receive this exemption. You may be injured, have urgent medical needs, or surgery scheduled.

Jury duty is one of the responsibilities of living in a democratic society.
Courtesy of Image Source/Corbis Images

If you are summoned for jury duty, you may think of it first as an inconvenience. However, think again of the remarkable fact that in our country, regular people from across society are allowed to listen to evidence and contribute to giving a fair trial. A juror—typically one out of twelve—has more power to influence society at that moment than most citizens do. You could argue that a juror's duty is more important than voting in an election. You might determine that a certain law is being unjustly applied, or help spare an innocent person from begin falsely convicted of murder. You could help determine that a rapist or thief is found guilty and put in jail, keeping society safer.

The Value of Volunteering and Community Involvement

Many of us have a tendency to focus more on our own needs and perhaps those of our immediate families and friends than about other groups and individuals. This tendency is human nature. However, our own welfare and that of our immediate circle depends in large part on the welfare of our larger community—our local, state, and national community. As you may have learned in a history or government course, the birth, growth, and continuing success of the United States and its states and cities have come about through individuals who stepped out of their immediate circle of family and friends to contribute to their communities.

Community involvement may not sound exciting at first. Just doing your schoolwork, going to sports or band practice, putting in your hours at work, and catching a movie once in a while with friends may seem like all you have time for. However, you may be surprised at the variety of ways and the ease with which you could a) contribute to the good of your community, b) grow as an individual, and c) have fun doing so.

You don't have to start from scratch. Many organizations already exist and are looking for people to get involved. You can search online for community service groups in your area. Find an activity you believe in, a group to help that you care about. Look for types of involvement that can use your skills or interests. Numerous organizations offer ways to serve. Some are aimed at special kinds of service such as repairing homes for people who can't afford to do so or serving meals to homeless people. Others are aimed at certain age groups, from tutoring kids in school to doing yard work for the elderly. Churches, synagogues, and other religious organizations often reach out to their communities with services as well. Military bases often organize events to help the local community and promote good will toward the military.

One of the largest youth organizations in high schools today is the Junior Reserve Officer Training Corps (JROTC), with over 500,000 students enrolled in over 4,000 schools worldwide. Students enrolled in JROTC are taught the value of giving back to their communities and nation. This all-volunteer high school program encourages service to community, provides leadership development opportunities, and imparts core values such as integrity and excellence. On average, JROTC students provide more than 8 million community service hours each year, completing projects such as trail restoration, gathering clothing for the needy, and providing volunteer services to their schools. JROTC has a proud tradition and continues to grow in enrollment and community service opportunities.

Lions Clubs International and Rotary International (RI) are two large, worldwide organizations with tens of thousands of local clubs. Both organizations aim to improve the quality of life for people in need in the US and all over the world. These well-known groups and others like them organize activities like collecting food and clothes for homeless families, repairing playgrounds, setting up after school programs, and raising money to help pay for immunizations. They seek help for the poor and promote health, education, and goodwill among the countries of the world.

Lions and RI clubs are run by adults in their communities, but both sponsor clubs especially for younger people: The Lions have *Alpha Leo Clubs* for ages 12–18 and *Omega Leo Clubs* for 18–30. RI has *Interact* clubs for ages 12–18 and *Rotaract* for ages 18–30. Both of these offer rewarding service opportunities, individual and leadership development, conferences, and valuable interaction with other like-minded young people. See *http://www.lionsclubs.org* or *http://www.rotary.org* for more information about Lions and RI and their many ways to help you serve.

You can also serve the global community with a short summer service project in another country. Most of the world's people are far poorer than even the poorest Americans. Volunteer organizations such as the Peace Corps, religious groups, ethnic groups, and school programs as well as the Lions and RI described above, serve those from less prosperous countries, building greater trust and understanding across cultures and governmental boundaries.

Volunteer work is a good way to meet others while contributing to your community.
Courtesy of KidStock/Corbis Images

In addition to the direct, inherent reward of putting a smile on someone else's face or knowing that someone will be healthier or better educated because of something you did, community involvement offers indirect benefits. Volunteer work can help you build skills and experience that may help you get into college or a job. You also grow from working with people you might not otherwise meet, and some of those people may turn out to be lifelong associates, mentors, and even friends.

Planning a Volunteer Event

So, what should you do if you want to get involved in your community? Where should you start? The types of groups (and there are thousands out there) suggested above usually have everything in place for you to step right up and help with a certain activity. Starting with something already organized will help you learn what volunteering is about and what kinds of things you enjoy doing. Through a service group, you might find, for example, that you really enjoy reading to the elderly—something you may never have thought of doing.

However, you may have a kind of service in mind for your community that an existing group doesn't offer. All of these groups were started by individuals with a passion, helping others to improve the world around them, people with a willingness and vision to sacrifice time and energy for something they believe in. You may be one of those people. Maybe you have noticed a local parking lot or field that never gets cleaned up. Perhaps there is a family with young children in your neighborhood who need new shoes? Volunteering doesn't mean you try to solve all the problems yourself; perhaps you could organize some friends to clean up the field or start a clothing donation project for those children.

Your school is a good place to start because it is already an established community with tools in place for getting people to work together. If you have an idea, talk to a teacher or school administrator. Bring it up with the student council, your sports team or other school program in which you participate. Maybe your art class could visit a home for the elderly and help them paint and draw for a couple of hours.

Once you have an idea in mind and some others to support you, sit down and make a plan. Every activity will be different, having its own challenges, but a few general planning steps will help you make the volunteer activity more rewarding and successful. (All of these may not apply, and you do not need to do them in the order given):

1. List your main objectives of the event—what do you really aim to accomplish?

2. Choose a location suitable to meeting your objectives.

3. Determine the minimum number of volunteers you will need.

4. Recruit your volunteers. Maybe you need just a few friends, but if your activity requires many, use email, school announcements, or other social media to draw volunteers, consider placing flyers at school, at church, or in your neighborhood.

5. Estimate the cost of any supplies, transportation, or facility rental fees.

6. Contact local businesses to ask for donations to help with any costs.

7. Use email, social media, and flyers to advertise the event itself (in addition to the need for volunteers) to your friends and community.

8. Consider the best time(s) and date(s) for your activity or event. Schedule it far enough in advance to give yourself the time to put everything in place.

9. Schedule and hold regular planning meetings with your main team of volunteers.

10. Don't forget to have fun!

On one hand, organizing a volunteer event or service may turn out to be more complicated than you first think. On the other hand, it can also be much less difficult that you expect, especially with the right team and the right planning.

Conclusion

As you move into adulthood, you become more and more responsible for the community you live in. Whether these responsibilities are required by law or voluntary, think of them as privileges not obligations. Remember that many others have dedicated their careers and lives to making it possible for us to vote, serve in the military, serve on a jury, or to make a difference as a volunteer. Successful societies depend on people willing to help those in need when they are unable to help themselves. Don't sit on the sidelines: Vote. Volunteer. Serve. Make your community better because of you, not in spite of you.

✔ CHECKPOINTS

Lesson 4 Review

Using complete sentences, answer the following questions on a sheet of paper.

1. Why do people need to register to vote if it is already one of their rights?

2. What is the Selective Service System?

3. Who must register for the draft?

4. How is a jury selected for a court trial?

5. You are a member of many communities; name three of these communities and the roles you provide in them.

6. Why is volunteering an important element to the success of a society?

APPLYING CIVIC RESPONSIBILITIES SKILLS

7. As with planning your finances and career path, you should also plan for fulfilling your role as a citizen. Doing so is important for you and the communities of which you are a part—from your neighborhood and town to your state and nation. Draft a plan for fulfilling your civic responsibilities, including both legal and other duties. Write a paragraph each on voting, military service, jury duty, and volunteer service. Include any other civic activities you think are worthwhile.

References

CHAPTER 1 Charting Your Financial Course

LESSON 1 Creating a Budget

Famousquotes123.com website. (n.d.). Retrieved 29 January 2012 from http://www .famousquotes123.com/zig-ziglar-quotes.html

Federal Deposit Insurance Corporation website. (2010). Retrieved 20 January 2012 from http://www.fdic.gov/deposit/deposits/index.html

High School Financial Planning Program Student Guide. Unit One. (2006). Denver, CO: National Endowment for Financial Education (NEFE).

InvestorWorks.com website. (2011). Retrieved 28 January 2012 from http://www .investorwords.com/tips/665/how-to-double-your-money.html

Madura, J. (2011). *Personal Finance.* Boston, MA: Pearson Education, Inc.

National Credit Union Association website. (2010). Retrieved 20 January 2012 from http://www.ncua.gov/DataApps/Pages/SI-FAQs.aspx

LESSON 2 Savings and Bank Accounts

Federal Deposit Insurance Corporation website. (2010). Retrieved 20 January 2012 from http://www.fdic.gov/deposit/deposits/index.html

Fighting Back Against Identity Theft. (n.d.). Retrieved 26 January 2012 from http://www.ftc.gov/bcp/edu/microsites/idtheft/law-enforcement/federal-laws-credit.html

Financial Responsibility (2012). Upper Saddle River, NJ: Pearson Education, Inc.

Frasca, R. (2009). *Personal Finance.* Boston, MA: Pearson Education, Inc.

Funinvest.com website. (n.d.). Retrieved 3 February 2012 from http://www.funinvest1 .com/quotes.html

High School Financial Planning Program Student Guide. Unit One. (2006). Denver, CO: National Endowment for Financial Education (NEFE).

Madura, J. (2011). *Personal Finance.* Boston, MA: Pearson Education, Inc.

Mitchell, N. L. (1999). *Leadership Education III: Life Skills.* Maxwell Air Force Base, AL: Air Force Reserve Officer Training Corps.

LESSON 3 Real-Life Issues in Buying and Selling

Automotive.com website. (n.d.). Retrieved 14 February 2006 from http://www .automotive.com/auto-loans/36/loan-tips/car-loan-tips.html

Financial Responsibility (2012). Upper Saddle River, NJ: Pearson Education, Inc.

Kelly Blue Book website. (2012). Retrieved 14 February 2012 from http://www.kbb.com/

Madura, J. (2011). *Personal Finance.* Boston, MA: Pearson Education, Inc.

Mitchell, N. (Ed.). (1999). *Leadership Education III: Life Skills.* Maxwell Air Force Base, AL: US Air Force Reserve Officer Training Corps.

CHAPTER 2　Managing Your Resources

LESSON 1　Avoiding the Credit Trap

Bankruptcy Filings Down in Fiscal 2011. (November 2011) Retrieved 20 February 2012 from http://www.uscourts.gov/News/NewsView/11-11-07/Bankruptcy_Filings_Down_in_Fiscal_Year_2011.aspx

Choosing a Credit Card. (2010). Retrieved 16 April 2012 from http://www.federalreserve.gov/pubs/shop/

Credit Card Loss Protection Offers: They're the Real Steal. (2000). Federal Trade Commission website. (2009). Retrieved 13 February 2012 from http://www.ftc.gov/bcp/edu/pubs/consumer/alerts/alt052.shtm

Federal Reserve System website. (2012). Retrieved 15 April 2012 from http://www.federalreserve.gov/releases/g19/Current/_

Federal Reserve System website. (2012). Retrieved 16 April 2012 from http://www.federalreserve.gov/creditcard/glossary.html

Federal Trade Commission website. (n.d.). Retrieved 22 Feb 2012 from http://www.ftc.gov/index.shtml

Financial Responsibility. (2012). Upper Saddle River, NJ: Pearson Education, Inc.

High School Financial Planning Program Student Guide. (2006). Denver, CO: National Endowment for Financial Education (NEFE).

Highlight Investments Group. (2012). Retrieved 16 April 2012 from http://www.trading-glossary.com/p0136.asp

Madura, J. (2011). *Personal Finance*. Boston, MA: Pearson Education, Inc.

Mitchell, N. (Ed.). (1999). *Leadership Education III: Life Skills*. Maxwell Air Force Base, AL: US Air Force Reserve Officer Training Corps.

The Project on Student Debt website. (2012). Retrieved 10 March 2012 from http://projectonstudentdebt.org/

LESSON 2　Insurance for Protecting Your Resources

Esurance.com website. (2012). Retrieved 12 August 2012 from http://www.esurance.com/faq/insurance-coverage-defined

Financial Responsibility. (2012) Upper Saddle River, NJ: Pearson Education, Inc.

Fowles, D. (2006). When Bad Things Happen to Your Good Name. Retrieved 12 April 2012 from http://financialplan.about.com/od/fraudandfinancialscams/a/IdentityTheft.htm

High School Financial Planning Program Student Guide. Unit Six. (2006). Denver, CO: National Endowment for Financial Education (NEFE).

Keown, A. (2013). *Personal Finance: Turning Money into Wealth*. Boston, MA: Pearson Education, Inc.

Madura, J. (2011). *Personal Finance*. Pearson Education, Inc.

Mitchell, N. (Ed.). (1999). *Leadership Education III: Life Skills*. Maxwell Air Force Base, AL: US Air Force Reserve Officer Training Corps.

　References

Senior Military Group, Mission Readiness—Military Leaders for Kids. Too Fat To Fight. (n.d.) Retrieved 7 February 2012 from http://www.missionreadiness.org/2010/too-fat-to-fight/

US National Highway Traffic Safety Administration website. (n.d.). Retrieved 7 February 2012 from http://distraction.gov/content/get-the-facts/facts-and-statistics.html

CHAPTER 3 Career Opportunities

LESSON 1 Researching Careers

Carnevale et al., *Help Wanted: Projections of Jobs and Education Requirements Through 2018*. (2010). Retrieved 21 February 2012 from http://cew.georgetown.edu/jobs2018/

Drexel University website. (n.d.). Retrieved 21 March 2012 from http://www.drexel.edu/scdc/coop/COOP101/materials/careerexploration.html

High School Financial Planning Program Student Guide. (2006). Denver, CO: National Endowment for Financial Education (NEFE).

Mitchell, N. (Ed.). (1999). Leadership Education III: Life Skills. Maxwell

Air Force Base, AL: US Air Force Reserve Officer Training Corps.

Occupational Outlook Handbook, 2012–13 Edition. Washington, DC. (2012). Retrieved 19 February 2012 from http://www.bls.gov/oco/

Office of Personnel Management website. (n.d.). Student Educational Employment Program. Retrieved 20 March 2012 from http://www.opm.gov/employ/students/intro.asp

PC Magazine website (n.d.). Retrieved 2 May 2012 from http://www.pcmag.com/encyclopedia_term/0,1237,t=social+networking+site&i=55316,00.asp

Pruitt B. E., Carter, C., & Sukiennik, D. (2005). *Foundations for Success in Life, Career, Health and Wellness*. (2005). Boston, MA: Pearson Custom Publishing.

Robbins, C. R. (2006). *The Job Searcher's Handbook*. Upper Saddle River, N.J.: Pearson Education, Inc.

Sherfield, R. M., & Moody, P. G. *Cornerstone: Opening Doors to Career Success*. (2010). Upper Saddle River, NJ: Pearson Education, Inc.

Sukiennik et al. *The Career Fitness Program: Exercising Your Options*. (2013). Upper Saddle River, NJ: Pearson Education, Inc.

University of California at Fullerton website. (2011) Retrieved 3 April 2012 from http://campusapps2.fullerton.edu/Career/students/jobSearch/Chapter1/BuildingNetwork.aspx

LESSON 2 Self-Discovery

California Careerzone http://www.cacareerzone.org/

The Multiple Intelligences Survey © Robert M. Sherfield, Ph.D., 1999, 2002, 2005, 2008, Sherfield and Moody, *Cornerstone: Opening Doors to Career Success* (2010). Upper Saddle River, N.J.: Pearson Education, Inc.

Shearer, C. Branton. (1999-2012). "The Theory of Multiple Intelligences, Career Development and The MIDAS Assessment December, 2004." Retrieved 24 September 2012 from www.MIResearch.org

Sherfield, R. M., & Moody, P. G. *Cornerstone: Opening Doors to Career Success.* (2010). Upper Saddle River, NJ: Pearson Education, Inc.

State of Georgia Career Resource Network (CRN) http://gacrn.gcic.edu/ToolsInformation/CareerClusters.htm

Sukiennik et al. *The Career Fitness Program: Exercising Your Options* (2010). Upper Saddle River, N.J.: Pearson Education, Inc.

US Department of Education career clusters. (2012). Retrieved 24 Sept 2012 from http://www2.ed.gov/about/offices/list/ovae/index.html

Using Multiple Intelligences Theory in Choosing a Career. Retrieved 24 Sept 2012 from http://www.teachervision.fen.com/intelligence/teaching-methods/2175.html

LESSON 3 Career Paths

America's Career Resource Network website. (n.d.). Retrieved 13 Mar 2012 from http://www.gcic.peachnet.edu/georgiacrn/ProfessionalResources/ACRN/ACRNbooklet.pdf

Association for Career and Technical Education website. (2012). Retrieved 20 March 2012 from https://www.acteonline.org/content.aspx?id=3654&terms=Frequently%20Asked%20Questions

Association for Career and Technical Education website (2012). Associates' degree earnings. Retrieved 12 March 2012 from https://www.acteonline.org/search.aspx?query=earnings

Construction Craft Training Center website. (2012). Retrieved 20 March 2012 from http://www.cctc.edu

Crosby, O. (2002). Apprenticeships: Career Training, Credentials—and a Paycheck in Your Pocket. *Occupational Outlook Quarterly*, Summer 2002.

Jacobson, L., et al. *Pathways to Boosting the Earnings of Low-Income Students by Increasing Their Educational Attainment.* Retrieved 11 March 2012 from http://www.nichejobworld.com/2012/03/05/union-apprenticeship-programs-an-open-door-to-some-very-good-jobs/

Payscale.com. (2012). Bachelors' degree earnings. Retrieved 15 March 2012 from http://www9.georgetown.edu/grad/gppi/hpi/cew/pdfs/collegepayoff-complete.pdf

Payscale.com. (2012). High school graduate earnings. Retrieved 15 March 2012 from http://www.payscale.com

Pruitt B. E., Carter, C., & Sukiennik, D. (2005). *Foundations for Success in Life, Career, Health and Wellness.* (2005). Boston, MA: Pearson Custom Publishing.

Sherfield, R. M., & Moody, P. G. *Cornerstone: Opening Doors to Career Success.* (2010). Upper Saddle River, NJ: Pearson Education, Inc.

Sukiennik et al, *The Career Fitness Program: Exercising Your Options.* (2010). Upper Saddle River, NJ: Pearson Education, Inc.

Universal Technical Institute, Inc., website (2012). Retrieved 28 March 2012 from http://www.uticorp.com/

US Department of Education website. Retrieved 10 March 2012 from http://www.ed.gov/news/speeches/new-cte-secretary-duncans-remarks-career-and-technical-education

US Department of Labor website. Retrieved 24 March 2012 from http://www.bls.gov/opub/ooq/2011/fall/art02.pdf and http://www.bls.gov/opub/ooq/2007/spring/art02.pdf

Vocational Information Center website. (2010). Retrieved 24 March 2012 from http://www.khake.com/index.html

CHAPTER 4 Aiming Towards a College Degree

LESSON 1 Financing for College

American Association of Community Colleges website. (2012). Retrieved 20 May 2012 from http://www.aacc.nche.edu/AboutCC/Trends/Pages/financialaid.aspx

American Association of Community Colleges website. (2012). Retrieved 20 May 2012 from http://www.aacc.nche.edu/AboutCC/21stcenturyreport/21stCenturyReport.pdf

College Board. (2012). College Costs. Retrieved 20 May 2012 from https://bigfuture.collegeboard.org/pay-for-college/college-costs/understanding-college-costs

College Board. (2012). Finding Your Big Future Starts with You. Retrieved 20 May 2012 from https://bigfuture.collegeboard.org/pay-for-college

College Board. (2012). Trends in College Pricing. Retrieved 20 May 2012 from http://trends.collegeboard.org/downloads/College_Pricing_2011.pdf

College Board. (2012). What is a Pell Grant? Retrieved 20 May 2012 from https://bigfuture.collegeboard.org/pay-for-college/scholarships-and-grants/what-is-a-pell-grant

FinAid.com. (2012). Number of Scholarships. Retrieved 20 May 2012 from http://www.finaid.org/scholarships/awardcount.phtml

FinAid.com. (2012). Scholarships. Retrieved 20 May 2012 from FinAid.com. (2012). http://www.finaid.org/scholarships/

FinAid.com. (2012). Scholarship Scams. Retrieved 20 May 2012 from http://www.finaid.org/scholarships/scams.phtml

FinAid.com. (2012). Student Loans. Retrieved 20 May 2012 from http://www.finaid.org/loans/

FinAid.com. (2012). US State Government Aid. Retrieved 20 May 2012 from http://www.finaid.org/otheraid/state.phtml

Free Application for Federal Student Aid (2012). Retrieved 20 May 2012 from http://www.2012pellgrant.com/pell_grant_eligibility.htm

Sallie Mae website. (1995–2012). Interest Rates and Annual Percentage Rates (APR). Retrieved 20 May 2012 from https://www1.salliemae.com/get_student_loan/apply_student_loan/interest_rates_fees/

Today's Military website. (2012). Education Support. Retrieved 20 May 2012 from www.todaysmilitary.com/military-benefits/education-support

US Department of Education website. (2012-2013). High School: The Guide to Federal Student Aid, Retrieved 20 May 2012 from http://studentaid.ed.gov/students/publications/student_guide/index.html

US Department of Education website. (2012). Student Aid on the Web. Retrieved 20 May 2012 from http://studentaid.ed.gov/PORTALSWebApp/students/english/index.jsp

LESSON 2 Selecting a College

CollegeData website. (2012). Getting Application Fees Waived. Retrieved 8 April 2012 from http://www.collegedata.com/cs/content/ content_getinarticle_tmpl.jhtml?articleId=10050

DistanceLearning.com. 2012) Online colleges. Retrieved 10 April 2012 from www.distancelearning.com/about_

Education Writers' Association website. (2012). Accredited Colleges and Universities. Retrieved 07 April 2012 from http://www.ewa.org/site/PageServer?pagename=resources_highered

Education Writers Association website. (2012) Accredited Schools. Retrieved 10 April 2012 from http://www.ewa.org/site/PageServer?pagename=resources_highered

Ezinearticles.com. (2012). Some Clarifications on the Differences Between a College and a University. Retrieved 9 Apr2012 from http://EzineArticles.com/6642578

Federal Student Aid Information Center website. (n.d.) Retrieved 06 April 2012 from http://studentaid.ed.gov/PORTALSWebApp/students/english/contactus.jsp

Mitchell, N. (Ed.). (1999). *Leadership Education III: Life Skills*. Maxwell Air Force Base, AL: US Air Force Reserve Officer Training Program, Junior Program Branch.

The National College Advocacy Group (NCAG) website. (2012). Preparing for College. Retrieved 8 April 2012 from http://www.ncagonline.org/main/timeline.aspx

Quotegarden.com (2012). Quotations about college. Retrieved 8 April 2012 from http://www.quotegarden.com/college.html

Quoteopia.com. (2012). Famous quotes on education. Retrieved 25 May 2012 from http://www.quoteopia.com/quotations.php?query=education

RTG & Associates website. ((2012). Retrieved 09 April 2012 from http://www.leadershipcredit.net

Schools.com. (2012). Accredited online schools. Retrieved 10 April 2012 from http://www.schools.com

Student Scholarship Guide website. (2012). Concurrent credit. Retrieved 11 April 2012 from http://sites.google.com/site/studentscholarshipguide/scholarship-basics/preparing-for-scholarships

US Department of Education website. (2011). College Costs. Retrieved 7 April 2012 from http://nces.ed.gov/fastfacts/display.asp?id=76

US Department of Education website. (2012). College Navigator. Retrieved 06 April 2012 from http://nces.ed.gov/datatools/

US Department of Education website. (2012). Dual enrollment. Retrieved 12 April 2012 from http://www2.ed.gov/programs/slcp/finaldual.pdf

Wecker, M. (2012). 10 Colleges with the Highest Application Fees. Retrieved 7 April 2012 from http://www.usnews.com/education/best-colleges/the-short-list-college/articles/2011/09/14/top-10-highest-college-application-fees

WorldWideLearn.com. (2012). US Regional Accrediting Associations. Retrieved 8 April 2012 from http://www.worldwidelearn.com/accreditation/accreditation-associations.htm

LESSON 3 Navigating the Testing Maze

ACT.org website (2012). What Is the Difference Between the ACT and SAT? Retrieved 18 May 2012 from http://www.actstudent.org/faq/answers/actsat.html

College Board. (2012). CLEP for Test Takers. Retrieved 18 May 2012 from http://www.collegeboard.com/student/testing/clep/about.html

College Board. (2012). SAT and SAT Subject Tests Overview. Retrieved 18 May 2012 from http://sat.collegeboard.org/about-tests

College Board. (2012). SAT Reasoning Test—Materials Available for License. Retrieved 18 May 2012 from http://sat.collegeboard.org/about-tests

College Options Foundation website (n.d.) JROTC Academic Challenge. Retrieved 18 May 2012 from http://www.collegeoptionsfoundation.net/JPACabout.html

Mitchell, N. (Ed.). (1999). *Leadership Education III: Life Skills*. Maxwell Air Force Base, AL: US Air Force Reserve Officer Training Corps.

Novapress.net (2012). Test prep center. Retrieved 16 March 2006 from http://novapress.net/sat/sat-information/

Peterson's website. (2012). A Brief History of the SAT and How It Changes. Retrieved 9 September 2012 from http://www.petersons.com/college-search/sat-scores-changes-test.aspx

Sherfield, R. M., & Moody, P. G. (2010). *Cornerstone: Building on Your Best*. Upper Saddle River, NJ: Pearson Education, Inc.

LESSON 4 Essays, Interviews, and Campus Visits

Bailyn, Evan (2006). How to Conceive, Create, and Perfect It. Retrieved 11 June 2012 from http://www.college-admission-essay.com/admission_essay.html

Cambridge Essay Service (2012). Seven Great and Unexpected Tips about College Entrance Essays. Retrieved 11 June 2012 from http://www.hbsguru.com/College.html#1

College Board. (2012).What to Do Before and After Your College Interview. Retrieved 11 June 2012from https://bigfuture.collegeboard.org/get-in/interviews/what-to-do-before-and-after-your-college-interview-admissions

Eagon, M. (1986). Writing the College Admission Essay. Retrieved 11 June 2012 from http://www.covington.k12.in.us/CHS/guidance/foundation_scholarship/docs_2007/section_4.pdf

Kaplan Test Prep website. (2012). Facebook Checking is No Longer Unchartered Territory in College Admissions. Retrieved 11 June 2012 from http://press .kaptest.com/press-releases/facebook-checking-is-no-longer-unchartered -territory-in-college-admissions-percentage-of-admissions-officers-who-visited -an-applicant%E2%80%99s-profile-on-the-rise

Mathews, J. (2010). Words to the Wise About Writing College Application Essays. Retrieved 11 June 2012 from http://www.washingtonpost.com/wp-dyn/content/ article/2010/06/29/AR2010062904105.html

Noel-Levitz website. (2012). 2010 E-Expectations Survey. Retrieved 11 June 2012 from https://www.noellevitz.com/papers-research-higher-education/2010/2010 -e-expectations-report

O'Shaughnessy, L. (2010). 36 Questions to Ask on a College Visit. Retrieved 11 June 2012 from http://www.usnews.com/education/blogs/the-college-solution/2010/ 10/19/36-questions-to-ask-on-a-college-visit

Sallie Mae website. (2012). School Interview Checklist. Retrieved 11 June 2012 from https://www1.salliemae.com/content/pdf/library/sm%20school%20interview %20checklist.pdf

Venable, M. (2011). Social Media and Your College Application. Retrieved 11 June 2012 from http://www.noodle.org/noodlings/college/social-media-and-your-college -application

CHAPTER 5 Charting Your Course

LESSON 1 Adjusting to College Life

Academic organizations. Retrieved 8 May 2012 from http://bmes.ec.illinois.edu/

Ainsworth BE, et al. 2011. Medicine & Science in Sports & Exercise. Retrieved 10 May 2012 from http://www.mayoclinic.com/health/exercise/SM00109

Campus religious organizations. Retrieved 8 May 2012 from http://studentaffairs.psu .edu/hub/studentorgs/orgdirectory/search.aspx and http://diversity.missouri.edu/ get-involved/religion/orgs.php

FamilyDoctor.org. (2010). Stress: How to Cope Better with Life's Challenges. Retrieved 10 May 2012 from http://familydoctor.org/familydoctor/en/prevention-wellness/ emotional-wellbeing/mental-health/stress-how-to-cope-better-with-lifes-challenges .printerview.all.html

Food Pyramid. Retrieved 8 May 2012 from http://www.foodpyramid.com

National Institute on Alcohol Abuse and Alcoholism website. (2005).College Drinking—Changing the Culture. Retrieved 20 April 2012 from http://www .collegedrinkingprevention.gov/NIAAACollegeMaterials/TaskForce/Intro_00.aspx

National Institutes of Health website. (2012). Managing Stress. Retrieved 10 May 2012 from http://www.nlm.nih.gov/medlineplus/tutorials/managingstress/htm/ index.htm

President's Challenge.org. (2012). Presidential Fitness Challenge. Retrieved 11 May 2012 from https://www.presidentschallenge.org/tools-resources/fitness-guides.shtml

Professional organizations. Retrieved 8 May 2012 from http://pharmacy.uconn.edu/alumni/alumni-association/professional-organizations/

Service organization participation. Retrieved 8 May 2012 from http://EzineArticles.com/6912473

Sherfield, R. M., & Moody, P. G. *Cornerstone: Opening Doors to Career Success*. (2010). Upper Saddle River, NJ: Pearson Education, Inc.

Starke, M. C. (1997). *Strategies for College Success*. Upper Saddle River, NJ: Pearson Education, Inc.

TeensHealth.org. (2012). Beating the Freshmen 15. Retrieved 11 May 2012 from http://teenshealth.org/teen/school_jobs/college/freshman_15.html

University High Schools of Indiana website. (2011) Commencement address. Retrieved 8 May 2012 from http://www.universityhighschool.org/blogs/graduation

University of Texas at Austin website. (2012). Electronic Game Developers Society. Retrieved 12 July 2012 from http://deanofstudents.utexas.edu/sa/vieworgs.php?org=2428

USAToday.com. (2002). Study: 1,400 Student Deaths Tied to Alcohol. Retrieved 13 May 2012 from http://www.usatoday.com/news/health/2002-04-09-drinking-deaths.htm

LESSON 2 Choosing a Major

Gordon, V. and Sears, S. (2004 and 2010). *Selecting a College Major: Exploration and Decision Making*, Fifth and Sixth Editions. Upper Saddle River, NJ: Prentice-Hall.

Sherfield, R. M., & Moody, P. G. *Cornerstone: Opening Doors to Career Success*. (2010). Upper Saddle River, NJ: Pearson Education, Inc.

LESSON 3 Planning Your Schedule

Dartmouth College Academic Skills Center (2001). Five Steps to Successful Time Management. Retrieved 30 May 2012 from http://www.dartmouth.edu/~acskills/docs/planning_well.doc

George Mason University. (n.d.). Time Management Tips. Retrieved 30 May 2012 from http://www.healthyexpectations.gmu.edu/rsrc_tm.htm

Nist, Sherrie L., & Holschuh, Jodi. *College Success Strategies*, 3rd ed. (2008) New York: Longman.

Sherfield, R. M., & Moody, P. G. *Cornerstone: Opening Doors to Career Success*. (2010). Upper Saddle River, NJ: Pearson Education, Inc.

CHAPTER 6 Applying for Jobs

LESSON 1 The Job Search Process

Careerjockey. org. (2010). Retrieved 2 July 2012 from http://www.careerjockey.org/4-classic-quotes-about-your-job-search/

EbizMBA.com. (2012). Top 15 Most Popular Job Websites. Retrieved 20 September 2012 from http://www.ebizmba.com/articles/job-websites

Goodreads.com. (2012). Retrieved 2 July 2012 from http://www.goodreads.com/quotes/
show_tag?id=goals

Mitchell, N. (Ed.). (1999). *Leadership Education III: Life Skills*. Maxwell Air Force Base, AL:
US Air Force Reserve Officer Training Corps.

Robbins, C. R. (2006). *The Job Searcher's Handbook*. Upper Saddle River, NJ: Pearson
Education, Inc.

LESSON 2 Preparing Your Résumé

Mitchell, N. (Ed.). (1999). *Leadership Education III: Life Skills*. Maxwell Air Force Base, AL:
US Air Force Reserve Officer Training Corps.

Robbins, C.R. (2010). *The Job Searcher's Handbook*. Upper Saddle River, NJ: Pearson
Education, Inc.

LESSON 3 Building Interviewing Skills

Robbins, C. R. (2006). *The Job Searcher's Handbook*. Upper Saddle River, NJ: Pearson
Education, Inc.

Virginia Polytechnic Institute and State University website. (February 2006).

Behavioral interviewing. Retrieved 20 September 2012 from http://www.career.vt.edu/
Interviewing/Behavioral.html

CHAPTER 7 Working for the Federal Government

LESSON 1 Military Careers

Battle, C. (11 January 2005). Commissioning Program Available for Active-duty Airmen.
Retrieved 2 May 2006 from http://www.af.mil/news/story.asp?storyID=123009581

The Black Collegian Online. (n.d.). Retrieved 30 December 2005 from http://www
.black-collegian.com

CareersintheMilitary.com website. (2012). Career fields in each service. Retrieved
29 May 2012 from http://www.careersinthemilitary.com

Community College of the Air Force website. (n.d.). Retrieved 1 January 2006 from
http://www.au.af.mil/au/ccaf/

Lopez, T. (21 April 2004). ASVAB changes will not mean lower standards. Retrieved
28 January 2006 from http://www.af.mil/news/story.asp?storyID=123007527

Military.com. (2012). Minimum enlistment age. Retrieved 29 May 2012 from
http://www.military.com/join-armed-forces/join-the-military-basic-eligibility
.html?comp=7000023451957&rank=5

Military.com (2012). Service missions. Retrieved 29 May 2012 from http://www
.usmilitary.com/which-branch-of-the-military/

Mitchell, N. (Ed.). (1999). *Leadership Education III: Life Skills*. Maxwell Air Force Base, AL:
US Air Force Reserve Officer Training Corps.

QuoteCove.com (2012). Retrieved 1 June 2012 from http://www.quotecove.com/famous-quotes/famous-military-quotes/

Today's Military website. (2012). Service academies. Retrieved 29 May 2012 from http://www.todaysmilitary.com/before-serving-in-the-military/service-academies-and-military-colleges/service-academies-and-military-colleges-at-a-glance

US Air Force Academy website. (n.d.) Admissions. Retrieved 30 January 2006 from http://www.academyadmissions.com/

US Air Force ROTC Scholarships. Retrieved 2 May 2006 from http://www.afrotc.com/scholarships/

US Air Force website. (2005). Brothers Meet at 25,000 Feet. Retrieved 30 January 2006 from http://www.af.mil/news/story.asp?storyID=123013323

US Department of Labor website. (2012). Military careers. Retrieved 30 May 2012 from http://www.bls.gov/ooh/military/military-careers.htm

US House of Representatives website (2012). Army mission. Retrieved 30 May 2012 from http://uscode.house.gov/download/pls/10C307.txt

LESSON 2 Careers in Aerospace

AvJobs.com. (2012). Retrieved 3 August 2012 from http://www.avjobs.com/table/airsalry.asp and http://www.avjobs.com/careers

Boeing website. (2012). Retrieved 6 August 2012 from http://www.boeing.com/stories/impact08_bwb_92flights.html

EmploymentSpot.com. (2012). Resources. Retrieved 3 August 2012 from http://www.employmentspot.com/vocations/aerospace/

Federal Aviation Administration website. (n.d.). . FAA Career Opportunities: Destination FAA. Retrieved 3 August 2012 from http://jobs.faa.gov/

Lockheed Martin website. (2012). Retrieved 6 August 2012 from http://www.lockheedmartin.com/us/who-we-are.html

Michigan Department of Civil Service website. (2000). Job Description: Aviation Specialist. Retrieved 30 January 2006 from http://www.michigan.gov/documents/AviationSpecialist_12110_7.pdf

Mitchell, N. (Ed.). (1999). *Leadership Education III: Life Skills*. Maxwell Air Force Base, AL: US Air Force Reserve Officer Training Corps.

NASA website. (July 2011). NASA Space shuttle missions. Retrieved 1 August 2012 from http://www.space.com/12376-nasa-space-shuttle-program-facts-statistics.html and http://library.thinkquest.org/5014/missions.html and http://www.nasa.gov/about/directorates/index.html

NASA website. (August 2011).What Does NASA Do? Retrieved 10 July 2012 from http://www.nasa.gov/about/highlights/what_does_nasa_do.html

Northrup Grumman website. (2012). Retrieved 6 August 2012 from http://www.northropgrumman.com/about_us/index.html

Smithsonian Air and Space Museum website. (n.d.). Retrieved 1 August 2012 from http://airandspace.si.edu/exhibitions/gal104/inplaneview/IPVBrochure08.pdf

US Department of Commerce website. (2012). Retrieved 6 August 2012 from http://selectusa.commerce.gov/industry-snapshots/aerospace-industry-united-states

WrightBrothers.info. (n.d.) Retrieved 8 August 2012 from http://wrightbrothers.info/quotes/

LESSON 3 Careers in Public Service

About.com. (2012). The Hiring Process in Criminal Justice Careers. Retrieved 12 July 2012 from http://criminologycareers.about.com/od/Job_Market/a/The-Hiring-Process.htm

Archives Networks website. (2012). Retrieved 12 July 2012 from http://www.outlookseries.com/A0992/Science/3911_Commencement_David_Petraeus_Dickinson_College.htm

CareerJusticeCareersNow.com. (2012). Retrieved 2 July 2012 from http://www.criminaljusticecareersnow.com/criminal-justice-career-schools.html

Careers in Homeland Security Occupational Outlook Quarterly (Summer 2006). Retrieved 3 July 2012 from http://www.bls.gov/opub/ooq/2006/summer/art01.pdf

CommunityPolicing.org. (2012). Police training. (n.d.) About Police Officer Training. Retrieved 2 July 2012 from http://www.communitypolicing.org/police-officer-training

Congressional Research Service website. (July 2011). Retrieved 29 May 2012 from http://www.fas.org/sgp/crs/misc/R41897.pdf

Criminaljusticedegreeguide.com. (2012). Retrieved 2 July 2012 from http://criminaljusticedegreeguide.com/criminal-justice-degree-and-career.asp

Degreedirectory.org. (2012). Fire science degree. Retrieved 16 July 2012 fromhttp://degreedirectory.org/articles/What_Can_I_Do_with_a_Fire_Science_Degree.html

Federal Emergency Management Agency website. (2012). Fire service. Retrieved 14 July 2012 from http://www.usfa.fema.gov/fireservice/research/dsn/index.shtm

IEEE website. (2011). Career Focus: Cybersecurity—A Growing Threat, a Growing Career. Retrieved 7 July 20102 from

http://www.todaysengineer.org/2011/Aug/career-focus.asp

Internal Revenue Service website. (2012). Definition of nonprofit. Retrieved 2 July 2012 from http://www.irs.gov

Lee, M. (2012). *Mass Spectrometry Handbook*. Hoboken, NJ. John Wiley & Sons, Inc.

Memphis Commercial Appeal website. (2011). After 9/11, Security Jobs Soar at Federal Level, but Thin Out Closer to Home. Retrieved 6 July 2012 from http://www.commercialappeal.com/news/2011/sep/11/assessing-risk-and-resources-economic-ills-force/

Myfootpath.com. (2011). Criminal Justice Careers. Retrieved 3 July 2012 from http://myfootpath.com/careers/criminal-justice-careers/

O*Net Online website. (2012). Firefighter jobs. Retrieved 14 July 2012 from http://www.onetonline.org/link/summary/33-2011.01

Public/private sector workers. Retrieved 29 May 2012 from http://abcnews.go.com/blogs/politics/2011/02/working-in-america-public-vs-private-sector/

Redorbit.com (2009). Applying Science to Firefighting. Retrieved 16 July 2012 from
http://www.redorbit.com/news/science/1779550/applying_science_to_fire_fighting/

ScienceDaily.com (2008). Fire Stopper Video. Retrieved 17 July 2012 from http://www
.sciencedaily.com/videos/2008/0804-fire_stopper.htm

SEMA website. (2012). Homeland Security training sites. Retrieved 7 August
2012 from http://training.dps.mo.gov/trainingwebsite.nsf/LinksView/
A87440DDFF5D4CB9862574F900080E11?Opendocument

Slate.com. (2012). We're in for More Wildfires than Ever. These New Technologies
Will Help Fight Them. Retrieved 17 July 2012 from http://www.slate.com/blogs/
future_tense/2012/06/29/colorado_springs_wildfire_new_technologies_to_combat_
forrest_fires_.html

Wet Feet.com Careers in Nonprofits. Insider Guide. Philadelphia, PA 2012

The White House website. (2007). Homeland security mission. Retrieved 20 September
2012 from http://georgewbush-whitehouse.archives.gov/infocus/homeland/nshs/
2007/sectionII.html

William Paterson University website. (2012). Dr. Martin Luther King, Jr. Retrieved 2 July
2012 from http://www.wpunj.edu/career-advisement/career-development/planning
-your-career/careers-in/criminal_justice.dot

CHAPTER 8 Developing Your Career Skills

LESSON 1 Planning Your Professional Development

Blanchard, K., & Peale, N. V. (1988). The Power of Ethical Management. New York:
William Morrow Co.

BrainyQuote.com (2012). Retrieved 10 May 2012 from www.brainyquote.com/quotes/
authors/m/michael_jordan.html

Pruitt B. E., Carter, C., & Sukiennik, D. (2005). *Foundations for Success in Life, Career,
Health and Wellness*. Boston, MA: Pearson Custom Publishing.

Tucker, M. L. (2002). *The Human Challenge: Managing Yourself and Others in
Organizations*. Upper Saddle River, NJ: Pearson Education, Inc.

LESSON 2 Learning to Work With Others

Hirsh, S. K. & Kummerow, J. M. (1990). *Introduction to Type in Organizations*. Palo Alto,
CA: Consulting Psychologists Press, Inc.

Mottet T., Bauer, S., and Houser, M. (2012). *Your Interpersonal Communication*. Upper
Saddle River, NJ: Pearson Education, Inc.

National School Boards Association website. (n.d.). Leadership Teams. Retrieved
15 April 2006 from http://www.nsba.org/sbot/toolkit/LeadTeams.html

Thinkexist.com. (2012). Retrieved 8 August 2012 from http://thinkexist.com/quotes/
henry_ford/

Tucker, M. L. (2002). The Human Challenge: *Managing Yourself and Others in
Organizations*. Upper Saddle River, NJ: Pearson Education, Inc.

LESSON 3 Seeking Feedback and Promotions

Aschaiek, S. (2006). Preparing for a Promotion. CanadianLiving.com. Retrieved 18 April 2006 from http://www.canadianliving.com/canadianliving/client/en/Family/DetailNews.asp?idNews=230214&idSM=428

Peter, L., & Hull, R. (1993). *The Peter Principle: Why Things Always Go Wrong*. Cutchogue, NY: Buccaneer Books.

ThinkExist.com (2012). Retrieved 10 July 2012 from http://thinkexist.com/quotes/ken_blanchard/

Tucker, M. L. (2002). *The Human Challenge: Managing Yourself and Others in Organizations*. Upper Saddle River, NJ: Pearson Education, Inc.

LESSON 4 Your Civic Responsibilities

Lions Clubs International website. Retrieved 1 October 2012 from http://www.lionsclubs.org

Rotary International website. Retrieved 1 October 2012 from http://www.rotary.org/en/Pages/ridefault.aspx

US Election Assistance Commission (EAC) website. Retrieved 1 October 2012 from http://www.eac.gov/voter_resources/register_to_vote.aspx

United States Selective Service System website. Retrieved 1 October 2012 from www.sss.gov

Glossary

360-degree feedback—a performance appraisal that comes from all levels around the employee—from a boss, coworkers, and subordinates, as well as the employee himself or herself. (p. 402)

A

ability promotion—a promotion based on your potential to do a new job, rather than how you did in your old one. (p. 403)

absentee ballot—a voting form sent by mail by voters who cannot visit a polling station in their community on election day. (p. 412)

academic adviser—a person who helps you make academic decisions about your collegiate education. (p. 216)

academic organization—a group that helps members learn about an academic subject and meet other people with a similar interest. (p. 211)

academic probation—means your grades have fallen below the minimum needed Grade Point Average (GPA) to graduate. (p. 219)

academic success center—a center that provides one-on-one or group study sessions, tutoring, specialized instruction, and self-paced tutorials. (p. 215)

account statement—a list of transactions in your checking or other accounts over the month. (p. 17)

accountability—being answerable for the outcomes of your words and actions. (p. 226)

accredited—a college that is approved as meeting certain standards. (p. 169)

achievement test—an exam that tests what a student has actually learned. (p. 186)

action verbs—verbs that give your résumé power and direction. (p. 278)

admissions officer—a person who helps decide whom to admit to a college. (p. 192)

aerospace—combines "aero," from aeronautics, or flight within Earth's atmosphere, and "space," or flight beyond the atmosphere. (p. 327)

alumni—people who have graduated from a certain school. (p. 174)

American College Testing (ACT)—a college entrance examination that is an alternative to the SAT. (p. 186)

analysts—workers who analyze situations and recommend solutions. (p. 364)

annual fee—a yearly fee that some companies charge in addition to the interest charge. (p. 56)

annual percentage rate (APR)—the yearly interest rate. (p. 53)

applied research—research focused on using previous findings to solve a practical problem or to develop a product. (p. 328)

apprenticeship—an opportunity to learn a trade on the job while also learning in class. (p. 134)

aptitude test—an exam designed to assess a student's talent, skill, or potential for learning, rather than his or her accumulated knowledge. (p. 181)

Armed Forces Qualification Test (AFQT) score—used to determine if someone is eligible to enlist in the military. (p. 312)

Armed Services Vocational Aptitude Battery (ASVAB)—the entrance test to enlist in the US military. (p. 312)

asset—something of value that you own. (p. 8)

astrophysics—the study of how Earth works and how the universe began and evolved. (p. 331)

asynchronous-mode course—a course in which students participate in activities and assignments whenever and from wherever it is convenient during the school week. (p. 175)

automated teller machine (ATM)—a 24-hour electronic terminal that lets you bank almost any time to withdraw cash, make deposits, or transfer funds between accounts. (p. 18)

B

balance—the amount of money after expenses that is left in your checking account. (p. 17)

balancing—comparing your bank statement to your checkbook register. (p. 23)

bank account—a formal relationship between you and a bank, where the bank keeps your money for you until you need it. (p. 15)

bankruptcy—a situation in which a court rules that a person is not able to pay his or her bills. (p. 55)

basic research—pure research that typically has no specific initial goals. (p. 328)

basic training—the period during which an enlistee enters the service and learns basic military skills. (p. 317)

behavioral interview—an interview during which the interviewer asks you to give examples of situations in which you demonstrated particular behaviors or skills. (p. 298)

benchmark—a standard by which to judge your progress. (p. 259)

beneficiary—a person who will receive insurance benefits. (p. 81)

benefit statement—a well-thought-out statement of your skills and abilities, with examples that illustrate them. (p. 262)

benefits—compensation you receive from your employer in addition to your salary. (p. 403)

blue-collar job—a job that often involves manual labor and for which people may need to wear a uniform or protective clothing. (p. 140)

board—the cost of food. (p. 152)

bodily/kinesthetic intelligence—(Body Smart) relates to the ability to connect mind and body, and often relates to excelling at sports. (p. 114)

body language—the nonverbal message that your facial expressions, physical stance, and gestures convey to a listener. (p. 295)

bond—a type of investment that helps a company or government agency raise funds for a return greater than the money invested. (p. 8)

brand—distinctive name identifying a product or manufacturer. (p. 34)

budget—a detailed summary of expected income and expenses during a given period. (p. 6)

burnout—the feeling of being worn out and unable to carry on usual activities. (p. 224)

C

cadet—a senior ROTC candidate or military academy appointee. (p. 323)

capitalizing—adding the interest payments to the loan balance. (p. 159)

career—a chosen field of work that has the potential for continuous growth and advancement by incorporating your interests, values, skills, and strengths to provide long-term fulfillment. (p. 92)

career clusters—an organized way to get information about a variety of different careers. (p. 112)

career ladder—a series of jobs that, over time, will take you higher and higher in an organization. (p. 373)

career-path strategy—a plan for how you will make progress in your career. (p. 406)

career path—a sequence of rigorous academic and career or technical courses leading to an associate's degree, baccalaureate degree and beyond, or an industry-recognized certificate and/or license. (p. 90)

career portfolio—a folder or notebook that contains information on you and your achievements over time. (p. 374)

cash advance—borrowed cash. (p. 56)

certificates of deposit—a type of bank deposit that typically pays higher rates of interest than a savings account, on the condition that you agree not to withdraw your money for a certain amount of time. (p. 18)

check—a written order that directs a bank to pay money. (p. 16)

checkbook register—a form on which you keep track of the money you deposit or withdraw. (p. 16)

checking account—a bank account into which you deposit money, and from which you can withdraw money by writing checks or using a debit card. (p. 16)

choice and select—less expensive grades of beef with less marbling in select than in choice grade. (p. 36)

chronological résumé—a résumé that lists your jobs, education, and other relevant accomplishments in reverse chronological order. (p. 274)

civic responsibilities—legal or social obligations to your community. (p. 411)

civilian—a person who is not on active duty in the armed forces. (p. 308)

civilian equivalents—jobs that are the same or similar to those in the civilian workplace. (p. 310)

claim—a demand for payment in accordance with the policy. (p. 71)

closing date—the cutoff point for an application. (p. 106)

collaboration—working with others in a team or group. (p. 393)

collateral—possessions that a borrower pledges in return for a loan. (p. 57)

College Placement Test (CPT)—a test designed to help schools place, or assign, students in classes where they'll learn most. (p. 187)

commercial world—also referred to as the private sector. (p. 307)

commissioned officers—personnel who enter the armed forces with a four-year college degree or higher, and who compete to enter and earn a commission from the President after confirmation by Congress. (p. 320)

communication—creating or sending of information, thoughts, and feelings from one person to another. (p. 384)

community—a group of people united by common government, location, interest, or activity. (p. 410)

community foundation—raises funds from donors and may support local programs through grants. (p. 349)

comparison shopping—comparing the prices and quality of different items to see which one is a better deal. (p. 33)

compassion—a feeling for and understanding of another person's situation. (p. 378)

competitiveness—the act of striving against others to achieve an objective. (p. 380)

compound interest—interest on accumulated unpaid interest. (p. 7)

conscription—the compulsory or mandatory enlistment of people in some sort of national service, most often military service. (p. 414)

continuing and adult education—evening or weekend courses for working adults who are not able to enroll in college full-time. (p. 141)

cooperative education (co-op) programs—programs in which you can work part-time in a career field in which you are interested, while taking job-related courses at school. (p. 133)

copayments—money paid for each doctor visit or other health service. (p. 79)

core requirements—required classes for majoring in an academic area. (p. 236)

corporate foundation—a separate entity of a corporation that makes charitable grants. (p. 349)

cosigner—a person with a good credit rating who signs a loan note along with a borrower. (p. 64)

courtesy—consideration and cooperation in dealing with others. (p. 377)

cover letter—gives prospective employers further information about you that is not in your résumé. (p. 285)

credit—offering to lend you money (p. 19); providing or lending money with the expectation of future repayment (p. 52); a point that a college assigns to a certain course. (p. 219)

credit bureau—a public or private agency that gathers credit information on people. (p. 64)

credit cards—cards that represent a promise that the bank will give you credit to buy things. (p. 19)

credit history—a record of paying your bills. (p. 59)

credit rating—an assessment of how trustworthy you are in paying your bills. (p. 53)

credit score—a rating that helps lenders decide whether and/or how much credit to approve to a borrower. (p. 64)

credit union—a not-for-profit bank that is owned by its members, often affiliated with some professional field or organization.(p. 20)

creditor—a bank, credit union, or other financing company that loans money. (p. 52)

criminal justice—a system of institutions and practices aimed at: maintaining social control; deterring crime; upholding the law; and giving fair punishments to offenders. (p. 350)

curriculum—a course of study. (p. 170)

cyberspace—the online world of computer networks, especially the Internet. (p. 306)

cybersecurity—the branch of computer technology known as information security as applied to computers and networks. (p. 364)

D

debit card—a card that allows automatic withdrawal of money you request from your checking account. (p. 16)

deductible—the amount that you must pay before the insurance company pays anything. (p. 71)

default—fail to your pay bill on time. (p. 63)

defensiveness—an effort to justify oneself. (p. 390)

deferment—the official postponement of military service. (p. 415)

deferral—a delay of your jury duty to a later time. (p. 417)

deficit spending—spending more than you earn. (p. 66)

dependability—the quality of being dependable or reliable. (p. 378)

direct deposit—a payment that is electronically deposited into an individual's account. (p. 18)

distortion—a distraction that interferes with communication. (p. 390)

distractions—activities, relationships or thoughts that draw your attention or interest away from what you should be doing at the moment. (p. 247)

down payment—partial payment that you make when purchasing something. (p. 47)

draft—action by the US Government for selecting eligible males to serve in the military. (p. 413)

drop/add—an option by which a student can attend a course for a week or two before deciding whether to take it or to drop it and substitute another course in its place. (p. 220)

dual enrollment/concurrent enrollment—when students enroll in college classes, and if they earn a passing grade, they receive credit that may be applied toward their high school diploma, a college degree, or a certificate. (p. 174)

E

early-admissions policy—colleges inform you by December whether or not you are accepted. (p. 178)

education—broad-based learning. (p. 94)

elective—a course you choose, or elect, to take. (p. 231)

electronic banking—a group of services that allows you to obtain account information and manage certain banking transactions. (p. 24)

electronic check conversion—converts a paper check into an electronic payment in a store. (p. 27)

electronic funds transfer (EFT)—a way to manage many banking transactions on your personal computer or other electronic device by accessing your bank account through the Internet. (p. 25)

electronic résumé—one prepared specifically for online use. (p. 274)

endowments—gifts, usually for specific community or global causes. (p. 349)

engineers—professionals who use the results of applied research, mathematics and other well-established principles to change ideas and theories into realities. (p. 328)

enlisted personnel—generally young men and women who enter the armed forces with a high school diploma or equivalent. (p. 312)

entrance examination—a standardized test that helps admissions officers determine who is qualified to attend their schools. (p. 180)

entry-level—beginning. (p. 265)

equity—the difference between the market value and the unpaid balance (p. 47); "equal justice or fairness (p. 380)

exemption—release from a requirement. (p. 417)

expenses—amounts of money you spend to pay bills or for other needs and wants. (p. 6)

extraterrestrial life—life originating, existing, or occurring outside the Earth or its atmosphere. (p. 327)

faculty—teachers or professors. (p. 169)

Federal Aviation Administration (FAA)—the government agency responsible for the safety of civil aviation. (p. 330)

feedback—the receiver's response to a sender's message. (p. 385)

field—an area of a profession. (p. 326)

filtering—hearing only what you want to hear. (p. 390)

finance—management of money. (p. 5)

finance charge—another term for interest and annual percentage rate (APR). (p. 53)

financial plan—a document that outlines your financial goals and how you plan to reach them. (p. 6)

financing—obtaining or providing money for a specific purpose. (p. 7)

first responders—personnel certified to provide urgent medical care and other emergency procedures before more highly trained medical personnel arrive on the scene. (p. 357)

forensics—the application of scientific knowledge and methodology to legal problems and criminal investigations. (p. 352)

formal communication—a structured, stable method of communication among people. (p. 391)

foundation—a public or private organization that acquires money from a range of contributors to support one or more causes. (p. 349)

fraternity—a men's student organization for scholastic, professional, or extracurricular activities, and having a name consisting of Greek letters. (p. 212)

functional résumé—a résumé that arranges your information under skill headings, without focusing on dates. (p. 274)

G

grace period—the time during which you can pay a credit card bill on new purchases without being charged interest. (p. 61)

graduate school—formal education after you graduate from college, which will give you in-depth knowledge about your specific career area. (p. 142)

grants—types of student financial aid that you do not have to repay. (p. 155)

grapevine—the informal channel of communication among people in an organization. (p. 391)

gross income—income before taxes and other deductions. (p. 43)

group interview—an interview in which several people will ask you questions. (p. 297)

H

halo/horn effect—the tendency to rate a person high on all performance factors or low on all of them because of an impression the evaluator may have of that individual. (p. 402)

hazing—any act that inflicts extreme physical, emotional, or psychological pressure or injury on an individual or that purposely demeans, degrades, or disgraces an individual. (p. 213)

heliophysics—understanding the Sun and how it interacts with Earth and other parts of the solar system. (p. 331)

high priority—something that you consider more important than other things. (p. 241)

higher education—study at a college or university—perhaps starting at a community or junior college. (p. 139)

Holland Interest Environments—a technique for exploring the ways that your interests can be grouped into job categories so you can begin to select specific career paths to investigate. (p.112)

"homegrown" terrorism—terrorism caused by persons native to, or citizens of, a region or country. (p. 364)

homeland security—a concerted national effort to prevent terrorist attacks within the United States, reduce America's vulnerability to terrorism, and minimize the damage, and recover from attacks that do occur. (p. 361)

honesty—the practice of being truthful, trustworthy, and sincere; it is refraining from lying, cheating, or stealing. (p. 379)

horizontal communication—communication among people at the same level in an organization, no matter what department they are in. (p. 391)

human resources department—the department that handles hiring, benefits, and other issues concerning employees. (p. 290)

hybrid résumé—a combination of the chronological and functional formats. (p. 274)

identity theft—when someone uses your personal information without your permission to commit fraud or other crimes. (p. 82)

income—what is earned or made available to you. (p. 6)

indemnity plan—a plan that provides payment to the insured for the cost of medical care but makes no arrangement for providing care itself. (p. 79)

independent foundation—a normally philanthropic organization with funds coming from a single individual or family. (p. 349)

industry—a group of productive or profit-making enterprises. (p. 328)

industry sector—the general field in which a company provides a product or service. (p. 291)

informal communication—social interactions among people who work together or are associated with one another in some other way. (p. 391)

informational interview—a conversation with someone working in the field you are interested in. (p. 264)

installments—monthly payments. (p. 56)

in-state resident—a legal resident of the state in which a college is located. (p. 154)

insurance—an agreement between two parties under which one party—usually an insurance company—guarantees the other that if an asset is lost or destroyed, the insurance company will pay for it (p. 8); the means by which people protect themselves financially against losses or liability incurred as a result of unexpected events (p. 70)

insurance agent—a person who sells insurance. (p. 76)

integrity—commitment to a code of values or beliefs that results in a unified, positive attitude and approach to life. (p. 379)

intelligence—the ability to acquire, understand, and use knowledge. (p. 113)

interest—a charge on borrowed money. (p. 7)

interest rate—the seller's or lending institution's charge on borrowed money. (p. 47)

intermediary—someone who shares communication between two or more individuals. (p. 392)

international organization—a group composed of people from a certain nation or part of the world or of students who have a special interest in such a place. (p. 214)

internship—a low-paying or volunteer job that provides supervised practical training in a field or skill. (p. 138)

interpersonal intelligence—(People Smart) involves the ability to comprehend others' feelings. (p. 114)

interpersonal values—values among people. (p. 259)

intramural athletics—sports competition between teams within a college. (p. 214)

intrapersonal intelligence— (Self-Smart) involves the ability to comprehend your own feelings. (p. 114)

intrapersonal values—values you feel inside you. (p. 259)

inventory—a list of your property and its value (p. 77); an evaluation or survey (p. 255)

investment—something you own that you expect to increase in value over time. (p. 8)

itinerary—travel schedule. (p. 204)

J

job—work you do to make a living. (p. 92)

job objective—a brief statement that describes the type of position you are seeking. (p. 281)

junior and community colleges—institutions that offer courses and programs leading to associate's degrees and training certificates. (p. 133)

junior enlisted personnel—enter at the lowest ranks, and focus much of their time on learning skills. (p. 312)

jury—a group of adult citizens who listen to the evidence in a court case and decides which side is in the right. (p. 416)

K

keyword—a specific word that a computer looks for when searching a database. (p. 284)

L

landlord—apartment owner. (p. 42)

laws—rules of conduct or action formally recognized as binding or enforced. (p. 410)

lead—an inroad or route to information before it is otherwise widely known. (p. 109)

learning style—the way an individual learns best. (p. 112)

lease—an agreement to pay rent and fulfill other obligations for a certain length of time. (p. 43)

liability—legal responsibility. (p. 70)

life insurance—a way to protect your family and loved ones from financial losses if you should die. (p. 80)

liquidity—access to funds to cover a short-term cash need. (p. 6)

loans—sums of money borrowed with interest. (p. 18)

logical/mathematical intelligence—(Number Smart) includes the ability to think abstractly, to problem-solve, and to think critically. (p. 114)

loyalty—being faithful to someone or something. (p. 379)

M

machinists—workers who make, assemble, or repair machinery. (p. 334)

major—the subject area on which you want to focus in college (p. 145); a subject or field of study representing a student's primary interest and which includes a large share of classes (p. 230)

managed care plan—a health-care plan that requires you to consult a primary care physician when you need medical care. (p. 79)

markup—the price added on above what the dealer paid for the product. (p. 31)

maturity date—the date by which you must repay the money you borrowed. (p. 53)

median—half the salaries are above the amount stated, while half are below. (p. 131)

mentor—a life coach who guides, advises, and advocates for you in your individual life path. (p. 139)

merit promotion—a promotion based on your performance in your current job. (p. 403)

minimum payment—the smallest amount due to the lender to keep your credit in good standing. (p. 55)

minor—a secondary focus for your academic studies. (p. 230)

multiple intelligences (MI)—the eight distinct areas of intelligence that everyone possesses. (p. 112)

multitasking—doing more than one thing at a time. (p. 246)

musical/rhythmic intelligence—(Music Smart) focuses on the ability to be aware of patterns in pitch, sound, rhythm, and timbre. (p. 113)

mutual fund—an investment that often includes a mix of stocks, bonds, or other securities purchased in shares. (p. 8)

mutual trust—develops when people and organizations know that they can rely on one another to do the right thing. (p. 379)

N

National Aeronautics and Space Administration (NASA)—the government agency responsible for the US space program and general aerospace research. (p. 330)

naturalistic intelligence—(Environment Smart) involves the ability to understand and work effectively in the natural world of plants and animals. (p. 114)

needs—things that you must have to sustain your livelihood. (p. 6; p. 256)

need based—funds that are given to students who have a documented need. (p. 157)

net income—income after taxes and other deductions. (p. 46)

network—the group of people you meet and maintain contact with. (p. 266)

networking—the process of making contacts and building relationships that can help you obtain leads, referrals, advice, information, and support. (p. 109)

no-fault—laws that make each person responsible for his or her own damages and injuries. (p. 74)

noncommissioned officers (NCOs)—have advanced leadership and technical skills. They often serve as specialists and supervisors. (p. 312)

nonprofits—institutions not organized to make a profit that operate to promote social welfare. (p. 346)

nonverbal communication—communication without words. (p. 389)

O

off-campus housing—includes apartments, houses, or rooms in someone else's home, located off the college campus. (p. 218)

on-campus housing—includes dormitories or residence halls owned and operated by a college. (p. 218)

online banking—a way to manage many banking transactions on your personal computer or other electronic device by signing on to your bank's website through the Internet. (p. 24)

open-admissions policy—a policy that permits enrollment of a student who has a high school diploma or equivalent, or in some cases, regardless of academic qualifications. (p. 141)

organizational values—combined personal values of the people in an organization and the values of the organization itself. (p. 380)

out-of-state students—students who are not legal residents of the state in which a college is located. (p. 154)

P

paralegal—a person trained to undertake legal work but not qualified as a lawyer. (p. 353)

patience—the ability to bear difficulty, delay, frustration, or pain without complaint. (p. 380)

pay-by-phone—a system that lets you call your bank with instructions to pay certain bills or to transfer funds between accounts (p. 27)

peer—a coworker at your level. (p. 297)

performance appraisal—a systematic review of how well an individual employee has performed during a specified period. (p. 400)

periodic rate—monthly rate. (p. 59)

perseverance—the quality of sticking to something until you achieve it. (p. 378)

personal finance—how you manage your money and other things of financial value. (p. 5)

personal identification number (PIN)—a code you enter to use a credit or debit card to make banking transactions like withdrawing cash, making deposits, or transferring funds between accounts from an ATM. (p. 18)

philanthropic—benefiting people through charitable aid or donations. (p. 348)

phishing—the creating of a website replica in order to trick users into submitting personal, financial, or password data online. (p. 84)

plagiarism—passing off someone else's work as your own. (p. 219)

policy—a contract that promises to pay for any losses. (p. 70)

political organization—a group of people with similar political interests. (p. 212)

polling stations—official locations for casting votes. (p. 412)

polygraph test—a test using an instrument to determine if a person is telling the truth. (p. 353)

portfolio—an instrument that gives employers a comprehensive picture of an applicant. (p. 287)

Preliminary SAT (PSAT)—a standardized test that covers the same areas the SAT does. (p. 189)

premium—the fee for being protected by the insurance. (p. 70)

prepaid debit card—a debit card for use at retail stores or for cash withdrawals. (p. 27)

prerequisites—courses required to enter a certain field of study. (p. 236)

primary election—the preliminary election for choosing the representative candidates from each political party. (p. 412)

prime—a cut of beef that has the greatest degree of marbling, or flecks of fat, that help make meat tender, juicy, and flavorful. (p. 36)

principal—the money you borrow. (p. 53)

priority—the value a person places on an activity, a goal, or another demand on time or energy. (p. 241)

private sector—businesses that are part of the nation's economy run by private individuals or groups, usually for profit. (p. 307)

private university—an institution of higher learning that is operated by a private organization. (p. 154)

procrastinate—to put off doing something, especially out of habitual carelessness or laziness. (p. 243)

produce—fresh fruits and vegetables (p. 34)

product expiration date—the date after which the item will be stale or no longer be at its finest quality. (p. 34)

professional development—includes all the activities necessary to have a successful career. (p. 370)

professional organization—helps its members learn about careers in a particular field. (p. 212)

promotion—a new job at a higher level. (p. 403)

public service—employment within a government or nonprofit organization that is for the benefit of the community. (p. 346)

public university—an institution of higher learning that is operated and funded by the state in which it is located. (p. 154)

R

rapport—a relationship or connection. (p. 297)

real estate agent—a professional who helps people buy, sell, or rent homes and apartments. (p. 43)

reconcile—verify that your checkbook register balances. (p. 23)

recreational organization—a group focused on a specific activity. (p. 214)

reference—a person future employers can contact to ask about what kind of worker you are. (p. 139)

religious organization—unites students with a similar religious faith or interest. (p. 212)

residential adviser—an adult or upper classman who lives in your dormitory and helps you solve living problems. (p. 218)

résumé—a brief summary of your work experience and qualifications. (p. 273)

retirement—the period (usually later in life) during which you no longer work full-time at a job. (p. 8)

risk—uncertainty as to the outcome of an investment. (p. 11)

risk taking—taking chances. (p. 381)

rolling-admissions policy—colleges make acceptance decisions as students apply. (p. 178)

room—the cost of a place to live. (p. 152)

rush—a drive each semester by sororities or fraternities to recruit new members. (p. 213)

savings account—an account for depositing money that you want to keep. (p. 16)

Scholastic Aptitude Test (SAT)—a widely used entrance exam that measures the academic skills and knowledge students most need for success in college. (p. 181)

scholarships—types of student financial aid that you do not have to repay. (p. 155)

scientific research—process of discovery. (p. 328)

scientists—those who seek answers to expand knowledge through discovery about why things happen the way they do. (p. 328)

security deposit—a payment to make sure you meet your obligations as a tenant. (p. 44)

security investigation—reveals information on any past arrests or questioning by law enforcement officers. (p. 314)

Selective Service System—the agency that keeps records of eligible males and executes the draft if it is ever needed. (p. 413)

semantics—achieving a desired effect on an audience especially through the use of words with novel or dual meanings. (p. 390)

senior NCOs—highly skilled and experienced noncommissioned officers. They carry significant authority and responsibility at the top of enlisted ranks as leaders and managers. (p. 312)

service organization—performs social or educational services for the community. (p. 214)

shares—equal parts into which company stocks are divided. (p. 8)

skill—the ability to do something that you have acquired through training or experience. (p. 258)

social network—a website that provides a virtual community for people to share their daily activities or interests, or to widen their circle of professional acquaintances. (p. 109)

social organization—focuses on bringing a group of people together for social activities. (p. 212)

sorority—a women's student organization formed chiefly for social or extracurricular purposes, and having a name consisting of Greek letters. (p. 212)

specialties—positions that are distinctive, or peculiar to a military career. (p. 307)

spending limits—the amount above which you should not spend if you are to meet your financial goals. (p. 11)

standardized test—one that is given and scored under the same conditions for all students. (p. 180)

stereotyping—holding a concept that is based on oversimplified assumptions or opinions, rather than on facts. (p. 390)

stocks—funds raised by companies through the sale of shares. (p. 8)

stress—a mentally or an emotionally upsetting condition that occurs in response to outside influences. (p. 224)

stress interview—an interview that deliberately creates an environment that puts you under pressure so that the employer can see how you behave in tense situations. (p. 298)

structured interview—a set of questions that the employer asks all candidates. (p. 297)

subjective meaning—personal significance. (p. 384)

subsidized—the government pays the interest while you're in school. (p. 158)

summary of qualifications—a brief overview of your skills, experience, and knowledge. (p. 281)

summons—a legal document requiring you to appear at the court on a specific time and date. (p. 417)

T

targeted résumé—includes the title of the actual job or career you are seeking. (p. 274)

teaching assistant—a graduate student who is specializing in the course topic. (p. 205)

teamwork—working together to identify and solve group-related problems and to achieve goals. (p. 381)

technical training program—a learning experience that will give you the knowledge and skills you need to start a technically oriented career. (p. 132)

technically oriented career path—a career path focused on mastering technical skills that do not require a college or university education. (p. 128)

technician—someone who translates the technical plans created by engineers into useful products and services. (p. 329)

technologist—does work similar to that of a technician, but at a higher level. (p. 329)

tenant—a person who rents an apartment. (p. 42)

term life insurance—a policy that you buy to cover a certain period of time. (p. 81)

term of enlistment—the number of years you agree to remain in the military before you have the option to leave or sign up for another term. (p. 308)

time management—keeping control of your time in a way that best enables you to achieve your goals according to your priorities. (p. 240)

training—prepares you to perform a function that requires a specific set of skills. (p. 94)

transcript—official record of your grades. (p. 198)

tuition—the fee for instruction. (p. 152)

U

unit price—cost per serving. (p. 34)

universal life insurance—insurance for a specific period that accumulates savings for policyholders during this period. (p. 82)

unsecured loan—a loan that does not require collateral. (p. 63)

unstructured interview—an informal session during which the interviewer will expect you to do most of the talking. (p. 297)

unsubsidized—you pay all the interest. (p. 158)

utilities—electricity, heat, gas, and water. (p. 44)

V

vacancy announcement—describes the skills and experience required to perform in a position. (p. 106)

variable rate—an interest rate that changes over time. (p. 61)

verbal communication—written as well as spoken words. (p. 386)

verbal/linguistic intelligence—(Word Smart) focuses on the use of language and words. (p. 113)

vertical communication—that which takes place between people at different levels within the same department. (p. 392)

visionary leadership—leadership exercised by people who have a clear sense of where they are guiding their organizations and who can persuade others to follow them. (p. 381)

visual/spatial intelligence—(Picture Smart) includes the ability to create mental images and transform them into an art form or useful product. (p. 113)

vocational school—a school that offers courses to prepare students in specific skills to enter a technical career field. (p. 134)

volunteer—an unpaid worker. (p. 138)

W

waiting list—a list of students who will be admitted if others choose not to come. (p. 179)

wants—things that you do not have to have, but would like to have, or own. (p. 6; p. 256)

want or classified ads—advertisements for job openings, services, or items for sale. (p. 254)

warrant officers— highly skilled officers who work in a single-track specialty throughout their military service. (p. 320)

white-collar job—a job that does not involve manual labor and for which people generally do not have to wear uniforms or protective clothing. (p. 140)

whole life insurance—provides coverage for your entire lifetime. (p. 81)

work ethic—taking into consideration the effects of your decisions and actions on all people connected with your organization—employees, customers, owners, suppliers, and competitors. (p. 378)

workers' compensation—a type of disability insurance that covers medical expenses and part, or most, of income lost due to injury in the workplace. (p. 80)

Index

Note: Page numbers followed by *b* indicate boxed text.